ESSAYS IN THE HISTORY OF CANADIAN LAW
VOLUME III

Nova Scotia

This third volume of *Essays in the History of Canadian Law* presents thoroughly researched, original essays in Nova Scotian legal history. An introduction by the editors is followed by ten essays grouped into four main areas of study.

The first is the legal system as a whole: essays in this section discuss the juridical failure of the Annapolis regime, present a collective biography of the province's superior court judiciary to 1900, and examine the property rights of married women in the nineteenth century. The second section deals with criminal law, exploring vagrancy laws in Halifax in the late nineteenth century, aspects of prisons and punishments before 1880, and female petty crime in Halifax.

The third, on family law, examines the issues of divorce from 1750 to 1890 and child custody from 1866 to 1910. Finally, two essays relate to law and the economy: one examines the Mines Arbitration Act of 1888; the other considers the question of private property and public resources in the context of the administrative control of water in Nova Scotia.

(Osgoode Society for Canadian Legal History)

PHILIP GIRARD is a University Research Professor and a professor in the Schulich School of Law at Dalhousie University.

JIM PHILLIPS is a professor in the Faculty of Law and the Department of History at the University of Toronto.

PATRONS OF THE SOCIETY

Blake, Cassels & Graydon LLP

Gowlings

Lax O'Sullivan Scott Lisus LLP

McCarthy Tétrault LLP

Osler, Hoskin & Harcourt LLP

Paliare Roland Rosenberg Rothstein LLP

Torkin Manes LLP

Torys LLP

WeirFoulds LLP

The Osgoode Society is supported by a grant from
The Law Foundation of Ontario.

The Society also thanks The Law Society of Upper Canada
for its continuing support.

Essays in the History of Canadian Law

VOLUME III

NOVA SCOTIA

Edited by

PHILIP GIRARD

and

JIM PHILLIPS

Published for The Osgoode Society for Canadian Legal History by

University of Toronto Press

Toronto Buffalo London

www.utppublishing.com
www.osgoodesociety.ca
Printed in Canada

ISBN 978-1-4426-1359-1

First published in hardcover in 1990 for The Osgoode Society for Canadian Legal History by University of Toronto Press.

Printed on acid-free paper.

Library and Archives Canada Cataloguing in Publication

Essays in the history of Canadian law / edited by David H. Flaherty.

Contents: v. 3. Nova Scotia / edited by Philip Girard and Jim Phillips
ISBN 978-1-4426-1359-1 (v. 3 : pbk).

1. Law – Canada – History and criticism. I. Flaherty, David H. II. Girard, Philip III. Phillips, Jim, 1954– IV. Osgoode Society

KE394.Z85E87 1981 349.71 C 810-95131-2

University of Toronto Press acknowledges the financial assistance to its publishing program of the Canada Council for the Arts and the Ontario Arts Council.

University of Toronto Press acknowledges the financial support of the Government of Canada through the Canada Book Fund for its publishing activities.

Contents

Foreword
R. ROY MCMURTRY AND PETER N. OLIVER vii

Acknowledgments ix

Contributors xi

Abbreviations xiii

1 Introduction
PHILIP GIRARD AND JIM PHILLIPS 3

THE LEGAL SYSTEM: AN OVERVIEW

2 'The Dayly Cry for Justice': The Juridical Failure of the Annapolis Royal Regime, 1713–1749
THOMAS GARDEN BARNES 10

3 The Superior Court Judiciary of Nova Scotia, 1754–1900: A Collective Biography
CLARA GRECO 42

4 Married Women's Property, Chancery Abolition, and Insolvency Law: Law Reform in Nova Scotia, 1820–1867
PHILIP GIRARD 80

THE CRIMINAL LAW IN SOCIETY

5 Poverty, Unemployment, and the Administration of the Criminal Law: Vagrancy Laws in Halifax, 1864–1890
JIM PHILLIPS 128

6 From Bridewell to Federal Penitentiary: Prisons and Punishment in Nova Scotia before 1880
RAINER BAEHRE 163

7 'Raised in Rockhead. Died in the Poor House': Female Petty Criminals in Halifax, 1864–1890
B. JANE PRICE 200

WOMEN, THE FAMILY, AND THE LAW

8 Divorce in Nova Scotia, 1750–1890
KIMBERLEY SMITH MAYNARD 232

9 Child Custody and Divorce: A Nova Scotia Study, 1866–1910
REBECCA VEINOTT 273

LAW AND ECONOMY

10 The Mines Arbitration Act, 1888: Compulsory Arbitration in Context
MARGARET E. McCALLUM 303

11 From Private Property to Public Resource: The Emergence of Administrative Control of Water in Nova Scotia
JENNIFER NEDELSKY 326

Index 353

Foreword

THE OSGOODE SOCIETY

The purpose of The Osgoode Society is to encourage research and writing in the history of Canadian law. The Society, which was incorporated in 1979 and is registered as a charity, was founded at the initiative of the Honourable R. Roy McMurtry, at that time attorney general for Ontario, and officials of the Law Society of Upper Canada. Its efforts to stimulate legal history in Canada include the sponsorship of a fellowship, research support programs, and work in the fields of oral history and legal archives. The Society publishes volumes that contribute to legal-historical scholarship in Canada and that are of interest to the Society's members. Included are studies of the courts, the judiciary, and the legal profession, biographies, collections of documents, studies in criminology and penology, accounts of great trials, and work in the social and economic history of the law.

The current directors of The Osgoode Society are Brian Bucknall, Mr Justice Archie Campbell, Douglas Ewart, Martin Friedland, Jane Banfield Haynes, John D. Honsberger, Kenneth Jarvis, Mr Justice Allen Linden, Colin McKinnon, R. Roy McMurtry, Brendan O'Brien, Peter Oliver, James M. Spence, and Richard Tinsley. The attorney general for Ontario and the treasurer of the Law Society of Upper Canada are directors ex officio. The annual report and information about membership may be obtained by writing The Osgoode Society, Osgoode Hall, 130 Queen Street West, Toronto, Ontario M5H 2N6. Members receive the annual volumes published by the Society.

This volume, our first devoted exclusively to Nova Scotia's legal history, will appeal to lawyers, legal academics, and historians alike. Some of the contributors explore the province's legal heritage in the areas of criminal law, family law, and labour law; others delve into judicial biography, law reform, the rise of the regulatory state, and the nature of British justice under the Annapolis regime. All combine seldom-used archival material with a variety of modern theoretical perspectives to bring fresh light to bear on the nature of Nova Scotia's legal culture. While adding an important dimension to Maritime historiography, these essays also contribute to a deeper and more critical understanding of Canadian legal history.

The Osgoode Society is grateful to Professors Girard and Phillips for their painstaking work in collecting and editing these studies, and to the authors for their important contribution to legal-historical scholarship. We especially thank the Law Foundation of Nova Scotia for its generous contribution in assistance of publication.

R. Roy McMurtry
President

Peter N. Oliver
Editor-in-Chief

Acknowledgments

Many people have provided assistance in the preparation of this volume. The staff at the Public Archives of Nova Scotia were unfailingly courteous and helpful, and Barry Cahill deserves a special mention for guiding us through the legal manuscripts. David Bell of the Faculty of Law, University of New Brunswick, saved us from many errors. Rebecca Veinott provided excellent research assistance at various points in the publication process. It was a pleasure to work with the editors of the University of Toronto Press.

Peter Oliver deserves our special thanks; an enthusiastic supporter of this enterprise from the outset, he provided much encouragement, useful criticism, and practical support. Financial support, in the form of generous publication subsidies, was provided by the Osgoode Society and the Law Foundation of Nova Scotia. The Faculty of Law, Dalhousie University, made substantial contributions towards research expenses.

Our warmest thanks must of course be extended to the contributors, without whom this volume would not exist.

Philip Girard
Jim Phillips

Contributors

RAINER BAEHRE is a member of the Department of History, Sir Wilfred Grenfell College, Memorial University of Newfoundland. His articles have appeared in *Ontario History*, *Historical Reports*, and *Histoire sociale/Social History*. At present he is studying nineteenth-century mechanisms of social control in Canada.

THOMAS GARDEN BARNES is a graduate of Harvard and Oxford. He is Professor of History and Law at the University of California, Berkeley, and Co-Chairman of the Canadian Studies Program there. Though primarily a legal historian of Tudor and Stuart Britain, his Nova Scotian background and his annual summer sojourns there have sparked an interest in Nova Scotia history.

PHILIP GIRARD is Associate Professor at Dalhousie Law School. He is working on a study of Beamish Murdoch's *Epitome of the Laws of Nova Scotia*.

CLARA GRECO is an associate with the firm of Blake, Cassels and Graydon, Toronto. She received a BA (Honours) in political science from McMaster University in 1983 and an LLB from Dalhousie in 1986.

MARGARET E. McCALLUM holds an LLB and a PHD in history from the University of Toronto. She has been awarded a Canada Research Fellowship in the Canadian Studies Program at Trent University, where she is studying and teaching about law and social change in the twentieth century. She is the author of several articles on labour and legal history.

KIMBERLEY SMITH MAYNARD is a member of the Bar of Manitoba. She received a Specialized Honours BA in History from York University in

1984, and an LLB from Dalhousie in 1987. She is currently at work on a history of the Manitoba Home for Boys.

JENNIFER NEDELSKY is Associate Professor of Law and Political Science at the University of Toronto. She received her PHD from the University of Chicago in 1977 and was formerly Assistant Professor of Politics at Princeton University. She has published numerous articles on American constitutional history and theory, Canadian legal history, and political and feminist theory. She is the author of *Private Property and the Limits of American Constitutionalism* (University of Chicago Press 1990)

JIM PHILLIPS is Assistant Professor of Law at the University of Toronto, where he is also cross-appointed to the Department of History and the Centre of Criminology. He received his PHD in 1983 and his LLB in 1987 from Dalhousie University. He has written on British imperial history.

B. JANE PRICE received a BA in history from Queen's in 1983 and an LLB from Dalhousie in 1987. She is currently working and studying in Toronto.

REBECCA VEINOTT holds an MA in history from Dalhousie University. She is completing her law studies at Dalhousie.

Abbreviations

Collections	*Nova Scotia Historical Society Collections*
DCB	*Dictionary of Canadian Biography* (Toronto: University of Toronto Press 1966–)
DHA	*Debates of the Nova Scotia House of Assembly*
DLC	*Debates of the Nova Scotia Legislative Council*
JHA	*Journals of the Nova Scotia House of Assembly*
JLC	*Journals of the Nova Scotia Legislative Council*
PANS	Public Archives of Nova Scotia
NA	National Archives of Canada
PRO	Public Record Office, London

Essays in the History of Canadian Law

1

Introduction

PHILIP GIRARD AND
JIM PHILLIPS

In exploring the legal history of Nova Scotia these essays move into relatively uncharted territory. The pioneering work of Thomas Barnes, Judith Fingard, Peter Waite, and others has given us glimpses of what the records have to offer, and Fingard and Louis Knafla promise more in the near future. None the less, a great deal is left to be done, including much basic research on the development of legal institutions. Filling this gap is perhaps the primary purpose of a work such as this one, but it is by no means the only purpose. Nova Scotia legal history may be a newborn child, but it has older siblings. One cannot study the history of the law in Nova Scotia without relying on, relating to, and contributing to three other areas of historical study: the 'new legal history' of Anglo-American jurisdictions, the emerging discipline of Canadian legal history, and the older, yet rapidly evolving, historiography of the Maritime provinces. Nova Scotia legal history must be placed in each of these contexts; it must draw from them and give something back to them.

These essays make an important contribution to the 'new legal history,' the growing body of work by Anglo-American (including Canadian and Australian) scholars, which has gone beyond the formalist bias of traditional legal history to consider the law in a multiplicity of historical settings and from a wide variety of political perspectives. Within this new tradition, the working of the criminal law, as seen from 'below,' has attracted by far the most attention, and this volume reflects that interest. Jim Phillips's work on vagrancy law in later Victorian Halifax shows that while Nova Scotia's response to the urban vagrant problem mirrored that of many American cities, the interpretation of that response advanced by some American historians is not valid for the province. The need for a reserve army of labour for the growth and maintenance of industrial capitalism was not present in the Nova Scotia of the 1860s, 1870s, and 1880s; Phillips looks to broader theories of social control to explain the resurgent interest in the 'vagrant problem' in that period. B. Jane Price focuses on the female petty offender; her contribution complements existing work, which has concentrated on the serious offender, or which has tried to isolate the prostitute from the pool of minor female offenders. Price shows that it may be misleading to define prostitution as a discrete category of criminality: women who worked as prostitutes also came into contact with the law for a variety of other reasons, such as drunkenness, brawling, profanity, and petty theft. Those were independent crimes, and should not be seen as surrogates for the offence of prostitution. Price gives us a rich portrait of the lives of the female underclass in later Victorian Halifax, and shows that many of the women were not mere pawns or victims but canny survivors who could on occasion manipulate the law to their own ends. Rainer Baehre's work on prisons and punishments in nineteenth-century Nova Scotia is a salutary reminder that the debate over penal reforms not only represented a clash of ideologies, but also posed some hard dollars-and-cents questions about how prisons would be built and maintained. From this viewpoint, fiscal policy was the real battleground; the debate over the efficacy of new modes of punishment appears to have engendered little controversy.

The new legal history has witnessed an explosion of interest in women's treatment by the legal system and their role in that system. We have travelled a long way since Sir James Stephen wrote in his history of English criminal law that 'the whole series of offences relating to the abduction of women, rape and other such crimes ... possesses no special interest and does not illustrate either our political or our social history.'[1] In the body of work that has sprung up to fill the gap, the law's role in shaping women's position in the family has received a great deal of attention. In her study of the origins and development of Nova Scotia divorce law, Kimberley Smith Maynard demonstrates that for women the divorce process could be a double-edged sword. Marriages 'tainted' by adultery were relatively easy for either partner to dissolve. In spite of express provisions for divorce on the ground of cruelty, however, the judges failed to articulate (at least until 1890) any standard for controlling domestic violence beyond imposing sanctions for conduct that seriously threatened the wife's life or physical health. By contrast, Rebecca Veinott finds that late nineteenth-century judges were receptive to the idea of enhanced, indeed equal, rights for women to custody of their children after divorce. Although the ideology of maternal feminism may have assisted in a reformulation of parental rights in late nineteenth-century Nova Scotia, it was not able to influence significantly the legal norms that shored up the patriarchal model of marriage. In fact, there seems to have been little pressure by anyone, maternal feminists or otherwise, to liberalize divorce law in Nova Scotia before 1900. This suggests that traditional views of marriage and the family retained a high degree of legitimacy among men and women alike, in spite of the not infrequent incidence of marital and family breakdown.

Although it is clearly situated within the context of the new Anglo-American legal history, this volume also finds its inspiration in the growing field of Canadian legal historical studies. In this respect it is instructive to contrast the contributors' preoccupations with those displayed in previous collections devoted mainly to Ontario and the West. The major themes of *Law and Justice in a New Land: Essays in Western Canadian Legal History*, for example, seem far removed from those of this volume: roughly two-thirds of *Law and Justice* is devoted to studies of aboriginal rights, natural resource issues, and the nature of law on the frontier.[2] While much remains to be written about the status of aboriginal peoples and their land rights within Nova Scotia's legal system, the issue did not concern contemporaries to the same extent that it did in the West or even in Ontario. Blacks, however, were a constant preoccupation of white Nova Scotians, and often came into contact with the law, usually on the receiving end of the criminal justice system. Nova Scotia was home to the largest black population in Canada until the 1960s, and their experience with institutionalized racism needs to be considered along with that of the aboriginal peoples in the search for dominant themes in the history of Canadian law. The subjects of the essays in the previous two volumes of *Essays in the History of Canadian Law* seem less alien, but there are still many areas of divergence.[3] Judicial divorce, for example, which was authorized by statute in Nova Scotia in 1758, was resisted in Upper and Lower Canada until the twentieth century, and Nova Scotia abolished its Court of Chancery only eighteen years after Upper Canada finally endowed itself with one. Meanwhile, Upper Canadians regarded with horror Nova Scotia's poor-relief system, which was a faithful reproduction of the Elizabethan poor-law, complete with pauper auctions and parish-based Overseers of the Poor. Nova Scotia's legal system was primarily a product of the eighteenth century; the West's and Upper Canada's were products of the nineteenth. This fact alone explains the high degree of local particularism that obtained in the legal affairs of the various provinces.

None the less, these regional studies reveal common themes. All of the essays in this volume touch on one or more of the issues that have intrigued Canadian legal historians: the respective influence of the British, French, and American traditions on the Canadian legal order; the nature of Canadian legal conservatism; and the role of the judiciary in responding to the social and economic change that transformed the country during the period from 1850 to 1930. Thomas Barnes uncovers a poignant example of the fruitful coexistence of French and English law in the judicial records of the Annapolis regime, a model that might have survived to challenge the two solitudes of common and civil law but for *les Grands Dérangements* of 1755. In his essay on law reform in the pre-Confederation period, Philip Girard probes the nature of Nova Scotia legal conservatism, and concludes that the phenomenon is more complex than has sometimes been asserted. Clara Greco provides us with only the second collective biography of a provincial judiciary; the inexplicable gap in this area of Canadian legal history clearly merits further work. Further research also is needed to determine whether the behaviour of the Nova Scotia judiciary bears out G. Blaine Baker's and David Howes's findings regarding the 'colonization' of the Upper and Lower Canadian legal mind in the later Victorian period.[4]

As with the new legal history, great strides have recently been made in Maritime historiography; in fact, it has become a commonplace to talk of its 'golden age.'[5] In particular, the rise and fall of Maritime prosperity, the development of politics and parties in the nineteenth century, relations with the new dominion, and the tribulations of the labouring classes have all come under detailed and sophisticated scrutiny. Here, Jennifer Nedelsky, writing on the establishment of regulatory control over provincial water-power, Rainer Baehre, writing on the changes in the nineteenth-century prison system, and Margaret McCallum, writing on the debate over compulsory arbitration in the mines, all contribute to the new historiography by exploring aspects of these and other developments not previously brought to light.

But the essays in this volume also contribute to continuing debates. The papers by Jim Phillips and B. Jane Price explore the tremendous social diversity that lay underneath the outward picture of a placid, stable, resource-based rural society. Halifax had an urban underclass throughout the nineteenth century; here it is dissected during one period, and the knowledge gained from the work of Judith Fingard and Ian McKay is thereby augmented. In addition, we can ask what significance is to be attached to the failure to reform commercial law – recounted by Philip Girard – in the development of Nova Scotia's economy after mid-century. When provincial historians have looked at these questions at all they have considered legal change, or the lack of it, as blindly derivative; yet the process of law reform had its own internal dynamic and must have affected other developments.

One important way in which the essays mirror recent changes in perceptions of Nova Scotia history is their confirmation of a tradition of innovation, one that is at least as significant historically as the 'innately conservative' stereotype. Kimberley Smith Maynard, Margaret McCallum, and Philip Girard demonstrate that in divorce law, compulsory arbitration, chancery reform, and married women's property law, the province's leaders were unafraid to propose (and at times to try) new directions. If many items on the reform agenda did not survive their immersion in the pool of politics, it was not necessarily because of any 'innate' conservatism or inertia. Vested interests played an important role, but older ideologies remained sufficiently powerful to brake the spirit of liberal progressivism that permeated the province.

Taken as a whole, the essays suggest some intriguing new directions for Canadian legal history. They demonstrate that a subtle and complex mixture of English, American, and indigenous influences was at work in shaping and reshaping our legal order from the earliest times until at least 1900. More specifically, they suggest that the weight given to English and American models depended upon the area of law in question: American influence seems to have been strongest in economic and commercial regulation in the nineteenth century, and weakest in substantive criminal law, in which the English model remained unquestionably dominant. With the decline of the mercantilist system, Nova Scotia set itself the task of combining American prosperity with 'British justice,' a mission that ultimately would be taken up by the new nation of Canada. David Flaherty has said that the Canadian legal system should not be treated as a tabula rasa upon which disembodied British and American 'influences' did battle;[6] still, a closer study of the selective use of American and British models will be necessary to elucidate the nature of Canadian legal culture as well as 'the function of law in the creation and expression of a distinctive Canadian identity.'[7]

It seems clear that Hurstian notions about the release of human creative energy are not especially helpful in the Canadian context. Canadian law in the nineteenth century displays a certain ambivalence towards the 'liberated' individual, amounting at times to outright distrust. Notions of liberal individualism became more influential as the nineteenth century progressed, but they never became the organizing principle of the law in the same way that they did, arguably, in the United States. While the facilitative role of law was important at some level, any freedom or privilege accorded by the law was hedged about with restrictions relating to the maintenance of prevailing notions of the collective good. Parties were permitted to exit from failed marriages, but divorce was strictly circumscribed lest the family, the fundamental unit of society, be threatened. Limited liability was accorded to corporations, but as a privilege, not a right, for most of the nineteenth century. Debtors could escape imprisonment fairly easily under insolvent-debtor legislation, but the debtors' prison had to stand as a reminder of the awesome sanctity of the debt obligation. Definitions of the public good were often, though not always, articulated by a narrow stratum of the community: white, well-educated, and relatively affluent older men. At times they represented a broad consensus, but often they were challenged – sometimes peacefully, sometimes violently – by liberals, Christian humanists, populists, trade unions, women, temperance advocates, and aboriginal protection groups. Out of this contestation there emerged a mentality of cautious reformism, best exemplified by figures such as Joseph Howe and Beamish Murdoch in Nova Scotia (Jonathan McCully was a little too experimental and technocratic to fit comfortably under this label) and William Hume Blake in Ontario. In their world-view, the law's function was to promote and protect a concept of 'ordered liberty' that allowed individuals a certain amount of autonomy while safeguarding the paramount interests of the community.

That this theme dominated the thought of individuals as different as W.D. LeSueur and W.L. Mackenzie King[8] suggests that it represented a distinctively Canadian approach to law, one that transcended the particularisms of the British North American colonies and indeed the cultural divide between English Canada and French Canada. This approach is consistent with a national identity that has led some literary critics to describe Canada as 'a dynamic and multi-dimensional mosaic of opposites in tension'[9] and a 'hope confronting both the anarchic and the totalitarian.'[10] More work at both the local and national levels will be needed to ascertain the significance of this legal ideology and its impact in the twentieth century.

NOTES

1 J.F. Stephen *A History of the Criminal Law of England* vol. 3 (London 1881) 117–18
2 L.A. Knafla, ed. *Law and Justice in a New Land: Essays in Western Canadian Legal History* (Toronto: Carswell 1986)
3 David Flaherty, ed. *Essays in the History of Canadian Law* vol. 1 (Toronto: The Osgoode Society 1981); idem *Essays in the History of Canadian Law* vol. 2 (Toronto: The Osgoode Society 1983)
4 G.B. Baker 'The Reconstitution of Upper Canadian Legal Thought in the Late Victorian Empire' *Law and History Review* 3 (1985) 219; D. Howes 'Property, God and Nature in the Thought of Sir John Beverley Robinson' *McGill Law Journal* 30 (1985) 365; idem 'From Polyjurality to Monojurality: The Transformation of Quebec Law, 1875–1929' *McGill Law Journal* 32 (1987) 523
5 G.A. Rawlyk 'A New Golden Age of Maritime Historiography?' *Queen's Quarterly* 76 (1969) 55; W. Godfrey 'A New Golden Age: Recent Historical Writing on the Maritimes' *Queen's Quarterly* 91 (1984) 35. Compare E.R. Forbes 'In Search of a Post-Confederation Maritime Historiography 1900–1967' *Acadiensis* 7 (1978)
6 D.H. Flaherty 'Writing Canadian Legal History: An Introduction' in Flaherty *History of Canadian Law* vol. 1, 6
7 R.C.B. Risk 'A Prospectus for Canadian Legal History' *Dalhousie Law Journal* 1 (1973) 230
8 A.B. McKillop *A Critical Spirit: The Thought of William Dawson LeSueur* (Toronto: McClelland and Stewart 1977), and P. Craven *'An Impartial Umpire': Industrial Relations and the Canadian State 1900–1911* (Toronto: University of Toronto Press 1980) chapter 3
9 D.M.R. Bentley 'A Sacramental Vision of Canada' *Dalhousie Review* 66 (1986–7) 537
10 M. Ross *The Impossible Sum of Our Traditions: Reflections on Canadian Literature* (Toronto: McClelland and Stewart 1986) 25

2

'The Dayly Cry for Justice': The Juridical Failure of the Annapolis Royal Regime, 1713–1749

THOMAS GARDEN BARNES

The most resounding proem to a work of jurisprudence in our civilization begins with a catalogue of barbarian tribes and great races conquered or reduced to obedience (as much promissory as real in AD 533) by Caesar Flavius Justinian, Ever Augustus, followed by a telling argument for law as an imperialistic tool: 'Imperial majesty should be not only embellished with arms but also fortified by laws so that the times of both war and peace can be rightly regulated and the Roman Emperor not only emerge victorious in war with the enemy but also, extirpating the iniquities of wrongdoers through the administration of justice, prove as solicitous of the law as he is triumphant over defeated foes.'[1] Clearly, Justinian the Legislator was also Justinian the Warrior, and the arts of peace were at one with the arts of war. Hammurabi, in 1750 BC, and Napoleon, in AD 1804, also warriors and legislators, understood and acted upon the premise that the conqueror's law was a means of imposing obedience, exacting allegiance, creating political dependency, and drawing the conquered to a greater or lesser extent into the dominant polity, society, and culture. British imperialists of the Golden Age, accepting this imperative unapologetically, made of that archetypal Whig Lord Macaulay, draughtsman of the Indian Penal Code (1838), one of the greatest imperialists.

British imperial authorities responsible for Nova Scotia between its acquisition by the Treaty of Utrecht in 1713 and the decisive imperial act of the founding of Halifax on Chebucto Bay in 1749 demonstrated no policy commitment to the role of law-making and law-doing in governing a conquered people. Granted, Nova Scotia was a novel challenge. Save for Jamaica in 1655 and New Netherlands (New York, New Jersey, and Delaware) in 1664, England had not acquired large territories in the New World by conquest of European peoples. In the case of Jamaica, at the time of conquest there were only a handful of Spaniards (who departed), a large number of slaves (who merely changed masters), and a sizable population of runaway slaves (the Maroons, who, though unconquerable, were not a routine menace). The Dutch had been in New Netherlands for less than a generation, and the indigenous population was fragmented among a number of tribes divided by deep traditional enmities. Nova Scotia possessed a French population of three generations' continuance and a single native people in a long and close political and (especially) credal alliance with the French. Moreover, the boundaries of Nova Scotia under the treaty were in dispute, and the British claim to present-day New Brunswick (beyond the Chignecto isthmus) was almost unenforceable. The colony stood menaced by the new French citadel at Louisbourg on Isle Royal (Cape Breton). The seat of government, France's Port-Royal (renamed Annapolis Royal) was a strategically remote site ill-suited to maintaining surveillance over, let alone governance of, the king's 'new subjects.'

There were influences at work that might have persuaded British authority to use law to imperial ends. Classical models were present and potent in Georgian England, and early eighteenth-century Britons fancied themselves Augustan, with the trappings, style, decoration, rhetoric, amplitude, and ambitions of imperial Rome. In an Augustan way their hegemonic thrust became more purposeful, even perhaps more militaristic, if not quite as self-consciously as one historian has argued recently.[2] Moreover, it was clear in English jurisprudence, following the law of nations, that the king might impose upon a conquered people what law he chose, subject only to the condition that until he did so, if the conquered were Christian, their existing law would obtain.[3] At least one Georgian imperialist, the man responsible for the routine governance of newly conquered Nova Scotia, early advocated a policy of juridical acculturation of the Acadians. Apropos the advantages to be gained by encouraging the Acadians to remain in the province, Thomas Caulfeild, lieutenant-governor of Annapolis Royal, wrote in 1715 that 'their numbers are considerable and in case they quit us will onlie strengthen our enemys when occasion serves by so much. And though wee may not receive much benefit from them, yett theire children in process of time will be brought to our Constitution.'[4]

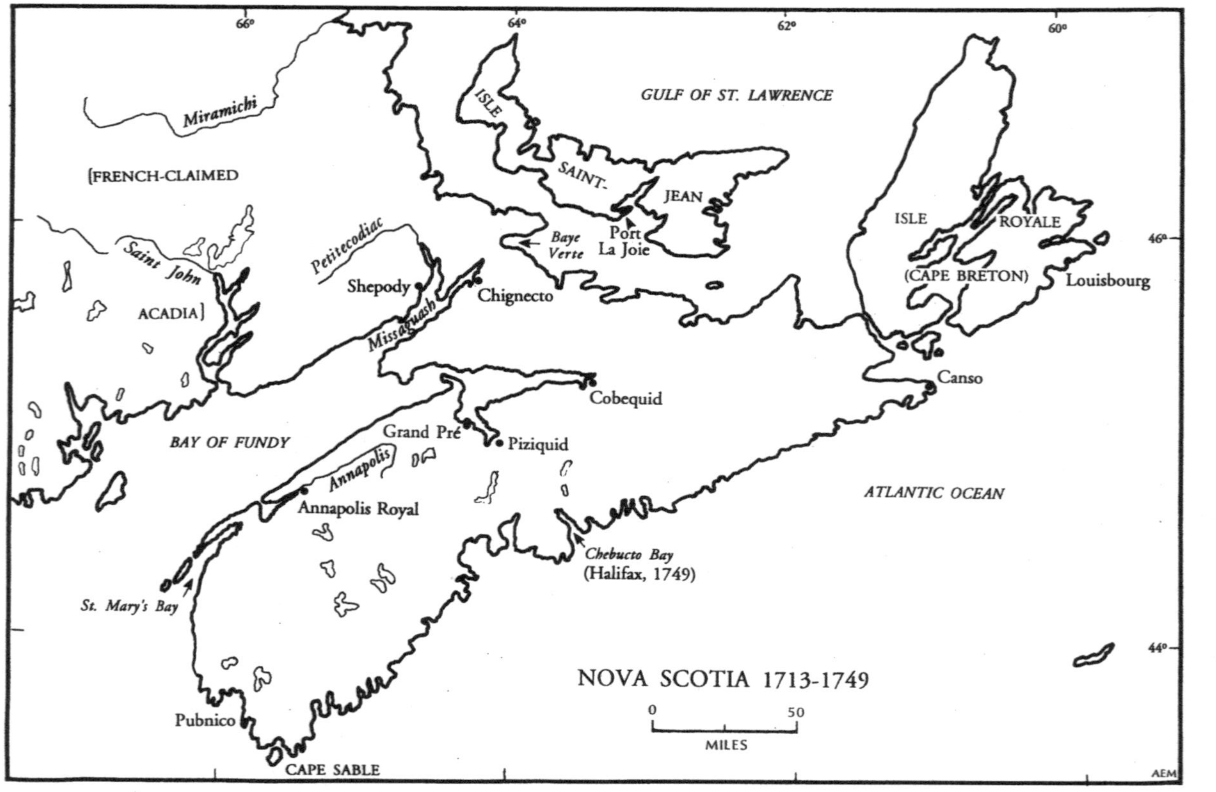

Map by Adrienne E. Morgan. Based upon a map in A.H. Clark *Acadia: The Geography of Early Nova Scotia to 1760* (Madison: University of Wisconsin Press 1968) 332. Used by permission

Caulfeild's prediction, 'theire children in process of time will be brought to our Constitution' did not strike a responsive chord at Whitehall. Neither did it prove prophetic. In 1755 a successor of Caulfeild expelled wholesale the 'children' of the Acadians of his day – men, women, and children neither brought within the British 'Constitution' nor afforded its protection.

Almost without exception, the conventional historical explanations for the tragedy of 1755 begin with the new regime's repeated attempts between 1713 and 1755 to exact from the Acadians an unconditional oath of allegiance.[5] The permutations of the oath-business still provide a bottomless well for historiographical creativity, despite the fact that Victorian historians exhausted the possibilities of any new combinations being adduced to establish the oath as an efficient cause of the expulsion. If most students of early British Nova Scotia have concentrated with singular (and perhaps excessive) intensity on the oath, there is no denying its contemporary importance: the spectres of a succession of governors and councillors can be summoned to testify to the time, effort, and anguish expended on it at Annapolis Royal and later at Halifax. This essay, though, suggests that there was a more fundamental shortcoming in British imperial governance than its failing to exact an unconditional oath or, wanting such, in its refusing finally to ignore the consequences. That shortcoming was in essence juridical, the failure to bring the French to 'our Constitution' as Caulfeild had suggested; and it was already well in place before the founding of Halifax in 1749.

The enduring (and now conventional) portrait of the Annapolis Royal regime was painted in bold colours by J. Bartlet Brebner sixty years ago. It is epitomized in three of the chapter titles in his published doctoral dissertation: 'A Phantom Rule and "Neutral" Subjects (1710–1723)'; 'Counterfeit Suzerainty (1724–1739)'; and 'Government by Analogy and Rule of Thumb (1710–1749).'[6] 'Phantom rule' referred to the handful of governing officials and the small garrison – four (or even fewer) understrength companies of the Fortieth Foot and some gunners – at the dilapidated fort at Annapolis Royal. Unsupported by any English-speaking settlers to form a militia reserve, without routine naval capacity and therefore reliant on New England merchantmen for communications and rapid extension of force, they were unable to control a hinterland peopled by francophone 'new subjects' whose avowed 'neutrality' was ambiguous, and by Indians whose movements were seldom detected and whose sporadic depredations were never interdicted.[7] In 1720 the garrison's officers reported that the orders of government 'loose their force at the distance of gun shot from this fort'; later, an eager subaltern's proposal for a punitive patrol against Micmac marauders twelve miles up the Annapolis River from the fort was disapproved: 'If any Accident should at such a distance happen to the Party, it would be of Ill Consequence to the Garrison.'[8] Indeed, the 'phantom rule' was not restricted to the period between 1710 and 1723. It was a constant, and it was further enfeebled by the 'counterfeit suzerainty' of the regime over a people whose population was growing rapidly along almost the entire length of the Fundy shore from Pubnico to Chignecto, whose allegiance was given always with reservation, who were unaccustomed to the trammels of external authority, whose credal loyalties were ultramontane (if not over the Alps to Rome, certainly over the Appalachians to Quebec), and who feared their Micmac nominal co-religionists more than they they did the British.[8]

'Government by analogy and rule of thumb' is a more questionable and even contentious description of how the Annapolis Royal regime governed. At most, it is only half true. The 'analogue' was Virginia. Article 9 of the instructions given in 1719 to Colonel Richard Philipps as governor of Placentia and captain general and governor of Nova Scotia directed him to return an assessment of the state of the province with respect to the people who lived there or were likely to come there, 'of what numbers it may be proper to constitute an assembly,' persons fit to be judges, justices of the peace, and sheriffs, and any other matter that might be of use 'in establishing a civil government' there. Article 10 covered the temporary exigency of governing until a representative assembly could be convened:

> In the mean time till such a government shall have been established you will receive herewith a copy of the instructions given by his Majesty to the governor of Virginia, by which you will conduct yourself till his Majestys further pleasure shall be known, as near as the circumstances of the place will admit, in such things as they can be applicable to, and where you are not otherwise directed by these instructions. But you are not to take upon you to enact any laws till his Majesty shall have appointed an assembly and given you directions for your proceedings therein.[10]

The Privy Council noted that it was necessary to include the Virginia instructions because Philipps's instructions were 'not to be so extensive as those for his Majestys other governors in America, in regard the said province hath not been hitherto peopled or settled by his Majestys subjects.'[11] The temporary exigency lasted until the first Nova Scotia assembly was finally convened in 1758, a decade after British settlement began.

The Virginia instructions referred to were those issued to George Hamilton, Earl of Orkney, on 15 April 1715. They were lengthy: something short of a codex, the 136 articles covered virtually all situations likely to arise in colonial governance.[12] They were less than ideally suited to the circumstances of Nova Scotia in the aftermath of the conquest of 1710, for they supposed British inhabitants living under English institutions. The sophisticated executive, legislative, and judicial structure called for was wholly applicable only to a province that had been in existence for over a century and that had had a representative assembly for ninety-six years. The instructions assumed the existence of a considerable substructure of sworn officers – judges, justices of the peace, sheriffs, a clerk of the assembly, clerks of court, a provost marshal, constables, parochial vestries, and militia officers – most of whom would not make an appearance in Nova Scotia until after the founding of Halifax. And they guaranteed fundamental rights and liberties which the experience of seventeenth-century English revolutions had dictated as essential in colonies of Britons: habeas corpus, speedy trial, jury trial, limitation of martial law, and appeals to the colony's council and the Privy Council. Above all there was the injunction of article 62: 'You are to take Care that no Man's Life Member freehold or Goods be taken away or harm'd in our said Colony otherwise than by establish'd and known Laws, not repugnant but as near as may be agreeable to the Laws of this Kingdom.'[13] Such guarantees could be extended to non-British inhabitants, and during the Annapolis Royal regime most were. But to have full force and effect they required the active participation of subjects in the political life of the colony. An ambiguous concession of toleration of Roman Catholicism by the Treaty of 1713 did not remove the impediment to Catholics' holding sworn office, which barred the Acadians from most executive service and any legislative role.[14] The king's 'new subjects' enjoyed the rights and liberties of Englishmen so far as they understood them and thought them advantageous, but they were passive recipients of them rather than vigorous partakers in them.

Brebner evoked the vivid image of the Virginia instructions 'thumbed almost to destruction by the perplexed soldiers' at Annapolis Royal: 'Many a time when unforeseen problems arose, the governor adjourned the Council for a day or two, while he retired to delve in the Virginian folios.'[15] There is only one such adjournment recorded. The litigious and fractious William Winniett, having lost a long-standing dispute over a house and garden in Annapolis Royal, accused the council of 'injustice' and threatened to 'appeal Home.'[16] The next day, Lieutenant-Governor Lawrence Armstrong informed council that from his perusal of the Virginia instructions Winniett was barred from appealing to the Privy Council. The council concurred, and confirmed the sentence of the day before.[17] That one boreal swallow doth not a Virginia summer make. The instructions were an ultimate resource, a fungible model, a convenient device, and a security-blanket for the governor and council in ambiguous and contentious situations, not living law routinely implemented. If there was no quorum in council, the Virginia instructions' sanctioning of three councillors to act in 'Extraordinary Emergencies' was expedient; the council, when intent upon requiring surveys of property, could roll out the Virginia instructions to reinforce those for Nova Scotia.[18] The Virginia instructions and the positive law of Virginia were implemented structurally and functionally only with the advent of the Halifax regime. Cornwallis's council accepted the 13 December 1749 report of the committee of three councillors for judicature, which expressly instituted the rules and regulations of the Virginia General Court and county courts for the new Nova Scotia cognates and which recommended that Virginia law be consulted in interpreting the Virginia court rules.[19] Even this 'reception' proved only partial.

If the Annapolis Royal regime did not govern 'by analogy,' it certainly did govern by 'rule of thumb,' and that most clearly in the matter of judicature. The report of the committee on judicature in 1749 puts the prior history in bold relief by its recommendations for a sophisticated judicial structure (a general court of superior first-instance and appellate jurisdiction and county courts for trial of lesser matters, including one at Annapolis Royal), and by its recommendation that 'all matters of fact be tried by jurys in the same manner as in England'; that all writs be in the same form as in England; and twice yearly commissioners of oyer and terminer (three or more justices of the General Court) go to Minas to hear causes of action brought by 'French subjects'; and that a regulated legal profession be established. Yet even these provisions erecting the glorious panoply of traditional English judicature pale before the report's schedules of fees – that concrete token of juridical maturity – for the new courts' clerks, the provost marshal, and attorneys.[20] In comparison, what the previous regime had done juridically appeared inchoate and ineffective.

Such was not the intention of the Annapolis Royal regime itself. From the outset, with the exception of Francis Nicholson's short and unblushingly personal rule from (August to October 1714), the institution of civil government was the objective of a succession of governors at Annapolis Royal. Nicholson's own lieutenant, Major Caulfeild, bemoaned the absence of courts of judicature and attempted to mediate causes between the inhabitants despite the absence of judicial powers.[21] The former governor, Samuel Vetch, scored his predecessors (and by implication Whitehall) for not 'having established any civil government there since its reduction, save what they may have empowerd Coll. Philips to doe, who only went thither thiss spring.'[22] Philipps had the power. It had taken him two years following his appointment in August 1717 as governor to obtain a full commission and instructions providing him with sufficient authority to establish civil government. In the meantime, his lieutenant at the fort, Captain John Doucett, had managed to avoid the prospect of soldierly disorder by reducing the discontent of the long unpaid and miserably treated garrison and to quiet the apprehensions of the Acadians by dealing forthrightly and irenically with them. Doucett admirably provided the transition from martial to civil government.

Philipps arrived at the fort in April 1720. He moved quickly to erect the frame of civil government, and within a month had appointed a council of twelve and summoned six 'representatives' (later 'deputies') of the Acadians around Annapolis Royal to make his first attempt at extracting an unqualified oath. He appointed Arthur Savage naval officer (maritime officer) and secretary.[23] He also commissioned three justices of the peace and appointed two captains of militia at Canso, which was about all the civil government provided to that wide-open fishing and trading port 350 nautical miles from Annapolis Royal. Within a year the system of Acadian deputies was firmly in place, and deputies were appointed from Minas and Cobequid as well as from the Annapolis River.

On 19 April 1721 Philipps convened the council to consider 'Establishing a Court of Judicature,' as in Virginia, that would consist of the governor and council. The next day, having noted that 'the dayly cry here is for Justice by many of the Inhabitants and residents of this Province,' they erected a Court of Judicature composed of the governor and council. The court was to meet at Annapolis Royal on the first Tuesday in May, August, November, and February, and was to have the style and to proceed in the manner of the General Court of Virginia.[24] This was the apex of Philipps's first tour in Nova Scotia as governor – indeed, of his entire three decades' governorship, twice present and mostly absent. Within a few months Philipps departed for Canso and thence to England, not to return until 1729, leaving government in the hands of Doucett (until his death in 1726) and, afterwards, Lawrence Armstrong.

The 'General Court,' with its neat quarterly sessions, never materialized. A comparison of council sittings over the years between 1721 and 1736 for which relatively full council records exist indicates that only thrice did council meetings correspond with the first-Tuesday dates, and two of those sittings did no judicial business. However, that does not mean that the council turned a deaf ear to the 'dayly cry for Justice.' On the contrary: after a modest start in the early 1720s (one to three cases per annum) there was a sharp increase in the amount of civil litigation (averaging eight cases per annum), and in the number of Acadian suitors, from 1724 to 1727. There are no council records extant from November 1727 to November 1729, and no civil judicial business was done by council from November 1729 until mid-1731. From 1731 to 1736, however, civil litigation increased markedly:

	British cases	Acadian	Mixed	Total
1731	5	14	0	19
1732	12	21	2	35
1733	6	13	0	19
1734	0	6	0	6
1735	1	7	2	10
1736	0	10	0	10

To these figures, of course, criminal cases must be added. Those were never as numerous: there were 63 (38 of them having Acadian defendants), as against 135 civil cases. The criminal cases were essentially prosecutions ex officio, even when moved by a party grieved and despite the fact that there was no one other than the governor or lieutenant-governor responsible for acting as procurator or Crown attorney. They were not much of a measure of popular resort to adjudication at Annapolis Royal.

The amount of time the council spent in judicature rose even more than the increase in the case load indicates, since the council became less summary and more procedure-bound over the course of time. Due process became, inevitably, slow process. No significant procedural differences existed between civil and criminal actions. An action began when the governor or the president put before the council for its 'advice,' or determination, a matter that had been brought to his attention by petition, complaint, or information. The very informal pleadings (the complaint and the defendants' answers) were submitted in writing. There is no hint of formalized special pleading. Both parties were given time to appear;

there was no trial absent either party. Parties in a civil suit could appear by attorney – that is, they could be represented by an agent, as there is no trace of a legal profession. The council openly heard both oral testimony and received written evidence. It found facts, determined law, gave judgment, and incorporated the 'sentence' in a written order. The usual remedies were restitution, possession, or specific performance; damages were rarely awarded. Costs were taxed for the fees paid the secretary of the council and the constable, according to a schedule of fees. Since procedure was simple, costs were modest, which enhanced the council's attractiveness to Acadian litigants. Costs for both parties in a typical civil suit, assuming one plaintiff and one defendant, including French translations, came to about 16s sterling (£2 16s 0d in New England currency).[25] The 'sentence' was executed by the Annapolis Royal constable (who was bailiff and marshal to the council, and the only sworn underofficer in the colony) or by the Acadian deputies, who were sometimes assisted by the Acadian notary appointed by the council for each settlement. Judgment was enforced by commitment for contempt. There no longer existed in English judicature an exact parallel to such conciliar jurisdiction and procedures; Chancery and Exchequer equity-side came closest. Its true cognate, the High Court of Star Chamber, had disappeared in 1641. The model was not despicable – it had served in early Massachusetts for the General Court.[26]

The council was the resident governor's or lieutenant-governor's instrument, and was convened by him to deal with such business as he saw fit to submit for its consideration. He determined how much juridical work it did. Governor Philipps convened his newly appointed council thirty-nine times between 25 April 1720 and 17 May 1721, and was present at and presided over it at all but three sittings. Of the twelve councillors an average of eight attended, and only once was the attendance as low as five. The business of the council was largely political-executive, with thirty-nine actions taken, six of them so general as to amount to 'legislation.' In seven consecutive sittings over five weeks two criminal matters and two civil matters came before the council; one of the latter was connected with one of the crimes. None involved Acadian parties.

Under the administration of Lieutenant-Governor John Doucett council meetings were no less regular, and judicial business became increasingly prominent beginning in early 1724 and continuing until Doucett's death in November 1726. From April to June 1725 six consecutive sittings dealt only with litigation – four Acadian, two English, and three mixed civil suits, and three Acadian criminal cases.[27] In the latter half of 1726, pressing political affairs (most of which centred on a resumption of the oath-business, Indian affairs related to ending Dummer's War, and the disruptive activities of a missionary to the Micmac, Abbé Antoine Gaulin, who was busily trying to prevent the Indians from making peace with the English) barred much judicial activity. It is not difficult to explain why, so far as circumstances allowed, Doucett's council undertook judicial business. Doucett personally took an interest in settling disputes, and often acted alone as a mediator among the Acadians. The council mirrored his concern for doing justice.

Lieutenant-Governor Armstrong continued Doucett's reliance on the council, especially for judicature, and also attempted to create a more sophisticated administrative substructure among the Acadians. Where Doucett was conciliatory, Armstrong was abrasive and suspicious of the Acadians to the point of paranoia. His mistrust moved him to tie the Acadians as closely as possible to government by an activist juridical policy intended to bind them in a web of law, law-doing, and law-enforcing. At his urging, the council became a relatively settled juridical instrument, increasingly sophisticated not only in its procedures but also in its substantive law. Armstrong's judiciousness and his commitment to due process were unusual in a soldier, his patience unexpected in a man with a dark side so desperate that he would ultimately stab himself to death.

While Armstrong's administration is best understood as a continuum from his arrival at the fort in September 1726 until his death there in December 1739, it was in fact interrupted by a disastrous second coming of Governor Philipps that endured from 20 November 1729 to his recall in August 1731.[28] The damage done by Philipps proved transitory, but it was very disruptive for a season. Philipps acted with unconcealed vindictiveness towards Armstrong, who left the colony as soon as Philipps arrived. He appointed Armstrong's arch-enemy, Major Alexander Cosby, president of the council in derogation of Major Paul Mascarene's better claim as senior councillor; he named as a councillor William Winniett, a man whom Armstrong had come to detest as early as 1715; and he made the slippery Alexandre Bourg, Winniett's agent and crony at Minas, notary and collector of rents there. The Philipps-Cosby-Winniett clique was a family affair: Cosby was Philipps's brother-in-law and Winniett's son-in-law.[29] The exceptionally harsh and degrading censure (pillory) meted out to two prominent Acadians for a 'notorious fraud' probably owed most to the fact that one of them, Francis Richards, had been appointed a high constable by Armstrong.[30]

Philipps treated the council with disdain. For the twenty-one months he was at Annapolis, Phillips attended and presided at council meetings only during the first nineteen; afterwards he remained in his house communicating imperiously through Cosby. In the first nineteen months there were only twelve sittings: twice, six months elapsed between meetings, and there were but four meetings in 1730. There were no civil trials and the few council meetings were brief and dealt largely with formalities: reading instructions, swearing in officers, appointing councillors, and 'approving' actions already taken by Philipps unilaterally and often arbitrarily without advice. Thus, Philipps doubled the number of deputies from the Annapolis River, appointed to the council 'upon ye Spot' a young officer to make up a quorum, and was wont to issue proclamations that were not only bombastic but also intemperate – actions detracting from what had become standard procedures that maintained the gravity of the council and introduced consistency in rule.[31]

Philipps's personal crusade to extract an unconditional oath from the Acadians – and his dishonest and perilous oral promise to the inhabitants of Minas and Chignecto exempting them from bearing arms – were characteristic of his methods in his second sojourn.[32] Indeed, during the long periods between council meetings in 1730 when Philipps was on extended perambulations up the Fundy about the oath, he was also conducting a kind of ancien régime *lit de justice*, or, since it was intensely personal and procedurally irregular, something like Saint-Louis's playing judge under the oak at Vincennes. In a number of cases he gave peremptory judgment alone, sometimes without hearing both sides, resulting in much confusion, some injustice, and the need for the council to undo the mischief after his recall.

The mischief took some undoing. While at Minas, Philipps had ordered escheat of the lands of an intestate to the defeat of his daughter-heir; council held that Philipps had been 'misinformed' about the non-existence of an heir and ordered the heir put in upon proof of her right.[33] Philipps's summary outlawry and confiscation of the property of Etienne Rivett for 'stirring up the savages,' which was based on the information of an adversary suitor, was reversed on a reading of the testimony of fifty-five of the inhabitants who swore to his innocence.[34] In two cases the council felt compelled to reiterate that the matters would not be heard until the adverse parties had had time given for their appearance, and in another a casual promise by Philipps to a claimant made in defeat of a title had to be undone.[35] A year after Philipps's departure, council reheard a complicated land dispute after overturning his solo 'sentence,' noting that it was given 'without the advice of the Council' and while on file was not of record in the minutes of council.[36] Indeed, the most eloquent testimony to the great distrust in which Philipps's personal judicial activism was held by both the British and the Acadians is the enormous number of civil cases tried by the council from 1731 to 1733 – seventy-three, all but two of which (both British) were heard after Armstrong began to preside again over council in September 1731.

The absence of anything approaching an adequate record of the council after August 1736 prevents a detailed analysis of its juridical function. What is extant indicates no cessation of activity and no significant changes in procedure.[37] Continuity in conciliar membership maintained its judicial role, which was further strengthened by the addition in 1736 of four new councillors (among them the devoted Edward How), three of whom attended regularly until the late 1740s. Major Paul Mascarene's defeat of Cosby for the presidency of the council (and for the post of civil administrator) after Armstrong's suicide in 1739 produced great continuity in policy and administration. Mascarene was no less committed than Armstrong to the juridical function of government. He could also articulate it better: 'Since I have had the honor to preside here, my study has been to make these French Inhabitants sensible of the difference there is between the British and French Government, by administering impartial justice to them and in all other respects treating them with lenity and humanity, without yielding anything wherein His Majesty's honor or interest were concerned.'[38] Mascarene has been hymned by historians in both tongues; nothing need be added to the encomia.[39] His native facility in French, his intellectual gifts, his almost academic curiosity and learning, his real interest in maintaining an active dialogue with missionary priests, and his temperate character commended him to the king's 'new subjects.' He was even readier than his predecessors to involve Acadians in government; he refined, defined, and as far as he could regularized the duties and roles of the deputies, notaries, and collectors of rents, thus advancing the administrative infrastructure begun at the outset of civil government. All this contributed to the maintenance of a remarkable degree of Acadian neutrality during King George's War (1743–8) and, in the years of fragile peace before and after it, to good and orderly government from Annapolis Royal.

What most plagued the Annapolis Royal regime was the paucity of English talent requisite to staff government. The pool was small: fewer than a score of garrison officers of the Fortieth Foot, plus the garrison surgeon, the chaplain (when there was one), for a time a deputy surveyor and a couple of other senior civilian officials of government, and a handful of English and New English civilians, merchants, and master mariners. Non-commissioned officers and civilian ordnance and stores personnel, a few sailors and clerks, were more numerous but of too low a rank to serve in offices higher than that of constable.

Nowhere was the staffing problem more evident than in the council. The fate of Philipps's first twelve councillors appointed in 1720 is instructive. Three were regimental officers (Doucett, Armstrong, and Mascarene); one was the chaplain (John Harrison); one was the surgeon (William Skene); two were civilian officials (William Shirreff, commissioner of musters, and Hibbert Newton, collector of customs); and five were merchants (Cypryan Southack, Arthur Savage, John Adams, Peter Boudre, and Guilliam Philipps), of whom Southack and Boudre were also master mariners. Guilliam Philipps, the son of a Boston merchant, attended only the council meeting at which he was sworn; Southack served two months, Harrison five, and Boudre from September 1721 to March 1723. Savage, the secretary and naval officer, fed up with factionalism, returned to his native Boston in 1722. Newton served faithfully until he moved to Boston in mid-1724. Armstrong, having taken an immediate dislike to Philipps, busied himself at Canso and then went to London to advance his political fortunes. When Armstrong returned as lieutenant-governor in September 1726, the council stood at Doucett (president), Mascarene, Adams, Skene, and Shirreff. Doucett's death two months later left four councillors.

Armstrong, while still away in 1725, had unsuccessfully moved for five new councillors.[40] By March 1727 the problem of finding a quorum of five was so serious that Armstrong issued commissions to Adams, Skene, and Shirreff to be justices of the peace, and 'also for want of Such a Quorum of the Council as is required by His Majestys Instructions ... to Examine and Enquire into all Pleas, Debates and Differences that are or may be amongst the inhabitants of Said Province and to make Reports of your Oppinions and Judgements thereof to the Gov. or Commander in Chief [lieutenant-governor] for Confirmation of your Said Judgements or Otherways.'[41] The creation of a 'judicial committee' merely recognized what was already a reality – the juridical work of Adams, Skene, and Shirreff – and neither added to nor subtracted from their powers or functions, though it did regularize the exercise of them. It did not solve the problem of numbers. Armstrong did that two months later by appointing to the council three captains and the civilian commissary-major of the fort, sparking a horrendous row by Shirreff over precedence (Adams and Skene remained neutral) that Armstrong cooled for a time, though he finally lost Shirreff's services for four years. One of Armstrong's new appointees proved useless; the three captains attended assiduously until sometime before Philipps's second coming, and then disappeared.

Shirreff's defection was a blow, because he, Adams, and Skene had borne the weight of council adjudication from the outset (and would do so again in the future). They had gifts for judicature that no other councillors possessed in like degree – patience, judiciousness, a willingness to work hard without tangible reward, a practical knowledge of law, and a sense of justice. Philipps assessed his new councillors in 1720: 'John Adams Esq. – Merchant and inhabitant of long standing in this place, and a man of sense. William Skeen Esq. – Surgeon to the garrison, a gentleman of learning and read in the Civil Law. William Sherriff Esq. – Commissary of the musters.'[42] Only Adams has found his way into the Canadian pantheon.[43] A Bostonian who came to Port-Royal in 1710 in the New England militia and stayed to trade, he was as prickly as he was sensible. An inveterate foe of the Philipps faction, as deputy collector of customs he pounced on Winniett for his shady dealings. He quit the colony in 1740 in high dudgeon after having been passed over for president of the council in favour of Mascarene. None the less, for twenty years, save for a year's sojourn in England (1734–5) and despite a worsening loss of sight, he faithfully attended 85 per cent of the council meetings for which minutes are relatively complete (1720–36). About Shirreff little is known. He was 'acting' secretary between 1722 and 1727; he ceased attending council in July 1727 after a dispute over precedence, and returned as secretary in July 1731. He achieved 87 per cent attendance (save for the hiatus), and remained just as active until 1749.

William Skene is hardly less shadowy a figure, but he had certain distinctions worthy of emphasis. His attendance rate from 1720 to 1736, during which he was continuously resident in the colony, was 94 per cent: he attended 288 of the 305 known meetings of the council in that period.[44] The minutes that exist for the period after 1736 indicate equally faithful attendance until his death, which occurred sometime after January 1747.[45] To such dutifulness must be added the significant fact that Skene was 'read in the Civil Law.' That a surgeon might also be legally learned was unusual but not unknown; that a Scot, a Skene of that ilk, of a distinguished Aberdeenshire family which had produced lords of session in the previous century, would be learned in civil law is not surprising.[46] Though nothing has been found out about William Skene's education, Philipps's ascription is not the only evidence of his learning. Because of the leading role he played in the juridical activity of the council, Skene probably supplied the distinctly civilian tone apparent in much of the council's adjudication. William Skene's 'thumb' provided a great deal of the 'rule.'

The civil law was evident in both rhetoric and doctrine. The council commonly and correctly used the terms 'moveables' and 'immoveables' when referring to Acadians' property.[47] 'Tutor' and 'tutorship' in their narrowly civilian meaning fell easily from the councillors' lips.[48] 'Right,' though it might admit of a common law meaning, more often had a distinctly Gallic civil law flavour about it. *Droit* connoted 'right' when it was coupled with 'equity' or 'possession.'[49]

Rhetoric went to substance, and for good reason. Two-thirds of the Acadian and mixed civil actions dealt with a 'right' to or possession of immoveable property; a further tenth, while in the nature of delicts, grew from property disputes and generally required a determination of right or possession before the delict could be adjudicated (if it was the object of the suit at all). Titles usually depended upon *contrats*; the earliest ones cited date from the 1680s. Originally such *contrats*, theoretically if not always in fact, were founded on seigneurial grants. From the outset the British regime tacitly equated 'right' with possession if supported by *contrat* or inheritance from *contrat*.

The regime's ultimate objective was to re-grant all old holdings and to allow no new ones without grant. Philipps took up this practice energetically during the last months of his second sojourn and Armstrong continued it. Neither man elicited much co-operation from Whitehall. Such an ambitious project depended upon (1) surveys and (2) the grantees' swearing an unconditional oath of allegiance. The second condition proved unattainable save in a few notable individual cases. Surveying awaited the belated arrival of a military surveyor in 1732.[50] Even then the Acadians were reluctant to pay the cost of surveys, and they occupied new lands by discreet squatting without any apparent fear of the (remote) consequence, forfeiture for want of title. A historian has argued recently that the repeated efforts of the council to exact surveys and settle titles was a device to pressure the Acadians into taking the oath.[51] Yet the council had other good reasons to quiet title and establish boundaries between holdings. In 1731 Armstrong's council issued a general order that no grants would be made without a survey first; otherwise it was 'Impossible ever to have Any Tollerable Account of their Estates or even to give Grants.'[52] A couple of months later a case brought the issue to the fore again, and each councillor was canvassed and minuted on the importance of surveys. William Skene was most perspicacious in observing that 'to prevent vexatious Suits, which daily happen, and the Better to Ascertain the Just Boundarys of Each mans property the lands ought to be Surveyed.'[53] The parties ignored the order, and council threw the case out until a survey was made.[54] A year later, an agreement disintegrated over an earlier amateur survey. Resigned, council left in the possessor until a proper survey was made.[55] The council, by not persisting in its resolve to re-grant all Acadian lands and by lessening even its judicial pressure for surveying before grant, produced the regime's signal juridical failure.

In the adjudication of Acadian suits involving immoveables, if the property was held by grant from the British regime, the title probably would have been determined according to common law – probably, because there is no Acadian action in which it is clear that the land was held by British grant, as it was in most British suits, where the common law ruled.[56] Absent a grant, the council demonstrated no preference for the common law in Acadian suits for immoveables (or even for moveables). Neutral principles might govern: it is unclear in the case of 'Widow Brossard's' nuncupative will whether the council held it proved by the French customary law or by English law, since both derived from the same canonical source and required only two or three witnesses (there were three).[57] More often, implicitly and sometimes explicitly, the council construed the right – *droit* – according to civil law or Acadian custom. The latter apparently was derived from the *Coutume de Paris*, though the rules the council followed were too imprecise to ascribe with certainty to any particular *pays*.[58] In accordance with French custom the council preserved equal partibility among heirs, and on abintestacy divided property between widow and children.[59] Tutorial powers were interpreted according to the civil law.[60] In one case the council emphatically and explicitly ordered possession 'According to the Custom of the ffrench Inhabitants' as propounded by Prudent Robichaud Sr, deputy and Acadian elder and attorney-in-fact for one of the parties. In the process Robichaud gave his case away because the custom went against his principal.[61] The custom was apparently the *vente à réméré*, which, though closer to the common law mortgage than to the civil law *hypothèque*, vested the equity of redemption in the mortgagor-and-family rather than in the mortgagor alone.[62] It was all very well for Armstrong to complain that '[w]ithout some Statutes this Province can never be rightly settled; Especially seeing the French here upon every frivolous dispute, plead the laws of Paris, and from that pretended authority contemn all the orders of the Government, and follow the dictates of their Priests and the Bishop of Quebec (or those of Cape Breton ...).'[63] There was nothing frivolous about the Acadians' suits per se. Without a thorough imposition of English property law (and the survey, re-granting, and settlement of title requisite for its implementation), the council's use of French custom and civil law fulfilled the guarantee to a conquered Christian people of its pre-conquest law. It was also appropriate, economical, and just.

It is hard to see at this remove how the lack of legislative capacity seriously hampered the regime's juridical activities. As party-and-party matters in English law were little governed by statute, it was not legislative incapacity that prevented the regime from uniformly imposing the common law in civil matters, but the small number of British settlers. It was the experience of English colonization – as the Halifax regime would discover later – that English law became indispensable only when there were Englishmen to be governed by it, and given enough Englishmen they could not be denied the power to make law.[64] Despite great talk (and less effort) about 'planting with British,' Nova Scotia to 1749 had so few British civilians that an assembly would have included almost every eligible male in its membership. Moreover, the council in effect legislated by general orders, usually with pains and penalties assigned, such as the three orders at one meeting which standardized the half-bushel of grain, standardized the cord of wood, and ordered the removal of encroachments on the highway.[65] One general order constituted a penal statute against export of provisions, with imprisonment, confiscation of vessel and cargo, and fine, to be prosecuted *qui tam*.[66] By proclamation the council exercised wide-ranging police powers: it regulated traders, controlled marshes around the fort, maintained French coin at established value (a power later quashed when it was found to be in conflict with an imperial statute), provided a supply of currency, prohibited the export of cattle and other provisions, and required surveys; all were enforced by commitment for contempt.[67] The council made enough local 'law' to deal with most contingencies.

Far more challenging to conciliar judicature was the absence of juries. Here the council was on shaky ground, not so much in civil matters, given the large majority of the suitors (Acadians) who were unfamiliar with the jury system, but in criminal cases. Misdemeanours could be tried without jury; the capital offences, felonies and treason, could not. There was no apparent bar to the council's empanelling a jury of life and death. Cornwallis's council did just that a little over a month after it was established at Halifax in 1749: a mariner, Peter Carsal (or Cartell), was sent to the gallows for murder after a verdict of a properly drawn jury of twelve fit and lawful men.[68] A petit jury might have been assembled in Annapolis Royal by empanelling every available British civilian. It would have been more difficult to empanel the equally necessary grand jury to hand up a true bill: there were probably not enough gentlemen (however loosely defined, and including garrison officers) to constitute twenty-four grand jurors. Excluded from either jury would have been all military other-ranks and Acadians. Prima facie, there were no trials for capital offences, though we know nothing about courts martial imposing death. Except for a Micmac hostage summarily ordered to be executed *pour encourager les autres*, there appear to have been no executions during the period.[69] A gallows was built in 1726, but only for the exemplary punishment of Armstrong's personal servant, who had assaulted him at Canso: he was to sit upon it for a half-hour on each of three days with a rope around his neck and a sign on his chest reading 'AUDACIOUS VILLAIN,' then be given five lashes each hundred paces over an undeterminable distance; finally, assuming he was still alive, he was to be 'turn'd over for a Soldier.'[70] Flogging and fine were the common punishments.[71] The council's solution to a difficult problem (and its tacit admission that the problem existed) was to proceed against all crime as misdemeanours, even where felony or treason was strongly suggested. When Lieutenant Amhurst's servant-boy, intending to murder Amhurst, his family, and the other servants, burnt down his house, it was not only Isaac Provender's youth (aet. ten or eleven) that saved his life, but the fact that his conviction for arson was rendered upon the council's sole finding of fact without a jury.[72] The point might have been borne in mind by a recent excoriator of Mascarene who saw as cravenness his confiscating the lands and goods of twelve prominent Acadians who gave aid and comfort to Duvivier's (1744) and Ramezay's (1746) invasions of Nova Scotia instead of trying them for high treason.[73] *Politique*, or perhaps a tacit confession of impotence, this leniency grew as much from a sense of the limitations placed upon judicature by the requirements of procedural justice.

Criminal prosecutions against Acadians were very few, and, excluding the ostensibly seditious and possibly treasonous activities during King George's War, none was more serious than grand larceny. Charges of contempt of proclamations and council orders were the most common: exporting cattle to Louisbourg, opposing the deputies in perfecting the highway to Minas, spreading false rumours to raise prices, refusing to appear, etc.[74] Such were ex officio prosecutions, even if moved by an informer. Openly moved prosecutions by Acadian parties were rare, and indicated either a feud or the breakdown of the community's internal mechanism for the maintainance of order. Jean Broussard's case against Francis Richards and his family for an assault on him on the highway was an example of the former (it grew from Richards's having taken wood from Broussard's land).[75] An example of the latter was a deputy's prosecution of Francis Raymond and Francis Meuse for theft and dropping trees over the highway to impede wood-hauling after a riot by the haulers provoked by them; it was clear that the community was fed up with Raymond and Meuse.[76] Two offences committed by a future Acadian hero, which came to the council on a complaint from within the community, illustrate both the motives and the guardedly internalized reserve of the Acadian community. Joseph Broussard, *dit* 'Beausoleil,' a guerrilla leader on the Petitcodiac after the Expulsion and the founder of New Acadia in Louisiana in 1765, abused Louis Tibeau, contemned the council's summons, and refused to appear when Tibeau and the deputies came. When he did appear, he was imprisoned. Even so, the deputies made excuses for him while distancing themselves from the twenty-two-year-old hot-tempered roughneck.[77] Two years later an entire council sitting was taken up with Broussard's refusal to provide support ordered by the council for a bastard he had fathered on Jacques Gousile's step-daughter. As the hearing progressed it became clear that while Gousile had the community's sympathy, he had breached its conventions in bringing the bastardy case to council in the first place. He backed off, however, and accepted a deputy's offer to keep the mother and child for a year in his own house. The parties and the council agreed that the sureties of the original bastardy order would pay arrears.[78] The council acted admirably in recognizing that such business was best left with the community, so long as public order and its own authority were preserved and the child maintained.

It was the internal machinery for self-government in the Acadian communities – their considerable, quietly asserted, and sometimes hidden autonomy – which the regime at Annapolis Royal found difficult to accept but even more difficult to change.[79] Armstrong's complaint that the inhabitants followed the dictates of their priests (and hence of the bishop at Quebec) reflected the impenetrability of the communities and offered an excuse for it. Some two dozen Roman Catholic priests, representing four orders of regulars (Jesuits, Récollets, Sulpicians, and Spiritans), and many of the seculars trained at the Missions Étrangères were at work during the period. In abilities, politics, loyalties, and sanctity they were a widely assorted lot, but few merited the distrust in which the regime held them. Abbé Jean-Louis Le Loutre, a missionary to the Micmac, was a genuinely dangerous incendiary; ever at war with the British he used the Micmac as his whip to try to keep in line the Acadians who did not share his zeal for resistance and battle. The priests who ministered to the Acadians rather than the Micmac were more benign and posed no real threat to peace and good order. The civil constitution under which the priests served – allowance and institution by the British authorities and sustenance by tithes from the Acadians, which the British enforced on parishioners – worked well overall. At one time or another Abbés René-Charles Breslay, Charles de La Goudalie, and Jean-Baptiste de Gay Desenclaves were punished for interfering in civil judicature: they appear to have used spiritual censures in attempting to keep disputes within the community, though how often and with what success is not clear.[80] The repeated accusation that the priests were full of 'insolence' was more a comment on their clerical arrogance and their general unhelpfulness to what they viewed as a foreign and heretical authority than a reflection on their probity. None was as brazen as Abbés Claude Chevreuil and Claude de la Vernede St-Poncy: asked by the council to intervene with the Cape Sable Micmac who had allegedly pillaged a wrecked vessel and perhaps killed some crewmen, they responded, 'Que Je Suis ici de la part du Roy de France ... Que Nous N'avons point D'ordres à Recevoir jci.'[81]

The priests' influence on the Acadians is easily (and often) exaggerated. None were Acadians: whether metropolitan or Quebec French, the priests were *étrangers* in a close-knit community. Parish priests were few and their parishes large in area and numbers of souls. Only Minas had two priests. Episcopal control was also a 'phantom rule': Acadians never saw a mitre, a diocesan court, a synod, a rural dean, or any of the apparatus of French ecclesiastical control so prominent in Quebec. The Bishop of Quebec's authority, such as it was in immediate terms, was exercised by his vicar general who, like La Goudalie, 1731–50, was kept busy with a cure (Minas), lived under British eyes, and, as was appropriate in a well-born agent of authority, was not given to rabble-rousing. There are enough hints of disputes between shepherds and flocks, especially over tithes and land, to reduce the prominence of clerical hegemony over the Acadians. And it cannot be overlooked that the three priests who were censured by the council for meddling in judicature were informed against by Acadian parties unwilling to accept clerical interference.

Acadia needed no priestly leaders. Its nucleated communities had evolved their own natural leadership over most of the previous century, when Acadia, ignored by France and mostly isolated from Quebec, had seesawed back and forth between French and English control. Even after

French regal government was created in 1670, the imposition of external control was largely superficial. The seigneurial system was underdeveloped, the social distinction between *seigneurs et roturiers* slight, and most *roturiers* treated their obligations with considerable disdain. The French governor often resided elsewhere than Port-Royal, and his authority was also merely a 'cannon-shot' long. The beginning of British rule saw Acadian leadership strengthened but not created. Annapolis Royal had perforce to rely upon that natural leadership for much governance, and not least for judicature.

Acadian leadership was centred in the deputies. In numbers and in constituency the deputies rapidly expanded from Philipps's original six, who had been appointed on 4 May 1720 for the area around Annapolis Royal (the River), to twenty-four elected annually on 11 October (the anniversary of the coronation of George II) – eight for the River and four each for Minas, Piziquid, Cobequid, and Chignecto – by the end of the regime. Because of the religious impediment, the deputies were not sworn officials: when they were confirmed in council the governor '[r]ecommended to them the Duty upon them, and the faithfull Execution of their office.'[82] Mascarene wanted the deputies to be 'men of good sense, upright, men of property and having the good of the community at heart, and sensible of the duty to which they are bound by their oath of allegiance ... [who] having fixed times for meeting and consultation should act together in the execution of the orders, &c., of the Govt. in the interests of justice and of the good of the community.'[83] Perhaps this reflected Mascarene's idealism more than the deputies', but the best of them came up to his standard and the worst of them were at least serviceable.

The deputies' role as spokesmen for the inhabitants was the most prominent because it was they who faced a succession of more or less menacing governors demanding an unconditional oath. The council minutes contain plenty of evidence of deputies' being punished for misfeasance and (though more questionable) malfeasance where they were involved in politically 'loaded' matters. No less important and more routinely time-consuming were their juridical responsibilities. Mascarene noted: 'They are invested with no judiciary power, but are appointed often as arbitrators in small causes, where, if any of the parties are not satisfied, appeal is made to the commander-in-chief, and council.'[84] The job-description is correct as far as it goes, but in fact the deputies' juridical duties were much more extensive. They disseminated council orders and proclamations. Because of the absence of a sheriff and bailiffs, they executed council orders and judgments, summoning parties, enforcing appearances, putting parties in possession, attending surveys to show lines and bearings, receiving road assessments paid on council order, and even arresting fugitives.[85] They also undertook duties usually discharged by commissioners or masters, notably in choosing 'Antient Inhabitants' to view and to find facts in property disputes and to report back with a site plan dividing property upon judgment, and settling suits on reference from council.[86] Once, the Minas deputies were empowered to appoint constables to aid them; in 1734 powers of assistance directed to all civil and military officers were given to the deputies in their inquiries in suppressing trade fraud.[87] Indeed, the responsibilities, if not the authority, that fell to the deputies were those of a justice of the peace. They undertook a wide range of administrative duties, such as overseeing the maintenance of fences, highways, and bridges, and police duties, such as keeping under surveillance 'restless spirits who could turn the *habitans* from their duty.'[88] No wonder Armstrong sought to commission as justices of the peace some of the deputies; the Board of Trade, quite properly in view of the Test Act, said no.[89] Yet already, without authority, Armstrong had done just that before Philipps's second coming, issuing a commission to 'Prudent Robichaud Senr. Esq. to be Justice of the Peace for Annapolis.'[90]

Armstrong's choice was sound, for Prudent Robichaud *l'aîné*, of the Cape at Annapolis, epitomized the Acadian deputy, and played more roles appropriate to that office than any other. He had the distinction of being one of the first six deputies elected in 1720, and the greater distinction of being one of two of them excepted against by Philipps on the grounds that he had but a 'slender propriety.'[91] Throughout the existence of the regime he was repeatedly a deputy for the River. He fared ill under Doucett's administration. He was twice accused of consorting with Micmac; the first time he was acquitted, and the second time he suffered the ignominious punishment of being put in irons 'amongst the Indians' in the fort.[92] His command of the Micmac tongue later made him the council's interpreter in its dealings with them. He was loyal and was prepared to go further than most of the inhabitants in warning of Indian threats. By the 1730s he was collector of rents for the River. he was continuously involved in the juridical work of the deputies. An active litigant in his own right, he also appeared more often than any other person as an attorney-in-fact in conciliar cases. The council members relied upon him to inform them of Acadian custom.[93] It is fair to say that Robichaud, unlike some other Acadian officials (deputies, notaries, collectors of rents), never gave the council cause to doubt his integrity.

At the same time, he appears never to have lost the confidence of his *compatriotes*. In serving the ends of justice in the manner which his Christian name implied, Robichaud served both government and *habitants*.

To assess the juridical failure of the Annapolis Royal regime one begins by appreciating its successes. For such there were: not only were they not negligible, but, given the circumstances in which the council and those Acadians who shared its responsibilities laboured, they were remarkable. Those successes were three in number.

The first and most important was that justice was done and it was seen to be done, as English judicature has consistently demanded since the mid-seventeenth century. It was done with exceptional even-handedness in view of the gulf that separated conquerors and conquered, governors and governed, without respect to parties, culture, or creed. The official record seldom trumpets injustice; yet the council's record indicates an admirable constancy in maintaining procedural correctness and substantive probity, and raises no suspicion of corruptness or partiality.

Second, the council managed by the judicious exercise of its juridical police-power to preserve the peace and public order among and between both the British and the Acadians. The Acadian communities' internal mechanism for order clearly made the task easier than it might otherwise have been. It is even possible that the inability of the council, real or supposed, to repress crime with the ultimate rigour of the noose proved an advantage rather than a hindrance: less sanguinary punishment created less resentment between the two cultures.

Third, the council, in responding to the overwhelmingly real-proprietal litigation of the Acadians, gave them assurance in their property that might technically have been denied them for having failed to take an unconditional oath of allegiance. Here, once, hopefully, the consequences of the failure of the oath-business and of the obduracy of the Acadians were ignored. The importance of that assurance cannot be exaggerated among an agrarian people whose cultivation of land was so intensive, despite the abundance of *Evangeline*'s 'forest primeval,' that Frederick Jackson Turner's famous 'frontier theory' may be applicable to every European settlement in North America except Acadia. In the greater political context, that assurance went a long way towards ensuring that the 'neutral French' remained neutral in King George's War. In the narrower social context, it permitted the Acadian communities to grow and to prosper, secure in their possession and their profits.

Until 1755 – and then 'waste are those pleasant farms, and the farmers forever departed!' *Le Grand Dérangement* was not the result of the juridical failure of the Annapolis Royal regime. It was primarily the political failure of the regime to settle the oath-business that led ultimately to the tragedy of the expulsion. Yet the juridical failure was symptomatic of the political failure, and contributed to it.

The juridical failure of the Annapolis Royal regime was its very benignancy. It demonstrated the difference between British and French government, administered impartial justice, treated the Acadians with lenity and humanity – Mascarene's explicit objectives and the implicit objectives of his predecessors and of Skene, Adams, and Shirreff. In doing so, however, it eschewed a certain stringency and rigorousness, even an aggressiveness, in judicature which would have clearly signalled the king's 'new subjects' that the British regime was permanent and that it wielded an authority and exercised a power with which they would have to deal and to which they must finally reconcile themselves. The council had brilliantly limned Justitia with her scales, but it had left out her sword.

Justitia's sword, not Mars's: while there were limitations on the military capacity of the regime, there were none on its juridical competence. Conciliar judicature would have been infinitely more impressive had more pomp and circumstance attended it; instead, meetings were held around the dinner table in the house of whomever its president was at the moment. Regular sessions at stated times would have attracted litigants. And justice should should have been taken out to the communities, instead of waiting for the Acadians to come to the fort. This was tried once – only once – and it worked splendidly. In April and May 1735 a council 'committee' comprising Armstrong, Skene, Shirreff, and an army officer-councillor held eight consecutive sittings at Minas. They handled a great deal of administrative business and a modicum of trials; they were a veritable eyre in the twelfth-century sense more than an assizes.[94] This should have been a feature of judicature from 1720 – certainly, continuously after 1735 – in the distant communities of Cobequid and Chignecto, where there was no British presence save New England merchants (and William Winniett). The council ought to have formalized the duties and responsibilities of the deputies and notaries, and devolved upon them greater powers as commissioners for arbitration, evidence-gathering, and implementation, in the process separating the deputies' perilous political activities from the routine and uncontentious travail of justice. Finally, the council in both its juridical and its executive capacities should have vigorously prosecuted the re-granting of lands along the lines of the well-established English procedure for the discovery of concealed lands. The task, though onerous for the regime, would have engaged the Acadians in a process of acculturation through political and legal activity. Moreover, they would have been caught up in litigation, plenty of it, and merely disputatious Acadians would have been turned into genuinely litigious 'British subjects.'

Such aggressive juridical activism from the fort would have reduced the impenetrability of the Acadian communities and would have brought more Acadians more often and on a more routine basis into contact with the British and their institutions. If nothing else, it would have made it more difficult, and less apparently pressing for Charles Lawrence and the council at Halifax to make that fateful decision of 28 July 1755.

Perhaps it was too much to expect a handful of overworked, uncompensated, isolated, ill-supported, uninstructed, amateur administrators and non-lawyers to undertake more than they did, let alone conceive and implement any grand scheme for more effective, more stringent, judicature. Their sights were low, but less through any shortcomings of theirs than from the total lack of vision or even much purpose on the part of the constantly changing factionalists at Whitehall, of whose ignorance and neglect they were the immediate victims. All that was most feeble, craven, and corrupt about the Whig Supremacy in the decades of the Walpole-Fleury peace beset and shackled the Annapolis Royal regime. Nothing changed until 1749. By then, too much time and too many opportunities had been lost to persuade the king's 'new subjects' that they neglected their duties to him at their peril.

On 12 July 1749 Paul Mascarene and five of the Annapolis Royal councillors waited upon Governor Cornwallis at Chebucto, among them William Shirreff, the only one besides Mascarene who had been present at the creation. Cornwallis felt uncomfortable with those shabby survivors of an old regime under a yet older dispensation. With youth's acuity (and its lack of charity) the thirty-six-year-old colonel would later remark that Mascarene, who was almost twice his age, had 'sold out, and is worn out.'[95] The insult was gratuitous: neither Mascarene nor the Annapolis Royal regime had sold out, though patently they were worn out. On the contrary, they had been sold out by Whitehall.

NOTES

1 *The Institutes of Justinian* J.A.C. Thomas, ed. (Amsterdam: North-Holland Publishing 1975) 1

2 S.S. Webb *The Governors-General: The English Army and the Definition of Empire, 1569–1681* (Chapel Hill: University of North Carolina Press 1979)
3 Per Coke CJ, in *Calvin's Case* (1608) 7 Co. Rep. 17b, 77 ER 377 (KB)
4 PRO CO217/2, ff 51–51v, Caulfeild to Board of Trade, 1 Nov. 1715
5 I have assessed the literature of this criticism in 'Historiography of the Acadians' *Grand Dérangement*, 1755,' *Quebec Studies* 7 (1988) 75–87.
6 John Bartlet Brebner *New England's Outpost: Acadia before the Conquest of Canada* (New York: Columbia University Press 1927). For the degree to which Brebner's portrait is engrained in the literature, see these recent works: Andrew Hill Clark *Acadia: The Geography of Early Nova Scotia to 1760* (Madison: University of Wisconsin Press 1968); Peter L. McCreath and John G. Leefe *A History of Early Nova Scotia* (Tantallon, NS: Four East Publications 1982); Robert Rumilly *L'Acadie Anglaise 1713–1755* (Montreal: Fides 1983); J. Murray Beck *Politics of Nova Scotia* vol. 1 (1710–1896) (Tantallon, NS: Four East Publications 1985). Brebner's other chapter, 'The Puritan Crusade and the Birth of a Policy (1740–1748),' has been no less fertile, stimulating and being reflected in George A. Rawlyk's *Nova Scotia's Massachusetts: A Study of Massachusetts–Nova Scotia Relations, 1630 to 1784* (Montreal: McGill-Queen's University Press 1973).
7 Beamish Murdoch *A History of Nova-Scotia or Acadie* vol. 1 (Halifax: James Barnes 1865) 351; Archibald M. MacMechan, ed. *A Calendar of Two Letter-Books and One Commission-Book, 1713–1741* (Halifax: Public Archives of Nova Scotia 1900) 91 (hereinafter 2 NSA)
8 PRO CO217/3, f. 165v, Philipps to Board of Trade, 27 Sept. 1720. The 'cannon-shot' was not figurative; it was three English miles, according to the Articles of Capitulation for Port-Royal, 1710: Archibald M. MacMechan, ed. *Original Minutes of His Majesty's Council at Annapolis Royal, 1720–1739* (Halifax: Public Archives of Nova Scotia 1908) 43, 13 Dec. 1722 (hereinafter 3 NSA).
9 The Acadian population was about 500 in 1671, 2,500 in 1714, 5,000 in the 1730s, and 10,000 by mid-century: Clark *Acadia* 201.
10 PRO CO218/1, 431–2, draft commission, 19 June 1719
11 PRO CO217/2, f. 318, Lords Justices in Council, 25 June 1719
12 Verbatim, in *Virginia Magazine of History and Biography* 21 (1913) 1–8, 113–21, 225–33, and 347–58, and 22 (1914) 14–15. Subsequent Virginia instructions were also sent to Annapolis Royal; those to Orkney, 22 Mar. 1728, superseded the 1715 instructions: see 3 NSA 211, council, 10 Jan. 1732.
13 *Virginia Magazine of History and Biography* 21 (1913) 228
14 Article 14 permitted the exercise of Roman Catholicism 'as far as the laws

of Great Britain do allow the same': quoted in Thomas B. Akins, ed. *Selections from the Public Documents of Nova Scotia* (hereinafter *SPDNS*) (Halifax: Charles Annand 1869) 15n.

15 Brebner *New England's Outpost* 134–5

16 3 NSA 282, council, 6 July 1733

17 Ibid. 283, council, 7 July 1733. It is not clear whether Winniett was barred on grounds of insufficiency of value of the property (quite likely, since the line was drawn at £300 sterling), want of timeliness, or failure to provide security.

18 3 NSA 124, council, 21 Sept. 1726; 211, council, 10 Jan. 1732

19 PANS RG1, vol. 186, 38

20 Ibid. 38–9

21 PRO CO217/2, f. 84v, Caulfeild to Board of Trade, 16 May 1716

22 PRO CO217/3, f. 111, Vetch to Board of Trade, London, 21 Aug. 1720

23 3 NSA 1–9; 2 NSA 169–70

24 3 NSA 28–9

25 Ibid. 273–4, fees schedule, council, 16 Feb. 1733

26 T.G. Barnes 'Law and Liberty (and Order) in Early Massachusetts' in *The English Legal System: Carryover to the Colonies* (Los Angeles: Clark Library 1975) 72–6

27 3 NSA 96–102

28 Philipps remained governor until 1749, but Armstrong came back as lieutenant-governor with Philipps's rate of pay and full powers.

29 For Cosby and Armstrong, see *DCB* vol. 3, 143–4; for Mascarene's protest, see 3 NSA 178–9, council, 24 June 1731. Winniett, a British officer at the conquest, became a successful merchant, using his marriage to a prominent Acadian woman (*familles* Maisonnat and Bourg) to gain something approaching a commercial monopoly with the 'upper Fundy' Acadians. Winniett's intimate relations with both the Acadians and the Micmac gave rise to doubts about his loyalty. He used his council office primarily to advance his own affairs. As early as 1715 Armstrong, as garrison captain, had tried without success to bar Winniett from dealing with the garrison: PRO CO217/2, f. 71, Winniett to Caulfeild, 30 Oct. 1715. Bourg was *procureur du roy* before 1710 and later notary at Minas, until he was sacked for 'Severall Misdemanours' and ordered to deliver in his notarial records: 3 NSA 106, council, 2 July 1725; 3 NSA 143, council, 23 May 1727.

30 3 NSA 177, council, 2 Apr. 1731; 2 NSA 171, commission to 'Francis Richards Esq.' as high constable, Armstrong, 5 April 1727

31 See 3 NSA 170, council, 21 Nov. 1729, for doubling the deputies; 172, council,

7 Dec. 1730, appointing Lieutenant Erasmus James Philipps; 176, council, 11 Mar. 1731, against the French for inciting the Indians in their attack on Cate's schooner.

32 This is well summed up in Maxwell Sutherland's notice of Philipps in *DCB* vol. 3, 517.

33 3 NSA 192–3, council, 11 Sept. 1731

34 Ibid. 194, council, 20 Sept. 1731; 2 NSA 185, order of reinstatement by Armstrong, 21 Sept. 1731

35 3 NSA 194–5, council, 20 Sept. 1731, *In re Bourg, Landry* v. *Boudrot*; 217, council, 27 Mar. 1732, *Le Blanc* v. *Hall*

36 3 NSA 237–8, council, 20 July 1732

37 What is extant has been gathered from a number of archives by C.B. Fergusson in *Minutes of His Majesty's Council at Annapolis Royal 1736–1749* (Halifax: Public Archives of Nova Scotia 1967) (hereinafter 4 NSA).

38 *SPDNS* 109, Mascarene to secretary of state, 15 Nov. 1740

39 A balanced and favourable recent Acadian assessment of Mascarene's administration is Neil Boucher 'Paul Mascarene et les Acadiens 1710–1748' *Revue de l'Universite Sainte-Anne* (1984–5) 14–22.

40 PRO CO217/4, f. 273v, Armstrong to Board of Trade, rec'd 17 Nov. 1725

41 2 NSA 171, commission, 28 March 1727

42 PRO CO217/3, ff. 47–48, accompanying Philipps to Secretary Craggs, 26 May 1720

43 *DCB* vol. 3, 3–4, notice by Barry M. Moody

44 There were 305 sittings of the council per se, or as a committee of the whole, or as a committee recorded in the minutes, from 25 Apr. 1720 to 17 Aug. 1736, with lacunae for 10 Oct. 1721 to 8 Oct. 1722 and 13 Nov. 1727 to 20 Nov. 1729: 3 NSA.

45 Skene was present at council on 15 Jan. 1747: 4 NSA 97. A memorial from Councillors Major Erasmus James Philipps and William Shirreff and John Hamilton on behalf of themselves and others for compensation for houses pulled down around the fort for defence during the war and a petition from 'Mrs Skeene' for the same for 'her father's House in the Lower Town' were submitted to the council on 4 Jan. 1749: 4 NSA 99. The latter document might indicate that William Skene's daughter (-in-law?) was acting as his heir.

46 See *Memorials of the Family of Skene of Skene* edited by William F. Skene, 1 New Spalding Club (Aberdeen 1887).

47 3 NSA 319, council, 24 Apr. 1735; 322, council, 28 Apr. 1735

48 Ibid. 190, n.d., ante 1726; 192, council, 11 Sept. 1731; 197, council, 13 Oct. 1731

49 Ibid. 192, council, 11 Sept. 1731; 277, council, 27 Mar. 1733

50 George Mitchell, 3 NSA 256, council, 25 Oct. 1732; see *DCB* vol. 3, 453
51 Rumilly *L'Acadie Anglaise* 120–2, 'La question des titres de propriété'
52 3 NSA 197, *In re Noel Duerong*, council, 13 Oct. 1731; 198, council, 14 Oct. 1731
53 Ibid. 209–11, *Depuis* v. *Boudrot, Landry et al.*, council, 10 Jan. 1732
54 Ibid. 218, council, 27 March 1732
55 Ibid. 280, *Trahan* v. *Trahan*, council, 23 June 1733
56 An English widow's right to the realty upon her husband's intestacy was strictly by common law dower: 4 NSA 41 *In re Anne Douglass* council, 7 Mar. 1744.
57 3 NSA 206 and 213, council, 30 Dec. 1730 and 22 Jan. 1731. Civil law, obtaining in *pays de droit écrit*, required Justinian's seven witnesses: Paul Viollet, *Histoire du Droit Civil Français* 3d ed. (Paris 1905; reprinted Aalen: Scientia Verlag 1966) 895.
58 For a comparison of *coutumes*, see Bourdot de Richebourg's *Coutumier General* (Paris 1724).
59 3 NSA 104–5, *Commeau* v. *Richards*, Council, 7 July 1725; 100, *Shirreff* v. *Robichaud*, Council, 29 Apr. 1725
60 Ibid. 190, *In re children of Charles Robichaux cadet*, n.d.; 192–3, *In re Abbé Gaulin ex parte heirs Deny*, council, 11 Sept. 1731, and 197, council, 13 Oct. 1731
61 Ibid. 237–8, *Hebert* v. *Robicheau*, council, 20 July 1732; the attorney was Prudent Robichaud Sr.
62 The French *Code Civil* preserves the device, *vente avec faculté de réméré: Dictionnaire de Droit* 2ème ed. (Paris: Dalloz 1966) 854.
63 *SPDNS*, 94, Armstrong to Board of Trade, 10 June 1732
64 See T.G. Barnes ' "As Near as May Be Agreeable to the Laws of This Kingdom": Legal Birthright and Legal Baggage at Chebucto, 1749' in Peter Waite et al., eds *Law in a Colonial Society: The Nova Scotia Experience* (Toronto: Carswell 1984) 1–23.
65 3 NSA 242–3, council, 27 July 1732
66 Ibid. 175, council, 16 Feb. 1731
67 Ibid. 34, 35, 142–3 (council, 19–20 May 1727, repeal based on 6 Anne c. 57 (1708), sections 174, 175, 315 (cattle and provisions), and 198
68 Petit jury in *R.* v. *Carsal*, 31 August 1749, PANS: RG39 'J', vol. 117, f. 1
69 3 NSA 56–7, council, 8 July 1724, following Micmac killing of a sergeant of the garrison; see Murdoch *Nova-Scotia* vol. 1, 409.
70 3 NSA 126–8, council, 22 and 23 Sept. 1726
71 Peter Guon and Jermine Doucett, for theft – grand larceny, a felony – fifty and twenty-five lashes respectively at cart's tail along the river, the whipping to be done by their young accomplice, Peter Pino (fined), with servitude for Guon and fine on Doucett as well: 3 NSA 328–30, council, 22 Dec. 1735.

72 4 NSA 11–14, council, 20 Apr. 1737; Amhurst asked the council to delay punishment of Provender until 'he could send to Boston to have the advice of some persons there learned in the Knowledge of the Law, after what manner he should proceed against & what could be legally done to such a Young Criminal.'

73 Robert Sauvageau *Acadie, La Guerre de Cent Ans des Français d'Amérique aux Maritimes et en Louisiane, 1670–1769* (Paris: Berger-Levrault 1987) 203–4, apropos 'Les douze Apôtres de la cause Acadienne.' A minute examination of their activities, building a strong case for their guilt, is in 4 NSA 49–99, council, 12 Oct. 1744 to 15 Jan. 1747.

74 3 NSA 160, 324, 313, 220

75 Ibid. 213–14, council, 5 Feb. 1732

76 Ibid. 261–4, council, 15 and 16 Jan. 1733

77 Ibid. 67–72, council, 10 and 12 Aug. 1724; see *DCB* vol. 3, 87–8 for 'Brossard' (Broussard).

78 3 NSA 112–13, council, 20 Apr. 1726; 121–3, council, 30 June 1726

79 The structure and dynamics of Acadian internal government and society in this period are brilliantly drawn in Naomi E.S. Griffiths *The Acadian Deportation: Deliberate Perfidy or Cruel Necessity*? (Toronto: Copp Clark 1969) and *The Acadians: Creation of a People* (Toronto: McGraw-Hill Ryerson 1973). My debt to these works is considerable and evident here.

80 Breslay: *SPDNS* 82, Armstrong to Board of Trade, 23 June 1729; La Goudalie, 3 NSA 225–6, council, 19 June 1732; Desenclaves: *SPDNS* 111–14, Mascarene to Desenclaves (three eloquent letters on the civil jurisdiction) June–Sept. 1741

81 3 NSA 343–4, council, 18 May 1736. The idea of the priests' going was Charles d'Entremont's at Pobomcoups (Pubnico), who also wanted them to celebrate mass at that isolated Acadian community, which might explain why Chevreuil finally did go. He reported back to the council: 3 NSA 360, council, 8 July 1736. The strange case of the brigantine *Baltimore* has been neatly closed by Donald F. Chard 'The Last Voyage of the *Baltimore*' *Nova Scotia Historical Review* 7 (December 1987) 63–70: the villains were the unmanifested Irish convict-passengers, who were led by a redoubtable Dublin prostitute, not the Micmac.

82 3 NSA 255, council, 11 Sept. 1732

83 2 NSA 241, memo. of Mascarene to [?], 27 May 1740

84 Murdoch *Nova-Scotia* vol. 1, 372, Mascarene to Governor Shirley, Apr. 1748

85 2 NSA 211, 249; 3 NSA 197, 212, 249, 285–6, 320

86 3 NSA 233, 308, 320, 362

87 2 NSA 201, order of Armstrong, 13 Sept. 1734

88 Ibid. 241

89 Ibid. 194, Board of Trade to Armstrong, 2 Nov. 1732. The Test Act disabled Roman Catholics from holding office.

90 2 NSA 172, commission, 5 Apr. 1727

91 3 NSA 7, council, 4 May 1720

92 Ibid. 47–8, council, 21 Sept. 1723; 100, council, 22 May 1725 (for entertaining Micmac at home, but because of his age and his long time in irons, his release was ordered upon surety)

93 Ibid. 237–8, council, 20 July 1732

94 Ibid. 318–23, council committees, 17, 19, 21, 24, 26, and 28 April, and 1 and 9 May 1735; the itinerancy required the secretary, Shirreff, to take the minute-book with him, which the council approved: 315, council, 1 Apr. 1735.

95 Quoted in Murdoch *Nova-Scotia* vol. 2 188

3

The Superior Court Judiciary of Nova Scotia, 1754–1900: A Collective Biography

CLARA GRECO

Despite the centrality of its role in the legal system, the Canadian judiciary has received little attention from legal historians. Although the literature is replete with individual biographies,[1] and there is now an increasing interest in the intellectual history of the judiciary,[2] collective analyses of the kind produced by American scholars are few and tend to concentrate on the Supreme Court of Canada.[3] The traditional reliance of legal scholars on formalist explanations of legal change and the much less overtly 'political' role played by the Canadian judiciary doubtless explain this lacuna. In particular, an emphasis on formalism in analysing doctrinal change denies the need to examine those persons responsible for the change.[4] Now that such assumptions are no longer tenable, judges, like legal processes and institutions, must be placed under the historian's microscope. Some years ago R.C.B. Risk included in his 'prospectus' for Canadian legal history the need to discover more about the structures of legal institutions.[5] In this essay I endeavour to fulfil that need for one Canadian jurisdiction. In part, at least, to study a court 'is to study men,' and 'a better knowledge of each Justice will mean a better knowledge of that mass personality,' the court itself.[6]

Collective judicial analyses are by now 'almost commonplace' for American courts.[7] The pioneering studies of C.M. Ewing and John R. Schmidhauser on the Supreme Court[8] laid the groundwork for a proliferation of work on lower federal and state courts.[9] Three major types of judicial studies have emerged. The first is the traditional biography. The second, the 'stepping-stone' or 'collection' study, is a descriptive collective biography of a particular group of judges. To the extent that conclusions about patterns of recruitment, experience, social status, and the like can be drawn from these, they go one step beyond the individual biography. The third type, the 'relational' study, draws on the first two in constructing hypotheses about the connections between judicial backgrounds and attitudes and judicial decisions.[10]

This last approach reveals the most about the relationship between legal change and social change, yet it cannot be undertaken in the absence of the groundwork provided by the collection study. We now have invaluable collection studies, not only for the various U.S. courts, but also for the Massachusetts bench in the pre-revolutionary period,[11] the English judiciary from 1730 to the present,[12] and the Quebec Superior Court between 1849 and 1974.[13] By examining factors such as social origin, legal training, incomes, political involvement, and the appointment process these works are able to draw conclusions about professionalization and the place of the judiciary in society. The former topic is particularly significant in the work of Peter S. Russell and Daniel Duman, both of whom chart the increasing professionalism of the judiciary in the years after 1750. Similar questions underlie this study, and similar methods are employed to answer them. A brief account of the evolution of the Supreme Court will set the stage for an analysis of specific judicial traits.

THE NOVA SCOTIA SUPREME COURT 1754–1900 AND THE OFFICE OF MASTER OF THE ROLLS 1825–55[14]

The Supreme Court had its origins in the founding of Halifax in 1749. Governor Edward Cornwallis's commission included instructions to 'erect, constitute and establish such & so many Courts of Judicature & publick Justice ... as you ... shall think fit ... for the hearing & determining of causes ... according to Law and Equity.'[15] Cornwallis founded, among others, the General Court, which consisted of himself and the members of his council and was styled after the judicial system of Virginia. This court exercised original and appellate civil, criminal, and exchequer jurisdiction. The system was soon found to be unsatisfactory, however, as the governor and council became absorbed in running the colony. London resolved the problem in 1754 with the establishment of a Supreme Court consisting only of the new chief justice, a Massachusetts-born barrister named Jonathan Belcher. The new court served as an appeal court, but also exercised original jurisdiction in major civil cases and in trials of serious felonies.

Growth of curial membership was slow. Belcher sat alone until 1764, and, like all chief justices until 1837, he was also a member of the executive council. He even served as lieutenant-governor and commander-in-chief of the colony from 1761 to 1763, but his general political and financial ineptitude resulted in a prohibition against one man's occupying this multiple role in the future.[16] In 1763 the Assembly asked that two assistant judges be appointed, since 'His Majesty's subjects ought not to rest satisfied with the judgment of one person only.' Governor and council agreed, and two councillors, John Collier and Charles Morris, were appointed. Belcher drafted their commissions and took good care to preserve his own position; he limited their powers so much that 'the intent of the Assembly was altogether frustrated.'[17] The assistant judges could not try a case without the concurrence of the chief justice until 1774, when the first circuits were established.[18]

As demands on the court increased, the number of judges was slowly augmented, but parsimonious assemblymen always resented paying for places in what was seen by many to be an expensive and overstaffed justice system. A fourth judge was added in 1810 and a fifth in 1816, but the position lapsed between 1836 and 1841 before being reinstated with the abolition of the Inferior Court of Common Pleas.[19] In 1870 provision was made for the appointment of two more judges, although the court had been made up of six judges since former premier James W. Johnston's appointment as judge in equity in 1864.[20]

Three different systems of appointment to the Nova Scotia Supreme Court were used during these years. Before 1848 the chief justice was selected by the imperial government and the assistant judges were appointed by the local authorities; they held office 'at pleasure' – that is, they could be removed by royal order for no cause assigned. In 1848 and 1849 the power of appointment was given to colonial politicians and the judges were made independent, holding their offices during 'good behaviour.'[21] After Confederation the federal government made the appointments. These different periods in the province's political evolution are reflected in the nature of its judiciary, as will be seen.

From 1749 the post of chancellor was held by the colony's lieutenant-governor, although from at least the 1790s Chancery in fact consisted of the governor and some Supreme Court judges as advisers.[22] In 1825 a master of the rolls was appointed, in effect divesting the governor of his original jurisdiction in equity matters; he retained, in theory at least, an appellate jurisdiction. Thereafter Chancery business was performed by the four holders of that office – Simon Bradstreet Robie, Charles R. Fairbanks, Samuel G.W. Archibald, and Alexander Stewart. Chancery was

TABLE 1
Years on the Bench

Position	Less than 5 years	5–10 years	11–19 years	20–29 years	More than 30 years
Chief justice only	3	2	0	4	1
Assistant judge or master of the rolls only	3	9	8	9	4
All	4	11	9	12	7

abolished in 1855 by reformers who had long considered it an 'abominable, heart-breaking, pocket-picking system,' and equity jurisdiction was transferred to the Supreme Court.[23]

JUDGES' AGE AND TENURE

The average age on appointment for the judges was 48.1 years; for the chief justices it was slightly higher, at 52.1 years.[24] The lack of a significant difference between the ages on appointment of chief justices and the assistants suggests that considerations other than age and experience determined appointment to the highest office. A substantial range of ages is represented within the average. The youngest was Thomas Strange, who was made chief justice in 1789 at the age of 33. His meteoric rise was assisted by family connections: his father dabbled in law before becoming Britain's premier engraver, and his mother was a friend of Lord Mansfield. He resigned from the Nova Scotia post when he secured the recordership of the Madras presidency in the new Indian empire; two years later he became chief justice of its newly created Supreme Court. The younger judges all appear in the colony's early years; one of Strange's predecessors, Bryan Finucane, was only 39 when he was made chief justice. The oldest judge was James W. Johnston, who was 72 when he was raised to the bench in 1864.

On average, the judges each spent 17.4 years on the bench.[25] If the time spent as assistants is included, they averaged precisely 15 years as presiding judges. Those who never became chief justices held office an average of 16 years (see table 1). Nineteen of the forty-three spent more than 20 years in that capacity alone, and some showed quite remarkable judicial longevity. Brenton Halliburton held the position for 27 years and was on the bench for a total of 53 years. Sampson Salter Blowers, who was appointed chief justice at age 55, sat for 36 years before resigning at age 91. No doubt this tenacity had something to do with the proprietorial notion of office then current;[26] it certainly created severe problems when ill health supervened. Blowers's longevity frustrated both his contemporaries and the Colonial Office, which wanted him to resign because of his advancing infirmity.[27] He admitted that he 'ought perhaps to have earlier relinquished a station for which age and the infirmities incident to it, were continually rendering him ... unfit.'[28] The assistant judges also clung to their offices; James Brenton had the distinction, if that is the word, of serving under five different chief justices; Lewis M. Wilkins Sr served for 32 years and William Blowers Bliss for 35. The masters of the rolls provided an exception to this pattern of extreme longevity; they served for an average of only 7.25 years. But there is no deeper meaning to this: Archibald and Fairbanks died in office, while Stewart had it pulled from under him with the abolition of Chancery in 1855. Only Robie was left to retire at the age of 64.

The lengthy tenures of most judges meant that the average age of the bench was usually elevated. It never fell below 54 in the nineteenth century and hovered around 60 before 1830 and again in the 1850s and 1860s. The oldest bench sat in 1870, just before the addition of two new places on the bench, when the incumbents averaged 72.2 years of age.

As can be seen from the appendix, over half the judges died in office – twenty-three out of forty-three. This reluctance to resign was much more characteristic of judges appointed earlier in the period than later, however. Of judges appointed prior to 1834, only six of nineteen (31.5 per cent) resigned; well over half of those appointed after that date did so (thirteen out of twenty-four or 54.1 per cent). Of those who resigned during the earlier period, two did so because they were moved to more prestigious positions: Strange went to India and John Duport became chief justice of Prince Edward Island. Three resigned for reasons of age or ill health: Blowers, Jeremy Pemberton, who died in England less than two years after his resignation, and Simon Robie. George Monk retired at age 68, but could not have afforded to do so had he not persuaded the Assembly to grant him a pension.[29] His situation provides a clue to the reluctance of many of the earlier judges to give up office: they lacked a source of post-retirement income. The Assembly was notoriously reluctant to grant pensions to retiring officials, and requests for them often led to nasty battles.[30] Without substantial independent means, which only Robie, Blowers, and presumably Pemberton had (none received a pen-

TABLE 2
Birthplace

Period	New England	Nova Scotia	United Kingdom	Other	Unknown
1749–1849	11	7	5	2	1
1849–67	0	1	1	1	0
1867–90	0	12	0	2	0
TOTAL	11	20	6	5	1

sion), it was often difficult for the judges to contemplate retirement.

The pattern changed after the dominion provided for judicial pensions by statute in 1868.[31] William Blowers Bliss, who had been in ill health for a number of years, offered to retire in 1864 if the Assembly would grant him a pension.[32] No doubt piqued by their refusal, he stayed on, and became the first Nova Scotia judge to take advantage of the new federal act in 1869. All fourteen of the judges appointed after the act's passage had died in office or resigned by the time they reached age 75, with the exception of Chief Justice James MacDonald, who resigned at 76. Their average age at death or resignation was 65, or 69 if Samuel Rigby, who died prematurely at 44, and John S.D. Thompson, who resigned at 41 after only three years on the bench, are excluded.

Nova Scotia's higher judiciary was a relatively elderly collection of men for most of these years. Although the average age on appointment was not especially high, an average tenure of almost twenty years and little turnover in personnel (a pattern similar to that which existed in Quebec), suggests that new ideas would have come slowly to the bench. If age and longevity in office can be associated with a tendency to support the status quo, this must have been a court unwilling to deviate from established principles.

GENERAL BACKGROUNDS

Birthplace

Birthplace, and what J.R. Schmidhauser calls the 'setting for the formative years of the justices,'[33] are of obvious significance in an examination of judicial backgrounds. In the period before 1830, eleven of the judges came from New England, the closest major legal centre (see table 2): the last of these was Robie, who was elevated in 1825. The first native-born judge was R.J. Uniacke Jr, who was appointed in 1830. Yet even before 1830 the movement towards an indigenous judiciary was underway. The last British-born place-seeker was Thomas Strange (1789). His successor, Sampson Blowers (1797), was a loyalist who had arrived in Nova Scotia at age forty-two, but all assistant judges from James Brenton (1781) on were 'locals' in spite of their New England birthplaces. Brenton himself and the next six assistant judges appointed during Blowers's long incumbency were all loyalists' sons who had arrived in Nova Scotia by the age of twenty; they spent their entire legal careers in the province. A few judges appointed after 1830 were born outside the province: Sir William Young (Scotland), James W. Johnston (Jamaica), Henry Smith (St Kitts), and Sir Robert S. Weatherbe (Prince Edward Island). All emigrated at an early age and received their post-secondary education or legal training in Nova Scotia.

Of the twenty Nova Scotia-born judges, only five were born and raised in Halifax. None of them became chief justices, which is surprising in the light of the dominance of the 'Halifax connection' in Nova Scotia politics.[34] Though rural-born, most judges were city-connected. Among the chief justices, four hailed from New England, four were from Britain or British subjects outside North America, one was from Switzerland (acting Chief Justice Isaac Deschamps), and one was from Nova Scotia (James MacDonald).

It is clear that in the Supreme Court's early years the New England presence, pre-loyalist and loyalist, was substantial. Belcher was born in Massachusetts and gave his imprint to the Nova Scotia court system; Blowers was a Harvard man and a Massachusetts loyalist; Halliburton, another New Englander, was the son of a prominent loyalist. Yet this early American influx does not appear to have resulted in a predominant New England influence in the early court system and early Nova Scotia law. The only substantial dispute over the use of New England law occurred in the early 1750s, before the inauguration of the Supreme Court.[35] The Massachusetts bar and judiciary had undergone a considerable degree of professionalization and Anglicization from the middle of the eighteenth century; the provincial law therefore came to reflect fewer of the customary rules of the early settlers and more of the established nostrums of the English courts.[36] Belcher, for example, did not plan to transplant New England institutions; rather, he modelled the Nova Scotia Supreme Court after the English system.[37]

TABLE 3
Parental Occupation

Government official/politician	8
Judge	8
Lawyer	4
Merchant	3
Artist	1
Farmer	6
Military	1
Clergyman	4
Medicine	3
Journalist	1
Unknown	4

Social Status

In obtaining judicial positions, these men joined the provincial élite. But did they also spring from it, as was the case with judges in other jurisdictions? Using fathers' occupations as reliable indicators of social status, Schmidhauser concludes that only 9 per cent of the American judges came from an 'essentially humble origin,' while 90 per cent had fathers with high-status occupations.[38] The same was true for the British judiciary and for that of colonial Massachusetts: land-owning families provided more than one-fifth of British judges before 1875, the professional class almost one-half; and the oldest and wealthiest New England families continually placed their scions on the bench in the pre-revolutionary period.[39]

The parental occupations of forty-three Nova Scotia judges comprise substantially all elements of Nova Scotia's élite; only the merchant group is underrepresented (see table 3).[40] The judiciary, the professions, and politics or government service are prevalent. Land-owning as a primary occupation was poorly represented even in the period before 1850; the 'farmers' were real farmers, not landed gentry, with the possible exception of Charles Morris's father.

Twelve (28 per cent) of the judges had fathers who were lawyers or judges. The figure clearly illustrates the usefulness of a legal pedigree in establishing a claim to a judicial post. That factor declines in importance over the period, however. Eight of these candidates appear before the granting of responsible government, making up 32 per cent of all appointments to that date, while only four (22.5 per cent) of subsequent appointments appear after that date. The post-1848 figure is very close to that given by Guy Bouthillier (20 per cent) for Quebec Superior Court judges appointed between 1849 and 1904,[41] suggesting similar patterns of judicial recruitment across British North America; but, since Bouthillier gives no figures for the years before 1849, trends cannot be compared.

The tendency to professional heredity among judges declines after 1848, and instances of non-élite recruitment begin to appear. Before responsible government, no appointees could be considered to have sprung from a non-élite background. Alexander Stewart's father was a poor immigrant Presbyterian clergyman, but his professional status gave him and his children a leg up over others. Young Alexander secured a post as clerk in the Ordnance Department, and shrewdly married Sarah Morse, sister of the prominent Amherst barrister J.S. Morse, with whom he finished his articles. A transfer of credal allegiance to the Church of England in the 1840s helped to confirm his social status. He was appointed master of the rolls in 1846.

The first appointee after 1848 who could be considered a non-élite candidate is Jonathan McCully (appointed in 1870); he was followed by Hugh McDonald (1873), John S.D. Thompson (1882), and Nicholas Meagher (1890). Meagher is perhaps the most striking example of non-élite recruitment. The son of an Irish immigrant who farmed in Cape Breton, Meagher worked as a grocery-store clerk in Windsor and first travelled to Halifax to care for lawyer, Hiram Blanchard's horses. He graduated to copying pleadings, and from there to an apprenticeship, a partnership, the bench, and a knighthood.[42] There is some debate about whether McCully came from a 'poor' background. References to his father as a 'farmer and shipwright' suggest a degree of financial security but not élite status, and McCully did have to teach for a few years to save enough money to survive his articling period. Thompson's background might best be described as one of genteel frugality, although his father's literary pursuits keep the family in professional circles. Alexander James (appointed in 1889) is difficult to label 'non-élite' in spite of his teaching stint in Dartmouth, because his father was connected with the British commissariat in Annapolis.

An élite background, although still enormously important, was not so rigid a prerequisite for elevation to the bench by the end of the century. In part this change reflects a growing emphasis on a more professional judiciary, whose qualifications must include a considerable number of years in the practice of law. It also reflects the increasing diversity of recruitment to the bar itself from the 1820s and 1830s, although the broader pool of candidates is a necessary but not a sufficient condition

TABLE 4
Religion

Period	Catholic	Anglican	Other Protestant	Unknown
1754–1849	0	21	4	1
1849–67	0	1	2	0
1867–1900	3	6	4	1
TOTAL	3	28	10	2

for the appointment of non-élite candidates to the bench. The 'sufficient' condition was undoubtedly the achievement of responsible government, which opened all government posts to groups of aspirants outside the traditional ranks of the Tory Anglican hierarchy. Religion and ancestral connection could be secondary for the candidate with irreproachable professional credentials.

Religion

In Nova Scotia a further indication of social status was religion: this is reflected in the Anglican dominance of the official establishment.[43] The poverty of most Scottish and Irish Catholic settlers, Catholic civil disabilities (removed in 1830),[44] and 'cronyism' all contributed to a bar and judiciary that were dominated by Anglicans. This was especially evident in the earlier period (see table 4). For some, Anglicanism was a faith necessary for advancement; Bryan Finucane, for example, converted from Catholicism at the age of twenty-one to qualify to study law in Dublin.[45] Although the Low Protestant sects were tolerated sufficiently to allow four of their number onto the bench before 1850, one of these, Charles Fairbanks, was a convert from Anglicanism who attended King's College but failed to get a degree when he refused to subscribe to the thirty-nine Articles.[46] There were no Catholic judges until 1873, when Hugh McDonald was appointed and only three Catholics sat on the bench in the 150 years covered here.[47] The dominance of what Schmidhauser terms the 'high social status religious affiliations' was also apparent in the U.S. Supreme Court: most of its judges were Episcopalian or Presbyterian.[48]

Education

About half of the Supreme Court judges pursued advanced studies (see table 5).[49] This figure is lower than those for pre-revolutionary Massachusetts (75 per cent) and for the British bench before 1875 (73.3 per cent).[50]

TABLE 5
Higher Education

	1754–1849	1849–67	1867–90
American university	4	0	0
British university	3	1	0
Nova Scotian university	4	1	7
Other university	1	0	0
None	10	1	7
Unknown	4	0	0

This figure might not be surprising in the pre-1850 period, given the different circumstances in Nova Scotia, but the proportion of highly educated judges did not change markedly over time. Aspiring judges tended early in their careers to look to the Assembly rather than to the academy as the primary route to preferment. What did change over time however, was the nature of their education. Whereas New England colleges, Oxbridge, and Edinburgh University provided seven of the early colonial judges, a local university education became prevalent after the mid-nineteenth century, paralleling the rise of a native-born judiciary.[51] Of the twelve judges who attended Nova Scotia colleges, seven went to King's College, three to Acadia University, and one each to Dalhousie and St Francis Xavier universities. King's, founded in 1789, was an Anglican school that exerted a great influence on 'the manners and morals of the country,' and was intimately connected to the Halifax political élite.[52] Yet five of the seven judges who went there were appointed before 1867; like membership in the Anglican religion, an Anglican college education became much less a mark of the judiciary after Confederation.

LEGAL TRAINING AND PRACTICE

A small number of judges received formal legal instruction as an aspect of their higher education; most (thirty-two) learned their law solely by apprenticing with practitioners (see table 6).[53] All three of the judges with no legal training were eighteenth-century appointees, and all were successful in other professions before their elevation to the bench.[54] Four of the six judges with formal legal training were also eighteenth-century men, three of them British-born place-seekers in the colonies. The other three were Belcher, Bliss, who went to study at the Inner Temple after admission to the bars of Nova Scotia and New Brunswick, and Hugh

TABLE 6
Type of Legal Training

University or Inns of Court	Law firm (Halifax)	Law firm (elsewhere)	No legal training
Belcher	Archibald	Blowers	Collier
Bliss	Fairbanks	Brenton	Deschamps
Finucane	Graham	Desbarres	Morris
Henry	Halliburton	Dodd	
Pemberton	Hutchinson	Haliburton	
Strange	James	Johnston	
	Meagher	McCully	
	Rigby	H. McDonald	
	J.W. Ritchie	J. MacDonald	
	Robie	Monk	
	J. Stewart	J.N. Ritchie	
	Thompson	Smith	
	Uniacke	A. Stewart	
	Weatherbe	Townshend	
	Young	Wilkins Jr	
		Wiswall	
6	15	16	3

Henry, who earned an LLB at Harvard after attaining his Dalhousie BA, perhaps at the behest of his father.[55]

For whatever reason, apprenticeship was much more a feature of the Nova Scotia bench's training than it was elsewhere. It was not uncommon for judges to take on apprentices who later rose to the bench themselves; at least ten did so. Robie's and Johnston's offices trained two each – Samuel Archibald and Charles Fairbanks and Robert Weatherbe and John W. Ritchie respectively. In turn, Fairbanks took on William Young, who later instructed Alexander James.[56]

The narrow practical base of the legal training of most of these judges, coupled with the importance of patronage in the judicial appointment process, led to a judiciary uneven in its intellectual quality. The celebrated 'judges' affair' of the later 1780s was at least in part an attack on judicial ignorance by an increasingly able bar.[57] Other judges had their competence assailed at times, including William Desbarres and James Stewart: John Marshall, a lower court judge and the author of a widely used JP manual, noted laconically that James Stewart 'could not be called eminent in his profession' when he was solicitor general.[58] Lewis M. Wilkins Jr apparently had to put up with being corrected by his lawyer brother

TABLE 7
Bar Membership

Years of practice	Before 1849	1849–67	1867–90
None	3	0	0
0–5	2	0	0
6–10	1	0	1
11–15	1	0	1
16–20	4	0	6
21–30	7	2	4
Over 31	3	1	2

Martin when the latter served as protonotary.[59] Some judges had their general knowledge questioned. When a lawyer argued before Edmund M. Dodd that a dispute between two friends brought to mind 'the case of David and Jonathan,' the judge apparently asked, 'Where do you find that case reported?'[60]

These examples can be countered by others that demonstrate greater legal and intellectual attainments and a broader cultural exposure. Foster Hutchinson, though not apparently eloquent, had an 'enlarged and solid legal knowledge';[61] Jonathan Belcher produced editions of the Irish and Nova Scotia statutes, and, in collaboration with John Duport, an edition of the Nova Scotia laws in 1767. According to one of the colony's early historians, the four leaders of the bar in 1830 were all men who later became judges – Fairbanks, Bliss, Johnston, and Archibald. Fairbanks was the profession's leading expert on commercial law.[62] Wallace Graham apparently had 'a wider knowledge of case law than any other man who ... sat on the bench in Nova Scotia.'[63] More esoteric were the interests of Strange, who wrote a treatise on Hindu law.[64] The best known of the literary figures on the bench, however, was Thomas C. Haliburton, who restricted his writings to non-legal subjects. Neither of the province's most accomplished legal writers, John Marshall and Beamish Murdoch, reached the ranks of the senior judiciary.[65]

Most of today's judicial appointees have spent substantial time as members of the bar. Without doubt membership in the legal profession serves 'as a conditioner of social, economic and political attitudes.'[66] Most Nova Scotia judges were experienced lawyers (see table 7).[67] Before 1849 at least fourteen of the twenty-six appointed had practised for more than fifteen years; thereafter, only two of seventeen practised for less than that. The longest-serving member was John W. Ritchie, who combined his legal practice with an involvement in provincial and national politics from his call in 1831 until his appointment to the bench in 1870. The shortest pre-judicial legal apprenticeships were served by Thomas Strange, who was called to the bar in England in 1785 and made chief justice of Nova Scotia in 1789, and Brenton Halliburton, whose legal training was interrupted by a nine-year stint in the army. Upon his return he qualified and practised in Halifax for only four years before his elevation to the bench in 1807. He was just thirty-three at the time; his appointment was perhaps meant to be compensation for the most recent death of his maternal uncle, James Brenton. The only three judges who had not practised at all – the ones with no legal training – were all early appointees. This was not uncommon in the colonies: in Massachusetts, for example, only ten of the thirty-two Superior Court judges selected between 1692 and 1774 had actually practised law.[68]

Halifax-based lawyers dominated court appointments. Excluding judges who had no legal training, those who were appointed from England, and those for whom there was inadequate information, nineteen of thirty-two judges practised primarily in the capital. The proportion was higher (eleven of seventeen) after 1849 than before (eight of fifteen), though not markedly. Similarly, while the eighteenth century saw the appointment of a number of members of other bars, the nineteenth century appointees were to a man 'home-grown.'[69]

Like apprenticeship, the practice of law often saw future members of the senior judiciary working together. Wallace Graham and Robert Weatherbe were partners, and after Weatherbe was elevated to the bench Graham joined John Thompson.[70] Other partnerships included those of Johnston, Bliss, and Alexander Stewart, Johnston and Robie, James and Young, James MacDonald and Rigby, and the Ritchie brothers.

POLITICAL ACTIVITIES AND JUDICIAL APPOINTMENTS

While information about the political careers of judges before their elevation to the bench is relevant to a study of patronage in the appointments process, I will not attempt to describe in detail that complex and multifaceted phenomenon.[71] My aim is a more modest one: to convey a sense of the prevalence of political activity in the average judicial life and the way in which that pattern changed over time.

When J.W. Lawrence's *Judges of New Brunswick* was first conceived in the 1870s, it was to be 'nothing less than a general constitutional and political history of the province to 1867 ... told through the vehicle of

TABLE 8
Previous Political and Judicial Offices

Judge	Attorney general	Solicitor general	MHA MP	Judge JP
1754–1849				
Archibald	x	x	x	x
Belcher (none)				
Bliss			x	
Blowers	x		x	
Brenton	x	x	x	
Collier				x
Desbarres		x	x	x
Deschamps			x	x
Dodd		x	x	x
Duport				x
Fairbanks		x	x	
Finucane (none)				
Haliburton			x	x
Halliburton (none)[1]				
Hill		x		
Hutchinson			x	
Monk			x	x
Morris				x
Pemberton (none)				
Robie		x	x	
A. Stewart			x	
J. Stewart		x	x	
Strange (none)				
Uniacke	x		x	x
Wilkins Sr			x	
Wiswall			x	
1849–67				
Johnston	x	x	x	
Wilkins Jr			x	
Young	x		x	
1867–1900				
Graham (none)				
Henry (none)				
James (none)				
McCully		x		x
H. McDonald[2]			x	x
J. MacDonald	x		x	
Meagher (none)				

TABLE 8 (continued)

Judge	Attorney general	Solicitor general	MHA MP	Judge JP
Rigby (none)				
J.N. Ritchie (none)				
J.W. Ritchie		x		
Smith	x		x	x
Thompson	x		x	
Townshend			x	
Weatherbe (none)				

1 Halliburton was appointed to the legislative council in 1816, nine years after his elevation to the bench.
2 Offered and declined the attorney generalship

judicial biographies.'[72] The intimate links between judicial and political history suggest that a similar approach to Nova Scotia's history would not be misplaced (see table 8). A previous political career was more the rule than the exception for the judges studied here. Seventeen were government law officers (attorney general or solicitor general) and twenty-five, or 58 per cent, were MHAS or MPS or both. Men like Blowers, Uniacke, Archibald, Johnston, and Young dominated the province's political history as much as they did the evolution of its courts of law. Blowers was attorney general, MHA for Halifax County, Speaker of the Assembly, and member of the council for nine years before his appointment and for thirty-six years thereafter; indeed, the chief justice was the president ex officio of the council until 1837, when its legislative and executive functions were separated. Johnston and Young competed not only in politics as leaders of opposing parties but also for the succession to Halliburton's post as chief justice. McCully and J.W. Ritchie were solicitors general, Confederation conference delegates, and senators, in that order. Hugh McDonald had been the minister of militia in the federal cabinet and at one point had declined the position of attorney general for Nova Scotia. This did not prove a handicap; an active campaign for the post, his long service to the party, and the importance of the Catholic vote in eastern Nova Scotia obtained for him Sir John A. Macdonald's recommendation.

The overall history of appointments to the bench was one of selection of high-profile political individuals. Before responsible government, political office had to be combined with some connection (preferably family) in

London. Later, advancement depended on one's own political party being in power, though after 1867 the politics of patronage became increasingly complex.[73] The importance of political experience may have been greater in Nova Scotia than in other jurisdictions, although direct comparisons are difficult because of variations in what is considered a prior political career. In Massachusetts, 'political' appointments declined after 1715, and although eight of the twelve judges selected after 1750 served in the House of Representatives, only two of them had been major political actors.[74] Just over half of the U.S. Supreme Court judges had been politically active, and about the same ratio of British judges were MPS, compared with the 65 per cent of Nova Scotia judges who had had significant political careers.[75] Bouthillier's study, which was based on holders of elected office only, revealed that 42.8 per cent of appointees between 1849 and 1873 had held such office. The Nova Scotia figures for the pre-1867 period are much higher than that (twenty of twenty-nine or 69 per cent); 56.8 per cent of the next group of appointees in Quebec (1874–98) held elective office, compared with 50 per cent in Nova Scotia (seven of fourteen, counting McCully and Ritchie, whose political contributions, albeit in non-elected offices, cannot be ignored).[76] It is not surprising to find that federal control of the appointments process led to a similarity in patterns of judicial recruitment across provincial boundaries after Confederation.

The progression of attorneys general to the bench merits special attention. English convention dictated that the attorney general, as the Crown's premier law officer, could expect 'any judicial post of sufficient eminence that fell vacant while he was in office.' While the chief justiceship was naturally the most prestigious post available, Nova Scotia's attorneys general seldom attained it. Only two, Sampson Blowers and William Young, did so before 1900, although James MacDonald was the dominion attorney general when he succeeded Young. It took more than a century for it to happen again: Lauchlin Currie, who served as attorney general from 1947 to 1949, became chief justice in 1967, but only because he was the senior puisne judge after nearly twenty years on the bench. Young's promotion did not occur in the normal way, as he was no longer attorney general when Chief Justice Halliburton died in 1860. Adams G. Archibald held the office, but had done so for only five months, a fact that probably counselled caution on his part. J.W. Johnston was the 'logical' candidate in every way, having served as attorney general from 1841 to 1848 and again from 1857 to 1860. Unfortunately for him, he belonged to the wrong party: the Conservatives had lost the 1859 election, and their defeat allowed Young, Johnston's nemesis, to claim the prize.[78] Johnston tried to assuage his loss by having himself styled 'chief justice in equity' when the new post was created for him in 1864, but his gambit was met with derision on all sides.[79] He was forced to settle for 'judge in equity,' although he was granted precedence next to the chief justice.

If attorneys general were usually frustrated in their aspiration to the chief justiceship, they regularly settled for puisne judgeships. Aside from the first two occupants of the office (the first, Otis Little, having 'left the province as an absconding debtor taking passage for the West Indies'),[80] all but two of the pre-Confederation attorneys general acceded to the bench.[81] After 1867 this career pattern became much less settled, and fewer than half of provincial attorneys general to 1983 acquired the ermine. J.M. Beck ascribes this shift to the 'stagnancy' of an office left mired in administration rather than policy-making duties after 1867.[82]

Joseph Howe is reported to have told Alexander James, while the latter was a practising barrister, that 'in order to ascend to the serene heights of the Judicial Bench, it was necessary to pass through the muddy waters of politics.'[83] It is ironic that James was one of the very few appointees discussed in this study who was virtually unsullied by political office or activity. It is said that he was appointed 'because the minister, when in Halifax, found the aspirant working in his shirt-sleeves.' This suggests that by the end of the nineteenth century professional excellence could occasionally make up for a lack of imperial favour or partisan enthusiasm. Actually holding political office was not the only means of establishing one's political credentials, however. Samuel Rigby held no office, but he did become involved in an election campaign before his appointment 'as a sort of qualification ... to his claim for preferment.' Benjamin Russell, a 1904 appointee to the Supreme Court bench, remembered that this qualification was 'desirable, although not altogether indispensable' at that time; he was correct, but only just.[84] Meagher does not seem to have had a high political profile, but he is the only one aside from James, about whom this can be said. John N. Ritchie was not politically prominent, but his family was staunchly Tory. Weatherbe's articling period with J.W. Johnston and his advocacy of colonial union in 1864 certainly would have marked him in political terms.

The last column of table 8 deserves further discussion. Most of the individuals shown as having had some judicial experience found it as justices of the peace or probate judges. Neither post can really be seen as training for higher judicial office, and in fact many JPs held their posts on a purely honorary basis. Only seven out of forty-three judges had judicial experience in any loftier capacity, and, ironically, three of these – Morris, Deschamps, and Collier – were also the three who had no legal training. Deschamps and Morris both sat on the Inferior Court of Common Pleas, the former for Kings County and the latter for Halifax County, while Collier was a judge of the Vice-Admiralty Court from 1753 to 1764. Of the other four, two (Duport and Haliburton) were also Common Pleas judges for eleven and twelve years respectively; Uniacke was acting chief justice of Cape Breton Island for a year; and Archibald was a non-resident chief justice of Prince Edward Island from 1824 to 1828. The failure on many occasions to turn to experienced lower court judges caused resentment among them. The lower courts were, from the early 1820s, headed by lawyers (even if partially staffed by laymen), but after 1800 only Haliburton was promoted through the court hierarchy. Even in this case, however, another Common Pleas judge considered himself better qualified and publicly denounced Haliburton's appointment.[85]

In addition to political considerations, family patronage networks also played a role in selection. Family connections were extensive among the judiciary, and helped to perpetuate its élite composition. We have already seen that many of the judges had fathers who were judges or lawyers. If this family history is taken further to include grandparents and relatives by marriage, the total of those connected to the law in their own generation or in previous generations rises to twenty-four; further research probably would reveal a higher total. Altogether eleven of the judges acquired a legal connection through marriage in addition to those they might have had before,[86] and at least fourteen of them had children, nephews, grandchildren, or great-grandchildren enter the profession.[87] The relationship between Sampson Salter Blowers and William Blowers Bliss typifies the close ties that bound the colony's legal élite. Bliss's father Jonathan was New Brunswick's attorney general and later chief justice and a friend of Blowers. When Jonathan Bliss died, William was adopted by Blowers and trained in the law by him; he eventually married Blower's adopted daughter. Upon his retirement in 1833, the aged Blowers sought to have Bliss appointed to the vacancy; he did not succeed – William Hill secured the post – but his efforts were rewarded in the following year when Bliss was named to the opening created after Richard Uniacke's premature death.

Such connections led to the rise of a number of distinct 'legal families' in Nova Scotia. Susanna Gibbons could claim to be the daughter of a chief justice of Cape Breton, the wife of a chief justice of Cape Breton, and the mother of a Nova Scotia Supreme Court judge, Edmund M. Dodd. The

Wilkins family is also notable: it provided the only father-and-son combination on the court, and was descended from a line of lawyers. Isaac Wilkins, the father and grandfather of the judges, married Isabella Morris, who also came from a legal family, and Chief Justice James MacDonald apprenticed with M.I. Wilkins and married his stepdaughter. Connections can be traced through generations. James Brenton's half-sister Susannah married John Halliburton, whose children were Brenton and Elizabeth Halliburton; Elizabeth married James Stewart. One of Alexander Stewart's daughters married a lawyer, Robert Dickey, and another became the mother of Chief Justice Townshend. Stewart's only son married Amelia King, whose father was a prominent barrister and judge of the Probate Court for Hants, and whose mother was Robie's adopted daughter. J.W. Johnston's sister Elizabeth was married to Thomas Ritchie, lawyer, member of the House of Assembly, judge of the Inferior Court of Common Pleas, and father of J.W. and J.N. Ritchie. The Ritchies, indeed, are the best known Nova Scotia legal family. In addition to the two Ritchies considered in this study, their father, their grandfather, and four of their brothers were all lawyers. One of them, William Johnston Ritchie, was chief justice of Canada from 1879 to 1892. Their descendants also included lawyers and judges, stretching over six generations and including the late Roland Ritchie, a puisne judge of the Supreme Court of Canada. If one accepts the contention that 'social transmission of attitudes, beliefs, values and aspirations has its most effective vehicle in the family,'[88] then families like the Ritchies and others will be of great importance to future studies of judicial attitudes.

Not only did Nova Scotia's legal families intermarry, they also formed links with other members of the province's élite to create a network reinforced by ties of blood and matrimony.[89] There was 'a tradition of intermarriage among the Ritchie, Johnston and Almon families'; the last-named were physicians and councillors.[90] Johnston married Amelia Almon; J.W. Ritchie, his nephew, married Amelia's niece, who was also named Amelia. James Brenton and Brenton Halliburton were connected to the Inglis family of clerics, Brenton through his children and Halliburton through his marriage to Margaret, the daughter of Bishop Charles Inglis. Blowers and Morris were connected to the Salter family of merchants. Numerous other relationships could be noted, but for our purposes the significance of these is clearly in the extent to which such relationships undoubtedly contributed to judicial appointment and very likely to conservative behaviour on the bench.

THE SPOILS OF OFFICE

It may be thought that one of the main reasons men coveted high judicial posts was the remuneration that accompanied them, but it is not clear that this was the case in the eighteenth century. Although the chief justice initially received £500 per year in salary, in 1776 the secretary of state worried whether a worthy successor to Belcher could be found 'to whom the Emoluments of the Office [would] be a sufficient inducement for quitting his situation.'[91] Indeed, Belcher's own estate was barely able to meet outstanding debts. His successor, Bryan Finucane, persuaded the Lords of Trade to pay him half his salary from the time of his appointment, despite the fact that he took sixteen months to arrive in Halifax. The acting chief justice, Charles Morris, received the other half.[92] There is evidence that in 1788 Chief Justice Jeremy Pemberton was actively seeking an increase in salary.[93] The high cost of living in Georgian Halifax, together with the necessity of maintaining a quasi-aristocratic lifestyle, doubtless taxed the incomes of eighteenth-century appointees who relied solely on their judicial salaries.

The chief justice's salary rose incrementally to £880 by 1848. With the coming of responsible government the colonial assembly set the incumbent's salary at the existing level, abolished fees, and decreed that future chief justices would get only £640 per year.[94] Just a year later Halliburton's salary rose to £1,000, although the £640 limit for his successor was retained; this arrangement was confirmed by future acts.[95] The dollar system was adopted in 1864, and Chief Justice Young's salary was fixed at $3,200.[96] The salary of the master of the rolls was also substantial; it rose from £600 for Robie to £650 by 1848, but was reduced to £560 in that same year. Among senior office-holders, only the treasurer received a comparable salary – £600 in the 1830s; the attorney general rated £225 and the solicitor general £100, although those offices possessed other pecuniary advantages.

Assistant judges were always placed directly on the Assembly payroll, not on the civil list. They received £350 in 1781, £400 in 1789, £500 in 1809, and £600 in 1822; the salary appears to have dropped to £560 in 1848.[98] In 1849 a special act gave the senior assistant judge, Bliss, a salary of £640, but kept the others at £560.[99] Three years later, assistant's salaries were reduced to £480 (except for Thomas Haliburton, who kept his £560).[100] A year previously, however, another act had confirmed the £640 paid to Bliss.[101] In 1859 Bliss's salary was raised to £650 and those of the others were returned to £560, the 1849 level.[102] After the conversion to dollars,

Bliss received $3,250 and the other assistants $2,800; Bliss was therefore earning $50 more than the chief justice.[103]

Confederation brought some increase in salary, with the chief justice's and the judge in equity's renumeration set at $4,000 each in 1868; the puisne judges received $3,200. Salaries rose steadily if not spectacularly until the end of the century, when the new scale in 1905 allocated $7,000 to the chief justice, $6,000 to the judge in equity and the puisne judges, and an additional $500 to the judge of the Court of Divorce and Matrimonial Causes.[104]

Even allowing for the pre-Confederation fluctuations, by the nineteenth century judicial posts were well-paid prizes for aged lawyers seeking financial security in an unsteady economic environment. It is likely that the purely financial attractions of the judicial post declined towards the end of the century, however, as lawyers' incomes rose with increased professional opportunities. P.B. Waite doubts whether John S.D. Thompson's income exceeded his $4,000 salary as a Supreme Court judge in 1877, but Thompson's friend, the lawyer-newspaperman Martin Griffin, thought it did. Wallace Graham's acceptance of a judgeship apparently did involve a financial sacrifice.[105] For a few individuals in the 1880s and 1890s, then, a judge's salary was not competitive with his professional income. Of course, even for those few, the attraction of a well-paid and not too strenuous position in one's golden years must have been great.

I have not been able to find information on all judges, but for twenty-seven out of forty-three I have collected data which, to varying degrees, give a sense of their financial success.[106] In somewhat crude fashion these men have been subdivided into four groups: the very wealthy, the wealthy, the moderately affluent, and the poor and insolvent. It is impossible to say whether, for some of those judges who died wealthy, their judicial salaries or other sources of income provided the bulk of their estates. A number of them, such as Robie and Uniacke, had undoubtedly inherited a good deal of wealth, while some spent only a few years on the bench. Others, such as J.W. Ritchie, had very successful law practices and held well-paid government offices.

At least nine of the judges appear to have died very wealthy men. Bliss turned his extra salary, his thirty-five years on the bench, and his shrewd investments into an estate of over $500,000 dollars at his death in 1874.[107] By the time he retired in 1834 Robie had accumulated some £60,000; when he died twenty-four years later that sum had increased substantially. His personal property alone at that time was worth over £80,000.[108] Young's total estate in 1881 was in the neighbourhood of $350,000, nearly one-third of which he devoted to philanthropic purposes.[109] The other five judges characterized as 'very wealthy' were Uniacke, who died possessed of 'an ample fortune';[110] J.W. Ritchie, who lived out his retirement years in his beautiful Belmont-on-the-Arm estate in Halifax; Haliburton, merchant, entrepreneur, and popular writer, who retired to England and became a conservative MP; McCully, who left $100,000 in 1877;[111] and Blowers, who was generally acknowledged to have left a substantial fortune even though he made bequests of just £4,000, with the residue of his estate going to his wife.[112] James Stewart's net worth is unclear, but it was probably a little over £30,000 in 1830.[113]

Less spectacularly rich, but still very comfortably off, were six of the judges. Strange married into the baronetcy, and lived out a comfortable retirement in England writing his law books.[114] Johnston too was clearly affluent, although the details of his fortune are not available. Like Thomas Haliburton, he died in England after having been appointed lieutenant-governor of Nova Scotia. Brenton Halliburton's estate was valued at a little over $40,000 at his death in 1860.[115] No such information exists for Archibald, but he was able to leave £600 to his granddaughter when she came of age and £300 a year to his wife for life, and to contemplate a bequest of a substantial residue to his children thereafter.[116] Hutchinson left £7,000 and a house when he died in 1815.[117]

The third category consists of six judges who died possessed of moderate fortunes. Fairbanks left some $10,500 in 1841, but acknowledged in his will that his debts would reduce that amount.[118] Peleg Wiswall's widow felt the need to petition for full payment of his salary in the year he died, but she did not go so far as to suggest that her circumstances were actually distressed.[119] Lewis Wilkins Jr's estate was worth $31,000 as late as 1885, John Thompson's only $20,000 in 1894; Edmund Dodd's will contained only moderate bequests and William Hill was worth no more than about £4,500.[120]

At least seven of the judges died in financially difficult circumstances. All of them were late eighteenth-century appointees; in general, they were insolvent because they had come to Nova Scotia poor, had enjoyed only limited or risky opportunities to augment their incomes, and had felt a need to maintain a quasi-aristocratic lifestyle. Finucane is a case in point: a combination of the debts he brought with him, a short career in Nova Scotia before his death in 1785, and his personal extravagance left him insolvent at the time of his death.[121] Both Finucane and Charles Morris found the economic problems of the American revolutionary years trying; Morris was put to 'great and heavy expense' by his son Alexander, so much so that his residuary estate in 1781 was only about £700.[122] When Belcher died, his estate had to be sold to pay his debts, as did Collier's; Deschamps left only a very small sum.[123] George Monk held a great variety of posts in Nova Scotia, from superintendent of Indians to judge of the provincial supreme court, but he was extravagant, a poor manager of money, and constantly in debt; his brother James, the chief justice of the Court of King's Bench for the District of Montreal, repeatedly came to his aid.[124] A decent old age was secured for George only because he was influential enough to have the Assembly vote him a pension upon his retirement.[125] The final judge in this category is James Brenton, who left an estate of £200 and debts of £600. His widow submitted a pathetic petition to the Assembly, noting that his 'low salary, warrants discounted at 25 per cent, [the] long illness of himself and his daughters' had used up all the money and left her with a house and 'four fatherless daughters.'[126]

Without more information it is impossible to draw a complete picture of judicial wealth in eighteenth- and nineteenth-century Nova Scotia. Nevertheless, it is clear that the judges ended their lives with widely varying fortunes, and that the lot of the eighteenth-century judge, who had to contend with conditions in a new colony and with the American and French revolutionary wars, was frequently a poor one. No such distress seems to have afflicted later judges, who were increasingly settled members of the colonial legal and political establishment rather than British office-seekers or New England loyalists.

CONCLUSION

Photographers know that group portraits are not easily taken. One subject has his eyes shut, another in the back row is obscured by those in front, a third is absent, and a fourth is blurred because he moved at the wrong instant. A portrait of a group that is constantly changing presents even more difficulties. None the less, if we restrict our inquiry here to objective characteristics we can discern the contours of the superior court judiciary.

With one major exception, changes in the judiciary can be traced to the achievement of responsible government at mid-century. No event better symbolized the dégringolade of the old Tory Anglican élite than the ouster of Alexander Stewart in 1855 (although the rise of his grandson Charles Townshend to the chief justiceship showed that such ties retained some utility even in a later era). After 1850 the judiciary began to reflect more accurately the religious diversity and social structure of the province, though not its ethnic composition. Acadians and Irish are notable for their absence, to say nothing of blacks or natives. Women remained absent because they were formally excluded from the bar.

One major change not traceable to the achievement of responsible government was the rise of an indigenous judiciary. The last British judge was Sir Thomas Strange, who served from 1789 to 1797, and the major legal metropolis, in terms of personnel, from then until 1833 was New England. A comparison with Upper Canada, where as late as 1833 a British-born vice-chancellor was imposed on the colony, is instructive.

The evolution of an indigenous judiciary seems to have been accompanied by a gradually increasing emphasis on professional qualifications and activities. The early 1870s marked a low point, if one accepts P.B. Waite's characterization of the reigning bench as 'idiosyncratic, at times crotchety, some no doubt vulgar, unwell, lazy ... old-fashioned [and full of] anachronistic ideas';[127] but a subsequent infusion of new blood brought in some younger men schooled in the new professionalism. Thompson, Weatherbe, Graham, and Meagher were all acknowledged leaders at the bar; Alexander James had attempted to form a Dominion Bar Society; and Hugh Henry held a Harvard LLB.

I have not attempted to relate the judges' careers to their legal opinions; much more work on the evolution of legal doctrines in the province must be done before that connection can be made. Nor have I traced in any detail the patterns of patronage in the appointment process. I hope that this essay will provide a starting-point for both projects.

APPENDIX

This list shows the appointment (a.) and death (d.) or resignation (r.) dates for each judge included in this article. The chronology is divided into eleven periods, marked by chief justices' terms, which include the periods when the court was headed by acting chief justices appointed locally until London's appointee arrived. Jonathan Belcher appears twice, once sitting alone and once with assistants.

1754–64:	Jonathan Belcher
1764–76	Jonathan Belcher, CJ (d.1776)
	Charles Morris (a.1764)
	John Collier (a.1764; d.1769)
	John Duport (a.1769; r.1770)
	Isaac Deschamps (a.1770)
1776–8	Charles Morris, CJ (acting 1776; superseded 1778)

	Isaac Deschamps
1778–85	Bryan Finucane, CJ (a.1776; d.1785)
	Isaac Deschamps
	Charles Morris (d.1781)
	James Brenton (a.1781)
1785–8	Isaac Deschamps, CJ (acting 1785, superseded 1788)
	James Brenton
1788–9	Jeremy Pemberton, CJ (a.1788; r.1789)
	Isaac Deschamps
	James Brenton
1789–97	Sir Thomas Strange, CJ (a.1789; r.1797)
	Isaac Deschamps
	James Brenton
1797–1833	Sampson Salter Blowers, CJ (a.1797; r.1833)
	Isaac Deschamps (d.1801)
	James Brenton (d.1806)
	George Monk (a.1801; r.1816)
	Sir Brenton Halliburton (a.1807)
	Foster Hutchinson (a.1810; d.1815)
	James Stewart (a.1815; d.1830)
	Lewis M. Wilkins Sr (a.1816)
	Peleg Wiswall (a.1816)
	Richard J. Uniacke Jr (a.1830)
1833–60	Sir Brenton Halliburton, CJ (a.1833; d.1860)
	Lewis M. Wilkins Sr (d.1848)
	Peleg Wiswall (d.1836)
	Richard J. Uniacke Jr (d.1834)
	William Hill (a.1833; d.1848)
	William Blowers Bliss (a.1834)
	Thomas C. Haliburton (a.1841; r.1856)
	Edmund M. Dodd (a.1848)
	William Desbarres (a.1848)
	Lewis M. Wilkins Jr (a.1856)
1860–81	Sir William Young, CJ (a.1860; r.1881)
	William Blowers Bliss (r.1869)
	Edmund M. Dodd (r.1873)
	William Desbarres (r.1881)
	Lewis M. Wilkins Jr (r.1878)
	James W. Johnston (a.1864; d.1873)
	Jonathan McCully (a.1870; d.1877)
	John W. Ritchie (a.1870)

	Hugh McDonald (a.1873)
	Henry Smith (a.1875)
	Sir Robert S. Weatherbe (a.1878)
	Alexander James (a.1879)
	Samuel Rigby (a.1881)
1881–1904	James MacDonald, CJ (a.1881; r.1904)
	John W. Ritchie (r.1882)
	Hugh McDonald (r.1893)
	Henry Smith (d.1890)
	Alexander James (d.1889)
	Sir Robert S. Weatherbe (r.1907)
	Samuel Rigby (d.1886)
	Sir John S.O. Thompson (a.1882; r.1885)
	John N. Ritchie (a.1885; d.1904)
	Sir Charles Townshend (a.1887; r.1915)
	Sir Wallace Graham (a.1889; d.1917)
	Sir Nicholas Meagher (a.1890; r.1916)
	Hugh Henry (a.1893; r.1904)

Masters of the rolls

1825–34	Simon Bradstreet Robie
1834–41	Charles R. Fairbanks
1841–6	Samuel G.W. Archibald
1846–55	Alexander Stewart

NOTES

1 Many of these are rather dated and belong in the category of genealogical or antiquarian studies. Among the better studies of individual Canadian judges are David R. Williams *Duff: A Life in the Law* (Toronto: The Osgoode Society 1984) and *The Man for a New Country: Sir Mathew Baillie Begbie* (Don Mills, Ont.: Fitzhenry and Whiteside 1980); Patrick Brode *Sir John Beverley Robinson: Bone and Sinew of the Compact* (Toronto: The Osgoode Society 1984); C. Berkin *Jonathan Sewell: Odyssey of an American Loyalist* (New York: Columbia University Press 1974); and L.F.S. Upton *The Loyal Whig: William Smith of New York and Quebec* (Toronto: University of Toronto Press 1969).

2 See G.B. Baker 'The Reconstitution of Upper Canadian Legal Thought in the Late-Victorian Empire' *Law and History Review* 3 (1985) 219–92; R.C.B.

Risk 'Sir William R. Meredith, C.J.O.: The Search for Authority' *Dalhousie Law Journal* 7 (1983) 713–41; D. Howes 'Property, God and Nature in the Thought of Sir John Beverley Robinson' *McGill Law Journal* 30 (1985) 365–413; idem 'From Polyjurality to Monojurality: The Transformation of Quebec Law, 1875–1929' *McGill Law Journal* 32 (1987) 523–58; R. Cook 'John Beverley Robinson and the Conservative Blueprint for the Upper Canadian Community' in J.K. Johnson, ed. *Historical Essays on Upper Canada* (Toronto: McClelland and Stewart 1975); J. Nedelsky 'Judicial Conservatism in an Age of Innovation: Comparative Perspectives on Canadian Nuisance Law' in D.H. Flaherty, ed. *Essays in the History of Canadian Law* vol. 1 (Toronto: The Osgoode Society 1981).

3 See, inter alia, G. Adams and P.J. Cavalluzzo 'The Supreme Court of Canada: A Biographical Study' *Osgoode Hall Law Journal* 7 (1969) 61–86; S.R. Peck 'The Supreme Court of Canada 1958–1966: A Search for Policy through Scalogram Analysis' *Canadian Bar Review* 45 (1967) 666–725; M. Bader and E. Burstein 'The Supreme Court of Canada, 1892–1902: A Study of the Men and the Times' *Osgoode Hall Law Journal* 8 (1970) 503–47. J. Snell and P. Vaughan, *The Supreme Court of Canada: History of the Institution* (Toronto: The Osgoode Society 1985) contains some useful information on the Supreme Court judiciary but is not intended as an analysis of it. See, similarly, H. Foster 'The Struggle for the Supreme Court: Law and Politics in British Columbia, 1871–1885' in L.A. Knafla, ed. *Law and Justice in a New Land: Essays in Western Canadian Legal History* (Toronto: Carswell 1986).

At the level of the provincial Superior Court judiciary, Quebec provides a major exception to the statement in the text: see G. Bouthillier 'Matériaux pour une analyse politique des juges de la Cour d'appel' *Revue Juridique Thémis* 6 (1971) 563; idem 'Note sur la carrière politique des juges de la Cour supérieure' *Revue Juridique Thémis* 7 (1972) 573; idem 'Profil du juge de la Cour supérieure du Québec' *Canadian Bar Review* 55 (1972) 436. Bouthillier's analysis owes more to political science and sociology than to history, however, and he is mainly interested in judges appointed since 1946. I.-J. Deslauriers provides a collection of individual biographies of all Quebec Superior Court judges, but no collective analysis, in *La Cour supérieure du Québec et ses juges 1849–ler janvier 1980* (Quebec: n.p. 1980). An older but still useful work is Pierre-Georges Roy *Les Juges de la Province de Québec* (Quebec: Imprimerie du Roi 1933). Outside Quebec there is J.W. Lawrence *The Judges of New Brunswick and Their Times* (1907; reprinted Fredericton: Acadiensis Press 1983) which covers judges appointed between 1784 and 1 July 1867. While there is little synthetic treatment of the judges, D.G. Bell in his introduction to the 1983 reprint edition praises the work for providing 'a unique omnium gatherum of rich Victorian detail' about them. For other provinces one must consult theses: see, for example, W.J. Klein 'Judicial Recruitment in Manitoba, Ontario and Quebec 1905–1970' (PHD thesis, University of Toronto 1975).

Treatment of the inferior courts has been even more sporadic: see R. Stubbs *Four Recorders of Ruperts Land: A Brief Survey of the Hudson Bay Company Courts* (Winnipeg: Pequis Publishers 1967); G. Bouthillier 'Profil du juge de la Cour des Sessions de la paix' *Revue du Barreau* (1978) 13; and I.-J. Deslauriers *Les tribunaux du Québec et leurs juges: Cour provinciale, Cour des Sessions de la paix, Tribunal de la jeunesse, Cour municipale* (Cowansville, Que.: Yvon Blais 1987) (biographies only).

4 One American author describes the 'emphasis upon personal qualifications and characteristics' as 'a manifestation of the twentieth-century shift in American jurisprudence from the unrealistic acceptance of the mechanistic theory of judicial interpretation to frank acknowledgement of the subjective element in the decision-making process': J.R. Schmidhauser 'The Justices of the Supreme Court: A Collective Portrait' *Midwest Journal of Political Science* 3 (1959) 1.

5 R.C.B Risk 'A Prospectus for Canadian Legal History' *Dalhousie Law Journal* 1 (1973) 228–9

6 J.P. Frank 'The Appointment of Supreme Court Justices: Prestige, Principles and Politics' *Wisconsin Law Review* (1941) 172

7 C.N. Tate 'Paths to the Bench in Britain: A Quasi-Experimental Study of the Recruitment of a Judicial Elite' *Western Political Quarterly* 28 (1975) 108

8 C.M. Ewing *The Judges of the Supreme Court, 1789–1937* (Minneapolis: University of Minnesota Press 1938); Schmidhauser 'Justices of the Supreme Court'

9 See the extensive listing in Tate 'Paths to the Bench' notes 1 and 2.

10 For a review of these in the United States, see J.B. Grossman 'Social Backgrounds and Judicial Decisions: Notes for a Theory' *Journal of Politics* 29 (1967) 334–51. See also, inter alia, S.S. Nagel 'Judicial Characteristics and Judicial Decision-Making' (PHD thesis, Northwestern University 1961); 'Political Party Affiliation and Judges' Decisions' *American Political Science Review* 55 (1961) 843–50; idem 'Ethnic Affiliations and Judicial Propensities' *Journal of Politics* 24 (1962) 92–110; J.B. Grossman 'Social Backgrounds and Judicial Decision-Making' *Harvard Law Review* 79 (1966) 1551–64; G. Schubert *Judicial Policy-Making* (Chicago: Scott, Foresman 1965); W. Murphy *Elements of Judicial Strategy* (Chicago: University of Chicago Press 1964); S. Goldman 'Politics, Judges, and the Administration of Justice' (PHD

thesis, Harvard University 1965); J.R. Schmidhauser 'Stare Decisis, Dissent, and the Background of the Justices of the Supreme Court' *University of Toronto Law Journal* 14 (1962) 194–212.

11 P. Russell 'The Development of Judicial Expertise in Eighteenth-Century Massachusetts and a Hypothesis concerning Social Change' *Journal of Social History* 16 (1983) 143–54

12 Tate 'Paths to the Bench' looks at the British judiciary from the 1870s. The earlier period is covered in D. Duman 'The Judges of England 1730–1875: A Social, Economic and Institutional History' (PHD thesis, Johns Hopkins University 1975, published as *The Judicial Bench in England 1727–1875: The Reshaping of a Professional Elite* [London: Royal Historical Society 1982]). On the British courts generally, see B. Abel-Smith and R. Stevens *Lawyers and the Courts: A Sociological Study of the English Legal System, 1750–1965* (London: Heinemann 1975); on the House of Lords, see R. Stevens *Law and Politics: The House of Lords as a Judicial Body, 1800–1976* (Chapel Hill: University of North Carolina Press 1978); L. Blom-Cooper and G. Drewry *Final Appeal: A Study of the House of Lords in Its Judicial Capacity* (Oxford: Clarendon Press 1972).

13 Bouthillier 'Profil du juge de la Cour supérieure'

14 The latter has been included in this section because the master of the rolls was also a member of the senior judiciary, ranking immediately after the chief justice in order of precedence. There was an office called the 'master of the rolls' from 1782 until 1813, when it lapsed, but its holders have not been included in this study because the nature of the office seems to have been much less important before the revival of the office with Robie's elevation in 1825. The amount of the salary itself, £600 per annum, bore eloquent testimony to the enhanced functions and prestige of the office. Before 1826 the 'Master of the Rolls, or Master's Fees' were set by statute, and the office seems to have carried no salary: see SNS 1802, c. 4, and SNS 1820–21, c. 40. For ease of reference, Robie will be considered the first master of the rolls for the purposes of this paper. See also Barry Cahill 'James Monk's "Observations in the Courts of Law in Nova Scotia," 1775' *University of New Brunswick Law Journal* 36 (1987) 131 n45; idem ' "Bleak House" Revisited: The Records and Papers of the Court of Chancery of Nova Scotia, 1751–1855' *Archivaria* 29 (1990).

The Court of Vice-Admiralty, although certainly an important court in the Nova Scotia context, is excluded here because of the peculiarity of its jurisdiction, which concerned mostly international law rather than domestic law, and the obscurity of its early history. On the latter, see J.M. Beck *The Government of Nova Scotia* (Toronto: University of Toronto Press 1957)

64–5. Many of its judges are included here, however, because all of them between 1821 and 1891 were also chief justices or masters of the rolls. They were Sampson Salter Blowers, CJ (1821–33); Charles Rufus Fairbanks (1834–41); S.G. Archibald (1841–6); Alexander Stewart (1846–65); Sir William Young, CJ (1865–81); and James MacDonald, CJ (1881–91). In 1867 admiralty affairs came under federal authority, and in 1891 the Courts of Admiralty were abolished and the jurisdiction transferred to the Exchequer Court of Canada.

Cape Breton was a separate colony with its own chief justice from 1784 to 1820, but the occupants of that office have not been included in this study.

15 'Cornwallis' Commission' in T.B. Akins, ed. *Selections from the Public Documents of Nova Scotia* (Halifax: Annand 1869) 501. Histories of the court include C.J. Townshend *Historical Account of the Courts of Judicature in Nova Scotia* (Toronto: Carswell 1900); M. Ells 'Nova Scotian Sparks of Liberty' *Dalhousie Review* 16 (1937) 476–92; Beck *Government of Nova Scotia*; T.G. Barnes 'As Near as May Be Agreeable to the Laws of This Kingdom: Legal Birthright and Legal Baggage at Chebucto, 1749' in P.B. Waite et al., eds *Law in a Colonial Society: The Nova Scotia Experience* (Toronto: Carswell 1984); J.B. Cahill 'The Judges' Affair: An Eighteenth-Century Nova Scotian *Cause Célèbre*' (unpublished monograph).

16 On his problems as governor and his disputes with the powerful merchant interests led by Joseph Mauger, see J.M. Beck *The Politics of Nova Scotia, 1710–1896* (Tantallon, NS: Four East Publications 1985) 27–9.

17 C.J. Townshend 'Jonathan Belcher, First Chief Justice of Nova Scotia' *Collections* 18 (1914) 33, 50; S. Buggey 'Jonathan Belcher' *DCB* vol. 4, 50

18 The circuits were originally at Halifax, Horton, Annapolis, and Cumberland. In 1794 the counties of Lunenburg, Sydney, Queens and Shelburne were added, and Cape Breton Island was included in 1820 when it was reunited with Nova Scotia.

19 SNS 1809, c. 15, s. 6; 1816, c. 2, s. 3; 1837, c. 54, s. 5; 1841, c. 3, s. 33. See the appendix for the dates of judicial appointments.

20 SNS 1864, c. 10; 1870, c. 2, s. 2. The 1864 statute specified that W.B. Bliss would not be replaced when his position was vacated; thus, upon his retirement in 1869 the court returned to five. The 1870 statute increased the total complement to seven. On the generally decrepit state of the bench in 1870 before the additions, see Beck *Government of Nova Scotia* 287–8.

21 SNS 1848, c. 21; 1849, c. 1. For the history of judicial independence, and the distinction between 'at pleasure' and 'good behaviour,' see B.A. Black

'Massachusetts and the Judges: Judicial Independence in Perspective' *Law and History Review* 3 (1985) 101–12.

22 For the history of Chancery in Nova Scotia, see the essay by Philip Girard elsewhere in this volume, and Townshend *Historical Account.*

23 SNS 1855, c. 23; quotation from J.M. Beck 'Alexander Stewart' *DCB* vol. 10 748. After the fusion of law and equity was effected by the Judicature Act, SNS 1884, c. 25, all the Supreme Court judges became bound to apply equitable principles and the title of judge of equity became an honorific only. It was retained until 1956, however.

24 The various tables, summaries, and calculations that appear in this essay are based on a large number of primary and secondary sources. Only a small minority of these appear in the footnotes. Space limitations prevent the publication with this essay of the full bibliography of sources, but it is available on request from the editors of the volume. The age calculation presented here does not include the ages for Collier and Duport, whose birthdates could not be established. The average age of the bench was calculated at ten-year intervals from 1801: (1801) 59.3; (1811) 62.0; (1821) 59.9; (1831) 64.2; (1841) 54.8; (1851) 58.2; (1861) 62.6; (1871) 70.1; (1881) 65.1; (1891) 54.0; and (1901) 60.7.

25 Calculating total time in judicial office, in whatever capacity. Included are years spent on the bench after 1900 for those appointed before.

26 On this notion, see P. Romney *Mr Attorney: The Attorney General for Ontario in Court, Cabinet, and Legislature 1791–1899* (Toronto: The Osgoode Society 1986) 36 and the references given therein. It is easy to give examples of the currency of this notion before 1850, but its decline thereafter is more difficult to chart. L.M. Wilkins Jr 'expected to inherit his father's seat on the Supreme Court in 1848' but was not appointed until 1856: L.K. Kernaghan 'Lewis Morris Wilkins' *DCB* vol. 11, 925, 926. The Reformers bitterly opposed the practice, which was castigated by Joseph Howe in his 'Letters of a Constitutionalist,' published in the *Novascotian* in June and July 1842. No doubt the dominion pension legislation of 1868 meant the demise of the concept, but Roy *Les Juges de la Province de Quebec* gives an example from 1933, when a Quebec Superior Court judge resigned and was succeeded immediately by his son. In 1922 one judge seems to have resigned only on condition that his son would replace him: Bouthillier 'Profil du juge de la Cour supérieure' 453

27 I. Longworth *Life of S.G.W. Archibald* (Halifax: Huestis 1881) 107–8. Blowers allegedly clung to office in order to frustrate the desire of his old rival, the elder R.J. Uniacke, to succeed him, and to enhance the chances of his

own preferred successor, the senior assistant judge Brenton Halliburton: B. Cuthbertson *The Old Attorney General* (Halifax: Nimbus 1980) 118. His status as attorney general should have made Uniacke's claim a strong one. Blowers's strategy succeeded admirably; he outlived Uniacke, who died in 1830 and thus cleared the way for Halliburton's appointment in 1833.

28 Executive council minutes, 1 Feb. 1833, PANS RG3, vol. 196

29 SNS 1816, c. 17

30 The worst was probably the dispute over Alexander Stewart's pension, necessitated by the abolition of Chancery: see the essay by Philip Girard elsewhere in this volume.

31 SC 1868, c. 33

32 *British Colonist* 14 April 1864

33 Schmidhauser 'Justices of the Supreme Court' 16

34 The 'Halifax connection' refers to the élite of Nova Scotia clergymen, councillors, and assemblymen centred in Halifax. See T.M. Punch 'The Halifax Connection, 1749–1848' (MA thesis, St Mary's University 1972) and Beck *Government of Nova Scotia* 21–2.

35 On this dispute see R. Rompkey, ed. *Expeditions of Honour: The Journal of John Salusbury in Halifax, Nova Scotia, 1749–53* (London and Toronto: Associated University Presses 1982) 47–50, 129–34.

36 J. Murrin 'The Legal Transformation: The Bench and Bar of Eighteenth-Century Massachusetts' in S.N. Katz, ed. *Colonial America: Essays in Politics and Social Development* (Boston: Little Brown 1971)

37 J. Lounsbury 'Jonathan Belcher, Chief Justice and Lieutenant-Governor of Nova Scotia' in *Essays in Colonial History Presented to Charles MacLean Andrews* (New Haven: Yale University Press 1931) 177

38 Schmidhauser 'Justices of the Supreme Court' 6–7

39 Duman 'Judges of England' 97; Russell 'Development of Judicial Expertise' 143, 145. It is worth noting, however, that over time fewer landed aristocrats were appointed to the bench in Britain as the judicial network became an élite in itself. See Duman 'Judges of England, chapters 2 and 7.

40 Punch 'Halifax Connection' 129–30

41 'Profil du juge,' supra note 3, 449–50. Bouthillier does not give these figures, but they can be calculated from the data he provides.

42 R.H. Graham 'Sir Nicholas Hogan Meagher' PANS MG100, vol. 170, no. 28. The knighthood was papal, not royal; Pius XI created him a knight of the Order of St Gregory the Great.

43 See J. Fingard *The Anglican Design in Loyalist Nova Scotia* (London: Society for the Propagation of Christian Knowledge, 1972), and S. Buggey 'Churchmen and Dissenters: Religious Toleration in Nova Scotia, 1758–1835' (MA thesis, Dalhousie University 1981) 33.

44 SNS 1830, c. 1

45 J.B. Cahill 'The Career of Chief Justice Bryan Finucane' *Collections* 42 (1986) 154

46 'C.R. Fairbanks,' PANS MG1, vol. 2140, no. 154

47 The other two were Meagher and Thompson; Thompson was a convert.

48 Schmidhauser 'Justices of the Supreme Court' 22.

49 This calculation omits four judges – Collier, Brenton, Dodd, and Duport – whose status is unclear.

50 Duman 'Judges of England' 81; Russell 'Development of Judicial Expertise' 143–4

51 Belcher and Blowers went to Harvard, Archibald to Andover College, and Wilkins Sr to King's College, New York (later Columbia University). Pemberton was a graduate of Cambridge, Strange of Oxford; James Stewart attended Edinburgh University.

52 T.C. Haliburton *An Historical and Statistical Account of Nova Scotia* (Halifax: Joseph Howe 1929) 153; Punch 'Halifax Connection' 81

53 John Duport, L.M. Wilkins Sr, and William Hill are not included in the table. Although they were lawyers, I could find no information on their legal training. The apprenticeship period was at first five years (four for university graduates), later four years, and finally three years for those with a BA or an LLB: RSNS 1864, c. 130; RSNS 1873, c. 108; RSNS 1884, c. 108.

54 Morris was Surveyor of Nova Scotia from 1745 to 1746, and with John Brewse laid out the city of Halifax in 1749. He is best known for his surveying career (he was the first Morris of a line of four to hold the post), but he also had a distinguished military career and was a judge of the Inferior Court of Common Pleas at Halifax. Deschamps was a merchant who learned his trade from Joshua Mauger, the city's most prominent entrepreneur, and who held a variety of official posts. Collier, one of the first settlers, was a retired army captain.

55 On his father W.A. Henry see P.R. Blakeley 'William Alexander Henry: A Father of Confederation from Nova Scotia' *Collections* 36 (1968) 96. W.A Henry was one of the first appointees to the Supreme Court of Canada.

56 The others were Blowers (apprentice Bliss), Wilkins Sr (Desbarres), J. Stewart (Halliburton), and J.W. Ritchie (Rigby).

57 Cahill 'Judges' Affair'; Ells 'Sparks of Liberty'

58 J.G. Marshall *A Brief History of Public Proceedings and Events* (Halifax: Wesleyan Printing n.d.) 3. Marshall was Chief Justice of the Inferior Court of Common Pleas for Cape Breton from 1823 to 1841 and the author of Nova Scotia's first manual for justices of the peace, *The Justice of the Peace and County and Township Officer in the Province of Nova Scotia* (1837). (A second edition was published in 1846.)

59 J. Doull 'Four Attorney-Generals' *Collections* 27 (1947) 1, 10
60 B. Russell 'Reminiscences of the Nova Scotia Judiciary' *Dalhousie Review* 5 (1925) 510
61 Marshall *Brief History* 3
62 D. Campbell *Nova Scotia in Its Historical, Mercantile and Industrial Relations* (Montreal: John Lovell 1873) 336; Longworth *Archibald* 55
63 R.H. Graham 'Sir Wallace Graham' PANS MG100, vol. 170, no. 28
64 Strange's *Elements of Hindu Law* 2 vols (London 1825) ran to four editions and was for many years considered the standard work.
65 Murdoch was the author of, among other works, *Epitome of the Laws of Nova Scotia* 4 vols (Halifax: Joseph Howe 1832–3).
66 Schmidhauser 'Justices of the Supreme Court' 34
67 The calculations tabulated here include pre-judicial years spent as assembly members, and years in government offices such as those of attorney general, solicitor general, and law clerk, because it was common to combine those offices with private practice. Not included are years spent in other judicial offices and as government ministers in a non-legal capacity. Five judges, all in the pre-1849 period, are excluded for want of sufficient information – Duport, Hill, Monk, James Stewart, and Wilkins Sr. Hill was appointed after the passage of an 1809 statute requiring that no assistant judge be appointed to the Nova Scotia Supreme Court unless he had been a member of the bar for ten years and had practised law for five. See SNS 1809, c. 15, s. 7.
68 Russell 'Development of Judicial Expertise' 144
69 They were Pemberton and Strange (England), Belcher (England and Ireland), Finucane (Ireland), Bliss (England, Nova Scotia, and New Brunswick), Blowers (Massachusetts and Nova Scotia), and Brenton (Rhode Island and Nova Scotia). Many judges had also received 'courtesy calls' to the bars of New Brunswick or Prince Edward Island or both.
70 *Acadian Recorder* 1 Nov. 1878
71 On the nature and meaning of patronage, see J.M. Bourne *Patronage and Society in Nineteenth-Century England* (London: Edward Arnold 1986). Detailed accounts of the operation of patronage in Canadian judicial appointments are rare; for an illuminating example, see J.G. Snell 'Frank Anglin Joins the Bench: A Study of Judicial Patronage, 1897–1904' *Osgoode Hall Law Journal* 18 (1980) 664.
72 Lawrence *Judges of New Brunswick* xi
73 For examples of this complexity, see J.M. Beck *Joseph Howe* 2 vols (Kingston and Montreal: McGill-Queen's University Press 1982) vol. 1, 257, 264.

74 Russell 'Development of judicial Expertise' 148

75 Schmidhauser 'Justices of the Supreme Court' 37; Duman 'Judges of England' 160

76 The Nova Scotia figures would be the same as Quebec's (eight of fourteen, or 57 per cent) if Sir Adams G. Archibald were included. He represented Colchester County in the provincial legislature and in Parliament, and served as the first secretary of state for the provinces after Confederation and as lieutenant-governor of Manitoba and the Northwest Territories before his appointment as judge in equity on 24 June 1873. Ever mobile, however, he resigned two weeks later when he was appointed lieutenant-governor of Nova Scotia: see J.K. Johnson *The Canadian Directory of Parliament 1867–1967* (Ottawa: PAC 1968) 10–11. In view of his brief tenure he has not been included in any of the tables here.

Bouthillier's restriction of 'previous political office' to elected office is too formalistic in view of the significant political careers of unelected members of Quebec's Conseil législatif. Had he added the Quebec equivalents of McCully and Ritchie, his figures undoubtedly would have been higher.

77 Romney *Mr. Attorney* 56

78 The competition is described in detail in J.M. Beck 'William Young' *DCB* vol. 11, 943

79 *Halifax Citizen* 14 April 1864

80 Doull *Sketches* 3

81 William Nesbitt (1753–79) did not obtain a judicial post, nor did R.J. Uniacke (1797–1830) or his son J.B. Uniacke (1848–54). Presumably, for the elder Uniacke it was the chief justiceship or nothing. Eight of the twelve pre-1867 attorneys general obtained judicial appointments, though not all were to the Nova Scotia Supreme Court. Richard Gibbons (1781–84) secured the chief justiceship of Cape Breton while it was a separate colony; S.G.W. Archibald (1831–41), who also lost out in the competition to succeed Blowers, became master of the rolls; A.G. Archibald (1860–3) is discussed in note 76 supra, and W.A. Henry (1864–7) went to the Supreme Court of Canada.

82 J.M. Beck 'The Rise and Fall of Nova Scotia's Attorney General: 1749–1983' in Waite et al., *Law in a Colonial Society* 132–3. Three of eight attorneys general between 1867 and 1900 were promoted to the bench: Henry Smith (1871–5), J.S.D. Thompson (1878–82), and J.W. Longley (1886–1905). M.I. Wilkins (1867–71) sought a judgeship but was denied one: *DCB* vol. 11, 927. If the attorney general's department was stagnant after 1867, it is hard to accept Beck's argument that 'by its very nature' this result followed.

Romney *Mr Attorney* (at 313) suggests that 'at the end of the nineteenth century the office of attorney general for Ontario 'probably enjoyed greater prestige than ever before or since.'
83 B. Russell *Autobiography* (Halifax: Royal Print and Litho 1932) 290
84 Ibid.
85 *Times* 6 April 1841; *Novascotian* 22 April 1841
86 They were Morris, Blowers, Brenton, Bliss, Desbarres, Dodd, both Stewarts, Townshend, Robie, and Graham.
87 They were Deschamps, Strange, Brenton, Wilkins Sr, Dodd, Desbarres, Johnstone, J. MacDonald, Meagher, Haliburton, J.W. and J.N. Ritchie, Townshend, and Graham.
88 Schmidhauser 'Justices of the Supreme Court' 13
89 Punch 'Halifax Connection' 126
90 N.J. Mackinnon 'John William Ritchie' *DCB* vol. 11, 754
91 Cahill 'Finucane' 154. The council resolved in 1778 to provide a house for the chief justice, but the Assembly did not agree to the measure: PANS RG1, vol. 301, no. 26.
92 Cahill 'Finucane' 155
93 Gregory Townshend to Ward Chipman Sr, 1788 (n.d.) New Brunswick Museum, Chipman S-38, F2, P1–3, 21. I am grateful to D.G. Bell for this reference.
94 SNS 1848, c. 24, s. 2. For the debate over judicial salaries and fees in the 1830s, see P. Burroughs 'The Search for Economy: Imperial Administration of Nova Scotia in the 1830s' *Canadian Historical Review* 49 (1968) 24, 41–4.
95 SNS 1849, c. 1, s. 2; SNS 1851, c. 34, s. 1; SNS 1859, c. 34, s. 1
96 RSNS 1864, c. 34, s. 1
97 *JHA* 1848, app. 35; SNS 1836, c. 1. The attorney general was allowed to retain his private practice and could also charge fees for certain services rendered to the government and to private individuals: see Romney *Mr Attorney* 36–7.
98 Resolution of Assembly, 23 June 1781, PANS RG5, series A, vol. 1b, no. 42; SNS 1789, c. 12, s. 1; SNS 1809, c. 15, s. 9; SNS 1822, c. 33; SNS 1848, c. 24, s. 2
99 SNS 1849, c. 1, s. 2
100 SNS 1852, c. 4, s. 1
101 SNS 1851, c. 34, s. 1
102 SNS 1859, c. 34, s. 2
103 RSNS 1864, c. 36, s. 1
104 RC 1868, c. 33; SC 1905, c. 31. The judge in equity was ex officio the judge

of the Divorce Court. After Confederation the title 'puisne judge' replaced the local title of 'assistant judge.'

105 P.B. Waite *The Man from Halifax: Sir John Thompson, Prime Minister* (Toronto: University of Toronto Press 1985) 117, 248

106 The missing judges are Desbarres, Duport, Graham, Henry, Hill, James, MacDonald, McDonald, Meagher, Pemberton, Rigby, J.N. Ritchie, Smith, A. Stewart, Townshend, Weatherbe, and Wilkins Sr.

107 P.R. Blakeley 'William Blowers Bliss' *DCB* vol. 10, 73

108 J.M. Beck 'Simon Bradstreet Robie' *DCB* vol. 8, 756; Robie Estate Papers, PANS RG48, reel 488, no. 167

109 J.M. Beck 'Sir William Young' *DCB* vol. 11, 948

110 *Novascotian* 21 Feb. 1834. See also Estate Papers, PANS RG48, reel 424, U5.

111 P.B. Waite 'Jonathan McCully' *DCB* vol. 11, 458

112 Blakeley 'Bliss' 73; Estate Papers, PANS RG48, reel 397, B83

113 Estate Papers, PANS RG48, reel 422, S165

114 *DNB* vol. 55, 27–8

115 Estate Papers, PANS RG48, reel 455, no. 926

116 Ibid. reel 430, no. 160

117 Ibid. reel 408, H184

118 Ibid. reel 429, no. 126; MG100, vol. 140, no. 2

119 Petition of Mary Wiswall, 13 Feb. 1837, PANS RG5, series P, vol. 6, no. 88

120 L. Kernaghan 'Lewis Morris Wilkins' *DCB* vol. 11, 926; Waite *Man From Halifax*; Estate Papers, PANS RG48, reel 132, no. 1 and reel 434, no. 285

121 Cahill 'Finucane' passim. He also died intestate: Estate Papers, PANS RG48, reel 404, F40.

122 Estate Papers, PANS RG48, reel 414, M154

123 Ibid. reel 397, B37; reel 402, D52; reel 400, C111; W.B Hamilton 'John Collier' *DCB* vol. 3, 130–1

124 PANS MG100, vol. 191, nos. 5–7

125 SNS 1816, c. 17

126 A.C. Dunlop 'James Brenton' *DCB* vol. 5, 108–9; PANS MG100, vol. 113, no. 49

127 Waite *Man from Halifax* 53

4

Married Women's Property, Chancery Abolition, and Insolvency Law: Law Reform in Nova Scotia 1820–1867

PHILIP GIRARD

A writer in Halifax's *Presbyterian Witness*, commenting upon a recent provincial act to amend practice in the Supreme Court, observed in 1853 that '[t]he present is, essentially, an age of progressive reform, – and in no department have greater changes been effected within the last few years, than in that of legal jurisprudence.' Until recently, professional men had offered 'the utmost resistance ... to any proposal having in view the abolition of antiquated legal forms and technicalities and the introduction of a cheaper and more uniform system.' They insisted on 'strict adherence to certain long established usages and forms of law which ... after all, were mere fictions and originated in the ignorance and semi-barbarity of past ages.' Professional conservatism coupled with lay inexperience meant that 'it was futile for the mass of the people to insist upon anything like "law reform." ' Eventually, however, public opinion forced the lawyers to alter their views. As a result, 'in England, a complete revolution [was] effected both in pleadings and practice, as well as in the law of evidence, – and that revolution ... originated entirely with the lawyers themselves.' The provincial act, which was expected to reduce court costs by one-half, was a local example of this welcome and overdue legal revolution, and in the writer's opinion was 'one of the most important and popular measures which has engaged the attention of the Legislature for some time.'[1]

Speedier legal decisions, a cheaper legal process, and comprehensible, up-to-date legal rules – these were the three major improvements which that writer saw as flowing from the law reform movement that had sprung up on both sides of the Atlantic after the close of the Napoleonic Wars. It was in the post-Waterloo common law world that the synthesis of Enlightenment values and Benthamite utilitarianism produced the modern concept of law reform – a concept that has remained essentially unchanged down to the present.[2] While legislation was the favourite tool of the period's law reformers (and remains so for today's reformers), not all changes to the statute-book constituted 'law reform.' The label was usually reserved for changes possessing three characteristics. First, a particular area of the law had to be considered out of step with current social needs or mores. Almost invariably, the law in question was castigated as 'feudal,' 'a relic of the Dark Ages,' 'medieval,' or 'barbaric.' This labelling assumed a sharp break between the past – the 'feudal' era – and the present – an age of 'progressive reform.' To state that a particular law was feudal in origin immediately implied that it was unsuitable for the present. Paradoxically, what was often advocated, at least for rhetorical purposes, as suitable for the modern age was a return to a pre-feudal law stripped of the canon, civil, and feudal encrustations that had been 'engrafted upon the body' of English jurisprudence.[3]

Second, the law under attack was usually castigated as the creature of special interests, be they aristocrats, the wealthy, or the lawyers themselves. Reform would make the law more uniform and thus, implicitly, fairer and more equal in its application: 'the mass of the people' would benefit. This resort to the language of populism was clearly a rhetorical ploy, as it was primarily the literate and propertied middle classes who needed a more efficient legal system to protect their interests. Finally, the discourse of law reform never omitted consideration of the legal machinery by which changes to the substantive law would be put into action. Court structures and rules of procedure, rules of pleading and evidence, and methods of enforcement were all part of the law reform process, either in themselves or as adjuncts to particular areas of the substantive law. It was here that the themes of decreased cost and increased speed, efficiency, and accessibility were often pursued most vigorously.

In England and the United States the Victorian era did indeed see considerable progress towards the attainment of those three goals in civil, criminal, and procedural law. Each country possesses a fairly substantial body of literature which analyses the law reform movement in general as well as particular reform campaigns. In Canada relatively little has been written at either the federal or the provincial level which considers in a sustained way this central feature of the nineteenth-century legal landscape.[4] What literature there is tends to look at a reform campaign aimed at the adoption or repeal of a specific law. In this paper I hope to contribute to the emerging Canadian literature by attempting to generalize about the theory and practice of law reform in nineteenth-century Nova Scotia on the basis of a consideration of reform campaigns in selected areas of the private law.

I will examine the origins of influences upon law reform in Nova Scotia between 1820 and 1867. These years were chosen for several reasons. They may be seen as the era in which 'modern' notions of law reform crystallized in legal thought and were reflected in legislative practice in most common law jurisdictions. On the material plane, these were years of great change in Nova Scotia as elsewhere; they were characterized by constant population growth, technological changes in transport and communications, and generally speaking, significant economic advances. Finally, ending the study in 1867 avoids the complicating factor of federalism. In examining how the Nova Scotia legal system responded (or did not respond) to these new ideas and changed circumstances, I hope to be able to assess whether it is possible to speak of a Nova Scotia legal tradition, and, if so, how it might be characterized.

The period between the 1820s and Confederation witnessed substantial economic growth, culminating in Nova Scotia's 'Golden Age' in the 1850s and 1860s. A diversified economy based on fishing, agriculture, and the merchant marine sufficed, with occasional reverses, to feed a growing population and enhance its standard of living.[5] Politically and intellectually, the period was one of ferment and accomplishment. The peaceful attainment of responsible government, the establishment of universities, the emergence of literary figures such as T.C. Haliburton, Thomas McCulloch, and Joseph Howe, and the greatly increased circulation of provincial newspapers all contributed to the creation of a provincial identity and a sense of local pride. One would expect to find a local legal culture emerging during this period when so much else that was distinctive about Nova Scotia was taking shape.[6]

While a considerable amount of work has been done on the political, economic, and cultural history of Nova Scotia during this period, local law reform efforts have received little attention. Yet there was a fairly vigorous and self-conscious debate over law reform during these years, which paralleled to a great extent contemporaneous debates in Britain and America. In the remainder of this article I will analyse that debate, its origins and effects, and finally its significance. A study of the campaigns for law reform in three areas of the private law – married women's property law, the fusion of the common law and equitable jurisdictions, and bankruptcy and insolvency law – will permit us to answer a number of questions about Nova Scotia's legal system during the period under review. What were the influences on and models for legislative change? Were they British, American, 'local,' British North American colonial, or some combination? What role did lawyers play in law reform? Were they enthusiastic proponents or reluctant participants? In a broader context, one can use these case studies to ask questions about the relationship between law and the economy, law and ideas, and law and 'public opinion.'

The three areas mentioned above were chosen for several reasons. They gave rise to considerable controversy in Britain and America in the period under review and have spawned a readily accessible secondary literature. As well, reform in the three areas tended to be interconnected, and it would be artificial to try to dissociate them. Finally, the chronology and motivations for reform in the United States and Britain were somewhat different, posing an interesting tension for the Nova Scotia legal historian.

MARRIED WOMEN'S PROPERTY LAW REFORM

The restrictions and incapacities imposed by the common law on married women vis-à-vis their property, which were based on the legal fiction of the unity of personality of husband and wife, are too well known to require a detailed cataloguing here. Upon marriage, the husband gained absolute control over his wife's personalty, including her earnings, and sole control over her realty during his own lifetime, though not the power to dispose of her freehold estates. In return, he became liable for her antenuptial debts and her support.[7] Equity allowed property to be conveyed to trustees to the separate use of the wife, but it is not clear to what extent this device was used outside the wealthy classes in Nova Scotia.[8] There is growing evidence that this type of settlement was frequently used in parts of the United States.'[9]

On both sides of the Atlantic the legal fiction of the unity of legal personality came under increasing attack by feminist reformers throughout the nineteenth century. In England the reform campaign slowly changed public attitudes on this aspect of 'the woman question,' resulting in the Married Women's Property Acts of 1870 and 1882, which instituted the regime of spousal separation of property. While the economic changes that resulted in increasing numbers of married women entering the work-force are acknowledged to have had a significant impact on the emergence and effectiveness of the reform campaign, historians have also stressed the history of ideas in accounting for the English experience.[10]

In the United States, economic change is conceded to have been at least as influential as changing attitudes towards women and marriage in spawning the first wave of married women's property reform statutes in the 1840s and 1850s. Historians have pointed to contemporaries' concern over the vulnerability of families to the instability of the ante-bellum economy as a key factor in the insulation of wives' assets from husbands' creditors. The reform of married women's property law is thus seen not as an attempt to enhance the economic independence of married women, but rather as a means of providing a lifeline for families suffering the vicissitudes of the commercial cycle. The impact of the wider campaign for law reform, with its anti-feudal ideology, is also acknowledged as a third factor in the emergence of the early American statutes.[11]

All Canadian common law provinces eventually adopted legislation modelled more or less on the English act of 1882, a fact that can be interpreted as demonstrating a lack of originality on the part of the Canadian legal community. As Constance Backhouse has shown, the existence of an earlier series of British North American statutes and reform efforts based on local conditions and using American models has been ignored. A closer study of this phenomenon will show that colonial Nova Scotians did not see themselves as dependent on Britain in the field of law reform.[12]

In Nova Scotia concern about the woman question dates from at least the 1820s. There may not have been a women's movement as such at that date, but there was certainly interest in the question of women's civil rights on the part of the educated élite. The 6 July 1826 edition of the *Novascotian*, for example, devoted two-thirds of a page to a letter on the topic sent by a female writer to an English newspaper. 'M.M' demanded legal changes to prevent domestic violence and the abuse by husbands of their wives' property, and sought better provision for widows from the estates of their deceased husbands. On each topic she presented various case histories known to her, from which she drew specific reform proposals. Why, she queried, were people so exercised about protecting Roman Catholics, slaves, and even animals while remaining silent about the physical and economic abuses to which married women were subject? She advocated the idea of marriage as an economic partnership, arguing that if a woman had some control over the marital assets, 'she [could] at least engage [her husband] to behave decently.' One can only speculate about the editor's motives, but the mere appearance of the letter would have served to stimulate reflection on the part of the paper's readership.

It is likely, too, that literate Nova Scotians would have been familiar with Sarah M. Grimké's indictment of the status of married women at common law contained in her *Letters on the Equality of the Sexes and the Condition of Woman.* These first appeared in the *New England Spectator* from June 1837, and were published in book form at Boston in the following year.[13] While many would have found Grimké's stance on female suffrage too radical, some of her proposals for reform of marital property laws found support even in eminently respectable American magazines such as *Godey's Ladies' Book,* which was popular with Nova Scotia matrons from at least 1850.[14] Direct evidence of attitudes on the woman question in the 1840s is scanty, but reaction to legislative initiatives in the next decade suggests that educated persons continued to take an interest in the issue.

On 30 January 1855 an 'Act for the benefit and better protection of the rights of married women' was given first reading in the Legislative Council. It declared that the real and personal property of any woman then married or to be married, including its rents and profits, should not be at the disposal of her husband or subject to his debts, but 'shall be her sole and separate property as if she were a single female.' Section 8 provided that any woman deserted by her husband or not adequately supported by him could, upon public notice, carry on business in her own name; she could then sue and be sued in her own name, and her husband was henceforth freed from liability for her debts and torts. Other provisions allowed a married woman to keep a bank account in her own name and to vote any stock she might possess in companies incorporated under provincial law.[15] Although it did not institute full separation of property, the bill seemed to embody a liberal approach to matrimonial property that would enhance the legal and social independence of married women.

The proponent of this bill was the Honourable Jonathan McCully, a future Father of Confederation, whose name had been synonymous with the Reform cause in the 1840s and 1850s.[16] His introductory remarks on the bill showed that he did not advocate a liberal approach to spousal property relations, as the bill might have suggested. Instead, he based his arguments on a conservative philosophy of the family, and emphasized avoidance of hardship in particular cases rather than the operation of any revolutionary change. Appealing to the loving father anxious for his married daughter's economic security, he made a special plea to the temperance advocates in the council, who knew all too well how alcoholic husbands 'not only [brought] about their own ruin, but [that] of their wives and families.' He singled out the machinery for the protection of female traders as particularly desirable, arguing that friends and relatives would be encouraged to aid a married woman in business if they could be assured that the husband's creditors would not snatch up any advances provided by them. Anticipating the argument that it was already possible to accomplish this end in equity, he demurred, stating that 'some of the most difficult [and] intricate cases, to legal minds, arise from the settlement of property with the view of protecting the rights of married females.' Chancery admittedly served the needs of the wealthy, but the object of the bill would be to place 'the humbler classes' on the same footing in this regard.

McCully was a firm believer in the ideology of separate spheres, and declared himself 'no defender of what are sometimes called the rights of women' (that is, political rights). On this ground he was prepared to drop the bill's provision for married women's voting of corporate shares, presumably because it smacked too much of female suffrage in the wider political world. Far from advocating reform of married women's property law to enhance the independence of the married woman, he justified it on the basis that it would 'induce her to be satisfied with the social position which God and nature designed for her influence ... retired from the noise and warfare of society, in which men engage.'

Opinion in council was divided, and the bill was ultimately given the three-month hoist in a thirteen-to-six division on 5 March. The objections were predictable. Several members feared that the balance of power within marriage would be upset; others thought it unfair that the wife had to consent to the husband's conveyances of realty in order to bar her dower while there was no analogous provision for the wife's conveyances of her own realty. Mather Almon teased McCully by suggesting that he had been 'swayed by a certain lecturer, who declaimed in Halifax recently,' presumably on the topic of women's rights. McCully testily denied that he had heard her. In a sense, though, he had the last word when he stated, prophetically, that 'at some time, if not now, [this bill] must become the law of the land.'[17]

Editorial opinion in Halifax and beyond was very favourable towards the bill. The *Morning Chronicle* thought it deserved 'grave and deliberate consideration' and predicted that 'thousands of females, in all parts of the Province ... will read its clauses with the very deepest interest.' If the complicated machinery of Equity presently required to protect a woman from the creditors of her unfortunate or dissolute husband could be obviated by this bill, said the editor, then 'the sooner some such law is enacted the better.' The anti-Chancery campaign in Nova Scotia was nearing its apogee, and it is not surprising that the editorial focused on the relative inaccessibility of Chancery as a major cause of dissatisfaction with the existing means of protecting married women's assets. The populist critique of legal institutions had been used with great effectiveness in the 1840s and 1850s, and here spilled over into the substantive law. A separate-spheres ideology was implicit in the article; the emphasis was upon avoiding cases of hardship rather than enhancing married women's independence.[18]

Pictou's *Eastern Chronicle*, however, was more inclined to see the bill as a frontal attack on the doctrine of marital unity, that 'ancient principle by which the civil rights of men and women are regulated.' Moreover, it approved entirely of this proposed legal revolution, and urged Nova Scotia to 'set a bright example to the rest of mankind ... [by] being among the first countries to declare the civil equality of the sexes, and that woman is not to be considered the serf or dependent of man.' While this language is not necessarily inconsistent with the philosophy of separate spheres, the tone of the article suggests that the editor perceived a more radical impetus behind the bill than its main proponents would have acknowledged. Taken as a whole, the newspaper reaction to the bill suggests that provincial opinion had been sensitized to the woman question and embraced a spectrum of responses to it.[19]

Where had the impetus for this bill come from? Certainly McCully himself was an ardent champion of law reform in general and reform of the law relating to married women in particular. In his personal life he practised what he preached by protecting his daughters' inheritances from their husbands' creditors by means of testamentary trusts to their separate use. Ironically, his own son became the paradigmatic alcoholic debt-ridden husband (and an Anglican parson at that) who loomed so large in McCully's arguments for reform. Perhaps his own experience in the 'humbler classes' – his father was a farmer of modest means in Cumberland County, and his own legal practice had begun there – had made him aware of the calamities that could befall families in cases of a husband's intestacy or profligacy.

In fact, McCully's bill was identical to the New York Married Women's Property Act of 1848, as amended in 1849, and was introduced in the Legislative Council of Nova Scotia a full two years before the first bill on the subject, also unsuccessful, was placed before the British Parliament.[20] During debate on a later version of his first married women's property bill in 1858, McCully mentioned that he had been corresponding with David Dudley Field, the leading advocate of codification and married women's property reform in New York state. On Field's recommendation he added a clause to the 1858 bill providing for protection of a married woman's wages or business earnings in cases where her husband could not support her because of drunkenness; the lack of such a clause, according to Field, had been keenly felt in New York.[21] Finding the British experience singularly unhelpful, McCully did not hesitate to turn to the south for legislative models to serve as vehicles for his reformist sentiments. In this he was not unique. Nova Scotia social reformers of the period looked to the south for guidance in many areas, such as temperance and treatment of the insane. Oddly enough, in his search for foreign models McCully overlooked New Brunswick, which had passed 'An Act to secure to Married Women Real and Personal Property held in their own right' in 1851. It is unclear whether this was an oversight or whether McCully chose to ignore the precedent.[22]

In any case McCully had anticipated the argument in favour of colonial inertia in 1855. Nova Scotia need not wait until Britain acts, he said, since the province had often deviated from the mother country's dispensations concerning real estate: primogeniture had been abolished nearly a century before, and the province's probate system was entirely different from Britain's. Either because of McCully's powers of persuasion, or because he need not have feared the argument to begin with, the debates do not reveal that any councillors objected to the bill simply because Britain did not have similar legislation. And as we shall see, the council did pass later versions of the 1855 bill in both 1857 and 1858.

Undaunted by his failure in 1855, McCully introduced a new bill in the council in 1857. This one omitted the more controversial provisions, such as those allowing married women to vote their own stock and to carry on businesses in their own names. Section 1 restated the basic principle that a woman's assets remained her separate property after marriage and could not be made liable for the husband's debts or disposed of without the woman's consent. Section 2 allowed a woman deserted by her husband to sue in her own name in a variety of situations to protect her own interests. Even in cases of continued cohabitation, section 3 allowed a woman who, de facto, had to support herself and her family because of her husband's 'drunkenness, worthlessness or other cause' to control and dispose of any property acquired during that period as if she were an unmarried woman, even to the extent of willing it. This bill was almost as far-reaching as the earlier one, but was couched in simpler and less elegant terms. This time McCully succumbed to the temptation to imitate New Brunswick as well as New York, and the bill passed the council. It died in the Assembly, as it would when reintroduced in the following year.[23]

The recourse to American legislative precedent suggests that we should ask whether the same factors motivated reform in Nova Scotia as in the United States: a sensitivity to the woman question; a general climate of law reform; and a desire to insulate the family from the worst effects of a boom-and-bust economy. The history of the woman question in Nova Scotia has yet to be written, but some evidence has already been presented which suggests that the province was by no means a backwater in this regard. It is doubtful, however, whether these ideas alone would have propelled the reform campaign of the 1850s. The same is true of general notions of law reform. One can find an identifiable group of reformers who were in the forefront of concern on many topical issues – abolition of Chancery, abolition of imprisonment for debt, reform of the bankruptcy, usury, and insolvency laws, codification, and reform of married women's property law. Yet reform proceeded differently in each of these areas. Radical change was effected in one case (the abolition of Chancery), partial change occurred in others (codification and married women's property), and a bankruptcy code was consistently resisted until Confederation. It is important to appreciate the general context of reformist sentiment, but we obviously need a way to explain why reform proceeded differently in different areas.

Can economic change explain the origins of attempts to alter married women's property law? It is tempting to interpret New Brunswick's 1851 act as a response to the panic of 1848–50, when the withdrawal of the British tariff preference for colonial timber and repeal of the Navigation Acts threatened to leave the provincial economy in ruins.[24] Joseph Howe remarked in 1849 that there was 'scarcely a solvent house from Saint John to Grand Falls,' while public sentiment began to favour incorporation of the province into the United States.[25] Without further research this hypothesis cannot be tested, but it would fit squarely within the current American analysis, which sees the emergence of reform statutes as directly linked to the nationwide depression that followed the panic of 1837.[26]

The liberalization of colonial economic policy, however, did not threaten Nova Scotia, with its more diversified economy, in the same way that it did New Brunswick. The years just before 1855 were prosperous ones in Nova Scotia. With the imminent implementation of reciprocity with the United States, mercantile opinion was highly optimistic. In the

1840s, however, progress had been very uneven; Nova Scotia suffered greatly from the boom-and-bust conditions that existed in both the British and the American economies. Numerous Halifax merchants had been driven into bankruptcy in the late 1840s, and their grim example probably remained to haunt the survivors even when prosperity returned.[27] Insulating their wives' assets from their own creditors would have seemed a prudent course to members of the Haligonian merchant oligarchy who sat as legislative councillors. If these were precisely the men who might have been expected to use complex marriage settlements to achieve this goal, it is likely that they did not feel comfortable entrusting such a critical task to the vagaries and eccentricities of Chancery or to the cantankerous master of the rolls, Alexander Stewart, who presided therein. Amendment of the common law offered a certainty of protection that equity may have seemed ill equipped to provide.

The same enlightened self-interest that encouraged the council to pass a married women's property bill twice in two years, however, did not seem to motivate the Assembly when it allowed the bill to die in both 1857 and 1858. When the subject was mooted in 1865 the Assembly took the initiative, but the bill died again.[28] Why this divergence between council and Assembly? If the bill's primary motivation is accepted to have been 'economic' rather than 'social,' then this split between the two houses of the legislature is consistent with their behaviour in other areas of debtor–creditor relations. The council, as we shall see, supported the adoption of a bankruptcy code and the abolition of imprisonment for debt; the Assembly, with its majority of country members, opposed those proposals. The rejection of the council's overtures in 1857 and 1858 may be seen as a rejection of a novel form of 'household limited liability.' Outside Halifax, where debtor–creditor relations were still overwhelmingly based on mutual trust and the creditor's personal knowledge of the debtor's worth, the notion that the total assets of the male debtor's household would not be available upon an execution seemed a dangerous innovation. There were no Assembly debates reported on the bills in 1857 or 1858, but in the debate on the 1865 bill Hiram Blanchard, a Liberal from Inverness, said it was 'a change startling to all of us who were accustomed to look upon the property of the wife as that of the husband.' That, of course, was precisely the point.[29]

It is not easy, however, to separate the 'economic' from the 'social' aspects of married women's property law. Resistance to reform took many forms: arguments couched in economic terms, such as Blanchard's, rested on a certain ideology of marriage, which in turn had at least in part a religious foundation. After the introduction of the 1865 bill in the Assembly, the *Presbyterian Witness* expressed the 'hope [that] the house will indulge in no more legislation in this direction,' it being a 'dangerous policy to create separate interests for husband and wife.' The reason was simple: the bill's tendency was 'at variance with the Scriptural theory of marriage.'[30] The *Witness* was not fooled by McCully's assertion that such a bill would actually help entrench a wife's place in her separate domestic sphere. This response did not mean that religious groups were opposed to any reform. The temperance movement, which included many women, began to advocate legal reforms in the 1850s and 1860s to protect wives from the physical and economic abuse committed by alcoholic husbands. Temperance petitioners accepted the common law doctrine that spouses' assets should be pooled for the benefit of the family, but requested that wives be permitted to act as guardians to manage family property in the place of alcoholic husbands. Protection, not 'independence,' was what these petitioners wanted, and protection was, eventually, what they got.[31]

By 1865, when a bill identical to the council's 1858 bill was presented in the Assembly by the member for Kings North, Dr Charles Hamilton, the debates reflected some ideas not expressed a decade earlier. The most noticeable change is the adoption of some of the feminist rhetoric on the doctrine of marital unity. The financial secretary thought that the members could not countenance the existing state of the law: 'The principle now was that a woman, on becoming married, was dead in law. No matter what her position in property might be, the moment the nuptial knot was tied, she was divested of all her rights.' S.L. Shannon, QC, thought that '[w]e had hardly in our existing law done justice to the position of a wife': the married woman 'was considered to have no rights at all, but to be merged in the existence of the husband.' Many of the opponents raised the old bugbear of domestic discord, but it was Henry Pryor, representing Halifax County (West), who best expressed the concern that had now become central. This ultra-Tory lawyer thought that the bill as a whole embodied too radical a change to merit his support, but he did approve of the clause that attempted to protect a married woman in cases of desertion. In other words, reform might be warranted in cases of failed marriages, but not where the marriage was healthy.[32] This was precisely the compromise that had been reached in England with the enactment of the Divorce and Matrimonial Causes Act of 1857. In essence, that act created separation of property for women after judicial separation, divorce, or desertion with respect to earnings and property acquired after the event. Lee Holcombe states that this 'compromise' was proposed precisely to forestall any demands for a more complete reform of married women's property law.[33]

The debate was resolved in 1866, with the enactment of 'An Act for the Protection of Married Women in certain cases.' It adopted almost verbatim those sections of the 1857 English act relating to separation of property upon desertion or divorce.[34] The legislative debates and newspapers of that year are almost totally given over to the issue of Confederation, and no official record remains of any debate on the bill. It is unlikely that the act involved the kind of scheming that Holcombe describes for its English counterpart. It is more likely that it reflected a genuine compromise between those who were prepared to go further and those who might have preferred no change at all. The singling out of 'failed' marriages sidestepped the objection several members had consistently voiced: if a husband had deserted his wife, presumably no creditor would be foolish enough to advance him money on the strength of his wife's assets. Once the potential prejudice to creditors was removed, only the churlish would press the absent husband's right to arrogate his wife's earnings to himself. The wholesale adoption of the English act, however, should not be interpreted simply as an example of colonial mimicry. It is clear that during the previous decade Nova Scotia legislators considered the American model and found it too radical on the domestic as well as the economic front. The consensus had crystallized around a halfway measure in 1865, and the adoption of the English act in the following year was an act of deliberate policy.[35]

REFORM OF THE LAW OF BANKRUPTCY AND INSOLVENCY

Credit was the lifeblood of capital-starved, specie-poor Nova Scotia through much of the nineteenth century. A pyramid of debtor–creditor relations bound the primary producers to the local merchants and the local merchants to their wholesalers, while Halifax merchants and entrepreneurs borrowed money to finance their own ventures. All were vulnerable to the unpredictable downturns that characterized the colonial economy after the end of the Napoleonic Wars. While the larger businessman survived occasional reverses and found insurance against various perils easier to obtain as the century wore on, a crop failure or sudden downturn in prices was likely to be catastrophic to the farmer and the fisherman, and sometimes to their suppliers. The experience of debt is central to the lives of Mephibosheth Stepsure's neighbours in Thomas McCulloch's *Stepsure Letters*, few of whom escaped 'going to live with the

Sheriff,' Mr Holdfast, at some point.[36] McCulloch's portrayal of Pictou County agricultural settlements in the early 1820s remained accurate for several decades. With the expense and difficulty of land transportation, farmers everywhere in the province found it difficult to harvest their crops, convey them to Halifax for sale, pay their debts, and still make a profit. 'A Farmer under Mortgage' from King's County writing to the *Acadian Recorder* in 1826 declared himself to be 'amused with the growing prosperity of the province' when 'hundreds ... have had their property ... completely swept away ... by the strong arm of the law and hardness of the times.' Six per cent interest – the maximum exigible under the provincial usury law of 1770 – left no profit for the farmer,[37] and there were hungry times in the 1840s after a series of crop failures.[38]

Given the universality of the experience of debt in nineteenth-century Nova Scotia, it is not surprising that in no area of the law did new and old ideologies clash with greater force or frequency than in the domain of debtor–creditor relations. Bills to abolish imprisonment for debt in whole or in part, to introduce a bankruptcy code, to repeal the usury laws, and to reform the insolvent debtors' relief system appeared constantly between 1825 and 1867. Yet Nova Scotia entered Confederation without a bankruptcy law, with imprisonment for even the smallest debt still legally authorized, with a usury law dating from Henrician times, and with an insolvent debtors' relief apparatus that first appeared after the Restoration and developed mainly under the Hanoverians. Cajole, expound, plead, and thunder as they might, the reformers made little headway. The rural magnates of the House of Assembly clung to imprisonment for debt, the ultimate weapon in the debtor–creditor arena, with impressive tenacity.

In one important particular the Nova Scotia code of debtor–creditor law diverged markedly from the English: land was subject to seizure for debts in the same way chattels were. The landed gentry in England had long preserved the immunity of their estates from attachment, resulting in the ludicrous spectacle of wealthy men living in comparative luxury on their rentals while in debtors' prison. With land pre-eminently an object of commerce in the New World, this anomaly was soon scotched in New England, and the early settlers in Nova Scotia followed suit as soon as they could, at the first session of the Assembly in 1758.[39]

In most other respects the code of debtor–creditor law that Nova Scotia had adopted in the eighteenth century reflected the English model on paper, and probably in practice. It was strongly creditor-oriented, and imprisonment of the debtor was available at the creditor's option before or after judgment.[40] Before judgment, the creditor might obtain the writ *capias ad respondendum* simply by swearing before a court official that a debt was overdue or that the debtor was about to abscond or conceal his property. The writ authorized the sheriff to seize the debtor. This pre-judgment procedure was referred to as 'mesne process.' If the debtor did not pay and the creditor's claim was upheld at trial, the debtor might remain in prison under a writ of execution *capias ad satisfaciendum*. This recourse to incarceration for civil debts was justified as affording the strongest possible deterrence to fraud and extravagance.[41]

If the debtor imprisoned under a writ of execution had no friends or relations willing to acquit his obligation, there were only two means of obtaining freedom: securing a private act of the legislature or applying for relief under provincial insolvent debtor relief legislation. The first course of action was always popular with debtors, but successful petitioners were few: on average one debtor per year was liberated in this way between 1820 and 1846.[42] An application under the Act for the Relief of Insolvent Debtors, first passed in 1763[43] and modelled on a series of English statutes beginning in 1729, was more likely to lead to freedom.[44] It allowed a debtor with total debts under one hundred pounds to be released provided that he assigned all his property (saving some personal effects) to his creditor and swore an oath that he had concealed none of his assets. His release did not extinguish the debt, and any after-acquired property was liable for its satisfaction, but the debtor could not be imprisoned again for the same debt. The act contained an important veto for the creditor, however: if he was not satisfied with the debtor's oath and wanted more time to investigate his situation, he could secure the remand of the prisoner if he supplied 'the full quantity of eight pounds of good and wholesome biscuit bread per week unto the said prisoner' (section 2). If upon investigation the creditor could discover no reason to impeach the debtor's oath, he was still entitled to maintain the unfortunate defaulter indefinitely upon payment of the bread allowance.

A glimmer of reform appeared in 1813, when the act was amended to control the creditor's discretion in two important ways. First, the debtor was to be discharged as soon as he assigned his property and swore the oath unless the creditor could show 'good and sufficient reason' why he should not be released, in which case he was to be remanded for three months. Further remands could be obtained, but only to a maximum of two years, at which point a non-fraudulent debtor had to be freed. The act also raised the debt ceiling to five hundred pounds from one hundred pounds.[45] This radical innovation was not to last, however. In 1819 the

1813 act was repealed in toto; the preamble to the later statute gravely declared that the 1813 act had been found injurious in its operation, as 'tending to encourage Debtors to defraud their Creditors.'[46] The 1813 innovation was restored after a fashion in 1832, when the creditor was once again obliged to show good cause to continue a debtor's detention. However, if the presiding justices felt that 'any circumstances in respect of [the] Debt, or the delay in payment thereof' justified an extension of the imprisonment, they could remand the debtor for a period of time they thought 'proper under all the circumstances of the case.' In other words, an uncontrollable discretion in the hands of the creditor was replaced with a virtually uncontrollable discretion in the hands of the justices. The creditor's option to maintain the debtor in prison at his whim on provision of the bread allowance, however, was finally ended.[47]

Later reforms attempted to control the judges' discretion, extended the eligibility for relief to those imprisoned under mesne process, removed the debt ceiling, and provided for commissioners to administer the act in each county.[48] An important restraint was imposed on the judges and commissioners in 1851, when the maximum period of imprisonment, even for fraudulent debtors, was fixed at one year. If we were to look only at this formal account of the evolution of the insolvent-debtor relief legislation, we might characterize the reform process as one of slow, incremental change. In one sense, it was; however, only by examining the gap between the reforms demanded and those actually obtained can we gain an idea of how hotly contested the issues were, and how the developments in Nova Scotia can be situated in the Anglo-American context.

Reform of debtor–creditor relations in Britain and the United States in this period took two main forms. One was the abolition of imprisonment for debt, initially for various classes of debtors, such as women,[49] and various classes of debts, usually small ones, and finally for all debts. More effective remedies against the debtor's property replaced recourse to his person. In the United States almost all of the states on the eastern seaboard had abolished debtors' prisons by 1870; in England the debtors' prisons disappeared in 1869, imprisonment under mesne process having been abolished in 1838. Humanitarian concerns played a part in the abolitionist movement, but it is generally conceded that imprisonment came to be viewed as an inefficient deterrent to default from the creditor's point of view and a burdensome solution from the community's point of view.[50]

The second strand in the reform movement was the spread of bankruptcy laws that allowed the debtor to be discharged from his old debts and begin a new economic existence. England had long had an involuntary bankruptcy system available only to traders; it was extended to non-traders in 1869, thus ending the distinction between bankruptcy and insolvency.[51] American state experiments with bankruptcy laws tended to prefer voluntary systems that could be invoked by the debtor himself. Progress tended to be slow, however, because of uncertainty about the constitutionality of state laws in view of the power of Congress to make uniform laws on the subject.[52]

No reformer sought modification of the laws regarding imprisonment for debt more assiduously in the Nova Scotia of the 1820s and 1830s than its foremost jurist, Beamish Murdoch. In 1827 he had arranged for copies of his *Essay on the Mischievous Tendency of Imprisoning for Debt and in Other Civil Cases* to be privately printed and circulated among members of the House of Assembly, presumably to coincide with the discussion of R.J. Uniacke Jr's Frivolous Arrests Bill, which was introduced on 3 February of that year. Uniacke's bill would have abolished arrest for debt unless the creditor swore that the debtor was about to leave the province; this would have brought the province into line with Lower Canada, where the English system of imprisonment for debt was unknown except with regard to absconding debtors.[53]

Murdoch seems to have been motivated by a combination of humanitarian feeling, pragmatism, and personal experience: his father had spent seven years in debtors' prison in Halifax.[54] His pamphlet, republished in 1831, marshalled every conceivable argument against the practice. It was clear that Murdoch had done extensive comparative research; he cited the Lower Canada example, Kentucky's experience with abolition, and reform attempts in Upper Canada, New York, and the American Congress. His main objection was the potential for abuse afforded by placing unrestrained power in the hands of a private party, and he summarized his complaint in constitutional terms: 'Trust any man with arbitrary power, and you tempt him to do wrong.' Even if some debtors were extravagant and reckless, he doubted that jail would cure those vices, and suggested that creditors themselves were often at fault for advancing money recklessly. He advocated the extension of creditors' recourses to the attachment of wages and choses in action, which were irrecoverable under execution at common law. Overall, one might say his objections were rooted in culture rather than economics: he believed that imprisonment for debt was inconsistent with the advance of enlightened Christian civilization, whose cardinal legal value was the checking of arbitrary power.

After Murdoch lost his seat in the 'Brandy Election' of 1830, he was no longer able to advocate his pet cause in the House; none the less, he continued his campaign from the outside. Inside the House his mantle passed to the Uniackes, Richard John Jr and James Boyle, while the Legislative Council began to champion the cause. An 1828 bill which bravely declared that the '[p]ractice of imprisoning the Person of Debtors for small debts is generally useless and often barbarous and inhuman,' would have abolished the practice for all debts under twenty pounds. It passed the council and was given the three-month hoist in the Assembly.[55] An 1831 bill with a ceiling of six pounds met the same fate.[56] Chastened, the council passed a modest bill in 1834 abolishing imprisonment for debts under three pounds: still the Assembly refused to budge, in spite of a clause in the bill declaring it to be operative for three years only. The process was repeated in 1836 and 1843; bills in the Assembly to abolish arrest under mesne process failed in 1841 and 1842, and bills regarding arrest upon execution failed in 1842, 1843, 1845, and 1846.[57]

The experience with bankruptcy legislation followed exactly the same course until 1860. Once again Murdoch was in the vanguard with an 1828 bankruptcy bill that was meant 'to relieve Insolvent Debtors from the distress to which they are often subjected from the obstinacy of one or more of their creditors to sign a release.'[58] The bill followed English tradition in its application to merchants or traders only, but reflected American practice in its provision for initiation of bankruptcy proceedings by the debtor himself. The creditors still retained substantial control, however; the consent of four-fifths of them by value was required to approve a certificate of discharge for debtors who had acted 'fairly and honestly.'[59] Uniacke's Frivolous Arrests Bill of the previous year appears to have contained the first bankruptcy provisions proposed in Nova Scotia; they were to be available on a voluntary basis to all insolvents, traders and non-traders alike, provided that they reached a certain level of indebtedness.[60]

In 1834 the Assembly appointed a committee to bring in a bankruptcy law, and a bill similar to Uniacke's 1827 bill was placed before the House; it failed in 1834 and again in 1838.[61] Local echos of the American financial panic of 1837 no doubt added an element of urgency to the bankruptcy debate. On 24 January 1842 Solicitor General Uniacke introduced a government bill in the House of Assembly that would have allowed merchants, bankers, insurers, shipwrights, and some others engaged in 'hazardous speculations' to declare bankruptcy when their total debts reached five hundred pounds. He stated that both American and English laws had been combined to produce the bill, and this was reflected in the combination of voluntary and involuntary means of invoking the bankruptcy procedure. Although he presented the bill as being urgently needed because of a recent 'monstrous' case upholding the right of an insolvent debtor to prefer one creditor to the exclusion of all others, this rationale was not discussed in the reports of the debate. The legislators' attention focused mainly on the machinery by which it was proposed to administer the law. The member for Guysborough County, William Frederick Desbarres, proposed that the act be amended to allow the appointment of commissioners for each county; otherwise rural residents would have to bring the entire matter to Halifax or wait for the Supreme Court circuit to arrive. Uniacke strongly opposed this notion; he argued that such appointees would wield too much power, power that could properly be entrusted only to a Supreme Court judge and jury. William Young agreed with Uniacke but urged that the assignees of the bankrupt's estate reside in the county where the assets were located, and that management of the estate continue there after the actual declaration of bankruptcy had issued.[62]

The spokesmen for urban mercantile interests who favoured the bill attempted to meet rural objections by maintaining that the law would not be used in the countryside in any case. Charles Fairbanks said that he had lived in the country for twenty years and never seen a case where the law would have been required; if the bankruptcy process was centralized in Halifax, that was only because the city would provide its raw material. Joseph Howe, descending from the Speaker's chair to proclaim the bill's merits, admitted frankly that if the country did not want it, the law would be a boon to Halifax. In a characteristic flourish, he declared that 'seven years ago [Halifax] was half depopulated for the want of some such law.' Such sentiments evidently failed to arouse sympathy in the Assembly; the bill was deferred by a vote of twenty-three to seventeen.[63] Although rural–urban tensions undoubtedly contributed largely to the bill's demise, many members, both rural and urban, probably agreed with the editor of the *Novascotian*, who feared that the bill 'would hold out temptation to speculate, and to evad[e] just demands.'[64]

The spate of mercantile bankruptcies in the later 1840s no doubt led to renewed agitation in the 1850s. The lieutenant-governor appointed five commissioners to prepare a bankruptcy law in 1854, with the ubiquitous Jonathan McCully as chairman. Their draft bill, sophisticated in concept and careful in its attention to detail, ran to an unheard-of ninety-one sections and thirteen pages of scheduled forms. It provided for a blend of English- and American-style provisions administered at the local level:

like officials of the probate court, judges and registrars of bankruptcy as well as official assignees were to be appointed in each county. Any person of full age and capacity with debts over two hundred pounds might petition for bankruptcy protection or be petitioned into bankruptcy by a certain number of creditors on the commission of certain acts. Time limits were set for various stages of the process with a view to minimizing costs and completing the distribution of creditors' dividends within a year from the launching of a petition. All orders and decisions of a bankruptcy judge were to be appealable to a Supreme Court judge in chambers. The judge's order would be final if it upheld the decision appealed from; otherwise, an appeal to the Supreme Court in banco was allowed, and the bill expressly provided that 'no decision shall be altered or reversed for any mere technical objection.'[65]

McCully's bill is perhaps the best example of the law reformer's craft to be found in pre-Confederation Nova Scotia. It judiciously selected those elements of foreign innovations that were deemed best suited to local conditions. It attempted to implement a new legal institution by means of a structure closely modelled on existing ones. It manifested the decentralist impulse and the concern for speed, efficiency, and accessibility that characterized the law reform movement on both sides of the Atlantic during this period. It reflected not a love of legal jargon and complex procedure, but a certain distrust of judicial discretion and a realization that brevity is sometimes the enemy of clarity. The appeal structures attempted a careful balance between the weeding out of errors and the checking of arbitrary action on the one hand and the guarantee of speedy resolution of the matter on the other.

Having passed the council in 1855, the bill, unsurprisingly, failed in the Assembly.[66] What explains this implacable opposition to changes in the status quo in debtor–creditor relations, this unwillingness to forgo imprisonment for even the smallest debt or to discharge the debts of 'honest but unfortunate' debtors? The arguments in fact changed little over the decades: in 1827 as in 1855 many members of the Assembly believed that there were two classes of debtors – the honest and the reckless or dishonest – but they doubted the capacity of any law, judge, or bureaucrat to distinguish between them and preferred to leave that power with the creditor. It was an article of faith that Nova Scotia creditors treated their debtors, at least the honest ones, with 'lenity and indulgence' and that the Insolvent Debtors Act was a 'mild, moderate, temperate law' which protected the debtor more than the creditor.[67] Where the reforming spirit of the age advocated general legislation and the levelling of distinctions and displayed a certain faith in human perfectibility and material progress, many assemblymen preferred to legislate for the particular case, saw no reason to erase the distinction between the honest and the dishonest, and tended to dismiss generalizations about 'human nature.' If pressed, they probably would have expressed pessimism rather than optimism about man's essential instincts. William Blowers Bliss, speaking to an insolvent debtor's petition for relief in 1834, declared his dislike of legislating for particular cases and used the case to illustrate the need for a general bankruptcy law.[68] Charles Rufus Fairbanks, a member for Halifax Township and later master of the rolls, declared his opposition to Uniacke's bankruptcy bill in 1827 on the ground that nothing was so dangerous as legislation based on some supposed general principles of humanity. Men were not alike, and it was a mistake to legislate as if they were.[69] Alexander Stewart, the member for Cumberland and also a future master of the rolls, took up the same theme: '[A] private bill for individual relief is acceptable, but not a bill for general relief. If all men were honest, this bill would be acceptable, but if all men were honest, it would in any case be unnecessary. [Pass it, and] the debtor would laugh at and despise your threats.'[70]

While the failure of bankruptcy bills before 1860 can be attributed largely to resistance on the part of rural members of the Assembly, this was not the only factor at work. Religious ideas also played their part, and they cut across rural and urban lines. The *Wesleyan*, for example, elaborated on the theme of 'The Religion of Paying Debts' in 1851: 'Men may sophisticate as they please; they can never make it right, and all the bankrupt laws in the universe cannot make it right, for them not to pay their debts. There is a sin in this neglect, as clear and as deserving church discipline, as in stealing or false swearing. He who violates his promise to pay, or withholds the payment of a debt when it is in his power to meet his engagement, ought to be made to feel that in the sight of all honest men he is a swindler.'[71] The depth of these feelings may be gauged from Sir Andrew Macphail's comments about the attitudes to debt prevalent during his childhood in post-Confederation Prince Edward Island: 'Apart from murder, there was no crime in that community except the crime of going in debt.' He recalled a neighbour who had been 'carried to gaol with fetters on his feet, as punishment for his failure to pay a debt ... legally adjudged against him.'[72]

The bankruptcy commissioners of 1854 had thought that the 'delay ... expense ... and the principles of centralization' contained in previous bankruptcy bills had been fatal to their success; in fact, the objections went much deeper than that. They were rooted in an ideology that accepted the efficacy of imprisonment as a deterrent to reckless borrowing and viewed the payment of debts as a moral duty, and in a rural lending practice that was not impersonal and formal, as it tended to be in Halifax, but highly personal and informal. To the high moral arguments of the humanitarian reformers, the rural gentry responded with one of their own. What was moral about allowing a dishonest debtor, even a petty debtor, to evade his obligations or to have his debts discharged by bankruptcy? If there were abuses under the existing system, there would be abuses of a different kind under the proposed system. The opponents of reform pointed to the widespread swindling that had allegedly plagued a national bankruptcy system introduced in the United States in 1841, and to the problems encountered in implementing a bankruptcy law in New Brunswick. Some alleged that abolition of imprisonment for debt would render credit unavailable to the little man. When imprisonment for debt was finally abolished, Macphail remembered his father as 'gravely apprehensive lest worthy men might be denied credit in the hour of their need.'[73] In the final analysis, what was 'moral' depended on one's point of view.

On the jurisprudential level, the opponents of reform were faced with a dilemma. Most of them bore the standard of 'tradition,' yet they had to face the fact that in the heartland of tradition, Britain, the reform cause had in some cases won the day. T.C. Haliburton, for example, who briefly sailed with the breezes of reform before tacking into the less dangerous gulf of provincial Toryism, had to accept that the system of English jurisprudence, 'one of the noblest structures which the wisdom of man had ever been able to rear,' recognized the concept of bankruptcy, which he opposed. He justified his own position by pointing out that conditions in England were different from those in Nova Scotia, and that the legal necessities of the mother country's vast commercial emporium were mere luxuries for a small, developing colony.[74] While he was correct in a general sense, he failed to recognize that the gap between conditions in England and Nova Scotia was reproduced to some extent within Nova Scotia itself in the differences between Halifax and the rural and outport settlements.

If the decades between 1825 and 1855 witnessed little change in the arguments or numbers of the anti-bankruptcy faction in the Assembly, the decade after 1855 saw a significant weakening of its influence. In 1858 bankruptcy bills were introduced independently in both the Assembly and the council; William Young presented the former and McCully the latter. The year had seen a commercial panic sweep across North America, and McCully was moved to observe that it was 'painful to see men who some months ago occupied a high position in this community ... now placed in the same condition as persons who would defraud others of their just claims. There is no possibility of their redeeming their position or their reputation, unless they go down to the common jail, and take the benefit of the Insolvent Debtors Act.'[75] McCully noted that when he introduced his 1855 bill there was not the same 'pressing necessity' as at present. Indeed, residents of Lunenburg had petitioned the Assembly in 1857 to pass a bankruptcy law.[76]

Neither bill passed, and the next bill, introduced in 1861, met the same fate. None the less, the identity of its sponsor provides a clue to shifts in attitudes within the anti-bankruptcy camp. Joseph Howe's Liberals were in power in 1861, but it was Samuel Leonard Shannon, the Conservative member for Halifax County (West), who presented a bankruptcy bill in the Assembly that year. Ironically, Howe had denounced Shannon as a Tory 'Obstructive' two decades earlier, at a time when Howe was ardently advocating the adoption of a bankruptcy law. A prominent Halifax lawyer with a large practice, Shannon was also a fervent Methodist. From his religion and political affiliation one might expect that he would have been disposed to disapprove of bankruptcy provisions. His law practice involved considerable work with corporations, however, and his experience with limited liability in that context may have suggested to him the desirability of similar protection for individual traders or entrepreneurs.[77]

Shannon's 1861 bill died, but he revived it, with some amendments, in 1862. He explained that the previous bill had allowed anyone with debts of at least $100 to avail himself of its provisions; after conferring with Chief Justice William Young, who appears to have given the new bill his imprimatur, he raised it to $1,000. This change allowed larger merchants to invoke the protections of the act but denied them to smaller traders. Any creditor with an unsatisfied judgment debt of at least $200 would also be allowed to petition the debtor into bankruptcy. All mortgages and preferences created up to thirty days before the petition were to be declared void. The bill vested most of the administrative powers in bankruptcy proceedings in the masters of the Supreme Court, who were appointed in each circuit. Thus most of the process would occur locally, although only a judge of the Supreme Court could issue a fiat declaring the petitioner bankrupt.[78]

In a reversal of precedents, Shannon's bill passed the Assembly on 4 April and was rejected by the council three days later.[79] Unfortunately, the newspaper reports of the session's debates give rather short shrift to this topic. It seems unlikely that any particular event inspired this change of heart on the part of some Assemblymen. Rather, the experiences of at least the previous quarter-century had finally convinced many people that the economy did move cyclically, removing much of the moral blame from those who foundered during periods of economic downturn. Absolution from personal responsibility for the quirks of the economy thus came to be seen as necessary even by those whose political and religious ideology normally would have led them in the opposite direction. On a broader level, this change of heart is also an example of the percolation of the values of liberal progressivism throughout the provincial body politic, a process that had finally eroded the strong moral–political consensus against the introduction of a bankruptcy law.

If the moral obloquy attached to non-payment of debts had now diminished in intensity, there was another reason, more immediate and utilitarian, for advocating a bankruptcy code: the retention of entrepreneurial talent in the province. 'Let leniency be the word, and prosperity the result,' exhorted a letter-writer to the *Morning Chronicle* in 1863, and the editor agreed, lamenting that businessmen were 'too often driven away from our shores' by the lack of a bankruptcy law.[80] Similar sentiments were expressed in the Legislative Council in the debates in 1862 and 1863 and were no doubt echoed in the Assembly.[81]

There may have been a simple explanation for the Assembly's conduct on this occasion. The clause that restricted the availability of bankruptcy protection to those owing debts of $1,000 or more meant that the vast majority of debtors within the province would be excluded from the act's purview. This in turn preserved the sanction of imprisonment for all but the most important debtors, a feature that may have forestalled the objections of many members to the adoption of a bankruptcy code. In other words, only when a bankruptcy law was framed in overt class terms could the Assembly accept it. This cannot be the sole explanation, however, because McCully's 1855 bill specified that a minimum of $1,000 in debts was necessary for one to qualify for bankruptcy protection.[82] None the less, the restrictive nature of the bill was probably enough to persuade some waverers of its merits where a general bill would have failed.

The very nature of the bill, aimed as it was at larger merchants and capitalists only, makes it more difficult to explain the council's spurning of this long-sought measure. Two official reasons were given for its rejection: the lateness of the session and the fact that several leading merchants considered the bill defective in some respects. The first obviously was an excuse rather than a reason, and it is doubtful whether the second had any real merit. Shannon's bill was similar to McCully's 1855 bill, which the council was happy enough to pass. There were no obvious provisions in the Assembly's bill that might have been expected to raise mercantile eyebrows. It is more likely that political divisions within the council overrode the mercantile consensus that had previously supported such a measure. A bitter rivalry existed during this period between two Cumberland County councillors – McCully, the Reformer, and Robert Dickey, an appointee of J.W. Johnston's Conservative administration. Their dispute was mainly over railway policy, but there is no doubt that it spilled over into other matters.[83] It is likely that the bankruptcy bill was a casualty of their feud in 1862, as it would be again in 1863.

Encouraged by the near success of the 1862 measure, both McCully and Shannon reintroduced their bills in their respective houses in 1863. This time, the debate both within and without the legislature was given more attention by the newspapers. The editor of the *Morning Chronicle* thought McCully's bill was simply 'common sense,' 'a code in itself ... a very concise and very plain bill' and urged merchants to consult copies of it at McCully's office.[84] This view was not surprising, as the editor of the *Chronicle* was none other than McCully himself. Joseph Howe urged that both bills be referred to a committee so that the views of the mercantile community could be ascertained. This was not done, and appears to have been unnecessary in any case, since the larger merchants, at least, had already had their say behind the scenes: Solicitor General McCully admitted that he had been under some pressure from them to draft his bill and shepherd it through the legislature.[85]

Friday, 13 March 1863, was an unlucky day for McCully: the council deferred his bill for three months on a vote of ten to nine. Councillor Brown, who was thought to be in favour, was absent, but McCully said he would not press ahead, given the lack of a clear majority. The editor of the *Novascotian* was 'sorry that the measure ha[d] fallen through, for many persons think that it was based upon sound principles, and would, after a trial, have been made to give satisfaction.'[86] Once again the McCully–Dickey rivalry had immobilized the council when a consensus normally would have been easy to achieve. Their dispute, however, was only one facet of a very disputatious session. The Liberal majority in the Assembly had shrunk to a perilous two or three, and with Howe's appointment in late 1862 as an imperial fisheries commissioner, the 1863 session was spent marking time until a spring election could be called.

The Conservatives, exhilarated by the the scent of blood, were eager to attack the government in any way possible, and the session deteriorated into partisan bickering.[87]

In this kind of climate the prospects for Shannon's bill in the Assembly were not good. In quieter times it probably would have been considered on its merits, but the political context meant that many Liberals who might have voted for it could not do so because it was proposed by a Conservative. At the very end of the session, the Assembly voted to defer by a majority of twenty-one to twenty.[88] With that, the advocates of a bankruptcy law finally gave up. The issue never again came before the legislature: after 1867 Nova Scotia lost the power to pass a bankruptcy law when the matter passed into federal jurisdiction.

The question to be answered with regard to the last round of bankruptcy debates is why Howe's Liberals, in power from 1860 to 1863, did not put forth a government bill on the matter. As recently as 1858 Howe had spoken of the great need for a good bankruptcy law. It is true that the bill introduced by McCully in the council in 1863 could be considered a government bill, but why were matters left so late? Howe had been a great advocate of bankruptcy legislation for over twenty years, and it is curious that he played so insignificant a role in the 1860s debates. On the one hand, it is possible that the matter was pushed into the shadows by the demands of 'high politics'; on the other hand, the lack of action may have represented a decision that public sentiment was not yet ready for such a measure, especially in view of the experience of the 1850s.[89]

Little has been said about the role of lawyers in the reforms discussed in this section. Some urban lawyers have been identified with the reform cause, notably Murdoch and McCully. Provincial lawyers such as Haliburton and Alexander Stewart were staunch advocates of the status quo. Many rural members of the Assembly were lawyers,[90] and it is well known that debt collection formed an important part of the business of colonial attorneys. They thus had a vested interest in opposing change whether or not they agreed with the attitudes towards debtor–creditor relations prevalent in the countryside.[91] However, a much more detailed analysis of voting patterns needs to be done before one can confirm this rural–urban variable as a significant factor in predicting lawyers' attitudes to reform of the law in general or to this area of the law in particular. It may be that the Halifax lawyers who favoured reform were exceptional individuals, and that lawyers in general, rural or urban, usually supported the status quo.

FUSION OF THE COURTS OF LAW AND EQUITY

If the partial success of attempts to reform the law of married women's property and debtor–creditor law illustrates the strength of traditional ideologies when challenged by newer ones, the history of the campaign to abolish the Court of Chancery and reform the equitable jurisdiction is one instance of the victory of the new over the old. It was during this campaign that the reformist themes of decreased cost and increased efficiency and accessibility found their most receptive audience. These ideas formed only one strand, however, in a rich tapestry of political intrigue, personality clashes, and populist discontent with the entire judicial system.

The Chancery court's jurisdiction included matters relating to the interpretation of wills, the powers of trustees under settlements of property, and – all-important in the colonial economy – the foreclosure of mortgages.[92] Masters in Chancery were appointed in each of the counties to perform some of the court's administrative tasks, but most of its business was carried on in Halifax, and the master of the rolls did not go on circuit. By 1825 the inordinate delay, expense, and obscurantism of the Chancery in England had made it the target of the nascent law reform movement there, and Nova Scotia newspapers eagerly printed accounts of the English developments. In 1833, for example, Howe's *Novascotian* noted that a savings of £56,000 had been effected in England by the abolition of various sinecures associated with Chancery, which was now known as the 'curse of the country.'[93] In the previous year he had published a series of articles attacking the Court of Chancery in Nova Scotia and the incumbent master of the rolls, Simon Bradstreet Robie. In his finest polemical style Howe recited the catalogue of complaints traditionally invoked by English reformers, and added a few local embellishments and suggestions for reform. He declared that there was not enough business to justify the public expenditure on such a court, and that the whole apparatus could be swept away and the money used more profitably to promote compromises between parties desirous of settling disputes coming under equitable jurisdiction. Lawyers conspired with the presiding judge to fleece the public: they had 'shared the plunder among them for years ... pluck[ing] one pigeon after another ... [while] Estates melt[ed] away from their clients.'[94]

Howe's most vitriolic criticisms, however, were reserved for Robie himself, a man who 'all his life [was] the enemy and oppressor of the People,' one who spouted reformist sentiment but in reality believed none of it.

It was almost treasonous, railed Howe, that Robie in seven years had done nothing to reform the 'body of costly absurdities' that constituted Equity while Lord Brougham had taken on the task with vigour and dispatch almost from the moment of his appointment as lord chancellor of England.[95] So intemperate was the attack that it is surprising that Howe was not charged with contempt of court or seditious libel. In reviling the master of the rolls personally, Howe illustrated a strand of the reform campaign in Nova Scotia that was not generally present in England: the fusion of an institutional critique of the Court of Chancery with a personal critique of its incumbent judge. In England most reformers were at pains to point out that they intended no disrespect for the current lord chancellor. In Nova Scotia some masters of the rolls were regularly excoriated in public, usually by those who had been their opponents while they were in active political life. It was not often easy to distinguish 'genuine' reformist sentiment from personal animosity and the settling of political scores.

It is not difficult to see why the office of masters of the rolls should have been so open to attack, even leaving aside the character or political colouring of those who occupied it. Endowed with a princely salary of six hundred pounds per annum and a rank second in precedence only to the chief justice himself, burdened with a modest workload and none of the circuit duties that exasperated the Supreme Court justices, the post was a prize plum in a province where good old-fashioned English sinecures were in relatively short supply. Given the competition among senior barristers for the appointment and the inevitable large numbers of keenly disappointed aspirants, a saint would have had difficulty occupying the office without adverse comment. It must be admitted, though, that some of its occupants hardly pursued a course of action likely to endear them to the public. Simon Robie, for example, anglophile and antiquarian, was the last person who could be expected to rouse the Court of Chancery from its lethargy. Alexander Stewart, arch-Tory that he was, did at least devote considerable energy to reforming the court's rules and procedures.[96] His rigidity and unpleasant manner, however, had made him 'one of the most detested of all Nova Scotia politicians.'[97] The man himself had few defenders when his position was abolished in 1855.

The 1830s saw some modest reforms, no doubt as a result of Howe's critique, Brougham's example in England, and the lengthy investigation into Chancery affairs necessitated by the petition to the House of Assembly of an influential dissatisfied litigant, Thomas King of Windsor.[98] An 1832 statute appointing commissioners to inquire into, inter alia, the practice of the Court of Chancery, resulted in some simplification of procedures in 1833 and the vesting of a rule-making power in the masters of the rolls.[99] A bill proposing more extensive reforms was prepared by a select committee of the Assembly chaired by William Young, the future nemesis of Chancery, in 1838.[100] It died in the Assembly, while a bill to regulate appeals in Chancery passed both houses but failed to obtain the royal assent in the following year.[101]

The momentum for Chancery reform petered out in the 1840s when the issue was eclipsed by the political struggle for responsible government and difficult economic times. Howe confirmed this in a debate on the state of the judiciary in 1849, in which considerable anti-Chancery sentiment was ventilated. It was pleasant, he observed, 'for a man to witness his own opinions coming up again after having slumbered for years.' A lack of accessibility in both economic and geographic terms was the main criticism levelled at Chancery on this occasion. William Alexander Henry, QC, member for Sydney, thought it a great inconvenience that country people had to resort to Chancery for the foreclosure of small mortgages, when the Supreme Court could hear their cases more cheaply on circuit. This observation reveals that the economic downturn of the 1840s had indeed taken its toll and had sparked new interest in and resentment of unresponsive legal structures. G.R. Young was prepared to take the point further, suggesting that each county could do its own business in all equity matters; Charles Harrington, the member for Richmond County and a Conservative, thought a union of the two courts desirable. John Hall, a Conservative from Kings, noted perceptively, if cynically, that lawyers would not introduce any reform 'unless they believed that some little [advantage] was to accrue to themselves from [it].' He pointed out that at present Chancery business benefited the metropolitan but not the country lawyers, and only the former supported it.[102] Hall was a barrister, and his outburst was presumably not a manifestation of anti-lawyer sentiment but a poke at the urban bar. The expectation of increased business on Supreme Court circuits after a union of the two courts may well have helped disarm any resistance from the country lawyers to such an apparently radical innovation.

By the late 1840s the disappearance of the Court of Chancery had already been engineered in several American jurisdictions. The New York constitutional convention of 1846 had approved a complete merger of law and equity, and by 1847 a separate Chancery court had ceased to exist.[103] Ohio had followed suit at its 1851 constitutional convention. Legislative precedents existed, then, for the union of law and equity, and the Nova Scotia reformers soon turned to them. With a Reform administration in power after 1848, matters moved swiftly: the abolition of the Court of Chancery presented the occasion for an irresistible combination of principle, pragmatism, and propaganda. In 1851 a bill to abolish the court, modelled on New York and Ohio legislation, passed the House of Assembly but was deferred by the council on the last day of the session. In an eleventh-hour gambit the Assembly responded by moving that the government create a law and equity commission to draft a plan for the union of the two courts and to consider how practice and procedure in them might be simplified.[104] It reported in 1852 on the latter topic and on the former in 1853.[105] In 1854 New Brunswick abolished its Chancery Court and transferred its incumbent to the Supreme Court as judge in equity, setting the stage for Nova Scotia's action in the following year.[106]

In an ironic counterpoint to the two examples of law reform previously studied, here we find the Assembly behind the 'progressive' innovation in question, and the council initially in favour of the status quo. A number of explanations are possible for the council's rejection of the 1851 bill. The councillors may have feared the populist, levelling overtones that characterized the anti-Chancery campaign in Nova Scotia, and acted to staunch such tendencies before they affected their own privileged positions. Bills to render the upper House elective, for example, were introduced soon after the achievement of responsible government.[107] Even though Alexander Stewart was not very popular, he had been a legislative councillor since 1837, and the attack on him and his court may have been seen as a prelude of things to come.

The knowledge that a bill would be introduced on the topic in the 1855 session provoked an extraordinary outpouring of editorials and letters to the editor in Halifax newspapers, many of them full of invective aimed at Chancery in particular and at courts and lawyers in general. Were it not for this wider critique one might begin to suspect that a politically orchestrated letter-writing campaign was underway. The old complaints of delay, expense, and incomprehensibility appeared regularly in these letters, coupled with some local concerns. "Manus Haec Inimica Tyrannis' thought that abolition was the only way to rid the province of 'this gigantic nuisance.' In England moderate reforms had effected some improvement in Chancery affairs; in Nova Scotia the judge invariably knew the parties, and nine times out of ten was influenced by political or external considerations, 'not to be overcome by either argument, reason or testimony of the clearest kind.'[108] Although this sounds like the classic tirade of the disappointed litigant, such sentiment was no doubt widely shared: in a relatively small jurisdiction such as Nova Scotia, single-judge courts were always vulnerable to perceptions of partiality. That there were some grounds for concern was suggested by a writer to the *Acadian Recorder*, who alleged that a lawyer related to the masters of the rolls, 'rather distinguished for the obtuseness of his moral perceptions, and with no native talent whatsoever,' represented litigants in almost every suit in Chancery. How, he wondered, could the public maintain confidence in its judicial institutions?[109]

A few correspondents came to the defence of Chancery or the masters of the rolls. One argued that the Supreme Court judges lacked expertise in equitable matters and that fusion of the courts would only lead to confusion of the law, all to the benefit of the lawyers; the writer seems to have been motivated more by antipathy to lawyers, however, than by any real pro-Chancery sentiment.[110] Another writer returned to the theme of expertise; he asked why Attorney General William Young did not replace the ailing Chief Justice Halliburton on the Supreme Court bench with Stewart, an admitted savant in equity matters. This step would permit the abolition of Chancery while allowing an untroubled period of transition until the practical problems involved in fusion of the two systems could be worked out. By dumping Stewart, he alleged, Young was simply preparing himself a place on the bench, waiting for the death of the old chief justice.[111] This was the criticism of the abolition bill most frequently heard in the Assembly, and appears to have been a just one: Young did succeed to the chief justiceship when Halliburton died in 1860.

It was left to the editor of the *British North American*, to put forth the most radical argument justifying the demise of Chancery and indeed of the entire judicial establishment as it was then constituted. Labelling 'the whole system of Court Houses, and Judges ... a monstrous fraud upon the public,' he outlined an alternative mode of administering justice in the province.

> We go in for the abolition of all Judges, and present Courts of Law, and the substitution of a Court of Justice in each county. Let every County select its own Judge for the year; to decide according to the law and the equity merits of every case; and as we have a Governor, who must always be an impartial man, and who has plenty of money and little to do under Responsible Government, let him stand as a Court of Appeal from each county; and decide as the Indian Chiefs, and the patriarchal Acadians did of old, on the just merits of each case, without allowing the interference of law-quibbles in any shape whatsoever.[112]

On the topic of lawyers, he added that there 'ought to be some other field open to the intellect of the country, besides the Bar. Lawyers monopolize almost every office in the country.' These sentiments are identical to those contained in the populist critiques of the legal system in Jacksonian America, with their emphasis on an elective judiciary, local rather than metropolitan control of the administration of justice, and the subordination of 'legal justice' to 'fairness.' Their presence in the Nova Scotia of the 1850s, shows that loyalty to things British, noticeable particularly at the outbreak of the Crimean War, did not necessarily exclude recourse to the alternative, and more democratic, conceptions of the legal system then current in the United States.[113]

Introduced in the House on 24 February 1855, the Act for abolishing the Court of Chancery and conferring Equity Jurisdiction on the Supreme Court passed, after some rather stormy debates, by a majority of twenty-eight to twenty on 26 March. The debates centred mainly on the fate of the incumbent master of the rolls, and especially on the question whether he should be awarded a pension if he was not transferred to the Supreme Court.[114] Certainly most, although not all, of the concern manifested in the press focused on these two issues. However, it would be wrong to interpret this evidence, as Townshend does, to explain the demise of the court solely in terms of political enmity and crass manoeuvring over the fate of chief justiceship. Writing privately to E.B. Chandler to inquire about the New Brunswick legislation, Young described the 1855 bill as 'a new and pretty bold experiment ... the fruit of a good deal of thought and labour.'[115] The ideas and ideals of the law reform movement were at least as important in motivating the anti-Chancery campaign as the personal rivalry between Stewart and Young.

In introducing the bill Young said that the experience of New Brunswick, New York, and Ohio had been considered. New Brunswick's attempt had been judged too timid – the creation of an equity side to the Supreme Court was simply 'Chancery under another name' – while the American states had too completely revolutionized the practice of the Supreme Court in order to effectuate the transfer of the equitable jurisdiction. Nova Scotia preferred to adopt a middle course by making some important changes in equity procedure on the basis of the select committee's 1853 recommendations, which were themselves based on the report that led to the Chancery Procedure Acts of 1852 in England. The practice of taking evidence in writing was abolished, and the Supreme Court judges were empowered to try any fact a jury could find in common law matters. Actions were henceforth to commence by a simple summons rather than by means of the verbose bills that had formerly initiated proceedings in equity.[116] Various other reforms too numerous to set out in detail meant that the act ran to seventy-odd sections.[117]

Taken as a whole, the act represents a careful attempt to unify two courts that had long been characterized by different procedures and different modes of thinking. Young was aware that the creation of an equity judge in the Supreme Court, without a degree of unification of common law and Chancery procedure, would be largely a formal measure. He sought to facilitate the unification of the two jurisdictions in a thoughtful, rational way; in this he went much further than New Brunswick had in 1854. It is true that nine years later the position of judge in equity in the Supreme Court was created and bestowed initially upon J. W. Johnston, who resigned as head of the government in 1864.[118] Townshend, on the basis of this and nothing more, declares that the abolition of Chancery in 1855 effected 'a serious muddle in the administration of justice' because its proponents had 'not grasped the basis on which the fusion of law and equity could be brought about.'[119] Subsequent commentators have been content to adopt this judgment.[120] Yet it is not clear that it represents anything other than Townshend's inability to accept that Nova Scotia might have innovated in this respect in advance of the mother country. In addition, Townshend suffers from two sources of possible bias: as a Conservative he would not have approved of the actions of William Young et al., and his mother was Alexander Stewart's daughter. In any case, the creation of the post of judge in equity has been interpreted as being simply an attempt to create a safe place for Johnston, and by implication as not responding to any genuine legal need.[121] It is thus difficult to see why its creation should be used to condemn retrospectively the 1855 action.

The truth probably lies somewhere in the middle. The act of 1855 could probably have been better implemented had Stewart, with his extensive equity experience, been transferred to the Supreme Court. That transfer was not effected for obvious political reasons, which Young himself did not scruple to hide at the time: in debate he asserted that 'the appointment of a Judge from the Liberal ranks would be a great public advantage.' The act had set up the appropriate machinery, but it may have been put to less than optimal use because of the judges' relative lack of experience with equitable doctrine.

Examination of the debate surrounding the 1864 measure confirms that the Supreme Court bench initially experienced some difficulty with its new jurisdiction. S.L. Shannon said he had brought the first post-reform case involving equitable doctrines and recalled Mr Justice Bliss's saying 'we would have to feel our way'; he now sought to avoid bringing such matters to court.[122] Uncertainty during a transitional period is only to be expected, however: even Stewart would have had to 'feel his way' for a while as bench and bar became familiar with the new procedures and doctrines. More serious were charges that the costs and delays of litigation had actually increased since the 1855 reform.[123] Even if such charges were true, however, it is not clear that they resulted from the reform. Chief Justice Halliburton's failing health had prevented him from fulfilling his duties for several years before his death in 1860. By then W.B. Bliss had become the court's weak link, admitting early in 1864 that his 'day of labor and usefulness [was] well nigh over.'[124] While some inconvenience may have followed the 1855 act, much of the responsibility for it must be attributed to the judges rather than to the legislation itself. Much more research needs to be done into judicial decisions and lawyers' records in the decade between 1855 and 1864 before Townshend's charges can be substantiated. In spite of some difficulties in implementing the change, the fusion of the courts of law and equity should be seen as an important victory in Nova Scotia's 'age of progressive reform.'

CONCLUSION

A consideration of the similarities and differences between these reform campaigns provides insight into both the relationship between law and politics in pre-Confederation Nova Scotia and the nature of Nova Scotia legal culture. Nova Scotia's political culture has been characterized as 'conservative' by her most eminent historian, J. Murray Beck, and this conservatism is said to comprise three major components: a general resistance to any change in the status quo; a specific attachment to British (as opposed to American or French) traditions; and an abhorrence of direct taxation.[125] It is difficult to quarrel with this generalization: this paper suggests important nuances in the thesis, however.

First of all, there is the matter of the Legislative Council's role in law reform. If Nova Scotia's political culture is conservative, one would expect the Legislative Council to behave as a traditional upper chamber, cautious at best and obstructive of the people's representatives at worst. One would expect to find this especially before 1848, and indeed there are many examples of caution and obstruction. Yet we also find the council in the vanguard of reformist sentiment in the campaign to abolish imprisonment for debt, adopt a bankruptcy law, and reform married women's property law. After 1848 there were Reformers such as McCully in the council, but they did not constitute a majority. I have argued that in their advocacy of these reforms there was an element of enlightened self-interest on the part of the council's Halifax merchants, but this suggests a certain adaptability in the face of changing circumstances rather than tradition-bound conservatism. The fact that the upper chambers in both Upper Canada and New Brunswick were also in the vanguard of married women's property law reform should cause us to reassess the traditional image of these unelected bodies as merely reactive and reactionary.

Second, what was the relationship between reform and Reform? In other words, what do the law reform campaigns tell about the role of responsible government in Nova Scotia's political history? For Beck the fact that 1848 came peacefully is evidence of the province's conservative political culture; while obviously important, the shift to responsible government did not amount to a sea-change in provincial history.[126] For others 1848 is a true watershed; in that year new political structures were created which allowed Halifax capital to impose its will on a reluctant hinterland.[127]

I have suggested that the heritage of responsible government was a complex one. The clearest evidence of the 'watershed' theory is the anti-Chancery campaign that got underway very soon after 1848. The destruction of Chancery combined a striking innovation in legal thought and practice with a dramatic uncrowning of the ancient regime; the campaign both reflected and exploited a rich vein of anti-legal sentiment unleashed in part by the achievement of responsible government. When the Liberal press could suggest that Alexander Stewart, then second in precedence to the chief justice, might yet have a useful future as a commissioner of bankrupts, it was clear that nothing was sacred any more. The abolition of Chancery was accomplished by peaceful means, but conservative it was not.

It is difficult to quantify intangibles such as anti-lawyer or anti-legal sentiment; none the less, the decade of the 1850s seems to have witnessed a peak in such attitudes. The year 1848 had raised expectations about what might be accomplished. The decade began with Joseph Howe's 'Free Trade in Law' bill in 1850, which broke the lawyers' professional monopoly by allowing any litigant to appoint any lay person to represent him in any court.[128] Important more for its symbolic value than its practical effect, Howe's bill set the tone for increasingly strident attacks on lawyers and the entire court system. The denunciation of all courts and law as a 'monstrous fraud upon the public' in 1855 was partly rhetorical excess, but it marked the distance travelled since Howe's charges of judicial corruption had resulted in a criminal libel charge two decades earlier. Again, these examples do not suggest a political or legal culture stolidly attached to the status quo.

When one turns to commercial law, however, the 'watershed' thesis seems to suffer an irreversible setback. One would have expected the men of 1848, imbued with the liberal and progressive spirit of the age, to have moved quickly to rationalize debtor–creditor law, adopt a bankruptcy code, abolish the usury laws, and promote the limited liability corporation, all in order to 'liberate' individual initiative and promote economic development. Yet they did not, or could not, accomplish these changes in spite of their twelve years in power between 1848 and 1867. An automatic right to limited liability via incorporation, for example, was not granted until 1883, under the administration of W.T. Pipes.[129]

The immobility in commercial law seems especially incongruous when set beside the enthusiastic embrace of the railway as a tool of economic development during the same decades. Nova Scotians seemed to want it both ways: one foot was firmly planted in the eighteenth century as the other stepped toward the twentieth. In many ways this is not surprising: we still tend to regard technology as a value-free tool that can be inserted into any social context without essentially altering it. Nova Scotians wanted the economic development the railways were supposed to supply, but they thought it could be attained without abandoning the protection afforded by maximum interest rates and direct legislative supervision of incorporations. They did not feel that enterprise would be encouraged by lessening the penalties for indebtedness. Pre-liberal ideologies stressing proper commercial behaviour and protection of the weak continued to attract many adherents well into the age of progressive reform.

Whether this state of affairs should be characterized as 'conservative' depends on whether one looks at the end result or at the process by which it was obtained. The debate over the reform of commercial law proceeded over four decades prior to 1867, at times vigorously, at times perfunctorily. If, generally speaking, pre-liberal ideologies continued to win the day, the victory was by no means uncontested. A mere glance at material conditions in the province shows why older ideologies should have retained their strength. Reform of debtor–creditor law in England and America was ultimately associated with both urbanization and increased commercial and industrial activity. Pre-Confederation Nova Scotia was still intensely rural – 92 per cent of the population lived in the country, according to the 1861 census[130] – and thus more comfortable with existing mechanisms.

No examination of the 'conservatism' of Nova Scotia's political and legal culture can avoid reference to the colony's loyalty to British traditions. In the rhetoric of political culture there was a strong tendency in Nova Scotia – indeed, across British North America – to reject the American model and embrace the British.[131] Yet in the legal culture, as has been seen in all three areas of law reform reviewed here, this resistance to American models diminished appreciably. If innovations based on American precedents were rejected, it was because of disagreement at the level of principle, not simply because they contained 'USA ideas.' The British example remained very influential, of course, but it by no means precluded consideration of American solutions to similar problems.[132] Thus we find William Young, acting in his capacity as Speaker of the House in 1852, sending copies of Nova Scotia's Revised Statutes of 1851 to the secretaries of state for Massachusetts and New York and asking for theirs in return. The 'intercourse between [the jurisdictions] is so rapidly and largely extending,' he wrote, 'that the legislative and social progress of one must always be regarded by the other of them with the feelings which spring out of a common origin and a mutual interest.'[133]

In short, I am suggesting that Nova Scotia's legal history reveals a genuine clash of ideologies – broadly speaking, eighteenth-century paternalism versus nineteenth-century liberalism – which renders the characterization of the province's legal culture as 'conservative' *tout court* misleading. No easy alternative label comes to mind, but S.F. Wise's observation that the English-Canadian style arises out of a 'contradictory heritage' best understood 'in terms of muted conservatism and ambivalent liberalism, of contradiction, paradox and complexity' accurately captures my meaning.[134] Those who have recently reminded us of the strongly conservative ethos of the British North American legal systems have done a valuable service, but sometimes at the risk of substituting a conservative consensus for the liberal one assumed by previous historians.[135] Once again I find S.F. Wise's insistence on 'the continued workings of a liberal-conservative dialectic' useful, at least for the pre-Confederation period.[136] Future research that incorporates these insights will prove fertile ground for an exploration of the legal cultures of British North America.

NOTES

1 *Presbyterian Witness* 2 Apr. 1853. All newspapers referred to herein were published in Halifax unless otherwise noted. I would like to thank Barry Cahill and David Sutherland for their comments on an earlier draft of this paper. Any errors are my own.

2 For a good example of the present-day rhetoric of law reform, see 'Statement of the Honourable Mr Justice Allen M. Linden, the president of the Law Reform Commission of Canada, upon the release of Report 30: *Recodifying Criminal Law*' 3 December 1986.

3 For an overview of the law reform movement in the United States, see C.M. Cook *The American Codification Movement* (Westport, Conn.: Greenwood Press 1981); Lawrence Friedman 'Law Reform in Historical Perspective' *St Louis Law Journal* 13 (1969) 351. For England, there are few works that emphasize law reform as such; most works dealing with the period focus on political reforms, the reform of governmental administration, or wider intellectual trends. See, however, Sir William Holdsworth *History of English Law* vol. 13 (Boston: Little, Brown 1922 –) chapter 4, parts 1 and 3; A.H. Manchester *A Modern Legal History of England and Wales 1750–1950* (London: Butterworths 1980) 10–20; A.V. Dicey *Lectures on the Relations between Law and Public Opinion in England during the Nineteenth Century* (London: Macmillan 1905) lectures 4–6; A. Birrell *A Century of Law Reform* (London: Macmillan 1901); B. Abel-Smith and R. Stevens *Lawyers and the Courts: A Sociological Study of the English Legal System 1750–1965* (London: Heinemann 1967), especially chapters 2 and 3. Curiously, there is no good overview of Lord Brougham's law reform efforts, even though his influence is acknowledged to have been enormous. The first volume of C.W. New's biography, *The Life of Henry Brougham to 1830* (Oxford: Clarendon Press 1961), ends just as Brougham's law reform efforts were getting underway. New died before completing vol. 2, and no subsequent biographer has dealt satisfactorily with Brougham's influence on the law reform movement.

4 A major exception is the path-breaking work of E. Kolish 'Changements dans le droit privé au Québec et au Bas-Canada, entre 1760 et 1840: attitudes et réactions des contemporains' (PHD thesis, Université de Montréal 1980), and 'The Impact of the Change in Legal Metropolis in the Development of Lower Canada's Legal System' *Canadian Journal of Law and Society* 3 (1988) 1. See also J.D. Blackwell 'William Hume Blake and the Judicature Acts of 1849: The Process of Legal Reform at Mid-Century in Upper Canada' in D.H. Flaherty, ed. *Essays in the History of Canadian Law* vol. 1 (Toronto: The Osgoode Society 1981).

5 Real economic growth ('intensive' as opposed to 'extensive') may have characterized only the latter two decades; it has recently been argued that the first half of the century saw only 'extensive' growth alternating with periods of stagnation: J. Gwyn ' "A Little Province Like This": The Economy of Nova Scotia under Stress, 1812–1853' in D.H. Akenson, ed. *Canadian Papers in Rural History* vol. 6 (Gananoque, Ont.: Langdale Press 1988).

6 W.S. MacNutt *The Atlantic Provinces: The Emergence of Colonial Society 1712–1857* (Toronto: McClelland and Stewart 1965); D.C. Harvey 'The Intellectual Awakening of Nova Scotia' *Dalhousie Review* 13 (1933–4) 1; J.M. Beck *The Politics of Nova Scotia* vol. 1 (Tantallon, NS: Four East Publications 1985); *Joseph Howe* 2 vols (Kingston and Montreal: McGill-Queen's University Press 1982–3); G.A. Rawlyk, ed. *Historical Essays on the Atlantic Provinces* (Toronto: McClelland and Stewart 1967).

7 For a good overview of the position of married women at common law, see L. Holcombe *Wives and Property: Reform of the Married Women's Property Law in Nineteenth-Century England* (Toronto: University of Toronto Press 1983) chapter 2.; N.A. Basch *In the Eyes of the Law: Women, Marriage and Property in Nineteenth-Century New York* (Ithaca: Cornell University Press 1982) chapter 1.

8 Simon Bradstreet Robie, master of the rolls from 1826 to 1834, left £400 in his will to Elizabeth Halliburton upon his death in 1858, with the direction to 'her father the Chief Justice to dispose of it for her own use': Harry King Papers, PANS vol. 4, file 12, 2117. Jonathan McCully, a judge on the Nova Scotia Supreme Court at the time of his death in 1877, had set up a testamentary trust for the separate use of his married daughters: P. Blakeley 'Jonathan McCully, Father of Confederation' *Collections* 36 (1968) 143, 151. This provision gave rise to litigation: *Foot* v. *Foot* (1888) 15 SCR 699, aff'g (1887) 20 NSR 71; *Borden* v. *James* (1894) 40 NSR 48. Settlements for married women are also mentioned in two decisions reported in B. Russell, ed. *The Equity Decisions of the Hon. John W. Ritchie* (Halifax: A. & W. Mackinlay 1883). In *Hunter* v. *The People's Bank of Halifax* a testator dying in 1861 left money to his daughter 'to be exempt from any debts or liabilities of her husband.' In *Silver* v. *Silver* the plaintiff widow had had property placed in trust for her benefit before her marriage, the income to be paid to her for life free of any *jus mariti* and not subject to her husband's debts.

9 S. Lebsock *The Free Women of Petersburg: Status and Culture in a Southern Town 1784–1860* (New York: Norton 1984) 57–67 (Virginia evidence)

10 Dicey *Law and Public Opinion* 369–96; compare Holcombe *Wives and Property* 8.

11 Basch *In the Eyes of the Law* 113–35; P.A. Rabkin *Fathers to Daughters: The*

Legal Foundations of Female Emancipation (Westport, Conn.: Greenwood Press 1980); R.H. Chused 'Married Women's Property Law: 1800–1850' *Georgetown Law Journal* 71 (1982–3) 1359

12 C.B. Backhouse 'Married Women's Property Law in Nineteenth-Century Canada' *Law and History Review* 6 (1988) 211.

13 Basch *In the Eyes of the Law* 119. *The Pearl*, a weekly literary magazine published at Halifax between 1837 and 1840, reproduced Grimké's petition against slavery, signed by 20,000 Massachusetts women, in its edition of 4 May 1838. Although the petition is not concerned with women's issues as such, its preamble ends with a clear statement on the right and duty of women to be involved in political affairs and seen as true citizens. *The Pearl's* editor, the Reverend Thomas Taylor, pronounced Grimké a 'lady of superior talents' but does not appear to have printed any of her *Letters on the Equality of the Sexes*.

14 G. Davies 'A Literary Study of Selected Periodicals from Maritime Canada 1789–1872' (PHD thesis, York University 1979) 175

15 Unpassed Bills, PANS RG5, series U, vol. 24. The progress of the bill in the Legislative Council can be found in *JLC* 1854–5.

16 On McCully's career see Blakeley 'Jonathan McCully' and P.B. Waite 'Jonathan McCully' *DCB* vol. 10, 456.

17 The debates on the bill in the Legislative Council can be found in *DLC* 1854–5; they are also reported in the *Acadian Recorder* of 3 Feb. and 24 Mar. 1855. Research has failed to reveal the existence of any petitions by women's groups who might have advocated the law. Their survival and classification is erratic, however, and their existence cannot be ruled out. Women did petition the legislature in Upper Canada in the 1850s, according to Backhouse 'Married Women's Property' 24.

18 *Morning Chronicle* 8 Feb. 1855 (reprinted in *Novascotian* 12 Feb. 1855). This editorial may have been written by McCully himself; he took up the editorship of the *Morning Chronicle* in 1855, but the exact date is unclear.

19 The Pictou paper's article was reprinted in *Acadian Recorder* 10 Feb. 1855.

20 The New York laws are reproduced in an appendix to Basch *In the Eyes of the Law* 233. Holcombe *Wives and Property* 90 reports that Lord Brougham presented the first such bill to the British Parliament in 1857. Women in Ontario were clearly aware of the New York law in the 1850s; numerous petitions were presented to the legislature by married women asking for the adoption of separate property statutes, some of which specifically asked for legislation on the New York model: see *JLC* 1865, vol. 14, 101, and the index to those journals covering the years 1852–66. (I am grateful to Professor Mary Jane Mossman, who shared her research on Upper Canada

with me.) No such petitions were found for Nova Scotia in the 1850s or 1860s, but the records are not complete.

21 *DLC* 1858, 18. On Field's role in the married women's property campaign in New York, see Basch *In the Eyes of the Law* 133–4. New York experimented with such a clause in 1860, but quickly repealed it in 1862; see the appendix to Basch, 234–7.

22 SNB 1851, c. 24, consolidated as c. 114 of RSNB 1854. The act provided that a married woman's property, whether accruing before or after marriage, was to be considered her separate property and not subject to seizure for her husband's debts, saving gifts from the husband during coverture. In case of desertion by the husband, the wife was entitled to take any actions in respect of her separate property in her own name, and any property she acquired by her own labour after desertion was to vest in her absolutely. On the insane, see D. Francis 'The Development of the Lunatic Asylum in the Maritime Provinces' *Acadiensis* 6 (1977) 23.

23 *JLC* 1857, *JHA* 1857. The bill does not appear in PANS RG5, series U, vol. 24, but it was said to be identical to a bill on the same topic introduced in the council in the following year; see *DLC* 1858, 17. The latter bill is found in PANS RG5, series U, vol. 25.

24 MacNutt *Atlantic Provinces* 235–6

25 Quoted ibid. 236

26 See especially Chused 'Married Women's Property Law' 1400–4.

27 D. Sutherland 'Halifax Merchants and the Pursuit of Development, 1783–1850' *Canadian Historical Review* 49 (1978) 1, at 13

28 *JHA* 1865. The bill can be found in PANS RG5, series U, vol. 27.

29 *DHA* 1865, 51

30 *Presbyterian Witness* 4 Mar. 1865

31 Compare Backhouse 'Married Women's Property' 24

32 *DHA* 51–4

33 Holcombe *Wives and Property* 102

34 SNS 1866, c. 33. The English Act was the Matrimonial Causes Act, 20 & 21 Vict. (1857) c. 85.

35 Later developments are discussed in Backhouse 'Married Women's Property,' and P. Girard and R. Veinott 'Married Women's Property Law in Nova Scotia 1850–1900' (unpublished 1990).

36 Thomas McCulloch *The Stepsure Letters* (Toronto: McClelland and Stewart 1960). The letters first appeared in the *Acadian Recorder* between 22 Dec. 1821 and 11 May 1822, and were published in book form in 1862 by Hugh Blackadar at Halifax. In these letters McCulloch is not at all concerned about the reform of debtor–creditor relations in general or imprisonment

for debt in particular. He believed that people got into debt because of laziness and extravagance, and he appeared to regard imprisonment as a natural and inevitable check on these tendencies.

37 *Acadian Recorder* 4 Mar. 1826, SNS 1770, c. 5. The act was consolidated in RSNS 1851, c. 52 but not in RSNS 1864, though it appeared in an appendix and was declared to be in force. Attempts to abolish the usury laws began as early as 1824 (*Novascotian* 1 Jan. 1824) but did not succeed before 1867, when the matter passed into federal jurisdiction as relating to 'interest.' McCully introduced a bill into the Legislative Council in late 1854, which the *Acadian Recorder* applauded (30 Dec. 1854): the usury laws were 'a remnant of a set of antiquated and silly regulations enacted at a time when legislation was made to protrude itself into all sorts of places where it should not have been.' For debates, see *Acadian Recorder* 10 and 17 Mar. 1855. Debate on a second bill in council can be found in *Acadian Recorder* 12 and 27 Feb. 1858. As with bankruptcy, the impetus then shifted to the Assembly, where bills failed in 1862 (*Novascotian* 7 Apr. 1862) and 1864: *DHA* 1864, 97–8. Supporters of the status quo argued that the law was 'intended to prevent the needy and reckless from being thrown into the hands of capitalists'; opponents maintained that it was evaded widely in any case, and that it exerted a dampening effect on trade and commerce. The affirmation of the law in 1864 was clear: the vote against the abolition bill was thirty-six to fourteen.

38 For conditions in the 1840s, see MacNutt *Atlantic Provinces* 213–16. Sutherland ('Halifax Merchants' 13–14) reports that Nova Scotia trade declined by 42 per cent during 1840–3, revived slightly, and fell to an all-time low in 1848.

39 SNS 1758, c. 15; Beamish Murdoch *Epitome of the Laws of Nova Scotia* (Halifax: Joseph Howe 1832–3) vol. 2, 120–3, 254–64

40 I.P.H. Duffy *Bankruptcy and Insolvency in London during the Industrial Revolution* (New York: Garland 1985) asserts that English debtors had a 'flippant attitude toward the insolvency process' and that creditors were not, on the whole, protected adequately by the debt laws (at 158, 162). Others have disagreed: see B. Kercher 'The Transformation of Imprisonment for Debt in England, 1828 to 1838' *Australian Journal of Law and Society* 2 (1984) 60. But whatever the case in England, imprisonment for debt was probably quite effective when used in Nova Scotia because there were fewer legal avenues for evading it, and the small scale of provincial society meant that creditors could control the process more directly. In the only recent Canadian study, E. Kolish 'Imprisonment for Debt in Lower Canada, 1791–1840' *McGill Law Journal* 32 (1987) 603, suggests that imprisonment

'was genuinely effective in many cases' (at 632), although it was resorted to relatively infrequently. I have not studied the actual incidence of imprisonment for debt in Nova Scotia, as did Kolish, mainly because the records appear to be much less complete than in Quebec.

41 Holdsworth, vol. 6, 407–8; vol. 8, 231–2, 245; vol. 9, 253

42 *JHA* 1820–46

43 SNS 1763, c. 5

44 Holdsworth traces the English legislation to 22 & 23 Car. II (1670–1) c. 20: vol. 8, 235. Subsequent statutes were consolidated in 1729 and 1759 (vol. 11, 597–601), and these served as models for the 1763 Nova Scotia legislation. All the features of the Nova Scotia enactment described in this paragraph were to be found in the English statutes, except that in England creditors had to pay an allowance in cash (set at 2s 4d per week in 1729) rather than in kind. The English acts, however, applied to debtors arrested on mesne process as well as final execution from 1678, while Nova Scotia did not extend its acts to the former cases until SNS 1837, c. 47.

45 SNS 1813, c. 14

46 SNS 1819, c. 22

47 SNS 1832, c. 58. No appeal was possible from the justices' decision until 1846 (SNS 1846, c. 12), although in theory certiorari probably would have been available before that date.

48 The acts were consolidated in 1846, at which time some of the reforms mentioned were adopted; the rest appeared in RSNS 1851, c. 137 (Of the Relief of Insolvent Debtors). The 1864 revision contained two minor changes to the 1851 scheme.

49 In Nova Scotia the imprisonment of women for debt was forbidden by RSNS 1851, c. 131, s. 7 (Of the Jurisdiction of Justices of the Peace in Civil Cases).

50 For the United States, see P.J. Coleman *Debtors and Creditors in America: Insolvency, Imprisonment for Debt, and Bankruptcy, 1607–1900* (Madison: State Historical Society of Wisconsin 1974). For England, see Holdsworth, vol. 11 600 and vol. 15, 114.

51 Holdsworth, vol. 8, 229–45; vol. 11, 445–7; vol. 15, 97–100

52 Coleman *Debtors and Creditors* 269–93

53 For the debate, see *Novascotian* 8 Mar. 1827.

54 K.G. Pryke 'Beamish Murdoch' *DCB* vol. 10, 539. Another reformer who was second only to Murdoch in his efforts to abolish imprisonment for debt was the MHA for Pictou, Jotham Blanchard. He too had occasion to dislike imprisonment for debt for personal reasons: the publisher of the *Colonial Patriot*, which Blanchard edited, was jailed for debt in 1829. See

R.H. Sherwood *Jotham Blanchard: The Forgotten Patriot of Pictou* (Hantsport, NS: Lancelot Press 1982) 31–5.

55 *JLC* 1828, *JHA* 1828

56 *JLC* 1831, *JHA* 1831

57 See *JHA* and *JLC* for the years in question. Most of the unpassed bills can be found in PANS RG5, series U. Imprisonment for debt was finally 'abolished' in 1890: SNS 1890, c. 17.

58 Debate on the bill in the Assembly is reported in *Novascotian* 28 Feb. 1828.

59 The bill can be found in PANS RG5, series U, vol. 10.

60 Ibid. Debate in the Assembly is reported in *Novascotian* 8 Mar. 1827.

61 See *JHA* for the years in question and the bills themselves in PANS RG5, series U, vols 12 (1834–5), 14 (1837–8), and 17 (1841–2). Debate on the 1834 motion is reported in *Novascotian* 23 Apr. 1834.

62 Debate on the bill is reported in *Novascotian* 26 Jan., 3 Feb., and 10 Feb. 1842.

63 *JHA* 1842, at 227

64 10 Feb. 1842

65 The bill is found in PANS RG5, series U, vol. 28. The report of the commissioners is reproduced as appendix 31 to *JHA* 1854. One of the five, L.M. Wilkins Jr, who had practised law at Windsor for over thirty years, 'acquiesc[ed] in the general character of the report, but [was] not satisfied of the indispensable necessity of a bankrupt law for Nova Scotia.' The other members were L. O'Connor Doyle, the Irish patriot and Reformer, and two merchants, William Pryor Jr and Frederick Charman.

66 Debates in the council can be found in *Acadian Recorder* 3 and 17 Mar. 1855.

67 Per Alexander Stewart in the debate on Uniacke's 1827 bill, reported in *Novascotian* 8 Mar. 1827.

68 *Novascotian* 5 Feb. 1834. Although he represented a rural riding, Bliss did not reside there. Bliss, who was born in Saint John and educated at the Inner Temple, was a law practitioner in Halifax; he had more urban than rural influences in his life.

69 Fairbanks later reversed his stand and supported passage of the bankruptcy bill in 1842.

70 *Novascotian* 8 Mar. 1827

71 *Wesleyan* 27 Sept. 1851

72 *The Master's Wife* (Toronto: McClelland and Stewart 1977) 36–7. The book, a memoir of Sir Andrew's childhood in Prince Edward Island during the 1860s and 1870s, was originally published in 1939, a year after the author's death.

73 Ibid. 37

74 *Novascotian* 8 Mar. 1827

75 *Acadian Recorder* 20 Feb. 1858. The Assembly bill is not available in PANS. One of McCully's fellow councillors, John Leander Starr, would go bankrupt in 1861 and be forced to give up his seat: *JHA* 1861, app. 48.

76 *JHA* 1857

77 Considerable material from Shannon's law practice can be found in PANS MG1, vols 799–804. An entry in the *Shannon Genealogy* (Rochester, NY: 1905) (available at PANS) provides much detail on his life and career, as does a long obituary in the *Acadian Recorder* 7 Jan. 1895.

78 PANS RG5, series U, vol. 26 (1860–4)

79 *JHA* 1862, *JLC* 1862

80 *Morning Chronicle* 14 Feb. 1863

81 Debates in the Legislative Council were reported in the *British Colonist* 12 Apr. 1862 and *Morning Chronicle* 19 Feb., 7 Mar., and 19 Mar. 1863.

82 McCully's bill specified two hundred pounds, but a new system of currency adopted in 1860 made one pound equal to five dollars: H.A. Flemming *Collections* 20 (1921) 111, 131.

83 *Morning Chronicle* 19 Mar. 1863

84 Ibid. 7 Mar. 1863

85 Ibid. 19 Mar. 1863

86 *Novascotian* 23 Mar. 1863

87 Beck *Joseph Howe* vol. 2, 157–69

88 *JHA* 1863, at 96

89 It is interesting to compare the experience of Lower Canada with Nova Scotia at this point. Kolish 'Imprisonment for Debt' 632 argues that the movement to restrict imprisonment for debt was a 'mild' one in Lower Canada, whereas I have argued that reform of debtor–creditor relations was a major point of conflict from 1827 to 1864. To some extent this is a difference of emphasis and chronology; I consider the whole field of debtor–creditor relations to 1867, while Kolish looks specifically at imprisonment for debt until 1840. However, there is a genuine difference between the two jurisdictions which may account for our different interpretations. The conflict over the adoption of a bankruptcy law in Lower Canada, which Kolish admits to have been acute in the 1820–39 period (see her 'L'Introduction de la faillite au Bas-Canada: conflit social ou national?' *Revue d'histoire de l'Amérique française* 40 (1986) 215) was resolved with the imposition of a bankruptcy law in 1839 by the British following the suspension of the constitution after the rebellions. This measure would have reduced the incidence of imprisonment for debt and probably defused the existing reform movement. Needless to say, no such *deus ex machina* was present in Nova Scotia.

90 The ratio of lawyers to laymen in the Assembly between 1820 and 1867 was never less than 1:4, according to S. Elliott *The Legislative Assembly of Nova Scotia: A Biographical Directory* (Halifax: Province of Nova Scotia 1984).
91 Coleman *Debtors and Creditors* 13–14
92 C.J. Townshend *Historical Account of the Courts of Judicature in Nova Scotia* (Toronto: Carswell 1900) 63–77. On the history of the office of master of the rolls, see Clara Greco's essay elsewhere in this volume. See also Murdoch *Epitome* vol. 4, 44–93.
93 16 Oct. 1833
94 *Novascotian* 19 Apr., 22 Aug., 20 Sept. 1832
95 On Robie's background, see J.M. Beck 'Simon Bradstreet Robie' *DCB* vol. 8, 756.
96 Townshend *Historical Account* 81
97 J.M. Beck 'Alexander Stewart' *DCB* vol. 9, 746, 748
98 It is difficult to tell whether King was a sore loser, a genuine Chancery reformer, or both. In any case, his complaints received extensive publicity in 1833–4 (see *Novascotian* 15 and 29 Jan., 29 Feb. 1834) and resulted in a lengthy investigation by a committee of the Assembly into his complaint. Its report, reproduced as appendix 61 to *JHA* 1833, concluded that King had no legitimate cause of complaint 'except such as result from the practice of the Court of Chancery, in occasioning unnecessary delay and expense.' While absolving the participants of any charges of bad faith, this conclusion hardly constituted a clean bill of health for the Chancery as a whole.
99 SNS 1832, c. 42; Townshend *Historical Account* 80–1
100 The committee's report is reproduced as appendix 86 to *JHA* 1838.
101 *JHA* 1839. After 1825 appeals went from the master of the rolls to the governor, who retained the title of chancellor. In theory, an appeal lay from him to the Judicial Committee of the Privy Council in matters of over £300, but it is not clear if this avenue was ever pursued: Townshend *Historical Account* 81.
102 This debate was reported in the *Acadian Recorder* 10 Feb. 1849.
103 Basch *In the Eyes of the Law* 149–50
104 *JHA* 1851, 7 Apr. 1851. Alan Sprague 'Some American Influences on the Law and the Law Courts of the Province of Nova Scotia from 1749 to 1853' (unpublished paper, 1935; available at PANS) states that parts of the 1851 bill were taken directly from the Ohio legislation (at 14–15).
105 *JHA* 1852, appendix 73; *JHA* 1853, appendix 16
106 SNB 1854, c. 18
107 *Novascotian* 17 Sept. 1849; see also *JHA* throughout the 1850s.
108 *British North American* 12 Mar. 1855

109 *Acadian Recorder* 10 Feb. 1855. The writer probably meant J.S. Morse, the brother of Stewart's wife Sarah, who had an extensive Chancery practice. Stewart's own son appeared in Chancery too, though less frequently. I am indebted to Barry Cahill for this information. Other critical letters and editorials appeared in *British North American* 26 and 31 Jan., 5, 9, and 14 Feb., and 23 Mar. 1855.

110 *British North American* 21 Mar. 1855. This letter appears as an editorial, but a correction appeared on 23 Mar. 1855.

111 *Acadian Recorder* 24 Mar. 1855

112 23 Mar. 1855

113 On Jacksonianism and its impact on the legal system, see M. Meyers *The Jacksonian Persuasion: Politics and Belief* (Stanford: Stanford University Press 1957).

114 The debates are reported in *British North American* 5 Feb., 19 Mar., and 20, 27, and 30 Apr. 1855. *Novascotian* of 26 Mar. and 30 Apr. 1855 also contains some of the debates. They also appear in *DLC* 1855, 96–108.

115 Young to Chandler, 24 Feb. 1855; Chandler to Young, 24 Mar. 1855, New Brunswick Museum, E.B. Chandler Papers 566, box 2, file 3–133, 134. I am indebted to D.G. Bell for this reference.

116 *British North American* 19 Mar. 1855. For the reforms effected in England by the Chancery Procedure Acts 1852, which inaugurated the modern system of equity procedure, see Holdsworth, vol. 15, 118.

117 SNS 1855, c. 23

118 SNS 1864, c. 10

119 Townshend *Historical Account* 96

120 For example, Beck, 'Alexander Stewart' *DCB* vol. 9, 746; Blackwell 'William Hume Blake' ibid. 139

121 Beck *Politics of Nova Scotia* vol. 1, 158–60

122 *Morning Sun* 20 Apr. 1864

123 *Morning Chronicle* 14 Apr. 1864; *British Colonist* 14 Apr. 1864

124 *British Colonist* 14 Apr. 1864

125 Beck *Politics of Nova Scotia* vol. 1, 266–72

126 Ibid.

127 This is suggested in Sutherland 'Halifax Merchants' 16, note 61.

128 SNS 1850, c. 13; Beck *Joseph Howe* vol. 2 28–9

129 SNS 1883, c. 24

130 Cited in A. Brookes 'Out-Migration from the Maritime Provinces, 1860–1900: Some Preliminary Considerations' *Acadiensis* 5 (1976) 26, 33

131 S.F. Wise and R.C. Brown *Canada Views the United States: Nineteenth Century Political Attitudes* (Toronto: Macmillan 1972) 121–30

132 Blackwell 'William Hume Blake' 166 also notes this tendency in Upper Canada.

133 William Young Papers, PANS MG2, vol. 733, nos. 303, 304

134 S.F. Wise 'Liberal Consensus or Ideological Battleground: Some Reflections on the Hartz Thesis' in Canadian Historical Association *Historical Papers 1974* 1, 13

135 G.B. Baker 'The Reconstitution of Upper Canadian Legal Thought in the Late Victorian Empire' *Law and History Review* 3 (1985) 219; idem ' "So Elegant a Web": Providential Order and the Rule of Secular Law in Early Nineteenth-Century Upper Canada' *University of Toronto Law Journal* 38 (1988) 184

136 Wise 'Liberal Consensus' 13

5

Poverty, Unemployment, and the Administration of the Criminal Law: Vagrancy Laws in Halifax, 1864–1890

JIM PHILLIPS

Vagrancy was one of the most common offences for which residents of late nineteenth-century Halifax were committed to the city prison at Rockhead; more than fourteen-hundred incarcerations occurred between 1864 and 1890. Prostitutes, strangers, professional mendicants, the able-bodied unemployed – all were susceptible to classification as vagrants. Like their counterparts in urban centres throughout North America, members of the Halifax middle class perceived in the vagrant a growing threat to social discipline and turned in part to the criminal justice system to impose their notions of order and respectability on this segment of the urban poor.

In this essay I will examine the characteristics of the vagrant class and the operation of vagrancy laws in late nineteenth-century Halifax, a period that witnessed the beginnings of industrialization, considerable population growth, out-migration from the rural hinterland of Nova Scotia, and new approaches to providing for the urban poor. Statistical evidence on rates of incarceration (garnered from the comprehensive city prison records available for this period), analyses of the ethnic, geographical, and religious origins of the convicted, sentencing practices, and official and popular reactions to vagrants are used to assess their place in society. Of particular concern is middle-class reaction to the emerging lower working class – unskilled labourers uprooted from traditional occupations and communities, transient and often unemployed, without a regular place in the new industrializing society. The administration of vagrancy laws in this period is best interpreted as part of a broader process of social control, which involved inuring those members of the lower classes to bourgeois notions of industry, sobriety, and respectability.

NOVA SCOTIA'S VAGRANCY LAWS

Colonial Nova Scotia enacted its first vagrancy law just a year after the establishment of the Assembly in 1758. A 1759 act providing for a workhouse in Halifax required justices of the peace to 'commit to the said house of correction ... all disorderly and idle persons, and such who shall be found begging ... common drunkards, persons of lewd behaviour, vagabonds, runaways, stubborn servants and children, and persons who notoriously mispend their time to the neglect and prejudice of their own or their family's support.'[1] The act was closely modelled on English statutes, which by the mid-eighteenth century focused on the vagrant as a status offender, one who threatened social order by living in a socially unacceptable though not otherwise illegal manner, or by appearing likely to commit other crimes.[2] In similar vein a successor statute of 1774 'for punishing Rogues, Vagabonds, and other Idle and Disorderly Persons' laid down eight categories of offenders deemed 'idle and wandering persons,' including those who ran away and burdened the community with supporting their families, those who, 'not having wherewith to maintain themselves, live idle and refuse to work for the usual wages,' and all beggars. Punishment was one month in the prison or workhouse with hard labour.[3]

These statutes provided a comprehensive vagrancy law for the colony and stayed in operation until their repeal at the time of Nova Scotia's first statutory revision in 1851. They were replaced by a single section of a short act dealing with 'madmen and vagrants,' which stated: 'Persons who unlawfully return to any place whence they have been legally removed as paupers, and idle and wandering persons having no visible means of subsistence, and persons going about to beg alms, shall severally be deemed common vagrants, and may be brought up and summarily convicted by a justice of the peace, and thereupon imprisoned for not more than one month.'[4] This provision was repeated in each subsequent statutory consolidation. It was supplemented for Halifax by the city charter, which permitted the City Court to sentence 'common beggars' to ten days for the first offence and ninety days for subsequent offences, and to imprison 'vagabonds' for up to a year.[5]

In 1869 the federal parliament passed a Vagrancy Act as part of the pre-codification campaign to consolidate the criminal law. It was intended primarily to punish immorality and control those who threatened to commit crimes, and secondarily to reduce begging and lessen the number of charges on poor-relief systems. Included in its sweeping definition were 'all common prostitutes or night walkers ... not giving a satisfactory account of themselves,' brothel-keepers, and persons who 'for the most part support themselves by gaming or crime or by the avails of prostitution.' All were to be 'deemed vagrants, loose, idle or disorderly persons,' as were, inter alia, '[a]ll idle persons who, not having visible means of maintaining themselves, live without employment.' The penalty upon conviction was a maximum two-month prison term, with or without hard labour, or a maximum fifty-dollar fine, or both.[6] In 1874 the maximum term of imprisonment was extended to six months. In 1881 judges' questioning of the power of the court to sentence offenders to hard labour brought another, one-section, amending act to confirm it.[7] Throughout this period vagrants were caught not only by federal law but also by provincial and municipal laws because the types of offences that feel under 'vagrancy' were susceptible to concurrent jurisdiction under section 92(14) of the British North America Act, which gave the provinces the authority to make laws to punish contraventions of provincial statutes enacted under another section 92 head. This authority was judicially confirmed in 1888 in *Winslow* v. *Gallagher* and again in *R.* v. *Munroe*.[8]

The new legislation was welcomed in a number of quarters. The chief constable of Toronto, for example, commented that 'if strictly enforced' it would 'tend more to the prevention of crime than any Acts hitherto passed by the legislature.'[9] A Halifax newspaper claimed that it would 'bring the street corner loafers and users of bad language within range of a healthy amount of judicious restraint and punishment.'[10]

HISTORIANS AND NINETEENTH-CENTURY VAGRANCY LAWS

Most studies of the operation of vagrancy laws in Britain and the United States have depicted the laws as overt instruments of ruling-class control. To orthodox Marxist historians they represent a mechanism for disciplining the large numbers of unemployed and underemployed necessary to the operation of a capitalist labour market. Industrial capitalism needed this 'reserve army' both to discipline its workers and to maintain low wages, and required also a means of controlling that army. Sidney Harring argues that the various 'Tramp Acts' passed from the 1870s on 'offer a classic example of class legislation – that is, laws specifically designed by one class to be used as weapons in controlling a weaker class.'[11] Others provide a subtler, but in many respects similar, interpretation, seeing the vagrancy laws as the means by which the Victorian middle classes imposed 'respectable' values on those who threatened the comfortable and settled bourgeois world of church, community, and industry. Paul Boyer presents a 'social control' thesis, which depicts an urban middle-class struggle to combat apprehended disorder in the new industrial cities through a mixture of repression, self-help-based charity, and institutions for the inculcation of morality and discipline. A similar interpretation is offered by a variety of local studies; Lawrence Friedman and Robert Percival, for example, conclude from the evidence of one California county that 'as the police patrolled the streets looking for vagrants, brawlers and drunks, they were also patrolling the moral and social edges of society, trawling for deviance, enforcing standard norms of good bourgeois conduct.'[12]

Despite such interpretive differences, common threads can be discerned in the work of all who have examined vagrancy in late nineteenth-century America. There is general agreement that America 'discovered' the vagrant problem in the depression years of the 1870s, and that the level of concern about the problem corresponded with fluctuations in the economy. The importance of the vagrant lay not in what he or she represented, be that social disreputableness, outlawry, or nascent labour radicalism. American society responded to the vagrant 'menace' principally with repression – long prison terms with hard labour – but also through an expansion of public and private charity, albeit charity that came increasingly to stress the importance of a labour test.[13] Vagrants presented similar problems in late nineteenth-century British society. David Jones argues that '[t]o many Victorians the vagrant was the most glaring affront to the trinity of work, respectability and religion,' even though 'a degree of mobility and homelessness was an inevitable part of the change from a rural to an urban and industrial society.'[14]

In the only Canadian work on vagrants in the later nineteenth-century James Pitsula paints a picture very similar to the American one: the number of vagrants greatly increased in the 1870s, the incidence of vagrancy fluctuated with economic conditions, and the presence of vagrants was met with a combination of middle-class private charity and public repression. Adopting a social control model, he argues that 'the tramp symbolised rejection of the work ethic and middle class values,' and that 'if social order was to be preserved, this rebellious figure had to be suppressed.'[15] In this essay I reach similar conclusions about another of Canada's major cities. While acknowledging that a variety of forces helped to shape the use of criminal sanctions against vagrants, I argue that the principal determinant was, as elsewhere, fear of the vagrant as a deviant, disruptive force, a fear that was manifested despite the limited degree of industrialization in Halifax during these years.

IMPRISONMENT FOR VAGRANCY, 1864–90

I have divided the incarceration statistics set out in table 1 into three principal categories – vagrants, drunks, and 'others.'[16] Vagrancy is shown as a percentage of all committals excluding those for drunkenness, which were always the most numerous. This separation demonstrates that 23 per cent of incarcerations for the more serious petty crimes were for vagrancy. In some years, notably 1867 and 1879, it was the most frequent cause of committals other than drunkenness, and rarely did it fall below second or third in importance. Measured by total committals men offended the vagrancy laws more often than women did, although only marginally so – 52.6 to 47.4 per cent. These are high rates for women. Rachel Vorspan demonstrates that 85 per cent of vagrants convicted in England during the second half of the nineteenth century were men; the equivalent figure for Massachusetts between 1866 and 1873 was 75 per cent.[17] Moreover, all historical and contemporary work on female criminals suggests that crime rates are much lower for women – 20 to 30 per cent of all crime.[18] The Halifax figures are skewed by two factors. First, the ratio of female to male crime is always larger for petty offences. Second, the substantial prostitute population typical of a port and garrison town must have considerably inflated the statistics. While it was not uncommon for women to be convicted because they were begging or had no place of residence, many of the female vagrants here were prostitutes. Given that approximately 30 per cent of all committals were meted out to women, it is reasonable to assume that prostitution accounted for the difference between that figure and the 47 per cent of vagrants who were female.[19]

The correlation between vagrancy committals and fluctuations in the economy is instructive. Like other major Maritime communities, Halifax was dependent on shipping, ship-repairing, and the lumber trade, and to a much lesser extent on ship-building. Ship manufacture dominated the economies of many of the Nova Scotia outports, towns that had been home to some of the vagrants imprisoned in the capital. The end of the American civil war and the abrogation of American reciprocity in 1866

TABLE 1
Returns of Committals to the City Prison, 1864–90

Year	Vagrants: Female	Vagrants: Male	Vagrants: Total	Drunks	Others	Total	Percentage*
1864	59	45	93	173	173	439	35.0
1865	49	29	78	264	172	514	31.2
1866	57	30	87	240	202	529	30.1
1867	53	46	99	119	215	433	31.5
1868	40	43	83	231	206	520	28.7
1869	22	38	60	255	184	499	24.6
1870	26	23	49	310	183	542	21.1
1871	14	21	35	304	170	509	17.1
1872	21	27	48	326	211	585	18.5
1873	31	35	66	246	210	522	24.0
1874	38	27	65	282	169	516	27.8
1875	28	27	55	302	171	528	24.3
1876	24	33	57	305	264	626	17.7
1877	22	33	55	265	214	534	20.4
1878	29	63	92	273	205	570	31.0
1879	37	50	87	243	205	535	29.8
1880	26	36	62	245	223	530	21.7
1881	11	15	26	186	175	387	13.0
1882	9	14	23	229	167	419	12.1
1883	16	9	25	167	140	332	15.1
1884	9	21	30	163	109	302	21.6
1885	6	18	24	199	145	368	14.2
1886	6	24	30	149	128	307	19.0
1887	5	15	20	100	115	235	14.8
1888	8	13	21	104	116	241	15.3
1889	15	16	31	142	150	323	17.1
1890	15	10	25	188	143	356	14.9
TOTAL	676	750	1,426	6,010	4,764	12,200	23.0

*Of vagrancy to all incarcerations, excluding drunkenness

reduced both the demand for and the competitiveness of Nova Scotia goods there, and a decreased British demand for lumber and ships after 1873 contributed to the decline and eventual eclipse of the principal traditional props of the export economy of the Maritime provinces. The 1870s was a decade of depression, but economic fortunes were restored by the introduction of the National Policy and, more important, by the global economic upturn of the late 1870s. The result was a growth in manufacturing in the Maritimes and a shift away from dependence on the traditional staples. While this growth represented no more than partial industrialization and was not sustained in later decades, in the 1880s industrial output in Nova Scotia increased by 66 per cent over the previous decade; indeed the growth rate was the highest among the eastern provinces.[20]

The rates of incarceration for vagrancy correspond closely to the performance of the local economy. The total number of men incarcerated was considerably higher in the depression years of the late 1860s (probably because of the failure of the fishery that sustained so many of the surrounding counties) and in the period from 1873 to 1879 than in the better days of the 1880s.[21] The incarceration totals for women display the same trends after 1867. Between 1864 and 1867 the rates for women were very high, almost certainly because they were greatly inflated by prostitution convictions in a period when the size of the garrison was much greater than subsequently. The general causal relationship between the state of the economy and vagrancy is illustrated by the figures for vagrancy as a percentage of non-drunkenness committals. Only in 1876 did they dip below 20 per cent during the period between 1873 and 1880, and they achieved that level only once in the next decade, in 1884.

The vagrant 'problem' was also partly the result of migration trends during these years. Halifax grew from a city of 25,026 in 1861 to 29,582 in 1871, to 36,100 in 1881, and to 38,556 in 1891.[22] This growth was not due, as it had been in earlier decades, to the large-scale immigration of trans-Atlantic paupers. During this period immigration from Europe was low, and the provincial government exerted itself to attract only the sturdy, well-founded immigrant.[23] Population growth had a localized economic origin – migration from the more depressed areas of the Maritimes, which from the early 1860s experienced a marked increase in out-migration. A first stop for many of those who would eventually travel south and west was the Maritime city. Urban growth and vagrancy convictions were highest during the 1870s, the decade of recession; the better times of the 1880s stemmed the flow of tramps and migrants.[24]

More incarcerations occurred during the summer months of May to September than at other times; the fewest people were jailed in the winter and early spring (see table 2). There are four probable explanations for this. First, more women were imprisoned as prostitutes during the months they were out on the streets and therefore visible. Women prisoners outnumbered men from May to July, and were only slightly less numerous in August; in all other months men predominated. Second, vagrants convicted in the fall, especially late in the fall, would often serve out their

TABLE 2
Monthly Incidence of Imprisonments for Vagrancy

Month	Males	Females	Total
January	56	28	84
February	52	47	99
March	56	44	100
April	50	43	93
May	50	67	117
June	70	72	142
July	61	79	140
August	73	70	143
September	76	71	147
October	76	46	122
November	63	53	116
December	67	56	123
TOTAL	750	676	1,426

sentences with little remission wanted or granted during the winter; consistent recidivists would therefore not be 'available' for reconviction until at least the following spring. Third, poor-relief was more generally available during the winter, which meant that fewer offenders had to court conviction for shelter. Fourth, it was easier to appreciate the plight of the resident poor in winter when jobs were few than to sympathize with the visible prostitute, the wandering tramp, or the able-bodied unemployed of the summer months, who represented the outsider and the non-conformer. Few tramped from community to community during the worst of the Nova Scotia winter.[25]

Most vagrants were in their late twenties and early thirties, and the relative consistency in age throughout the period suggests a considerable turnover in the vagrant population (see table 3).[26] Vagrants were not merely an incorrigible rump of Halifax society, but a renewable class of prostitutes, strangers, and able-bodied unemployed. As the vagrants of one generation either moved on or became old or infirm enough to qualify for public poor-relief, they were replaced by others unable or unwilling to find a regular place in society.

Most vagrants were of prime working age, but the laws were also applied to the very old and the very young. Michael McCarthy was in his seventies when he was sent up in December 1864 and again in July 1867. On each occasion he remained in prison for only two weeks; in 1864 he was released on Christmas Eve by order of the lieutenant-governor,

TABLE 3
Age, Religion, and Ethnicity of Imprisoned Vagrants – Selected Years

Year	Average age	Roman Catholics	Protestants	Blacks
1864	29.7	36	39	16
1867	28.1	59	22	8
1870	34.4	35	8	2
1873	35.1	35	22	6
1875	30.2	29	18	6
1877	32.6	27	19	2
1880	34.1	28	21	8
1883	29.0	10	9	1
1885	32.5	12	11	2
1887	29.2	11	2	1
1890	31.7	9	11	4
TOTAL	31.4	284	188	56

and in 1867 he was sent to the poor asylum.[27] Similarly, John Colbert was seventy when he was imprisoned in March and again in April of 1875. On each occasion he received a short sentence (ten and twenty days respectively), which was much lighter than the average at the time. Pat Cody was imprisoned twenty-two times between 1864 and 1880, by which time he was in his late seventies.

A total of eighty-one, or 5.6 per cent of the committals were children aged sixteen and under. Andrew George and Susan Scott, both aged fourteen, received twelve-month sentences in September 1867, although both served their time in the reformatory and the poor asylum respectively. While most of the very young and the very old did end up in institutions more suitable than the city prison, Halifax society often dealt with them initially through the criminal law. Eleven-year-old Harry Fuller served almost all of a three-month sentence imposed in August 1880. James McMaster, a boy of twelve, was sentenced to a year in October 1880, and stayed in prison for seven weeks until his father in Saint John sent three dollars to pay for his return to New Brunswick. The Holihan brothers, eleven-year-old Edward and fifteen-year-old John, were both given twelve-month sentences in November 1875 for the dual offences of vagrancy and 'leaving the Poor House.'

A substantial majority, some 60 per cent, of the imprisoned vagrants were Catholic at a time when Catholics made up approximately 40 per cent of the city's population. Moreover, they generally comprised either a minority or a narrow majority of persons arrested for all petty offences.[28] It appears that their economic status caused them to be singled out by a law aimed primarily at the unemployed. They were a relatively impoverished group within the city, and had long been the major recipients of public and private poor-relief.[29]

Blacks, the city's most visible and discriminated-against minority, also appear in disproportionate numbers: 3 per cent of Halifax residents, but at least 11 per cent of imprisoned vagrants, were black.[30] Again, we can look for the cause of their overrepresentation in their status as an economically disadvantaged community; racial prejudice, of course, would also have rendered them susceptible.[31] Yet they do not seem to have been arrested every time they offended. One Halifax newspaper reported in 1872, 'The coloured people that one sees in this city, all beg, with few exceptions.'[32] This comment, though obviously an exaggeration, suggests that begging by blacks was highly visible, and that the vagrancy laws could have been applied more rigorously against them. They may have been charged with lesser offences, or perhaps the community felt that it was acceptable for members of the long-established resident black population to panhandle on the streets, but not for whites. The small number of blacks and their long history as a depressed minority within the city may have resulted in their not being considered a threat, which may have meant that they were not expected to conform to white middle-class standards.

Vagrants whose place of origin was designated 'Ireland' in the registers were not necessarily recent Irish immigrants; the designation probably stood for first- or second-generation Catholics of Irish origin (see table 4). Occasionally individuals reappeared on subsequent convictions as having been born elsewhere, or they were sent to other communities on release. The use of this designation probably reflects the preponderance of Catholics among convicted vagrants, and the desire to categorize vagrants as aliens. More than 20 per cent of vagrants were said to be from Ireland. This stands in marked contrast to figures for all arrests; in 1886–7 persons of Irish origin numbered 120 out of 1,552 and in 1888–9 53 out of 1,244 (7.7 and 4.2 per cent respectively).[33] In fact a substantial minority of convicted vagrants were local people. Halifax consistently appears as the most frequently named single place of origin: over the years some of those imprisoned altered their place of origin to Halifax. The migration patterns discussed above are confirmed by the 28 per cent who came from other Atlantic Canadian communities.

Analyses of sentencing and release practices reveal trends similar to

TABLE 4
Place of Origin of Convicted Vagrants – Selected Years

Year	Halifax	Ireland	Nova Scotia	Atlantic provinces	USA	Other	Total
1864	21	16	17	12	2	7	75
1867	28	20	12	11	4	6	81
1870	10	16	11	6	0	0	43
1873	18	16	5	9	2	7	57
1875	21	8	7	5	1	5	47
1877	16	11	5	3	3	8	46
1880	20	10	7	4	3	5	49
1883	1	3	10	0	1	3	18
1885	14	1	2	1	1	5	24
1887	9	1	1	1	0	1	13
1890	9	2	7	0	1	1	20
TOTAL	167	104	84	52	18	48	473
PERCENTAGE	35.9	21.6	17.5	10.8	3.9	10.3	100

TABLE 5
Sentencing and Time Served – Selected Years

Year	Average sentence (months)	Average time served (months)
1864	5.48	4.07
1867	7.74	3.73
1870	6.00	3.42
1873	9.46	5.38
1875	10.84	4.61
1877	10.95	4.56
1880	10.45	2.34
1883	2.15	na
1885	3.54	na
1887	3.00	na
1890	3.30	na

those for conviction rates (see table 5). Through the 1870s sentences of up to a year were common, and nine to ten months was the average duration. Forty-five of the fifty-five sentences given out in 1875, for example, were for twelve months. In the 1880s the length of sentences decreased drastically, demonstrating a more lenient attitude to vagrants in better economic times.

The statistics for average time served are instructive in a number of ways. Like all petty offenders, vagrants received substantial remission of their sentences.[34] The average time served decreased sharply after 1880; in 1880 sentences remained long but the average time served fell to less than 2.5 months. Release dates are not given after 1882, but time served throughout the 1880s must have been less than time imposed and must therefore have been substantially down from the 1870s.

Within the broad trends indicated by the statistics, considerable inconsistencies occurred. Mary Mackenzie, aged twenty-one, and Ann Mahony, aged twenty-three, were each sentenced to twelve months on 5 July 1867. Mackenzie was out a month later, while Mahony remained incarcerated until 10 April 1868. Some clues to the reasons for such inconsistencies can be drawn from the cases of six prostitutes who were each awarded six-month sentences in September 1864. Four of them stayed in jail until the middle of the following March; the other two were let out in December to go to the poor-house and to the female reformatory. Some inconsistencies can be explained by recidivism; Ann Mahony, for example, was a consistent offender,[35] as was Eliza Cahill, who was convicted three times in 1867 (5 March, 14 August, and 1 November); she served two months on the first two convictions and eleven on the third. In many cases, however, the records do not provide such logical explanations for differences in release dates.

A major question to be answered before a vagrant was released was whether he or she could be sent elsewhere. On at least 126 occasions during these years the old, the young, the sick, and the indigent were variously dispatched to the poor-house, the hospital, reformatories, or the industrial school very shortly after committal.[36] Pat Cody is recorded as having been sent almost immediately to the poor-house on eight of the twenty-one occasions that he was imprisoned for vagrancy; Edward Sheehan, who was committed thirty-two times, was sent there five times. Others served varying amounts of their sentences before being moved. John Mahony and John Warren, sentenced in early December 1879, were set to the poor-house just after Christmas, perhaps in a spirit of seasonal charity. It was not uncommon, however, for a vagrant to serve a longer portion of the sentence before being sent to another institution.[37] The provincial hospital received a number of ex-prisoners. When forty-seven-year-old William Devines was sentenced to twelve months in July 1868, he served only a little more than a quarter of that time before being sent to hospital 'broken in health.' The practice of sending children to reformatories was commonplace, and drew applause from city officials.[38]

Other vagrants obtained their release by agreeing to accept a job or to leave the city. This method of disposing of offenders was implemented at least 114 times. Most women went into domestic service, although Ann Mahony had served only two weeks of a twelve-month sentence in March 1873 when she agreed to go to work as a nurse in a smallpox hospital. She could not have stayed long, since she received a ninety-day sentence on 9 July of the same year. Annie Gore was given the same dubious privilege in March 1878. Among those who got their release by agreeing to go elsewhere was Barbara Gibson, aged thirty, from Saint John, who was sentenced to twelve months in December 1876. She stayed in prison through the worst of the winter, and was released and sent back to New Brunswick in early April 1877. In all she was 'expelled' from the city five times.[39] Mary Barry, twice imprisoned in 1867, was sent to Antigonish by order of the stipendiary magistrate. Following her second conviction in 1867 and her bad conduct in prison, Ellen Hawke was put on a ship for her native England. Robert Boyle, from Prince Edward Island, served half of a three-month sentence in 1867 before being released and sent to New Brunswick. The overall reduction in time served in 1880 can largely be attributed to a greatly increased tendency to remove vagrants from the area. The three vagrants convicted in January 1880, for example, were released and sent away after having served two to three months of their twelve-month sentences.

Many of Halifax's vagrants were repeatedly institutionalized in prison, the provincial hospital, the poor-house, or reform school. The impression of lives of poverty, unemployment, and misery is confirmed by the fact that many of the vagrancy committals were meted out to repeat offenders. While 540 (74 per cent) of the 731 individuals who appear in the registers were imprisoned only once for vagrancy, they represented 38 per cent of the total committals; 62 per cent were accounted for by the 191 individuals who were imprisoned more than once (see table 6). Recidivism was thus a significant feature of the vagrant population; in fact these figures underestimate it, since they do not include incarcerations that occurred before and after the period between 1864 and 1890 or those imposed for other offences. The importance of recidivism should not be exaggerated, however. The city's 'old lag' population, those who were constantly in and out of prison as vagrants, numbered only eight men and eleven women. They represent a relatively small proportion (21.2 per cent) of the total number of incarcerations. Within this group women were the more likely recidivists; they also accounted for a higher proportion of the offences than their numbers warranted. The women were imprisoned an

TABLE 6
Recidivism

Number of committals	Number of offenders			Total committals			Percentage of total committals
	Male	Female	Total	Male	Female	Total	
1	341	199	540	341	199	540	38.4
2	45	44	89	90	88	178	12.7
3	16	19	35	48	57	105	7.5
4	8	6	14	32	24	56	4.0
5	5	6	11	25	30	55	3.9
6	2	4	6	12	24	36	2.6
7	2	6	8	14	42	56	4.0
8	0	3	3	0	24	24	1.7
9	3	0	3	27	0	27	1.9
10	1	2	3	10	20	30	2.2
11–15	5	6	11	63	77	140	10.0
16–23	3	5	8	61	97	156	11.1
TOTAL	431	300	731	723	682	1,405	100.0

average of 2.27 times each, the men 1.67 times; women were liable for imprisonment as vagrants both because they were poor and homeless and because they were prostitutes.

For some, the cycle of poverty, vagrancy, and petty crime proved impossible to break. Four blacks – George Diminus, and John, Martha, and Henry Killum – were incarcerated 16, 11, 8, and 13 times respectively during these years; the three men usually appeared together. Edward Sheehan was jailed 23 times for vagrancy; he was frequently sent to the poor-house, and was once dispatched to his brother in Shubenacadie. The hapless Pat Cody went up on 22 occasions for vagrancy and many more times for drunkenness and other offences. In 1874 a newspaper noted that he had been 'before the Court a score of times' and approved a sentence of one year for being drunk and disorderly and assaulting a policeman.[40] John McDonnell, aged forty-nine, was in and out of prison for vagrancy 5 times in 1867–8 alone. First convicted and given a thirty-day sentence on 29 March 1867, he was released on 27 April, recommitted on 7 May, released in mid-August, convicted three days later and given an indefinite sentence, let out after a week, and picked up again on 11 September and sentenced to ninety days; he served his sentence, but received another one shortly after Christmas and stayed in prison until late March 1868. He appeared 9 times in the years between 1866 and 1870, but never after 10 June 1870 when, at the age of sixty-three, he was released upon the death of his wife.

Most vagrants were unskilled labourers, the marginal poor, the outcasts of Halifax society. Their numbers were swelled in the winter months by transient workers from among the idle ships' crewmen and the outports.[44] Only thirty-two of those imprisoned for vagrancy paid their fines and got out early during these years; most of those were women who had been convicted as prostitutes. The registers reveal many pathetic life histories in their terse descriptions and comments. They tell us about Patrick Maloney, a young man of about nineteen, a little over three feet tall and a cripple, who was jailed four times as a vagrant between August 1864 and October 1866. Some of these people died in prison, such as Johanna Freeman and William Flinn, who died on 26 October 1867 and 25 April 1880 respectively. Two young men, Robert Jones and Thomas Smith, might have died in mid-November 1878 had they not been put inside for vagrancy; they were spending the cold nights in a large packing-case.[42] An apparently happier fate befell Anne Burke and Thomas Drew. Burke was committed twelve times for vagrancy between 1869 and 1879, by which time she was in her mid-forties. Some of her convictions were for prostitution. On 13 November 1879 she was released early from her most recent incarceration so that she could marry her fellow inmate Drew and go with him to Saint John. Drew was a little younger than Burke, and had been jailed only twice before for vagrancy. Unfortunately, Burke appears again; she was sentenced to ninety days in July 1880.

The degradation of those made subject to the vagrancy laws is shown by the extent to which the prison was used as a winter refuge. People listed as going in 'at own request' appear consistently in the registers. Not everyone appreciated the regime, however; at least thirteen vagrants escaped during these years. James MacDermott, a twenty-four-year-old Halifax Catholic, asked to go to jail in late November 1879, and was not released until the following February. On 4 September 1879 the *Herald* reported that the groom-to-be Thomas Drew went to the police station asking for shelter and 'was kindly granted one for 12 months.' Later that year two men were discovered 'in an unfurnished rookery ... sitting down around a coal scuttle in which there was a fire burning.' Because they had no place of residence they were sent up for ninety days.[43] Mary and Martha Killum 'applied to be sent up to Rockhead' in December 1879 because 'dere was nuffin' doing' and 'the twain went up to board at the City's expense until the end of May.'[44]

The use of jail as refuge, by no means unusual in North American cities during the later nineteenth century,[45] was also reflected in the pattern of time-serving. Persons sentenced in spring or summer served less time than those convicted after 1 November, who rarely emerged before late March. Johanna Power, for example, was given a twelve-month sentence with the option of a fine in January 1879; she went to prison until April, then paid the fine and left. One of the clearest examples of this practice is the case of Mary Walsh, whose sentence for vagrancy in December 1864 is given as 'for the winter.'[46]

Many of the city's respectable citizens disapproved of the jails' being used as shelters. The *Acadian Recorder* thought it 'singular' that prison should be 'preferred to the Poor House by numbers of that class of persons, male and female, who figure in the annals of the Police Court.'[47] In 1885 the mayor of Halifax argued that hard labour would discourage the practice.[48] There was much hypocrisy in such views, considering that many of those sent to prison for vagrancy were guilty of nothing more than having no home, and should have been admitted to the poor-house. In 1886 the prison governor was moved to make this very point in his annual report.[49] The use of the prison as a place of refuge is stark proof of the dislocated, hopeless lives of many of Halifax's vagrant class.[50]

HALIFAX SOCIETY AND THE DISCIPLINING OF THE VAGRANT

During these years the Halifax middle class responded to vagrants in much the same way as their counterparts in other North American cities. The vagrant was viewed as a dangerous element in society who should be treated severely by the police and courts. There was some recognition that unemployment and endemic poverty were in part responsible for the vagrancy problem, but most public and private poor-relief schemes emphasized the distinction between the deserving and the undeserving poor. Prison work and discipline were toughened up to discourage the use of prison as a refuge, public poor-relief underwent some reorganization, and private charitable agencies strove, principally through the medium of the labour test, to force the vagrant population to conform to middle-class notions of the work ethic and labour discipline.

This reaction to vagrancy mirrored that of many American cities, where increasing attention was being paid to the phenomenon. Lawyers, academics, charity officials, and law enforcement agents all took an interest, and the vagrant was condemned in many forums. He or she was 'lazy' and 'shiftless,' 'a barbarian, openly at war with society' who would refuse to work if '[c]ertain charitable eccentricities – such as soup-houses, night shelters, and depots for the free distribution of articles of subsistence' were made readily available.[51] The vagrant was not merely deviant but dangerous, always likely to commit other crimes. Although the depressions of the later nineteenth century also brought an acceptance of the need for some measure of relief for vagrants and other members of the urban unemployed, a labour test was generally insisted upon. In part, of course, this was done so that charitable institutions and societies could produce a saleable product to encourage contributions. But behind this policy there also lay a belief that the fundamental cause of the vagrancy problem was character.[52] Rare indeed were the sentiments of one author who complained that Americans 'make the chief causes [of vagrancy] ignorance, intemperance, thriftlessness, and indiscriminate charity,' and reminded his readers the 'the poorer classes of the United States had recently emerged from at least seven years of unparalleled misery.'[53]

Canadian approaches to the vagrant problem differed little from American ones. Before 1850 crime and poverty had frequently been blamed on immigrants, especially Irish Catholics, and on the seasons. The second half of the century saw in Ontario a 'critical transition from a perception of the seasonality of poverty to an apprehension of a permanent class of dependent urban poor.' The result was an increasing gulf 'between the respectable classes who define what society is and the disreputable elements who exist beyond their reach,' and a concomitant 'explosion of concern' about crime and poverty and 'the institutional remedies ... to meet them.'[54] Against this background James Pitsula's study of tramps in Toronto tells a familiar story. The *Globe* typically characterized the vagrant as 'dissipated, shiftless, and it is to be feared vicious,' while the *Star* recommended the lash as a suitable punishment.[55] Charity organizers fought hard for a labour test – stone-breaking – and approved its financially and morally beneficial results. The 1891 report of the Royal Commission on Prisons admitted that vagrants were not universally idle, that some were genuinely travelling in search of work.[56] But a series of petitions sent to the House of Commons in the 1880s demonstrates that in Canada, as in the United States, the general trend was towards a harsher, more disciplinary approach to vagrancy. A total of twelve municipalities in Ontario, Quebec, and British Columbia asked the House to amend the law to allow vagrants to be sentenced to hard labour on the roads outside the prison.[57] While this request may in part have reflected municipal parsimony, it also represents a perception that vagrants should be forced to make a contribution to society.

In Halifax local newspapers and city officials took a keen interest in poverty and crime; the underside of Halifax society was plainly visible and the activities of its members widely reported in the press.[58] The Halifax élite nevertheless took a special pride in what they saw as the peaceful nature of the city. Newspapers and the *Annual Reports* repeatedly stressed the city's 'character for being ... orderly.' Halifax was 'the most orderly city in the world for its population,' and it was 'a subject for congratulation' that 'there is a marked absence of serious crimes.'[59] These smug assertions did not paint an accurate picture; the prevalence of warnings about the dangers of criminals testify to that.[60] But they do suggest a middle-class longing for a safe, comfortable, and respectable city.

In these circumstances it is not surprising that attitudes towards vagrants were harsh. They were depicted as dishonest characters, idlers who hoped to get a free ride from society. Bitter denunciations and ironic accounts of their activities appeared frequently in the press. In 1880 the *Herald* reported that a 'most delapidated specimen of the *genus* tramp' had been found in Point Pleasant Park, and that he had claimed in a foreign accent to have walked from Chicago. This was clearly a ploy to excite 'a greater compassion with his forlorn condition.' The following day the paper noted succinctly that he had been put away for twelve months.[61] One writer was amused that the town of Dartmouth had 'kindly agreed to entertain' a vagrant, while another man, 'going to the [police] Station for shelter and having no fixed abode, was kindly granted one for 12 months.'[62] In 1879 residents were warned that 'a delegation of tramps' was on its way from Saint John. Their arrival may have prompted an article in the same newspaper three days later: entitled 'Begging and Beggars,' it warned that 'this is the season of the year when most frequently is heard the voice of the professional street beggar.' Residents should avoid succumbing to a seasonal charitable urge, lest 'the habit of professional begging, which seems to be on the increase in this city ... be encouraged.'[63] Begging children attracted particular attention; the newspapers claimed that parents trained them in the art and that the result would be a generation of professional vagrants.

At the root of these attitudes was a perception of the vagrant as someone who contributed little or nothing to society. One alderman in 1866 condemned the practice of sending vagrants to prison at public expense when they might more usefully be employed on public works.[64] Mixing its condemnation of vice with its self-interest, the *Citizen* suggested that 'loafers' who relied on charity could be employed selling newspapers. Such work was always available, and there was no excuse for the unemployed to refuse it: '[W]e submit that people who can get work – and light work at that, and won't work, deserve to starve, and boys who would rather beg and steal than earn an honest living should be arrested and punished without the alternative of a fine. Give them three months with hard labour and an occasional flogging, and it will have wonderful effect on their future career.'[65]

Although more compassionate references to seasonal unemployment and the plight of the poor do appear,[66] it was generally considered that unwillingness to work was the root cause of the problem. A fear of the danger the vagrant posed to society dominated middle-class attitudes. The following is typical:

> If one of these robust and healthy-looking beggars is asked to do a job of work for remuneration, he, or she, will sheer off immediately ... It is a notorious fact that it is almost impossible to get any person, old or young, in this city, to go an errand, or do any other casual job; and when such labor is secured, it has to be paid for at twice, or thrice, its worth. This is not an indication of much poverty in Halifax. The crowds of dirty loungers in the City Court House of a morning, or about the street corners, who contemptuously decline employment when offered them, would lead any stranger to suppose that poverty was unknown here.[67]

This attitude towards vagrants was reflected in three aspects of city policy: an emphasis on police efficiency and curial strictness; an attempt to render prison a less hospitable environment; and, most significant, a mobilization of citizens to impose a labour test for charitable relief.

The city court structure underwent significant change at the beginning of this period. From 1841 the court had been presided over by the mayor and aldermen. This system came under attack in the 1860s because of inconsistencies in procedure and sentences and alleged bias.[68] In 1867 the elected officials were replaced by a stipendiary magistrate, who had security of tenure during good behaviour.[69] The magistrate from 1867 until 1886 was Henry Pryor, a barrister and a former mayor of the city, who had judicial experience in the old Mayor's Court.[70] As stipendiary he had jurisdiction over all cases except those involving treason, homicide, burglary, and arson, and at first his appointment was expected to be 'of great good as regards the morality of the city.'[71] He did not entirely live up to that expectation. He ruled his courtroom with an iron hand and with little regard for the niceties of procedure, but his sentencing, which was often 'tailored ... to fit the person, not the crime,' caused him to be regarded as 'arbitrary, unprofessional and irascible.'[72]

Pryor's treatment of vagrants fitted this general pattern. Long sentences were frequently imposed, especially in the 1870s, and some offenders were particularly unlucky. Anne Weston left Rockhead prison on 31 July 1879; she was picked up that day for being drunk and disorderly and a vagrant, and sentenced to sixty days more. Yet on other occasions the accused were treated more leniently. When John Carey promised to leave the city to find work, he was allowed to go. Julia Martin and Margaret Chandler both received twelve-month terms for vagrancy 'with the understanding that they might be let out if they behave themselves.' Mary McNamara was told to leave the city after having been out of prison only two weeks.[73] Some offenders escaped the prison, without having to go elsewhere, through what seems to have been a hallmark of Pryor's court – the granting of 'a chance.' All classes of offenders, including vagrants, regularly appealed for 'a chance' and on occasion got it, with a strict warning that the next offence would bring a year in prison. Hannah Baker got a chance because she had been released only a few days previously; Henry Downey was also let off, but when he asked for shelter at the police station a week later Pryor sent him up. When Thomas Drew came to the police station in July 1879 complaining that he had no work and nowhere to live, he was let off with the warning that 'if he came back again he would get work at Rockhead for 12 months.' Margaret Schofield, charged with being drunk and a common vagrant, was given a chance when it was shown that she had stayed clear of police-court trouble for fourteen months and was living at the Female Inebriate Home run by Mrs Harrison, who was prepared to take her back.[74] Leading citizens may have been dissatisfied with some of Pryor's decisions, but they could do nothing about a judge with security of tenure. Perhaps more important than the individual cases of leniency, however, was the fact that the consistently harsh sentences meted out to vagrants were as much Pryor's work as the granting of 'chances.'[75]

The second public institution concerned with vagrants, the police force, witnessed considerable growth as well as increased public demands for more efficient policing. The force grew from 33 men in 1864 to 40 in 1867; it reached a high of 49 in the mid-1870s, and was reduced again to between 40 and 44 throughout the 1880s.[76] It is tempting to ascribe the growth in police numbers simply to the increases in population, but to do so would be to disregard the fact that the size of the force decreased in the 1880s while the population continued to grow. In fact, policing policy was influenced not only by population but also by public concern over crime rates and the constraints of municipal finances. While calls for more policemen from the press, the city marshal, and the mayors were not uncommon, the desire for protection conflicted always with municipal parsimony.[77] Economy nevertheless seems to have taken a back seat during the 1870s, the years when public concern about vagrants was at its highest.

Of more concern than an increase in the size of the force was a perceived need to improve the force's quality. On many occasions the Halifax police seem to have been little more acceptable to their masters than those whom they were supposed to control. Reports and complaints about policemen drunk on duty and neglecting their offices appear frequently, negating City Marshal Cotter's claim that the men under his command were 'steady and sober.'[78] The city council's police committee spent most of its time dealing with the officers' derelictions of duty.[79] The prevalence of such complaints makes clear the public's desire for a better force, and a variety of reforms were introduced. Pay rates were raised in the early 1870s, which produced a discernible improvement, although the men petitioned council again in 1884 for further increases.[80] Cotter also tightened internal discipline; while abuses did recur, complaints lessened through the 1880s, although there was a considerable fuss made in 1884 when a new appointee turned out to be a man who had resigned from the Dartmouth force rather than be dismissed.[81]

The culmination of the campaign for a more 'respectable' and efficient police force came in 1888 with the passage of a provincial statute regulating the police. It tightened entry requirements, made pay increases dependent on good behaviour, and specified punishments, especially suspension and dismissal, for violations of the regulations.[82] The period from 1870 to 1920 was one that saw an increasing emphasis on professionalism in urban American police forces, and to some extent Halifax followed this pattern. As elsewhere, the increased desire for 'law and order' in the city emanated in part from the vagrant problem. Better policing and stricter sentencing were measures to control the petty offenders who came from the lower working class, including vagrants. If Halifax saw less large-scale violence than other cities, it was because tramps and vagrants did not present as great a threat. But that is not to say that they were not perceived as a danger to accepted standards; the distinction is one of quantity, not quality.

This conclusion is strengthened by an examination of changes in the prison regime. At all times the regulations imposed strict standards on those 'sentenced to imprisonment' and on 'persons condemned to be confined ... as vagrants.'[83] By municipal ordinance 25 the sexes were strictly segregated, prisoners were kept in solitary confinement except when working, and all were put to work on the prison farm or, for those sentenced to hard labour, at stone-breaking.[84] Yet it seems that theory and practice were not always aligned, and that the regime was not enforced entirely to the council's liking. I have already noted the practice of using the prison as a winter refuge, and despite efforts to stop it the mayor could still complain in 1885 that '[m]any idle and vicious vagabonds looked upon the city prison as a home during the winter.' The governor of the prison was ordered to tighten discipline, and especially to increase hard labour; the mayor was subsequently pleased to note that 'under the present management these individuals prefer to look elsewhere' for winter shelter.[85] In addition, in order to make the maximum use of prisoners, a provincial statute of 1881 permitted Nova Scotia municipalities to employ prison labour outside the grounds of the institution.[86]

The most direct evidence of the public perception of vagrants comes from those engaged in the relief of the poor. The Halifax poor-house served for most of the nineteenth century as both poor-house and workhouse, caring for the sick, aged, and disabled as well as the able-bodied unemployed. Conditions were kept harsh lest some should prefer the poor-house to life outside an institution.[87] The public system was supplemented throughout the century by private societies, often affiliated with a religious denomination, which 'fulfilled a basic middle-class instinct for collective efforts as well as for emulating the fashionable course.'[88] This period saw both an expansion of public institutions for caring for society's unfortunates and a degree of consolidation and reorganization.[89] There emerged also a perception that some persons used the system to avoid working, a belief that transcended both genuine concern for the blameless poor and the ample evidence that the asylum supported primarily 'the aged, those whose constitutions have been broken down by dissipation and disease, and ... children.'[90] Nevertheless, the need for a labour test was constantly reiterated. Officials thought their able-bodied charges fundamentally work-shy, and put them to stone-breaking for their moral benefit and to compel them 'to contribute to their own support.'[91] This perception was echoed in the public debate over the choosing of a site for a new poor-house after the old one burned down in 1882. Many letters to the press urged that it be located outside the city so that the able-bodied would enjoy the life less: there were even suggestions that it simply be combined with the prison.[92]

Private charity reflected much the same attitude. The Night Refuge for the Homeless, established in May 1876 by James Potter, was intended initially to provide shelter, prevent crime, and most of all to 'check imposition.' Its avowed purpose was to discipline both beggars and almsgivers. Citizens were urged never to hand out money, but to direct vagrants to the refuge. A genuine case in need of shelter would go there; an 'impostor' would not. Thus the able-bodied would be forced to work for a living, and the middle classes could collectively provide alms and salve their consciences by indulging a charitable urge without risking the moral character of the recipient. Potter claimed to have reduced the problem substantially by 1879, and concentrated thereafter on his other charitable enterprise, a sailors' home. His claim is not supported by the evidence.[93]

The major voluntary organization of the period, the Halifax Association for Improving the Condition of the Poor, founded in 1866, espoused the same message. Run by some of the city's wealthiest and most influential citizens, including the industrialists Samuel Brookfield and John Doull, its aims were twofold: to relieve 'the temporary distress of the deserving poor' and to provide a 'check upon the vicious in their too generally successful schemes of imposture,' for 'many evils' resulted from 'indiscriminate almsgiving.'[94] Temporary outdoor relief was provided to those who warranted it, a visitor system was established to assess need, and male recipients of the association's largesse were put to work breaking stone, which was then sold to the city. These projects were supplemented by a soup-kitchen and by a service providing washing and cleaning work for women. The association operated form January to March every year. Citizens were constantly urged not to yield to the importunities of beggars but to direct them to the association's office. It was a scheme designed to co-ordinate and make more effective private charity in the city, to force the unemployed to work for their welfare, and to remove the unseemly spectacle of begging from the city streets.[95]

The work of the association received much favourable comment from the Halifax press. 'A scene of busy activity meets the eye of the visitor to the stone-breaking sheds,' the *Morning Chronicle* reported on 20 January 1875, adding that the association was performing 'a noble work.' When the council discussed its purchase of the broken stone in 1878, the mayor 'stated his willingness to personally guarantee $1,000 of the cost should the amount required not be forthcoming.'[96] Urging the council not to abandon its policy of buying the broken stone, the *Citizen* found 'no need ... to remind the citizens of the amount of good' the association had done.[97] Many citizens clearly believed that there were deserving poor and that duty required that such people be taken care of; one correspondent to the *Acadian Recorder* chided his fellow residents for ignoring their duty to God and their fellow man by not giving generously enough to the association.[98] For all contributors there was the satisfaction of seeing their names announced in the press.

In its attempt to maintain the often delicate balance between charity and discipline, the association did not receive universal or complete approval. A correspondent of the *Herald,* calling himself 'Syndicate,' noted in 1881 that the aim of private charity should be 'to elevate not to degrade,' which meant 'the decrease not the increase of begging.' He approved of the association's work, but wanted it and other relief organizations to establish a registry of recipients so that none could apply to more than one society. He argued that 'indiscriminate giving' was 'the cause of half the poverty in this City' because 'as long as the lazy and intemperate can get fuel and food, work for them is out of the question.'[99] When in January 1879 the city council refused to buy any more of the association's broken stone, 'A Ratepayer' complained that the result would be that 'all tests as to the willingness of the unfortunate applicants to work will cease, and thus one of the main objects of the Society will be frustrated.' He demanded that the council buy the stone, for the alternative would be increased expenditures to house the destitute in the prison or the poor-house.[100]

The association claimed some success. 'Street-begging in the winter months is much less common than it was formerly,' it boasted in 1874.[101] Yet begging by residents and transients alike continued, for at every annual meeting the members railed against the practice.[102] Two problems in particular hampered the association's work. First, on a number of occasions it had to fight to persuade the city to purchase stone; this happened in the winters of 1874–5, 1877–8, 1878–9, and 1885–6.[103] Second, charitable contributions were often in short supply. In March 1875 the funds of the society were exhausted before it had met all the demands on it; in March 1877 the funds were so depleted that 'visitors would have to exercise very great discrimination in giving relief.' In January 1878 the treasurer issued an urgent appeal for money, as 'barely one-third of the amount usually subscribed has been received.'[104] The unsurprising result was that poverty remained endemic and highly visible in the winter months. An apocryphal story in the *Acadian Recorder* in October 1879 showed how much more needed to be done. The paper recounted that John May and his wife were forced to live in 'a shanty' at the rear of a house on Grafton Street. The building had no glass in the windows and uneven floors and ceilings; it had been used as a wood-house, and was described by the reporter as a 'kennel.'[105]

The importance of the association lay in its perceived solution to the problems of vagrancy and poverty. It acknowledged that there were deserving paupers, but refused to accept that all those who sought relief were unable to work. The labour test, the demand that citizens not give alms indiscriminately in the street, and the calls for the punishment of those who would not work all point to middle-class desires to mix charity for the unfortunate with reformation and punishment for those who would not conform to accepted standards of industry.

CONCLUSION

In late nineteenth-century Halifax men and women of all ages were imprisoned on the basis of the vagrancy laws, most for 'crimes of poverty' – being homeless, wandering about, prostitution, and begging. Two principal conclusions emerge from this study. First, there was a correlation between economic conditions and the incidence of incarceration for vagrancy. Although not all crime can be explained by reference to changes in economic trends, the historian of crime cannot ignore such developments and the concomitant changes in social attitudes. In Halifax the depression of the 1870s accelerated economic and demographic trends already under way as the city adjusted both to the transition to industrial capitalism and to a redefinition of its role within the British North American and continental economies. Individuals shaken loose from their traditional employment roles as a result of this process contributed to the unemployment problem, and society was forced to reassess both the nature of the problem and the nature of the solution. The ways in which the vagrancy laws were administered formed a part of that solution.

This contemporary reassessment serves to introduce the second major conclusion of this paper, which concerns the attitudes of those at the forefront of disciplining the working class through the vehicle of the criminal law. Laws and institutions that had evolved gradually over centuries were increasingly perceived as inadequate. This perception did not represent so much a sharp break with the past as a redefinition of the seriousness of the problem, for society still focused on the inadequacy of the individual vagrant and his or her lack of moral fibre and commitment to the work ethic. There was none the less a greater emphasis on inculcating appropriate industrial attitudes and in restricting the definition of the worthy poor. Yet these developments took place in Halifax, a city that was only beginning the process of industrialization. The still predominantly commercial metropolis of Halifax reacted in much the same way as the advanced industrial cities of the U.S. eastern seaboard and the midwest.

This suggests that the importation of fears about vagrants was as important as any actual threat to the progress of the new industrialism. Yet whatever the cause, in Halifax as elsewhere, vagrancy laws were an important tool in the control of the non-conformist and the unemployed.

NOTES

1 SNS 1759, c. 1, s. 2

2 Between the fourteenth and the eighteenth centuries, when some forty-eight vagrancy statutes were passed in England, the definition of 'vagrant' underwent a number of changes. According to Sir James Stephen's analysis, which has remained largely unchallenged, from the late fourteenth century to the mid-sixteenth century the overriding function of vagrancy laws was labour control. From then until the mid-eighteenth century they served primarily as a criminal sanction to support the administration of the poor-law. Although this aspect remained important thereafter, it gradually gave way to a perception that the vagrant population represented a threat to order and morality. This change was marked by the case of *R* v. *Branworth* (1704) 6 Mod. 240, 87 ER 989, which established that although idleness per se was not sufficient to ground a conviction for vagrancy, the law should be used to control those likely to support themselves by crime or immorality rather than by industry. For the development of the law see, inter alia, J.F. Stephen *A History of the Criminal Law of England* (London: Macmillan 1883) vol. 3, 266–75; W. Chambliss 'A Sociological Analysis of the Law of Vagrancy' *Social Problems* 12 (1964–5) 67–77 and 'The Law of Vagrancy' in Chambliss, ed. *Criminal Law in Action* (New York: John Wiley 1984); A.L. Beier *Masterless Men: The Vagrancy Problem in England, 1560–1640* (London: Methuen 1986); and J.F. Pound and A.L. Beier 'Debate: Vagrants and the Social Order in Elizabethan England' *Past and Present* 71 (1976) 369–85.

3 SNS 1774, c. 5. In addition, a 1787 statute regulating servants included a provision that 'disorderly and beggarly persons' found 'strolling in any part of this Province' who could not demonstrate how they made their livelihood could be jailed and/or indentured to a master for up to seven years: SNS 1787, c. 6, s. 6.

4 RSNS 1851, c. 104

5 SNS 1864, c. 81, s. 134

6 SC 1869, c. 28; SC 1874, c. 31

7 SC 1881, c. 43. Its sponsor MacDonald noted that the latter measure was

'simply a short amendment required by the omission in an amendment to the Vagrant Act to insert the words "with or without hard labour" ... [because] one of the Judges, in administering the Act, held that without these words hard labour could not be imposed.' House of Commons *Debates* 1881, 1403. In 1886 the first federal statutory revision repealed the Vagrancy Act, and brought the offences in it into an Act Respecting Offences against Public Morals and Public Convenience. The same provisions formed sections 207 and 208 of the first Criminal Code in 1892: RSC 1886, c. 157, s. 8; H.E. Taschereau *The Criminal Code of the Dominion of Canada* (Toronto: Carswell 1893) 140–2.

8 (1888) 27 NBR 25 (SC); *Canadian Law Times* 9 (1989) 378; (1911) 19 CCC 86. See also P. Hogg *Constitutional Law of Canada* 2d ed. (Toronto: Carswell 1985) 399.

9 Cited in P. Craven 'Law and Ideology: The Toronto Police Court, 1850–1880' in D. Flaherty, ed. *Essays in the History of Canadian Law* vol. 2 (Toronto: The Osgoode Society 1983) 264.

10 *British Colonist* 18 Jan. 1870

11 S. Harring *Policing a Class Society: The Experience of American Cities 1865–1915* (New Brunswick, NJ: Rutgers University Press 1983) 201. In more detailed studies of Buffalo he demonstrates that the police used vagrancy laws to cope with large-scale protests by unemployed and immigrant workers and to suppress strikes. See Harring 'Class Conflict and the Suppression of Tramps in Buffalo, 1892–1894' *Law and Society Review* 11 (1976–7) 874–911. See also Harring and L.M. McMillin 'Buffalo Police, 1872–1900: Labor Unrest, Political Power and the Creation of the Police Institute' *Crime and Social Justice* 4 (1975) 5–14, and D. Rodgers 'Tradition, Modernity and the American Industrial Worker' *Journal of Interdisciplinary History* 7 (1977) 660.

12 P. Boyer *Urban Masses and Moral Order in America, 1820–1920* (Cambridge: Harvard University Press 1978); L. Friedman and R. Percival *The Roots of Justice: Crime and Punishment in Alameda Country, California, 1870–1910* (Chapel Hill: University of North Carolina Press 1975) 85. See also P. Ringenbach *Tramps and Reformers, 1873–1916: The Discovery of Unemployment in New York* (Westport, Conn.: Greenwood Press 1973).

13 In addition to the works by Boyer, Harring, and Ringenbach cited above, see also E. Monkkonen *The Dangerous Class: Crime and Poverty in Columbus, Ohio, 1860–1885* (Cambridge: Harvard University Press 1975); *Walking to Work: A History of Tramps in America* (Lincoln: University of Nebraska Press 1984), and *Police in Urban America, 1860–1920* (New York: Cambridge University Press 1981); R. Lane *Policing the City: Boston 1822–1885* (Cam-

bridge: Harvard University Press 1967) especially 193–4 and 206; J.F. Richardson *The New York Police: Colonial Times to 1901* (New York: Oxford University Press 1970) especially 264–7; D.R. Johnson *Policing the Urban Underworld: The Impact of Crime on the Development of the American Police, 1800–1887* (Philadelphia: Temple University Press 1979) passim; and K. Kusmer 'The Underclass: Tramps and Vagrants in American Society' (PHD thesis, University of Chicago 1980).

14 D. Jones 'The Vagrant and Crime in Victorian Britain: Problems of Definition and Attitude' in D. Jones, ed. *Crime, Protest, Community and Police in Nineteenth-Century Britain* (London: Routledge 1982) 178. See also D. Garland *Punishment and Welfare* (Brookfield, Vt: Gower 1985) 64, and D. Jones ' "A Dead Loss to the Community": The Criminal Vagrant in Mid-Nineteenth Century Wales' *Welsh History Review* 8 (1977) 312–43. Rachel Vorspan argues that concern about vagrants was so great by the late nineteenth century that, but for the First World War, Britain might have established penal labour colonies for the 'undeserving poor.' See 'Vagrancy and the New Poor Law in Late Victorian and Edwardian England' *English Historical Review* 92 (1977) 59–81.

15 J. Pitsula 'The Treatment of Tramps in Late Nineteenth Century Toronto' *Historical Papers* (1980) 116

16 This essay is based on prison records primarily because they are extant for this period, whereas local court records are only inconsistently available before 1880. My purpose is to examine trends over time, and thus I have chosen not to reproduce partial court statistics which would not be comparable to preceding decades. It should not be assumed from the use of prison records that all vagrants were imprisoned; the evidence presented later in this essay demonstrates clearly that this was not the case.

I have divided the statistics into three categories to isolate the offence of vagrancy and to delineate its importance in relation to the total number of offences that brought incarceration and to offences other than the most minor and most common one, drunkenness. Where an individual is noted in the records as having been guilty of more than one offence, including vagrancy, I have treated that as a vagrancy committal. The offences designated 'others' include assault, larceny, prostitution offences (lewd conduct, keeper or inmate of bawdy house), disorderly conduct, nuisances, breaches of the licensing laws, and a number of other infrequent crimes. Tables 1 and 2 are compiled from the City Prison Registers, PANS RG35-102, series 18B, vol. 2 (1864–73) and vol. 3 (1873–90). The registers are almost complete, although three months are missing from 1881 and 1882, and the figures for these years were averaged upwards accordingly. This accounts for the discrepancy between the total number of committals given in tables 1 and 2 (1,426) and that noted in table 6 (1,405).

17 Vorspan, 'Vagrancy and the New Poor Law' 60; M. Hindus *Prison and Plantation: Crime, Justice and Authority in Massachusetts and South Carolina, 1767–1878* (Chapel Hill: University of North Carolina Press 1978) 83.

18 See the essay by B. Jane Price elsewhere in this volume.

19 *Acadian Recorder* 10 July 1879; see also the essay by B. Jane Price elsewhere in this volume.

20 For Halifax's economy during this period see T.W. Acheson 'The National Policy and the Industrialisation of the Maritimes, 1880–1910' in D. Frank and P. Buckner, eds. *The Acadiensis Reader: Volume Two* (Fredericton: Acadiensis Press 1985) 176–201, and L.D. McCann 'Staples and the New Industrialism in the Growth of Post-Confederation Halifax' *Acadiensis* 8 (1979) 47–79.

21 See *Acadian Recorder* 30 Aug., 20 and 25 Nov. 1867; *Unionist* 5 and 18 Dec. 1867; *Morning Journal and Commercial Advertiser* 13 Mar. 1868; and *British Colonist* 9 Jan. 1868.

22 Canada *Censuses of Canada, 1608–1876* (Ottawa: Queen's Printer 1878); Canada *Census of Canada 1880–1881* (Ottawa: MacLean, Roger 1881); Canada *Census of Canada 1890–1891* (Ottawa: MacLean, Roger 1891).

23 See *JHA* 1879, app. 14 (Immigration Report), which announces the government's intention 'to discourage pauper immigration in whatever phase it may prevent itself' (at 2). Similar comments reappear frequently in subsequent years, along with laments that 'good' immigrants were not forthcoming.

24 A. Brookes 'Out-Migration from the Maritime Provinces, 1860–1900: Some Preliminary Considerations' in Frank and Buckner *Acadiensis Reader Two* 41. On labour mobility generally see S. Thernstrom and P. Knights 'Men in Motion: Some Data and Speculations about Urban Population Mobility in Nineteenth Century America' *Journal of Interdisciplinary History* 1 (1970) 7–35.

25 Contrast this with California, where vagrancy increased during the winter months as vagrants were attracted there by the climate: Friedman and Percival *Roots of Justice* 84.

26 The information in tables 3–6 has been abstracted from a complete name-list of all those imprisoned. The prison registers list age, religion, place of origin, offence, sentence, and release date. While the information provided by convicted persons was not always strictly accurate, a sample of this size is large enough to eliminate any significant errors. Where there was doubt as to identity, I counted a common name as representing more

than one person. The discrepancies between the totals for each year recorded here and the annual totals in table 1 are the result of incomplete information, or, more generally, of counting an individual only once for some purposes, such as place of origin, no matter how many times he or she offended in one year. Statistics were unavailable for average time served after 1880 in table 5 because release dates were not recorded after 1881.

27 The references to individuals discussed in this and subsequent sections of the essay are found in PANS RG35–102, series 18B, vol. 2 (for 1864–73) and vol. 3 (for 1873–90). They can be located in the registers by date.

28 See the city marshal's (police chief's) reports in the *Annual Reports* of the City of Halifax (hereinafter *Annual Reports*) for 1884–5, 1886–7, and 1888–9 at 118, 169–70, and 112–3 respectively.

29 P.B. Waite *The Man from Halifax: Sir John Thompson* (Toronto: University of Toronto Press 1985) 42; J. Fingard 'The Relief of the Unemployed Poor in Saint John, Halifax and St. John's, 1815–1860' in Frank and Buckner *The Acadiensis Reader: Volume One* (Fredericton: Acadiensis Press 1985) 193–4; Poor Asylum Commissioners, *Annual Report* 1874–5, 155

30 This is a minimum figure; increasingly in the 1880s the registers stopped noting details of race.

31 For examples of prejudice towards blacks in the operation of the courts, see *Acadian Recorder* 8 Sept. 1879 and 12 Dec. 1884.

32 Ibid. 19 Feb. 1872

33 City marshal's reports, *Annual Reports* 1886–7, 170, and 1888–9, 112–3

34 J. Fingard 'Jailbirds in Mid-Victorian Halifax' in T.G. Barnes et al., eds *Law in a Colonial Society: The Nova Scotia Experience* (Toronto: Carswell 1984) 84

35 Ann Mahony was imprisoned a total of eleven times: see the entries for Dec. 1864, Oct. 1866, July 1867, Aug. 1868, Mar. and Nov. 1869, Mar. 1870, Mar., July, and Oct. 1873, and May 1874.

36 See the cases of Thomas Johnston (convicted 30 Dec. 1867, sent to the poor-house 6 Jan. 1868(; Michael Donovan, convicted 21 Nov. 1867, sent to the poor-house 27 Nov.); Anne Richards (convicted 2 June 1880, sent to the poor-house 10 June); and Mary Gaffney (convicted 5 Oct. 1864, sent to the poor-house 15 Oct.).

37 See the cases of Daniel Harvey (convicted 3 May 1880, sent to the poor-house 16 June) and Ellen Murphy (convicted 9 Oct. 1867, sent to the poor-house 9 Dec.).

38 See mayor's address and city prison reports, *Annual Report* 1885–6, xxix–xxx, 121.

39 In June 1875, Apr. 1877, Apr. and Nov. 1878, and Sept. 1879

40 *Morning Chronicle* 25 Dec. 1874

41 See the complaints of the prison governor that no skilled mechanics were available for maintenance work: city prison report, *Annual Report* 1880–1, 112–3. The best study of 'outcast Halifax' is I.G. Mckay 'The Working Class of Metropolitan Halifax, 1850–1889' (Honours thesis, Dalhousie University 1975) chapter 5. For skilled labourers' concerns that the rural semi-skilled threatened their position, see *Royal Commission on the Relations of Labour and Capital – Nova Scotia Evidence* (Ottawa 1889), evidence of P.F. Martin.

42 *Acadian Recorder* 12 Nov. 1878

43 Ibid. 15 Dec. 1879. Not all the Halifax homeless were so lucky. Reports of death from exposure were not uncommon: see *Novascotian* 9 Dec. 1867.

44 *Acadian Recorder* 22 Dec. 1879. For a similar attitude to the prison in other offenders, see the cases of Robert Wiseman and Henry Turner, 'two roughs' who tried to extort money by posing as policemen. Given the option of a fine or a prison term, the 'decided to go up as times is hard': *Citizen* 8 Feb. 1878.

45 H. Graff 'Crime and Punishment in the Nineteenth Century: A New Look at the Criminal' *Journal of Interdisciplinary History* 7 (1977) 477–91. Judith Fingard's work on Halifax also notes the use of the jail as a winter refuge, but comes to different conclusions about the significance of this and about the role of the criminal law and petty criminals in society. She proposes an analysis of the criminal that places more stress on individual failings than social dislocation or economic hardship: see 'Jailbirds' 101.

46 See also similar examples in *Acadian Recorder* 7 Aug. 1879 and *Citizen* 8 Feb. 1878

47 11 Dec. 1867

48 Mayor's address, *Annual Report* 1884–5, x–ix, and 1885–6, xxx

49 Prison governor's report, ibid. 119–20

50 Fingard notes that this can also be seen as one way in which the victims of the law exerted a measure of control over the justice system: 'Jailbirds' 101.

51 Rev. F. Wayland 'The Tramp Question' *Proceedings of the National Conference of Charities and Corrections* (1877) 112; E.R.L. Gould 'How Baltimore Banished Tramps and Helped the Idle' *Forum* 17 (1894) 497–504. For similar attitudes see also, inter alia, J. Flynt *Tramping with Tramps* (New York 1899); J.J. McCook 'The Tramp Problem: What It Is and What to Do with It' *Proceedings of the National Conference of Charities and Correction* (1895); 'A Tramp Census and Its Revelations' *Forum* 15 (1893) 753–66; O. Thanet 'The

Tramp in Four Centuries' *Lippincott's Magazine* 23 (1879) 565–74; and A. Pinkerton *Strikers, Communists, Tramps and Detectives* (New York: G.W. Carleton 1878).

52 Monkkonen *Dangerous Classes* 150. Similar fears in Britain are discussed in B. Weinberger 'The Police and the Public in Mid-Nineteenth Century Warwickshire' in V. Bailey, ed. *Policing and Punishment in Nineteenth Century Britain* (London: Croom Helm 1981) 85. For the Charity Organization movement of the Gilded Age see Boyer *Urban Masses* chapter 10. A social worker warned her colleagues, 'I would not in my enthusiasm for the work of friendly visiting, lose sight of the old adage that it is hard to make a silk purse out of a sow's ear. The best we can do is a sorry patchwork often ... In many cases the more heroic treatment of cutting off supplies must be resorted to. So long as charitable people insist that they must forestall the possibility of "letting the innocent suffer" ... just so long the lazy man has society by the throat': M. Richmond 'Married Vagabonds' *Proceedings of the National Conference of Charities and Corrections* (1877) 516.

53 S. Leavitt 'The Tramps and the Law' *Forum* 2 (1886) 192

54 S. Houston 'The Impetus to Reform: Urban Crime, Poverty and Ignorance in Ontario, 1850–1875' (PHD thesis, University of Toronto 1974) 5. See also Craven 'Law and Ideology' 293, and J.J. Bellomo 'Upper Canadian Attitudes towards Crime and Punishment, 1832–51' *Ontario History* 64 (1972) 11–26.

55 Pitsula 'Treatment of Tramps' 119–20

56 Cited ibid. 122

57 For these see House of Commons *Journals* 1880, 31; 1885, 164, 204, 237, 255, 265, 268, 290, 310, 465, and 555; and 1886, 52.

58 Local newspapers and visitors to Halifax commented frequently on the taverns, brothels, and slums congregated in the streets running north and east from the citadel. The streets were still largely unpaved, dusty and smelly, and peopled with 'beggars and old drunks.' The combination of the northern winter and an economy geared to seasonal pursuits meant that the winter months were especially desperate for those without resources to fall back on, who were forced to live in 'common houses' that were 'the meanest of their kind to be found anywhere in this vast Dominion.' Quotations from Waite *Man from Halifax* 35 and C. Roger *Glimpses of London and Atlantic Experiences* (Ottawa: MacLean, Roger 1873) 12. See also Fingard 'Jailbirds' passim; idem 'The Winter's Tale: The Seasonal Contours of Pre-industrial Poverty in British North America, 1815–1860' Canadian Historical Association *Historical Papers 1974* 65–94; *Morning Chronicle* 7 Jan. 1873; *Herald* 15 Jan. 1884; and *Acadian Recorder* 3 May 1867.

59 City marshal's report, *Annual Report* 1871–2, 55; *Herald* 10 Aug. 1889; City

prison report, *Annual Report* 1881–2, 1882–3, 100. See similar comments in the *Annual Reports* for 1871–2; 49; 1879–80, 128; 1880–1, 122; 1884–5, xviii–xix; 1885–6, 149–50; and *Herald* 27 Dec. 1883.

60 *Morning Chronicle* 21 Jan. 1873; *Citizen* 1 Feb. 1878; *Herald* 11 June 1884

61 *Herald* 19 and 20 Jan. 1880. See also the many stories about crimes committed by tramps elsewhere on the continent. Examples can be found in *Novascotian* 2 Dec. 1867 and *Citizen* 16 Jan. 1878.

62 *Herald* 29 July and 4 Sept. 1879

63 *Acadian Recorder* 19 and 22 Dec. 1879

64 Ibid. 3 Feb. 1866

65 3 June 1876

66 See, for example, *Presbyterian Witness* 20 Dec. 1868 and 20 Nov. 1869.

67 *Acadian Recorder* 19 Feb. 1872

68 See ibid. 3 Feb. 1866; *Unionist* 16 July, 15 Oct., and 7 Dec. 1866 and 29 Mar. 1867.

69 SNS 1867, c. 82; SNS 1870, c. 38

70 See P.V. Girard 'Henry Pryor' *DCB* vol. 12.

71 City marshal's reports, *Annual Report* 1866–7, 49. Marshal Cotter claimed that the new system and the uniformity it introduced had made 'the class known as old offenders ... much more chary of making an appearance in the dock, knowing that there is a record of previous convictions always at hand to confront them.'

72 Girard 'Henry Pryor.' On at least one occasion Pryor received a death threat for his harshness towards those convicted of selling liquor without a licence. On another occasion in 1879 an offender was considered 'fortunate ... that there was an acting Stipendiary, with whom the quality of mercy is not strained': *Herald* 9 June 1884; *Acadian Recorder* 13 Dec. 1879. See his summary treatment of litigants reported in *Acadian Recorder* 8 and 21 July and 18 Dec. 1879. When Nova Scotia's Chief Justice Sir William Young spent a morning on the bench with Pryor, he 'seemed surprised at the expeditious manner in which the judgments of the Court were given': *Acadian Recorder* 4 July 1879.

73 *Acadian Recorder* 4 Jan. 1886, 3 Sept. and 9 Aug. 1879

74 Ibid. 29 Sept., 26 Dec. 1879; 9 July 1878. For references to offenders' being 'given a chance' see, inter alia, ibid. 8 July, 29 Aug., 15 Sept., and 2 Dec. 1879, 27 and 30 Dec. 1886; and *Herald* 12 Aug. 1879.

75 This practice might fit Douglas Hay's interpretation of the criminal law as an ideological construct that combined harshness with mercy to legitimate social relations: see D. Hay 'Property, Authority and the Criminal Law' in Hay et al. *Albion's Fatal Tree: Crime and Society in Eighteenth-Century England* (London: Penguin 1975). For a more detailed attempt to apply

Hay's thesis to the Toronto Police Court, which seems to have exhibited many of the characteristics of Halifax's Stipendiary Magistrate's Court, see Craven 'Law and Ideology.'

76 See PANS MG100, vol. 156, no. 28 (history of the Halifax Police Department).

77 See, for example, *Citizen 16 Nov. 1869; Acadian Recorder* 4 Dec. 1884; city marshal's reports in *Annual Reports* 1876–7, 208, 1879–80, 172, 1885–6, 149, and 1886–7, 48–9; mayor's address, ibid. 1884–5, xix–xxi. See also *Acadian Recorder* 18 Nov. 1867 and 24 July 1879; *Unionist* 18 Dec. 1868; and *Morning Chronicle* 30 Jan. 1873. Municipal finances were a constant problem in Halifax during this period; the city came close to bankruptcy in 1881: McKay 'Working Class' 12.

78 *Royal Commission on the Relations of Labour and Capital supra note 41*, 225. For complaints about the force see *Citizen* 16 Nov. 1869 and 6 and 21 Feb. 1878; *Acadian Recorder* 19 May 1888; city marshal's report, *Annual Report* 1879–80, 127, 1880–1, 122; and mayor's address, ibid. 1866–7, 11. The press published a variety of stories that did not reflect well on the police. Policeman Brennan was fined by the magistrate for assault and false imprisonment; Policeman Charles Lang's ten-year-old son fatally stabbed a fifteen-year-old boy in a knife-fight: *Acadian Recorder* 21 and 29 Aug. 1879. Earlier in the decade one newspaper complained that a man who had assaulted two policemen with a knife was released on an alderman's order: *Morning Chronicle* 21 Oct. 1872.

79 PANS RG35-102, series 16, section G, police committee minutes 1884–90

80 There were thirty-five applications for three vacancies in 1874: *Morning Chronicle* 30 Dec. 1874. See also *Acadian Recorder* 20, 26, and 31 Dec. 1884.

81 *Acadian Recorder* 12 and 17 Dec. 1884; see also police committee report, *Annual Reports* 1871–2, 33–4 and 1874–5, 131; city marshal's report, ibid. 1877–8, 99, and 1878–9, 161–2.

82 SNS 1888, c. 52

83 SNS 1864, c. 81, s. 538

84 Ibid.; *The Charter and Ordinances of the City of Halifax* (1864) 170–1

85 Mayor's address, *Annual Report* 1884–5, xlix. See the discussion above about the use of the prison as a refuge.

86 SNS 1881, c. 14, 1. The prison governor objected to doing this because it was less profitable to employ prisoners on the streets, taking into account the additional security expenses.

87 See G. Andrews 'The Establishment of Institutional Care in Halifax in the Mid-Nineteenth Century' (Honours thesis, Dalhousie University 1974) 3–4; Fingard 'Winter's Tale'; idem 'Relief of the Unemployed Poor'; SNS 1864, c. 81, ss. 567–9.

88 Fingard 'Relief of the Unemployed Poor' 193

89 Institutions such as the inebriate home, the industrial school, and the insane asylum were founded at this time. In 1878 a Board of Public Charities was constituted to take over the hospitals, the insane asylum, and the poor asylum. When it was abolished in 1886 these institutions were kept under one authority – the commissioner of public works and mines: SNS 1878, c. 16, SNS 1886, c. 5; Mayor's address, *Annual Report* 1885–6, x, xxxiii.

90 Report of poor asylum commissioners, *Annual Report* 1874–5, 156; B. Potter 'Poor Relief in Nova Scotia in the 1880s' (Honours thesis, Dalhousie University 1978) 5, 8–13. Potter demonstrates that most inmates of the asylum were over fifty and/or genuinely indigent. See also the comment by a reporter in the *Herald* 9 May 1884: '[L]ife at Rockhead seems infinitely preferable to life in the asylum for the poor.'

91 Mayor's address, *Annual Report* 1885–6, xxxv. See also Report of poor asylum commissioners, ibid. 1874–5, 156, and 1876–7, 191.

92 Potter 'Poor Relief' 37–9

93 *Citizen* (Apr. 1876; Night Refuge for the Homeless *Annual Report* 1879, 3, 5; J. Fingard *Jack in Port: Sailortowns of Eastern Canada* (Toronto: University of Toronto Press 1982) 235

94 Halifax Association for Improving the Condition of the Poor *Report* 1867, 5. Doull was president of the association for many years; he was apparently worth some $150,000 in 1884: *Herald* 1 Jan. 1884.

95 See the *Annual Reports* of the association, which continue to 1890. See also the many press reports of its work, including *Herald* 9 Jan. 1879, 8 and 16 Jan. 1884; *Acadian Recorder* 5 Dec. 1879, 19 Jan. 1886; and *Morning Chronicle* 23 Dec. 1874. For similar British campaigns to drive beggars from the streets, see G. Stedman-Jones *Outcast London* (Oxford: Clarendon 1976) 272–3, 296.

96 *Citizen* 9 Jan. 1878

97 Ibid. 3 Jan. 1878

98 23 Dec. 1879; see also ibid. 10 Dec. 1879.

99 *Herald* 31 Jan. 1881

100 Ibid. 13 Jan. 1879

101 *Report* 1874

102 See, for example, *Report* 1883, 7–8, 1889, 5.

103 *Morning Chronicle* 23 Dec. 1874; *Citizen* 3 Jan. 1878; *Acadian Recorder* 13 Jan. 1879 and 13 Jan. 1886

104 *Morning Chronicle* 12 Mar. 1875; *Christian Messenger* 21 Mar. 1877; *Citizen* 18 Jan. 1878

105 12 Oct. 1879

6

From Bridewell to Federal Penitentiary: Prisons and Punishment in Nova Scotia before 1880

RAINER BAEHRE

The Halifax penitentiary, which received its first prisoners in 1844, was one of three Canadian penitentiaries existing at Confederation.[1] Preceded from the early 1750s by a bridewell in Halifax and a system of county jails, it was finally replaced in 1881, along with the penitentiary at Saint John, New Brunswick, by the federal Dorchester penitentiary. A modest edifice in comparison with its Upper Canadian counterpart at Kingston, the Halifax penitentiary nevertheless symbolized the transformation of criminal punishment evident during the early to mid-nineteenth century in Canada and other western countries.[2] In this essay I will attempt to shed light on Nova Scotia's institutional response to crime in the context of that transformation.

The literature on crime (recently described as having assumed 'the status of a boom industry')[3] and on the study of penal institutions is extensive, diverse, and sophisticated. The study of crime and punishment is but one aspect of a broader interest in the role of the state and social control.[4] Stanley Cohen provides an excellent discussion of approaches to and research on social control, 'the organized ways in which society responds to behaviour and people it regards as deviant, problematic, worrying, threatening, troublesome or undesirable in some way or another.' He identifies four main features of its historical development. The newly secular state became increasingly involved in developing centralized, rationalized, and bureaucratic social institutions to deal with deviancy. Deviants became differentiated and classified by means of 'scientific knowledge' utilized by a growing body of experts. Institutions such as the prison and the asylum were used to change the behaviour of deviants. Punishment became less physical and more psychological; the focus of reform became the deviant's mind. While there is broad agreement among scholars that these changes occurred everywhere, albeit at different times and in slightly different forms, there is a wide difference of opinion as to why they took place.[5] This essay, though informed by the new histories of crime and punishment, does not attempt to provide a definitive or comparative explanation of the interrelationship between crime, society, and social control in Nova Scotia. Rather, it offers an overview of the process that culminated in the establishment of a penitentiary in Nova Scotia, and examines the operation of that institution during its thirty-six years of existence.

CRIME AND PUNISHMENT IN EARLY NOVA SCOTIA

For more than half a century after the founding of Halifax in 1749 imprisonment played only a minor role in Nova Scotia's regime of crime and punishment. Various other types of punishment worked to extirpate crime and to serve as instruments of social control. They included, in ascending order of severity, fines, the pillory, public whipping, mutilation, transportation (most often to New South Wales or Bermuda), and hanging. The framework for the colony's criminal law was established in 1758 during the first session of the new Assembly. Five statutes laid out a wide variety of offences with specified capital and non-capital punishments.[6] Capital offences included high treason, murder (including infanticide), buggery, rape, blackmail, stabbing, aggravated assault,[7] and the malicious firing of a gun, all of which were non-clergyable, as well as manslaughter, grand larceny, arson, and polygamy, for which benefit of clergy was available for first offenders.[8] Added later to the catalogue of capital offences were petit treason, breach of quarantine regulations, offences related to wrecks and wrecking, breach of a dyke which caused flooding, and impersonating another at a bail hearing. Only the last offence attracted benefit of clergy.[9]

Non-capital offences named in the 1758 enactments were punishable either by corporal punishment or by a combination of imprisonment and fine. The principal corporal punishments were whipping and the pillory. Petty larcenists and all felons who received benefit of clergy were subject to whipping.[10] It was also prescribed, in combination with time in the pillory, for some forgery offences and, in combination with mutilation, for women who made false accusations of paternity. The pillory, alone or with other punishments, was generally imposed on those who had committed crimes considered particularly morally abhorrent – incest, blasphemy, and assault with intent to commit buggery, as well as perjury and counterfeiting. Perjurers who were unable to pay a fine of twenty pounds faced the prospect of having their ears nailed to the pillory. A convicted counterfeiter was subject to one hour at the pillory, to the nailing of one ear, and to a public whipping. Branding, another form of corporal punishment, was reserved for felons in receipt of benefit of clergy. Offenders guilty of manslaughter had an M burnt 'upon the brawn of the left thumb'; other felons received a T. Women and men were punished in the same manner, and the branding was performed by the jailer in open court. There was only one major amendment to this statutory table of punishments in the second half of the eighteenth century: in 1787 'any clergyable felony, grand larceny, or other [offence]' was made additionally punishable by the perpetrator's being bound out to an employer for a maximum of seven years. This provision applied also to all 'disorderly and beggarly persons.'[11]

The 1758 statutes contained relatively few provisions for punishment by lengthy imprisonment. Unspecified prison terms faced individuals who committed assault with intent to commit buggery or who received stolen goods. Parents of illegitimate children who refused to provide security to the Overseers of the Poor or anyone who enticed a seaman or marine to desert could be imprisoned for six months. Blasphemers and petty larcenists could be jailed for three months. In all these cases imprisonment appears as a supplement to a regime of fines, whippings, and periods in the pillory. Fines ranged from as low as five shillings for a first conviction for drunkenness to twenty pounds for concealing a sailor or helping him to desert and one hundred pounds for running an illegal distilling-house in Halifax.

Traditional corporal sanctions were the dominant mode of punishment during the eighteenth and early nineteenth centuries. Men and women alike were whipped. Jane Tolmy, tried in 1774 for petty larceny, was sentenced to be publicly whipped twenty-five times; she applied for a pardon because she was pregnant, and the executive council decided to 'pardon, release, acquit and discharge' her. Some first-time felons received benefit of clergy, and were branded. On 5 May 1808, for example, George Ingat was found guilty of stealing a mare; he was 'given clergy' and the letter T was branded on his left thumb.[12] Second offenders in clergyable crimes risked the gallows. As is evident from Jane Tolmy's case, the severity of sentences could vary. Supreme Court judges, the executive council, and the Colonial Office could all play a mitigating role – the first at the sentencing stage and the last two through the executive pardon system.[13] Judicial compassion was evident in the case of Nancy O'Neal of Liverpool, who was charged with the murder of a bastard child. She was acquitted of the original charge on the basis of her testimony that the baby was stillborn, and was instead found guilty of concealing a birth. She was sentenced to fourteen days' imprisonment on 21 November 1814 because she had already spent fourteen months in jail awaiting trial.[14]

Prisons played a role in the system almost from the founding of Halifax. According to contemporary accounts the first British settlers in the town included numerous 'vagabonds' and assorted criminals. These were the remnants of the three thousand discharged soldiers and sailors, 'the King's bad bargains,' introduced to the colony by Governor Cornwallis in 1749. An influx of former indentured servants from Newfoundland and Virginia, whom some officials also viewed as wastrels, helped swell the town's population to about five thousand in 1755.[15] Such economic and social dislocation contributed to the crime and poverty noted by observers, as did wartime conditions and the transient nature of the port city's population.

In 1752 the Halifax justices, supported by the *Gazette*, which was concerned to suppress the '[p]etty Larcenies and other Evils that daily happen through the Idleness of several Persons,' demanded not only a proper jail but a bridewell, or reformatory.[16] This institution, common in England for the previous century and a half,[17] was designed to enable offenders to perform hard labour. In Nova Scotia it served as a jail – a place of pretrial and prepunishment detention – for the town and county of Halifax, and, more important, as a house of correction, a place of confinement and punishment. Magistrates decided whether the convicted person should be confined to the jail to await non-carceral punishment, or sentenced to imprisonment in the bridewell. In 1754 a stone house formerly owned by one Richard Wenman was purchased and turned into a bridewell. A variety of petty offenders were sentenced to imprisonment at hard labour supplemented, if necessary, by whippings.[18] A few years later, in 1758–9, a second multi-purpose bridewell was established to house together the poor, the criminal, and the insane, all under the control of the magistrates.[19] The framers of the statute governing the house of correction clearly saw the institution as a tool for social control. Magistrates could commit there 'all disorderly and idle persons, and such who shall be found begging, or practising any unlawful games, or pretending to be fortune-telling, common drunkards, persons of lewd behaviour, vagabonds, runaways, stubborn servants and children, and persons who notoriously misspend their time to the neglect and prejudice of their own or their family's support.' If necessary the inmates were to be fettered and shackled, and given ten lashes on entry or whenever they were found to be stubborn or idle so that they would be 'reduced to better behaviours.' Poor children and orphans without support were to be bound out as apprentices.

In 1763 some distinction was made between different classes of inmates. The workhouse remained directly under the jurisdiction of the magistrates; three rooms in it were reserved for paupers and placed under the control of the Overseers of the Poor. Inmate labour was intended to defray all costs, with anticipated profits accruing to the institution.[20] When a third Halifax bridewell was opened in 1790, its predecessor was left abandoned and in a state of disrepair.[21] By this time other communities, such as Shelburne, had followed suit.[22] Two years later, in 1792, grand juries were given the power 'to provide proper buildings, or to appropriate a certain part of the county or district jail, as a work-house, or house of correction.' In part, this initiative resulted from Halifax's refusal to continue to accept responsibility for non-Haligonian paupers and vagrants.[23]

From its inception the Halifax bridewell was a house of indiscriminate confinement for criminals, delinquents, debtors, and other social undesirables, such as prostitutes and vagrants. It lacked a regulated system of penal discipline and classification of prisoners, although from 1801, when the Commissioners of the Poor were established to deal with paupers and vagrants, longer-term criminals only were kept in the jail quarters.[24] The building was cold, damp, and unhealthy, and prisoners slept on straw. The quality of clothing, blankets, and food depended on a prisoner's ability to pay. The poorest inmates were sustained on a diet of molasses and tea. The jail-keeper, whose treatment of prisoners was often arbitrary and sometimes brutal, supplemented his income by selling liquor to prisoners. Debtors had to pay rent for their cells and a fee to the jailer before their release.[25]

Whatever the conditions in the bridewell, they were never as severe as they were in Halifax's other principal carceral institution of the period, the military prison. Opened on nearby Melville Island in 1808 – a site that twenty-one years later also saw the establishment of a lazaretto – the prison was moved to the Citadel from 1847 until 1857, when it returned to the island.[26] It held roughly the same number of prisoners as the bridewell, but they were treated much more harshly. Blood began to flow after one hundred lashes, yet Private Frederick Schmidt, who had been absent at tattoo roll-call, was sentenced on 28 January 1805 to receive four hundred lashes, two hundred per day on two consecutive days. Private Martin Sweeny, convicted by court martial of stealing a shirt from a prisoner of war, was sentenced to eight hundred lashes, of which five hundred were to be given the second day. The British military use of flogging, especially for desertion, did not decline until the 1830s, when reformers began to stress prevention rather than punishment. It was not entirely abolished until 1881.[27] In contrast, in 1814–15 the grand jury recommended the dismissal of several keepers at the Halifax jail for cruelty and of the jailer, William McMillan, for excessive flogging.[28]

THE RISE OF IMPRISONMENT, 1815–1835

Punishment in Nova Scotia underwent gradual but significant changes in the first third of the nineteenth century. The use of traditional corporal and capital punishment was reduced as imprisonment was increasingly imposed on serious offenders. At the same time new ideas emerged about the reformatory role of a prison. None of this was manifested in a sudden break with the past; indeed, during this period old and new ideas about punishment coexisted. Changing attitudes and policies are none the less clearly discernible, and they set the stage for the eventual establishment of a penitentiary in the early 1840s.

Two events that followed closely on the Napoleonic Wars served as harbingers of the new order. The first was the passage of an 1816 statute that allowed the courts to impose lengthy prison sentences, rather than the traditional fines and corporal punishments, for a substantial number of offences.[29] The second was the construction in 1818 of a new bridewell separate from but immediately adjacent to the county jail.[30] While the new building was meant to relieve the overcrowded and inadequate conditions of the old one, it was also a response to changed social and economic conditions. The post-war depression saw a greater incidence of vagrancy and petty crime in the city. There had been an influx of refugee blacks after the War of 1812, which led the xenophobic Halifax magistrates to complain of the 'greatly increased ... [numbers] of Black people among us many of which evinced the most vicious habits.'[31] In addition, Britain expected its colonies to accept emigrants to ease the pressures created by the transition to commercial and industrial capitalism. Poverty-stricken highland Scots embarked for Cape Breton and elsewhere, while the destitute Irish who arrived in St John's were shipped to Halifax, adding to the anxieties of colonial officials and drawing new attention to the bridewell.[32] The new prison, however, was more than a response to changing social conditions in the 1820s and 1830s; it also represented an acknowledgment of changes in attitudes. It symbolized a transitional phase in modes of punishment, one in which imprisonment was gradually displacing older forms and becoming the dominant response to criminal convictions.

This development was reflected in two aspects of penal practice. First, the courts began increasingly to use their new power to impose prison sentences on serious offenders. A comparison of lengths of sentences confirms this change. In 1790 forty-two persons serving sentences of one to fifty-two days were imprisoned in the bridewell; in 1825 the length of sentences ranged from six months to two years.[33] Second, discipline took on a different emphasis; in particular, solitary confinement was used to control unruly prisoners. Magistrates began calling for the mitigation of 'the old form of punishment' through imprisonment, while jail officers forced inmates to work on roads, to cut stone, and to learn skills, habits of industry, and religion.[34] Liquor sales to prisoners were discontinued. John Fielding, the jailer, petitioned the grand jury in December 1828 for a salary increase. Many of the inmates, he said, were members of 'the lowest classes' and 'unable to provide for their subsistence while confined'; they were debtors imprisoned for amounts 'generally ... trifling.' 'Feelings of humanity' and the lack of facilities led him to feel sorry for them, and he allowed them to use the yard. But in doing so he became liable for their debts if they escaped, a personal economic risk and one that obviously made him nervous. In addition, he wanted to discontinue the 'most lucrative' practice of selling liquor from the tap, 'for the preservation of decency among prisoners and for the prevention of riot, disorder, and drunkenness.' The grand jury's response was to recommend a raise of twenty-five pounds per annum on the condition that Fielding refrain from selling liquor at the prison.[35]

Changes in other areas confirm the movement away from eighteenth-century penal practices. In the prepenitentiary period Nova Scotians convicted of capital felonies occasionally had their sentences reduced to transportation to various British colonies or to England itself. This practice had originated at the end of the eighteenth century, but fell into disfavour in the 1830s. Transportation was an inexpensive alternative to long-term incarceration for the struggling colonies, and an attractive one as long as its costs were borne by the imperial government. When the Colonial Office embarked upon a period of economic rationalization in the early

1830s, it began to insist that the colonies foot the bill. In a dispatch of 2 March 1835 the colonial secretary, Lord Aberdeen, informed Lieutenant-Governor Sir Colin Campbell that Nova Scotia convicts should no longer be sent to Bermuda or England but to New South Wales, and at colonial expense.[36] This directive was repeated several times in the following year by Lord Glenelg, Aberdeen's successor, with the additional stipulation that convicts not be sent 'without being supplied with an adequate provision of Clothing and Maintenance properly adapted to the Season of the year,' again at colonial expense. Glenelg also provided the colonial government in 1837 with regulations governing the transportation of military prisoners, and informed Campbell that the imperial government was now willing to pay transportation costs only of those persons sentenced by a formal court martial, which excluded convicted members of the local militia corps.[37]

Other imperial and colonial objections to the system of transportation led to its virtual abandonment. Its 'evils,' according to Glenelg, consisted in its failure 'to possess most of the essential qualities of an efficient Secondary Punishment.' In other words, little was done to reform the convict. But Glenelg raised other important and perhaps overriding considerations. Before being transported, some convicts were detained, sometimes for years, at considerable expense. Some sentences were later discovered to have been illegal, resulting in a pardon for the convict and in the additional expense of his passage home. Moreover, the Australian colonies now wanted fewer convicts. Glenelg therefore asked Campbell to find a substitute punishment and to commute sentences, or to do 'whatever practicable,' in the meantime. This direction apparently did not apply to military prisoners, who continued to be transported until the practice was abolished in 1857.[38]

By the 1830s the curtailment of capital punishment in Nova Scotia met with general approval. At the end of that decade a committee of the House of Assembly noted that new attitudes had virtually put an end to 'the sanguinary and vindictive laws which were dictated by the barbarism of the dark ages.'[39] The trend had been noted by Mr Justice Brenton Halliburton in 1829, a staunch Tory who became chief justice four years later; he commented with satisfaction that during the previous twenty-two years not a single native-born Nova Scotian had been executed for a capital felony, including, presumably, homicide.[40]

Despite reforms in sentencing and carceral practices, until the later 1830s imprisonment shared the stage with more traditional sanctions. Corporal punishments continued to be meted out. John Lewis Puttum, a

Halifax man found guilty of forging provincial notes in July 1825, was sentenced to one year in jail and one hour in the pillory, and was to have one ear cut off. Sometimes judges sentenced criminals to be mutilated for lesser crimes. On 18 February 1828 one guilty party had 'part of his ear cut off at Halifax for cheating in measuring potatoes.' Hangings also continued. John Hynds, convicted of burglary on 20 January 1826, was sentenced to be hanged because he was a repeat offender; he had previously been branded.[41] Moreover, despite the apparently small number of executions carried out in the province during the post-Napoleonic period, a total of twenty-five capital treasons and felonies remained on the statute-books.

There was opposition to the continued use of corporal and capital punishments in the 1820s and 1830s. At both the official and unofficial levels there were those who hoped to build on the changes already made and to extend them into a more thoroughgoing reform. The official effort was represented by a law reform commission, established in 1833 and consisting of four distinguished members of the bar – S.G.W. Archibald, James B. Uniacke, Beamish Murdoch, and William Hill. The commissioners were asked to look at reforming the practice and proceedings of the courts of law and equity, a mandate that included an examination of criminal laws. They recommended a consolidation of such laws and a limitation on the number of capital crimes. They argued that '[i]t would be proper to confine the number of Offences of an atrocious nature, as at present many of those enactments are a dead letter. The lenient administration of Justice in this Province has, for a very long period, restricted capital punishment in effect almost exclusively to cases of Murder, where the proof of guilt has been complete, and where no palliating circumstances tend to mitigate the crime.' In addition, they called for the abolition of transportation, mutilation, branding, and pillory, all of which should be replaced with imprisonment at hard labour. They urged that all defendants receive the assistance of counsel in addressing grand juries. Legal and penal reform, then, extended beyond the nature of punishment to a questioning and a proposed rationalization of existing criminal justice practices.[42]

Unofficial efforts at reform were primarily represented by a movement for the abolition of capital punishment. In 1834 the *Acadian Recorder* described at length the public hanging of one John Lee for highway robbery.[43] The writer's tone was decidedly critical. He referred to the event as 'the melancholy exhibition, of the sacrifice of a human being to the majesty of the laws.' Lee himself was depicted as 'the miserable being who was about to suffer the utmost penalty which man can inflict,' the 'wretched man to mount the ignominious ladder.' Remorseful and frightened, he 'seemed lost in anguish, clinging with melancholy tenacity to the last dregs of life ... until after several convulsive motions, [he] was at rest as regards this world.' The deterrent value of this 'very fearful drama' to young and old alike was mentioned. The newspaper congratulated the community that it had been thirteen years since the last execution in Halifax.

By the end of the 1830s the *Colonial Pearl*, reflecting popular opinion, openly attacked capital punishment in a lengthy and well-argued piece, 'Fifteen Reasons against Death Punishments.'[44] The article was based on a work by Thomas Wrightson, 'On the Punishment of Death.' The writer pointed out that on the basis of statistical evidence, trials of capital crimes resulted in proportionately more acquittals than was the case for lesser crimes. This suggested to him that juries were often reluctant to convict capital offenders. But, the writer continued, there were fifteen other sound reasons for doing away with executions. These included the argument, based on the experiences of the French Revolution, that capital punishment was 'dangerous to liberty,' especially in the hands of tyrants. It was incompatible with the idea of reforming the offender. It was not always an effective deterrent: the loss of one's life was often less terrible to the very poor than to the higher classes, and 'the example [was] momentary.' A public execution tended to harden and brutalize 'the *bad*,' while offending and disgusting 'the good,' and 'strong minds triumphed over it.' Moreover, the process created an 'infamous office – that of the hangman.'[45] The writer emphasized the point, asking rhetorically whether, 'politically speaking, it is good to accustom the people to the spectacle of blood?' Capital punishment frustrated the ends of justice by removing a source of legal evidence, and encouraged crime among the friends of the executed and perjury among witnesses. It also gave 'neither restitution nor satisfaction to the party injured.' In a broad psychological and cultural sense, capital punishment alienated 'the best feelings of human nature' and formed 'a standard of severity which generate[s] national cruelty and vindictiveness'; it even encouraged murder, for only 'gentle laws produce gentle manner.' Finally, such punishment was 'irremissible': how did a wrongful execution of an innocent person ultimately reflect on a society?

The changes in penal attitudes and practices that took place in Nova Scotia during the 1830s and 1840s were similar to the reforms in Upper Canada, Britain, and the United States. Yet one is left asking why these changes took so long to be manifested in the establishment of a penitentiary. Penitentiaries began to be built in the United States and in England in the 1820s, and in Upper Canada the penitentiary at Kingston was completed by 1835.[46] Three factors were probably responsible for the dilatoriness of the colonial legislators. First, not all segments of society were converted by the new ideas. The reformed system of prison discipline established in the 1820s, for example, met with some resistance, as evidenced by the comments of a Halifax grand jury in 1823. They did not see the reformation of inmates by means of imprisonment at the bridewell as an effective deterrent, and they recommended a return to traditional forms of public punishment.[47] There were complaints that convict labour on road construction undercut employment opportunities for free labour in the recession, and members of the Assembly more than once debated the introduction of a treadmill (a proposal defeated by only one vote in 1824).[48] Until the late 1830s no single mode of punishment prevailed, and the further development of the bridewell as a distinct method of punishment was neglected.

Second, the issue of crime and punishment probably was not of great importance in people's minds. The numbers of convictions do not reflect the full extent of criminal activity, but they do provide a useful, if somewhat crude, measure of the way in which citizens gauged the prevalence of crime. During a six-year period from 1815 to 1820 only 58 felons were convicted in the Supreme Court; another 50 were found guilty in the courts of quarter sessions. An average conviction rate of 16 felons per year suggests the relative absence of major crime in Nova Scotia. A further 658 minor offenders were convicted in the Halifax Police Court or by individual justices of the peace out of sessions.[49]

In 1829 the grand jury for Halifax County, noting a rise in crime, commented that 34 males and 10 females were imprisoned in the bridewell, 'a larger number than has been known at any former period.'[50] This proved to be a temporary increase, however, and through most of the 1830s the crime rate did not particularly concern contemporaries, in contrast to Upper Canada, where substantial immigration raised fears of increased serious crime (even though this did not occur in practice).[51] During the early years of the decade the *Blue Books* recorded the state of the seventeen county jails throughout Nova Scotia. In 1832, a typical year, there were 74 convicted criminals and 211 debtors in the jails. Halifax always had the largest number of inmates, and some county jails had no prisoners.[52] A Halifax grand jury in 1833 was quick to blame poverty, crime, and the declining health and morals of 'the People' on alcohol, but noted also that there appeared to be little cause for anxiety.[53] Sixty criminal trials took place in the Supreme Court during the five-year period from 1835 to 1839, only a 25 per cent increase over the previous generation. Of those, forty trials led to convictions. The majority were for crimes against property; only ten were for crimes against the person – two for murder, three for manslaughter, and five for assault.[54] In 1839, when the decision was made to build a penitentiary, there were only twenty-two persons in the bridewell: seven men, fourteen women, and one infant. Only three individuals had been imprisoned for two years or more.[55] These low crime rates strongly suggest that in Nova Scotia ideology played a more significant role than either social crisis or class conflict in the evolution of new ideas about crime and punishment.

The third and perhaps the most significant reason for delay in the adoption of the Halifax penitentiary as a principal mode of punishment and the introduction of new forms of prison discipline was the ignominious state of the Halifax bridewell in the mid-1830s. The economic tensions between metropolitan Halifax and its hinterland that contributed to its condition are discussed below.

THE BRIDEWELL CRISIS OF THE 1830S AND REFORM IDEAS

The Halifax grand jury, composed of members of the middle class, was responsible for the inspection of the jail, the bridewell, and the poorhouse. In 1828 the jurors found all three institutions to be 'clean and comfortable and in compleat order.' In the following year they again praised the management of both the jail and the bridewell. In 1830 they found poor drainage conditions and inmates ill with influenza at the bridewell; two years later, following an unannounced visit, they reported 'order and cleanliness prevailing.' The same general comment appeared in the year-end report for 1833.[56]

These were difficult years for the town, which suffered a cholera outbreak in 1832 that left four hundred dead, a deepening recession in 1833, and another onslaught of cholera in 1834. Socio-economic problems were exacerbated by charges of maladministration against the Commissioners of the Poor and the county treasurer. Dominated by an oligarchy of government officials and merchants, and mired in what J.M. Beck has described as a 'bureaucratic maze,' town government seemed incapable of undertaking social reform without first reforming itself.[57] Beginning in 1832, problems at the bridewell were added to this catalogue. In that year an intoxicated inmate died in his cell, and it was discovered that prison supplies were bought at the highest rate without tenders or contracts. From 1834, a year that saw failing businesses, increased unemployment, a growing jail population, and a heightened general anxiety about the future, positive comments on the bridewell were few. On 23 April 1834 it was recorded that the building was 'in a miserable condition and totally unfit to give Shelter to Human Beings.' The convicts lacked clothes and the building leaked badly. The grand jury accused Acting Commissioner William Roach of not keeping proper accounts, using the yard for his horse, having a convict make shoes for his family, and mixing flour short.[58]

This scandalous situation, and other problems with the administration of the Commissioners of the Poor, provided a platform for Joseph Howe to attack Halifax's ruling clique of magistrates and merchants, some of whom in turn initiated a charge of criminal libel against him.[59] Despite the government's appointment of a new Board of Commissioners for the bridewell, matters did not improve as the decade advanced. A committee of the grand jury in 1837 condemned the neglected state of the institution. Apart from its continuing leaky condition, the building was insecure; nineteen prisoners had escaped its confines during the previous year. One commissioner had been remiss in his responsibilities by not paying a visit for six months. No medical attendant had come in five or six weeks, although a diseased prisoner needed assistance. The inmates' clothing was inadequate in cold weather and could not be washed, and the bedding swarmed with vermin. The publicity surrounding this report prompted the lieutenant-governor to make an immediate inspection of the premises and to order that attention be given to the prisoners.[60]

The bridewell's problems were not solely the product of poor management and lack of concern for prisoners. They also symbolized the rift between town and country. Since 1816 inmates had been sent to the bridewell from the other counties, and Halifax County felt that it shouldered a disproportionate tax burden as a result. Since 1835, in protest, it had contributed 'nothing from the County funds towards [the Bridewell's] support.'[61] This was a tactic similar to one used by a Halifax grand jury in 1833 when it refused to levy a tax assessment in order to force the county treasurer to collect back taxes.[62] The bridewell was kept going on grants from the Assembly. Yet by the mid-1830s it was used almost exclusively to confine persons convicted in the Halifax courts, and it was now the other counties that were expected to bear an unequal burden. Aware of Halifax's reluctance to shoulder the operating costs and critical of rural attitudes, the Halifax grand jury argued in 1836 that the bridewell 'should be abolished being a heavy burthen on the County – with a

Building scarcely habitable from decay and possessing no Regulation, whereby the labour of Criminals is made available to their support.'[63]

Two years later financial concerns still dominated discussions. The bridewell continued its decline, 'inefficient' and 'destitute' because the Assembly refused to erect a new building or provide additional operating funds. By May 1839 an impasse had been reached, and the committee on the bridewell believed it had 'no alternative to prevent the starvation of the Persons now in confinement, but their discharge.'[64] In an attempt to force a political resolution, another select committee recommended 'that this delapidated [sic] and inefficient Establishment' no longer receive legislative aid, with the exception of a small operating fund; any extra expenses were to be charged to the County of Halifax. Consequently, the bridewell lacked the funds to operate for more than a week at a time.[65] The underlying issue was still taxation. Politicians outside Halifax were not interested in supporting 'a Town establishment,' although convicts were sent to the institution from throughout Nova Scotia.[66] In turn, officials considered closing the bridewell doors to non-Haligonian offenders to reduce costs. It appears that the extraordinary practice of releasing offenders from other counties before the expiration of their sentences was used increasingly because of the bridewell's general condition and lack of time.[67]

In addition to the physical decline of the bridewell, the 1830s also saw an important change in the way in which criminals were viewed. Increasingly, they were seen as fellow human beings deserving of humane treatment and reformation. This change mirrored contemporary penal reform movements in the United States and Britain. In 1835 the Colonial Office urged Lieutenant-Governor Campbell to bring to the attention of the Assembly the report of the Committee of the House of Lords 'to enquire into the state of the Gaols and Houses of Correction.' Colonial Secretary Glenelg was anxious to standardize prison practices throughout the empire. To effect his purpose he wanted information on the numbers of jails, prisoners, regulations, labour, convict earnings, and daily allowances for food. He also inquired into medical treatment, classification of prisoners, instructional materials, visitors, and exercise facilities. In response to Downing Street's urgings to introduce more effective prison discipline, a bill was laid before the Assembly for a new penitentiary and house of industry. But arguments over who should pay, not over the merits of the institution, prevented its passage.[68]

The *Blue Books* already supplied much of the information requested by Glenelg. They showed that in the early 1830s no prisoner in any provincial jail was forced to do hard labour. The jails continued to serve primarily as 'holding-tanks,' and even the bridewell was used for that purpose. No exercise facilities existed. No systematic punishments were employed, except for the placing of refractory inmates in irons. Although no insane persons were found in any jail, they were commonly put into the poorhouse. No classification of prisoners other than by sex and as debtors or criminals was attempted, 'prisoners not being sufficiently numerous to make it necessary.' Prisoners were allotted seven pounds of bread per week, bibles, and prayer-books, but no clothing or bedding.[69]

An 1838 select committee of the Assembly acknowledged the influences of the United States and England in shaping colonial opinion. It linked denunciations of the disgraceful state of the bridewell with contemporary penal ideology:

> The decayed and ruinous state of the Building is such, that were it not for the Military Guard, and the fetters with which the wretched beings are loaded, the prisoners could not be kept, and even with these, it is well known that they frequently do escape. But were there no danger in this respect, the unwholesome noxious effluvia arising from Sewers, and other nuisances, connected with the present wretched Establishment, which no cleanliness on the part of the Keeper can prevent render it not only unfit for human beings, but absolutely disgraceful to a civilized community. For, while good government requires that crime should be punished, humanity, and reason, and Christianity, require that even Criminals should be treated as fellow Mortals and Immortals, and not as irrational beasts.
>
> Respect for our common nature demands this of every well ordered mind, and of every properly organized government.

The committee members called for a new bridewell 'suited to the objects for which under every good and well ordered Government, such places are designed, viz. – The safety of the Community – the prevention of Crime – the lessening or the removal, of possible, of the burden on the public for their support – and, the reformation of the Criminal.' While the committee rejected making such a prison a 'Manufactory,' as some American prisons were, because local artisans would disapprove of the competition, they nevertheless hoped that it could be made self-supporting by means of convict labour. The new prisons, according to the committee, emanated from 'the genial and meliorating influence of Science and Christianity,' which gave rise to 'a more humane and philanthropic system' that was based on the idea that certainty of punishment, not severity, was the best deterrent. Reformation, 'correcting but not destroying the guilty,' in the form of solitary confinement of prisoners who were subjected to 'moral culture' was the best way to protect the community from crime.[70] The committee's emphasis on 'reformation' was typical of other social welfare ideas in the decade: interest in reform extended to the lunatic asylum and to the bridewell's sister institution, the poor-house. To ensure the 'moral regeneration' of its charges, the poor-house was to operate as a house of industry, thereby reflecting the transformation of poor-relief practices in England following the passage of the Poor Law Amendment Act of 1834.[71]

The immediate crisis at the bridewell and the climate of reform gave force to the recommendations of the 1838 committee and spurred the creation of the Halifax penitentiary. By 1839, at the urging of judges of the Common Pleas to grand juries in counties throughout the province, town and country politicians finally agreed that the bridewell should be taken out of local hands and made a provincial institution. In 1839 another committee recommended that a provincial bridewell, or penitentiary, be built. A bill to this effect was tabled in the following year. Authorization to proceed was given, and a grant of four thousand pounds was made in 1840, the money to be borrowed at 5 per cent interest or less.[72] The preamble to the legislation reiterated the positions of earlier committees: 'the punishment of Criminals ought to be applied with a view to their reformation and restoration to Society, for which Object the Penitentiary System adopted in Great Britain and the United States, is justly applauded.' The act also established a penitentiary commission to oversee the construction and operations of the institution.

The laying of the corner-stone and the first stages of penitentiary construction took place in 1842, when the legislature granted six thousand pounds and the penitentiary commissioners contracted with George Jones, a local 'mechanic,' to build the outer walls. Unfortunately, construction was delayed when the contractor was unable to pay several creditors and was temporarily jailed as a debtor. Construction was finally completed later in the year.

THE HALIFAX PENITENTIARY, 1844–1880

The architectural features of the new institution were modest. The hewn ashlar granite building was 148 feet long and 42 feet wide, and was initially intended to be three storeys or 48 feet high, though only two storeys were completed. Eventually it would have two cell-blocks running longitudinally, each containing thirty cells. The entire edifice was to be contained by a wooden enclosing wall. But in 1844 it consisted only of thirty cells for male inmates and another nine cells for females, in addition to apartments for the keepers and a prison workshop. When the first prisoners arrived in June, they found the building in an unfinished state.[73] During its inaugural year the penitentiary usually contained between fifteen and twenty persons drawn from a population of nearly three hundred thousand. These figures were 'gratifying' to the commissioners who managed the institution, 'particularly when they consider[ed] that imprisonment ... [was] now almost the only punishment for the higher class of crimes.' The commissioners described the penitentiary as less a place of punishment and 'more a work of benevolence for the reformation of the criminals.'[74]

By the end of 1845 the institution held thirty-one inmates. There were four women with no occupation listed, eight labourers, four farmers, three carpenters, and three fishermen; the rest were mostly artisans. Twenty-two inmates, or 71.1 per cent, had been convicted of larceny. Other crimes listed included arson, concealing a birth, assault with intent to commit rape, horse-stealing, and forgery. Eight convicts, or 25.8 per cent, were pardoned before the expiration of their sentences. The prisoners came from all over Nova Scotia, from Cape Breton to Digby.[75] The statistics for 1850 reinforce the impression that there was relatively little serious crime in the province. Only three murder charges were laid: one resulted in a conviction, another in a reduced verdict of manslaughter, and the third in an acquittal. Only eight felonies committed in Halifax County resulted in penitentiary terms.[76] The penitentiary was also used to house thirteen military prisoners because of its efficient security and its arrangements for isolating prisoners from one another.[77]

Thirty-five years later, when the Halifax penitentiary closed, there was still no explosion of crime. The daily average number of prisoners in 1879–80 was seventy-seven. During the preceding decade approximately 10 per cent of the inmate population had been military offenders, most of whom were guilty of insubordination.[78] Among the 49 people incarcerated on 30 June 1880, 85.7 per cent were designated 'white,' the rest 'coloured.' One prisoner was Irish; the rest were Canadian-born. Fifteen were Roman Catholic, 13 were members of the Church of England, 9 were Baptist, 9 were Presbyterian, and the rest were Methodist, Lutheran, and Adventist. Twenty-eight inmates, or 57.1 per cent, could read and write. Forty, or 81.6 per cent, were under the age of thirty, and 13 of the 40 were less than twenty years old. Forty were single or widowed. Most inmates (36.7 per cent) had been convicted of larceny or compound larceny. The remaining convictions consisted almost equally of receiving stolen goods, breaking and entering, burglary, and counterfeiting. There were also single instances of murder, wounding with intent, arson, maliciously wounding, forgery, stabbing, assault, and sheep-stealing. Only 4 inmates served sentences longer than seven years; 11 served between three and seven years, and 31, or 63.3 per cent were sentenced to two to three years.[79]

PENAL IDEOLOGY IN NOVA SCOTIA

In its design the Halifax penitentiary did not rely on 'moral' architecture to the same extent as the Kingston Penitentiary, although that model might have been desirable.[80] R.C. MacLeod has explained that such prison architecture 'was designed with elaborate care that each room, almost each block of stone, should contribute to the rehabilitation of the prisoners.'[81] But design merely facilitated the workings of the overall penitentiary system, which was based more on social relationships than on physical setting. Penal reformers in Nova Scotia tended to emphasize the disciplinary mode, or what Michel Foucault has called the 'micro-physics of power,' and Bentham's panoptic model, which influenced the development of nineteenth-century penal institutions, was ultimately conceptual and psychological, not structural. The system of discipline at Halifax initiated in 1844 by legislation was a direct borrowing from the Auburn State Prison of New York; its main features were silence, labour, and instruction.[82]

The Halifax penitentiary, like other prisons of the day, was organized according to a hierarchical yet self-regulatory method of control. Supreme Court judges were to make and publish prison rules and regulations,[83] but there is no evidence that they ever did so. Until 1852 the task fell to commissioners, who supervised the operations of the penitentiary as a whole. The convict's immediate overseers were a governor (later renamed 'superintendent'), a matron, a keeper, a night keeper, and a messenger. A physician came when necessary, and there was also a visiting chaplain.[84] Initially, staff were supervised by the Board of Commissioners; the board was dissolved in 1852 and replaced with a committee responsible to the Board of Works.[85] The original board and its successor, the advisory committee, were ultimately accountable to the lieutenant-governor. On the next rung of this hierarchy stood the prison governor-superintendent, who was responsible for carrying out and enforcing the commissioners' edicts as well as for supervising convicts and staff; he was required to report regularly to the committee on the state of the prison. All staff members performed distinct duties and had specified rights within the penitentiary system; these were itemized in the rules and regulations. Lowest in the prison hierarchy were the inmates themselves, but in theory they too were protected by these same rules.[86]

Everyone, staff member as well as convict, was expected to conform to the general mode of prison discipline. For example, employees were told to be vigilant, 'never [to] give way to passion, but always remain self possessed and calm but resolutely and undeviatingly enforce the discipline of the prison.' They were also expected to be punctual and sober, to preserve harmony among themselves, and not to talk to anyone except in the performance of their duties. The model penitentiary, it was hoped, would run like a well-oiled and self-regulated machine, and the expectation was that 'the executive management of the Prison must be precise, rigid and undeviating, subject to no confusion or irregularity.'[87]

Observation, inspection, supervision – the key elements of Bentham's panoptic model – became the corner-stones of good order and discipline in the penitentiary. In silence, it was thought, lay the inmates' only hope for reformation. The staff members were 'never' to allow the rule of silence to be broken by the convicts. Furthermore, constant vigilance ensured domination. The behaviour of the inmates was constantly checked and redirected. Any prisoner who broke the rules was punished by being made to sleep in a hard bed in a darkened cell, to subsist on bread and water for up to three days, and to wear shackles. The lash, which was still used at the Kingston penitentiary, was absent in Halifax. The 'micro-physics of power' structured the entire life of the convict during his prison term. The procedures were outlined in the following terms:

> [I]n no case shall any hope of pardon or favour be held out to them, they will not be permitted to engage in any other kind of work than that assigned to them, nor shall they leave their stations to range about the shops or go into the yard. In passing to and from the cells, to and from the shops, and to and from their meals, the convicts must move in close single file with lock step, in perfect silence, and facing towards the officer in immediate charge of them, their working tools and instruments must be left in the shops, and their knives in the eating room. Each convict must wash his hands and face at least daily, his feet once a week, and he must change his clothes once a week, every male convict shall have his beard shaved weekly, and his hair cut monthly; the females shall have their hair cut as often. The men and women shall always be kept separate, and no possible

opportunity of intercourse be allowed them. They shall have three meals a day of such plain wholesome food as may be decreed proper by the Commissioner.[88]

In sharp contrast to the bridewell, almost every aspect of the penitentiary inmate's routine was highly structured and regulated. Although the manner in which the regime was implemented was not identical to that of Kingston, there were many similarities to the other colonial penitentiaries. This suggests some degree of consensus on the nature of crime and the object of punishment in mid-nineteenth-century British North America. So strict was the discipline at the Halifax penitentiary that a Newfoundland visitor to the city in 1845 found the regimen too severe. Lord Stanley, an advocate of stern penitentiary discipline, recommended reducing the prisoner's work day from twelve hours to ten lest there be too little time left 'for the moral and religious instruction, meals, and exercise of prisoners.'[89]

Perhaps the most significant aspect of the new regime was the insistence on prison labour. It was believed that labour, instruction, and moral reformation together would bring about wholesale rehabilitation of offenders. In 1846 the commissioners expressed their satisfaction that 'this work and labour has been performed by men who have received all their instruction in cutting and laying stone since they have been in prison, many of whom will return to the world useful Mechanics, and (from their behaviour while in prison) the Commissioners trust they will become better members of society.'[90] Despite these fine words, there was a second and more important reason for prison labour – the reduction of costs. In 1847, for example, Superintendent George Carpenter explained an increase in operating costs to the board by noting that cost estimates for the penitentiary had assumed the presence of a blacksmith among the inmates, but this hope had not been realized, and 'for want of such a Tradesman a great deal of Blacksmith work had to be given out.'[91] Fiscal restraint was emphasized even to the detriment of the institution. Carpenter had been promised a salary of £150 in addition to board and lodging. The actual provisions he received were 'the same as a convict,' and his salary was less than a tradesman's although he worked six days a week and often acted as a clergyman.[92] A parsimonious government did little to meet Carpenter's demands, and its preoccupation with 'economy' shaped much of the institution's history.

Convicts were kept occupied with construction work in the interior of the prison – stone staircases, cells, columns, a wooden platform, a kitchen. Outside, they put up walls, fenced, cleared, filled, and cultivated the land,

and worked the smithy. Male inmates made the prison dress and shoes; females were put to work carding, spinning, knitting, washing, and mending clothes for fellow prisoners.[93] The convicts learned no trades apart from cutting stone, completing the construction of the institution, and performing cost-cutting tasks such as farming. In 1853, when the Board of Works took over the penitentiary, Chairman Hugh Bell remarked that 'no work to any extent of a manufacturing kind can be engaged in, – indeed it is doubtful whether any other labour [than work done to facilitate the penitentiary's operations] would be so profitable.'[94] Nevertheless, Bell boasted in 1854 that several prisoners had managed to acquire mechanical skills, and he noted with pride that 'a young boy' at the prison, apparently the only minor among the inmate population, had been learning both the blacksmith's and the stone-cutter's trades.[95]

In the 1860s it was generally believed that convict labour at the prison should be self-sustaining, especially when 'very nearly all [prisoners] seem hearty and able to labour.'[96] The convicts were put to work producing goods that could be sold to outside agencies or businesses. They made barrels, tubs, and buckets; they worked as carpenters; they made fisherman's boots, shoes for the inmates of the Dartmouth Provincial Hospital for the Insane, and, later, boots for the military. They did tailoring and worked in the blacksmith's shop making and repairing tools and grates for the Nova Scotia Railroad.[97] But working conditions at the penitentiary had little to recommend them. In 1862 a committee found that the 'working apartments' were too small, and that smoke belched upwards from the blacksmith's shop into the workshops, thereby interfering with the convicts' work as well as '[prejudicing] their health and comfort.'[98] During the 1870s convicts engaged in activities such as broom-manufacturing. In promoting prison labour, officials always assumed that the convicts were learning useful trades, so that upon their release they would 'not be thrown on society without, at least, having learned the means of supporting themselves by honest industry.'[99] Those prisoners incapable of performing heavy work were left to pick oakum and make shoes.

Apart from the adoption of an Auburn-inspired regimen and an overriding emphasis on convict labour, there were several other important ways in which the Halifax penitentiary differed significantly from the bridewell. It reduced, if it did not entirely eliminate, congregate confinement; prisoners were now classified and their routines were largely determined by their personal characteristics and the seriousness of their offences. Congregate confinement could not be eliminated completely, however. In 1845, for example, an Assembly committee called for the penitentiary to take in more convicted offenders from the old bridewell (which was now used as the jail), to which offenders were sent by the Court of Sessions for the County of Halifax. The penitentiary committee rejected the suggestion: '[R]eformation of offenders being one great end which the Regulations of the Penitentiary seek to ensure and promote ... the reception of Vagrants and transient offenders, committed by the City Courts cannot be admitted, as thereby that wholesome design would be frustrated, offenders hardened in guilt, or confirmed in immoral practices, might thus retard the reformation of inmates committed for a longer period.' They suggested adding a wooden building to the penitentiary to house vagrant and disorderly persons.[100] It appears that this suggestion was not taken up.

In time, however, the problem largely solved itself. In 1860 the new city prison, Rockhead, was opened, and in 1865 and 1867 respectively a new county jail and a poor-house were added to the city's carceral institutions. They provided adequate and suitable space for many vagrants and minor offenders. Some later Halifax penitentiary reports contain no mention of vagrants, though after Confederation some other short-term prisoners were included in descriptions of the prison population. It is likely that traditional congregate confinement was virtually eliminated in the penitentiary.

Another feature that distinguished the penitentiary and the bridewell eras was prison conditions. Although complaints continued, they differed both in kind and degree from those levelled previously. Cleanliness and order were strictly maintained, but in an effort to same money convict rations were reduced in 1851. The standard ration had consisted of 'two Plates Mush, Soup and hard Biscuit, with one lb. Beef on Sundays.' Two years later Dr Rufus Black, a medical attendant, reported 'sickness to a considerable extent among the inmates,' probably as a result of prisoners' being more susceptible to disease.[101] The extent of sickness that year must have come as a surprise; in the wake of a typhoid and dysentery epidemic that seized Halifax in 1845, the prison recorded only one death, proportionately a lower mortality rate than in the city. At that time Black had attributed the general good health of the inmates to the 'diet and discipline.'[102] Some changes to diet must have been carried out, however, because in 1861 Black said that he could vouch for the 'wholesome nature of the food, and the cleanly manner in which it was prepared.' Later the commissioners admitted that the convicts' general health was 'not good' because of the 'poor atmosphere,' the cold, and the unchanging diet; they thought that potatoes might be used to supplement the regular fare of hard biscuit and bread.[103]

Any unpleasant conditions at the penitentiary were structural and economic in origin rather than a result of discrimination against inmates because of their inability to pay for amenities. Prisoners now suffered equally. The cells at the front of the building were damp and cold because they were far from the stove. When the building was only ten years old the roof began to sag. Troublesome or uncooperative inmates were confined in narrow cells, and, 'unable to exercise their limbs and breathing from week to week,' were left in 'an extremely vitiated atmosphere.'[104] No major structural improvements were made; repairs were carried out on a piecemeal basis. In 1880 a fire destroyed the blacksmith, carpentry, and tailor shops and the wash-house. By that time the decision to move all Nova Scotia convicts to Dorchester had already been made, and the devastation was of little consequence.[105]

Another significant change occurred when the penitentiary's original Auburn system was modified in 1851 and 'a mark system for good behaviour of the prisoners,' a forerunner of the Crofton system, was introduced by the commissioners.[106] The commissioners became convinced that rewards for prisoners in the form of privileges would have a beneficial effect. From 1845 Superintendent Carpenter had been evaluating the behaviour of each prisoner in his annual reports. Almost always that behaviour was described as 'good'; the phrases 'making himself very useful' and 'works well this month' also were prevalent. The exceptions were prisoners who escaped, or a case like that of Number 31, William MacLean, who struck 'a good and quiet Black Boy' and used 'bad language,' and whose conduct was 'most outrageous' after he was put in irons. On that occasion Carpenter made use of two or three 'dark cells' in the basement to deal with the problem. On the whole, he claimed, 'as far as practicable every effort has been exerted to make the convicts good members of Society and useful tradesmen, without losing sight of the best means of turning their Labour to the advantage and interest of the Province.'[107]

In 1852 the high expectations of the committee received a sharp blow when several inmates preferred charges of mistreatment and cruelty against the superintendent. The commissioners accepted the prisoners' allegations, and Carpenter was discharged. Also, according to the committee, Carpenter had not carried out 'the good conduct medal system' that was considered to be essential in improving the behaviour of the prisoners.[108] That system was implemented by William Fish, the new superintendent, and his wife, the prison matron. Fish also removed the traditional chains and shackles from all but the most unmanageable prisoners.

Initially, Fish also displayed 'evenness of temper, and kindness yet firmness of manner.'[109] His demeanour earned him the 'respect and gratitude' of the prisoners, and the harmony that prevailed made the penitentiary easier to run and more productive. But underlying friction was also evident, and it peaked in the 1860s. A harsher discipline was instituted by the superintendent in 1861–2, which brought complaints from the inmates. In defending the necessity of these 'reforms,' a legislative committee on the penitentiary argued that the prison must be 'not merely a place of punishment, but, as its name imports, a penitentiary, where penitence for past offences and reformation of character might be promoted; – that fallen and degraded as the greatest criminals may be, they are still members of the human family, possessing minds and susceptibilities akin to our own, and having therefore a kindred claim to our sympathy. The rule in this view has been "as much kindness as is consistent with the strictest discipline." '[110]

The committee submitted 'rules of some of the best regulated prisons in England' forwarded by Lord Carnarvon, the president of the select committee of the British House of Commons on the state of prisons, to the Nova Scotia government. But the British system too was harsh. Carnarvon proposed eliminating all contact between prisoners, alternating military shot-drill with hard labour during the first six months of imprisonment, creating three different categories of prisoners to be distinguished from one another by earned privileges, increasing the severity of punishment, reducing the quality of food to that below workhouse fare, and photographing every convict. The third class, or the least reformed category of prisoners, was to be treated especially harshly. Everyone who entered the penitentiary was put into this category initially. The prisoners were 'not to be allowed the use of matrasses [sic],' and were to be given 'hard labour, hard beds, and hard fare, [they] being strong deterring elements, which ought only to be alleviated by good conduct.' In its insistence on hard labour, the committee reasoned that 'an aversion to regular labour is one of the chief sources of crime, and it is therefore of the utmost importance that the system of punishment to which convicts are subjected should be one calculated to teach them habits of steady labour, and to associate industry in their minds with the advantages to be obtained by it.'[111] The committee further explained that 'the chief object of a prison is not solely to punish crime, but to inculcate the right principles and to let the prisoner see that an interest is taken in his welfare, and by good advice and kindly admonition, endeavour to convince him of his error and encourage him to future good conduct.' At the same time, Upper Canadian prison officials were expressing similar views on the Kingston penitentiary.[112]

Although the committee considered these measures to be progressive, they were more severe than those practised in the past. It is not surprising that 'a great spirit of insubordination [prevailed]' in 1866 when the prison superintendent further implemented the new system. To counter the collective hostility of the convicts, it was suggested that the revised rules be posted in order to 'relieve the Superintendent of a great deal of unnecessary trouble.'[113] On 18 August 1867 a riot led by convict soldiers was quelled by troops. This 'rising' quickly drew the attention of federal authorities who, under the terms of the new British North America Act, were responsible for penitentiaries and who were ordered by the governor general to investigate. Inquiries conducted by the federal inspector James Ferres found that the riot had followed the serving of tainted meat at dinner; in addition, Ferres discovered an 'utter want of discipline' among both inmates and guards. The near anarchy was attributed to political patronage in the hiring of guards, some of whom were described as 'old and feeble' men more fit to be committed to an almshouse than to carry out duties in a penitentiary. The warden was 'sensible of the shameful state of discipline,' but the guards 'knew that they did not owe their appointment to him; that he could not dismiss them, and that, therefore, he possessed no control over them.' Moreover, the guards apparently were afraid of the inmates and refused to impose discipline. The riot had been an exercise in intimidation.

What Ferres saw 'staggered' him. Not only was he able to walk unattended and unhindered into the penitentiary on arrival, but the Auburn system was nowhere evident. Convicts wore what they liked, talked, smoked, laughed and bantered, and even chatted freely with the guards. Walls and floors were dirty, patched, and ripped. Some of the guards were 'fully as bad as the convicts, whom by a fiction they were presumed to be set over to inspire with respect.' Ferres's observations on the state of the corridors and cells were telling:

> All the cell-doors stood wide open. Observing that some of the men had gone into them, I also, by and bye, strolled down the corridors in the crowd, to see what those men were about. I found one particular blackguard, whose prison character was indicated by his having a chain riveted to either ankle – stretched

on his bed at full length – perusing his newspaper. Another was deep in a novel which, at my request, he obligingly handed me, which bore the title, 'Bella Trelawney; or, Time Works Wonders'; and, as I looked around me, I thought truly Time had worked wonders with convicts in one penitentiary at least. Another convict was as earnestly absorbed in another novel, 'The Young Crusader; A Tale of the Middle Ages.' He had retired to the comfort and quiet of his bedchamber to enjoy the story – secluded from the noise and boisterous mirth of his fellow prisoners in the corridor. I opened the door of one cell, which I saw shut, and disturbed the inmate by the creak of the door while in an enviable snooze. Two were on one bed, half sitting, half reclining, with their dirty boots on the blankets; one was seated on his bed, with a jack-knife in hand, mincing a piece of beef which he had taken from the dinner table to feed the cat which purred alongside of him. The floors, of course, were filthy, and variegated with different hues of tobacco squirts.

A campaign to clean up the prison and restore discipline was immediately begun. For the first time officials recommended the closing of the penitentiary, because of its inadequate 'moral architecture', in favour of a regional institution in the Sackville, New Brunswick, area. But while the Nova Scotia attorney general was happy to cede jurisdiction to the federal government, there was 'no machinery' whereby Ottawa could undertake the supervision of such an institution.[114] In the meantime the revamped system was rigorously enforced, although this lasted only until 1868 when George MacGregor, the warden, died. 'A young man named Stamper' served as interim warden, but permitted a slackening of the rules. He was replaced, and the commissioners reintroduced 'a more thorough discipline.'[115]

A change of heart on the part of the commissioners soon became evident, however – perhaps because after federal legislation placed the institution under the authority of the Board of Inspectors of Asylums and Prisons[116] the Halifax officials could draw on the knowledge and experience of their federal counterparts. Whatever the reason, when Robert Dunkin, the new warden, took charge in 1870 he removed the shackles worn by several prisoners, the 'hard ones.' In his view, harsh measures were to be considered only when moral suasion failed. He castigated two guards for their 'very objectionable bearing,' which was calculated merely to 'exasperate the prisoners, and goad them to acts of insolence and insubordination.' Dunkin emphasized kindness, a kindness not incompatible with discipline; convicts had 'feelings like other men, to be acted upon for good and for evil.' Apparently, Dunkin's system of 'kindness and conciliation' was practised to good effect.[117] In 1872, for example, the directors reported that 'the general conduct of the prisoners has been creditable.' No serious offences were committed and therefore no severe punishments were inflicted that year.[118]

The more compassionate attitude towards inmates illustrated by the decline in the use of corporal punishment extended beyond the matter of penitentiary discipline, for the directors also pleaded with the government to give released convicts some money and clothes in order that they might 'with their little capital and decent appearance be able to obtain some employment by which to earn an honest livelihood' instead of being driven to commit new crimes. Such support, they argued, was especially necessary in the case of military ex-convicts, who either lost their good-conduct rating if they returned to the service or suffered a dishonourable discharge. For the latter group especially the adjustment to life outside the prison could be difficult: '[O]n the expiration of their sentence, usually without friends, they have to face a world utterly new to them, in a strange country; they are penniless; they have no other clothing than the scanty uniform left them when sent to prison.'[119]

Problems surfaced again after yet another change of warden late in 1874. John Flinn, the latest senior officer, encountered 'a great deal of trouble and annoyance' in 1876 owing to the 'very bad, insubordinate and indecent conduct' of several female inmates. With the aid of the matron Flinn had their diets reduced, placed them in solitary confinement, and had their hair cut short. In 1877 he requested an assistant matron. Relative harmony was then restored at the institution, and Flinn was able to report general satisfaction with the conduct of the inmates.[120] During the first six months of 1877 only forty-two punishments were meted out. In increasing order of severity, they included 'admonishment'; suspension of privileges; confinement to cell; confinement to cell with loss of privileges; confinement to dark cell on bread and water; breaking stone; and confinement to a dark cell with loss of stripes and remission. Only eight instances of the last three forms of punishment were tabulated.[121] Of all these punishments the most severe was the loss of remission. The remission system practised in the penitentiary had been introduced in the 1868 Penitentiary Act; the scheme enabled prisoners to earn reductions in sentences of five days per month.[122]

Sixty-one inmates of the Halifax penitentiary, described as 'cheerful' and enlivened at the prospect of change, departed on 16 July 1880 for the newly built regional penitentiary at Dorchester, New Brunswick. They were accompanied by ten other officers and guards, two of whom were armed with Remington repeating rifles. There was only one convicted murderer among them, although the party included two men convicted of manslaughter and two rapists. Thirty-four of the prisoners were larcenists. The murderer had been incarcerated since 1851 and was by 1880 considered quite harmless and an 'exemplary' inmate. Thoroughly institutionalized, he was thought to be better served by imprisonment than by pardon. Of the other prisoners, one man was serving ten years, seven others between five and six, and most of the rest two to four. There were also five 'common prisoners' whose sentences ranged from one year to eighteen months; one had been convicted of perjury, the others of larceny. Two female convicts were left behind at the county jail, and two others were discharged, their sentences having expired.[123]

The afternoon before the transfer, the federal inspector of penitentiaries, J.G. Moylan, had lectured the prisoners on the need for good behaviour; he had held out the prospect of executive clemency for some. In the evening the prison officers had presented Warden Flinn with gifts, including an ice-pitcher engraved with an inscription that expressed their appreciation, affection, and esteem, and reflected the 'good feeling' that had existed at the penitentiary for the previous five years. The convicts had breakfasted at 5:30 A.M. Dressed in conspicuous yellow and black uniforms and marked underwear, all designed to inhibit escape, they had paraded manacled and handcuffed two by two to busses that took them to the railway station. Upon arrival at the 'new era' penitentiary, which was still in the final stages of construction and in a 'confused state,' the convicts were ushered into the dining-hall. Inspector Moylan, who had accompanied them on the trip, complimented them on their good conduct during the transfer. They were given dinner and locked into their cells. The staff then divided them into two gangs, one to repair roads and the other to clean up the prison.[124]

CONCLUSION

The development of the Nova Scotia prison system in the nineteenth century illustrates the social-control thesis propounded by historians of other jurisdictions. A single central, bureaucratic institution was constructed and operated on 'scientific' principles for the purpose of taming and reforming the deviant. Yet the Nova Scotia experience was not an uncomplicated story of a simple, linear march towards modernity. Owing to the peculiarities of local politics and administrative structures, the penitentiary was not built until long after its desirability was generally accepted. Even after its establishment the penitentiary did not always function smoothly. There was uncertainty about its goals and about the methods that should be used to achieve them. On the surface the primary goal was always the reformation of the inmates. In 1845 the penitentiary commissioners stated their objective to be 'that great reformation among the prisoners, both moral and religious, as well as the formation of industrious habits,'[125] and similar sentiments were expressed throughout the period. The Halifax officials reflected a consistent Canadian philosophy: in 1858 a New Brunswick commission noted that 'while the Law punishes crime, its merciful design is – while protecting the great interests of the community – to benefit and reform the criminal.'[126] In a similar vein the inspector of penitentiaries informed Sir Alexander Campbell, the minister of justice in John A. Macdonald's Conservative government, that

> [t]he notable features which we have been slowly but steadily seeking to introduce into our Penitentiary management are, in brief, reformation as the supreme end to be kept in view; hope, as the great regenerative force in prisons; industrial labor as another of the vital forces to be employed to the same end; religion and scholastic education and training as a third force belonging to the same category; abbreviation of sentence, good conduct marks and certain minor indulgences – within the power and discretion of the Wardens to grant – as incentives to be held out for diligence, good conduct and effort at self-improvement; the enlistment of the will of the prisoner in the work of his moral regeneration; and the introduction of a variety of trades and industries as supplying the means of honest support on his discharge.[127]

Provincially, regionally, and nationally, the idea of the penitentiary remained remarkably consistent during this period. No calls were heard in Halifax or Ottawa for a return to the pre-penitentiary model. While it sometimes appears as if the system of penal discipline varied according to the person in charge, there was actually a consistent effort to make the penitentiary conform to the spirit of prevailing British and American ideas, architecture, and practice – the bridewell, Auburn, and Crofton systems. Individual views held by wardens were subsumed in the models, rules, and regulations introduced by local, federal, and imperial governments.

Yet attitudes about the purpose of the institution were always a mixture of the idealistic and the pragmatic, and the history of the Halifax penitentiary is a chequered one. Idealism about the reformation of criminals was consistently tempered and undermined by other considerations, such as administrative self-interest, fiscal rationalization, an emphasis on institutional self-sufficiency, and the maximization of productive forces entailing the use of convict labour and the prison as a manufactory. The most obvious and significant secondary consideration was protection of the public. The criminal class was consistently depicted as disorderly, idle, obstinate, lawless, depraved, dangerous, vengeful, and violent. As W.A. Calder has noted in a study of federal penitentiaries after Confederation, 'the most common justification of punishment advanced in Parliament [was] ... the need for deterrence.'[128]

The result of such a bifurcated version of the penitentiary was that while the apparent principal purpose of confinement remained consistent, the necessary institutional will and certainty of practice needed to implement that purpose was at times lacking. The penitentiary ideal failed to influence the city's other carceral institutions. In December 1875 H. Whitaker, JP, visited the county jail and then resigned in protest at what he had found there. He had discovered prisoners, including some awaiting trial, locked up in total darkness after sunset, and kept in their cells sometimes for sixteen hours at a stretch. Owing to inadequate facilities, the only female prisoner was kept in solitary confinement for months. The one meal a day given all inmates consisted of barley-broth, and there was no work to keep prisoners occupied during the day. He concluded that this treatment was 'enough to make a prisoner desperate or to deprive him (or her) of his senses.' Whitaker agreed that a prison should not be a place 'to be desired' by criminals, yet he was equally certain that prisoners 'should *not* be tortured.'[129] In this case, as with the penitentiary, there was a rift between the hope and ideology of prison reform and the realities of prison practice.

NOTES

1 This essay is an extensively revised version of a previous study, 'The Prison In Atlantic Canada Before 1880,' User Report no. 1985–25, prepared under contract with the Ministry of the Solicitor General of Canada as part of the Federal Corrections History Project. I am grateful for the ministry's financial support and for permission to use portions of that study here.

2 See D. Rothman *Discovery of the Asylum* (Boston: Little Brown 1971) especially 79–108; M. Foucault *Discipline and Punish* (New York: Pantheon 1978); M. Ignatieff *A Just Measure of Pain: The Penitentiary in the Industrial Revolution, 1750–1850* (New York: Pantheon 1980); and D. Melossi and

M. Pavarini *The Prison and the Factory: Origins of the Penitentiary System* (London: Macmillan 1981).

3 J.L. McMullan 'Crime, Law and Order in Early Modern England' *British Journal of Criminology* 27 (1987) 252. See also D. Garland and P. Young 'Towards a Social Analysis of Penality' in Garland and Young, eds *The Power to Punish* (London: Heinemann 1983) 1–36.

4 See, for example, S. Cohen and A. Scull, eds *Social Control and the State: Comparative and Historical Essays* (Oxford: Oxford University Press 1983), especially J.A. Mayer 'Notes towards a Working Definition of Social Control in Historical Analysis' and M. Ignatieff 'State, Civil Society, and Total Institutions: A Critique of Recent Social Histories of Punishment.'

5 S. Cohen *Visions of Social Control* (Cambridge: Cambridge University Press 1985) 13–14

6 SNS 1758, c. 12, c. 13, c. 17, c. 19, c. 20, and c. 25. See also Beamish Murdoch 'On the Origins of Nova Scotia Law' (1863) reprinted in P.B. Waite et al., eds *Law in a Colonial Society: The Nova Scotia Experience* (Toronto: Carswell 1981) 190. I am very grateful to Jim Phillips for sharing his notes and his unpublished work on the early bridewell and the development of criminal law in Nova Scotia.

7 Offenders who committed aggravated assault were defined as those who 'unlawfully cut out or disable[d] the tongue, put out an eye, slit the nose, cut off a nose or lip ... [or] disfigure[d] any such person': SNS 1758, c. 13, ss. 2 and 3.

8 Benefit of clergy was a legacy of medieval criminal law, by which initially the clergy could save themselves from execution for a first offence. It was extended first to all who could pass a simple literacy test, and then effectively to everyone when that test became pro forma in 1706.

9 SNS 1768, c. 3, s. 3; SNS 1799, c. 3, s. 11; SNS 1801, c. 4, ss. 1, 2, and 7; SNS 1766, c. 1, s. 1

10 In 1774 petty larceny was made punishable also by a maximum of three months' imprisonment with hard labour: SNS 1774, c. 7.

11 SNS 1787, c. 6

12 Pardon to Jane Tolmy, PANS MG100, vol. 239, no. 7; Trial of George Ingat, 5 May 1808, PANS RG1, vol. 343

13 C. Ward 'Punishments of Seventy Years Ago' *New Brunswick Magazine* 3 (1899) 84. See also Administration of Justice Records, PANS RG34–312, series J12; Pardons, RG50; Papers Relating to Criminal Prosecutions, RG1, vol. 343; Halifax County Records, RG34–312, series C, vols 3–4, 10–11; and Executive Council Petitions, RG3, vol. 1.

14 Nancy O'Neal, 2 July 1813, PANS RG1, vol. 343, no. 4

15 Executive Council Minutes, 22 Dec. 1752, PANS RG1, vol. 186, 276, and 27 June 1754, vol. 187, 77–9; W.S. MacNutt *The Atlantic Provinces: The Emergence of Colonial Society* (Toronto: McClelland and Stewart 1965) 53–4; T.H. Raddall *Halifax: Warden of the North* rev. ed. (Toronto: McClelland and Stewart, 1971)
16 *Halifax Gazette* 23 Dec 1752
17 See Ignatieff *Just Measure of Pain* 11–12.
18 Executive Council Minutes, 27 June 1754, PANS RG1, vol. 187
19 SNS 1759, c. 1, ss. 4, 6, and 7.
20 SNS 1759, c. 1, s. 5
21 Account of Persons Committed to the Workhouse ... of Halifax, 1 Jan. – 31 Dec. 1790, PANS RG34–312, series J4
22 House of Assembly Papers, PANS RG5, series P, vol. 80, no. 4
23 SNS 1792, c. 5, ss. 1, 2, 4, 6, and 13
24 SNS 1801, c. 6; SNS 1802, c. 6
25 R.E. Kroll 'Confines, Wards and Dungeons' *Collections* 40 (1981) 95–6
26 H.M. Logan 'The Military Prison in Halifax' (1932) in PANS, and 'Melville Island, the Military Prison of Halifax' United Services Institute of Nova Scotia *Annual Journal* 6 (1933) 12–34
27 Garrison Court Martial, 28 Jan. 1805 and 25 Feb. 1805, Military Orders, Halifax, PANS MG1, vol. 706, no. 44, 31; P. Burroughs 'Crime and Punishment in the British Army, 1815–1870' *English Historical Review* 396 (1985) 561, 571. For military punishments generally in this period, see Burroughs 'Crime and Punishment.' See also Raddall *Halifax* 51.
28 Grand Jury Report, 19 Sept. 1815, PANS RG34–312
29 SNS 1816, c. 9
30 County Papers Relating to Sherriffs, Boundaries and Jails, 1808–36, PANS RG1, vol. 381
31 Petition of Halifax Magistrates to Assembly, 28 Feb. 1823, PANS RG1, vol. 411, no. 107
32 MacNutt *Atlantic Provinces* 71, 156–7; Raddall *Halifax* 154–5
33 Account of Persons Committed to the Workhouse ... of Halifax, 1 Jan.–31 Dec. 1790; Quarterly Return of the County Bridewell of Halifax, 5 Sept. 1825, PANS RG34–312, series J4
34 Magistrates' Petition, PANS RG1, vol. 411, no. 108; Grand Jury Reports, 15 Mar. 1824, PANS RG34–312, vol. P8
35 John Fielding, Petition to the Grand Jury, 11 Dec. 1828, Grand Jury Reports, 12 Dec. 1828, PANS RG34–312
36 Aberdeen to Campbell, 2 Mar. 1835, PANS RG1, vol. 73, 65–8
37 Glenelg to Campbell, 16 Mar. 1836; 18 Mar. 1836; 20 Oct. 1836; 25 May 1837, PANS RG1, vol. 74

38 Burroughs 'Crime and Punishment' 560

39 *JHA* 1839, app. 18, 12

40 *Novascotian* 14 Jan. 1829. Much more research needs to be done on the incidence of capital punishment in Nova Scotia, but anecdotal accounts do appear to bear out Halliburton's analysis: not only were there very few executions, but also those that were carried out involved strangers – sailors, new immigrants, and transients.

41 Ward 'Punishments' 84; Court Cases, 18 Feb. 1828, PANS MG4, vol. 239, no. 4; John Hynds, 20 Jan. 1826, RG1, vol. 345, no. 4

42 Commissioners' Report 1833, PANS MG100, vol. 100, no. 37

43 *Acadian Recorder* 8 Feb. 1834

44 *Colonial Pearl* 1 Mar. 1839

45 Perhaps indicative of public sentiment is Raddall's account of how the body of an accidentally deceased public hangman, nicknamed 'Tomahawk,' was thrown into a latrine and left there with a noose around his neck: Raddall *Halifax* 66

46 For Upper Canada see R. Baehre 'Origins of the Penitentiary System in Upper Canada' *Ontario History* 69 (1977) 185–207; J.M. Beattie *Attitudes towards Crime and Punishment in Upper Canada, 1830–1850: A Documentary Study* (Toronto: University of Toronto Centre of Criminology 1977); C.J. Taylor 'The Kingston, Ontario Penitentiary and Moral Architecture' *Histoire Sociale/Social History* 12 (1979) 385–408; and J.J. Bellomo 'Upper Canadian Attitudes towards Crime and Punishment, 1832–1851' *Ontario History* 64 (1972) especially 11–12.

47 Grand Jury Reports, 15 Dec. 1823, PANS RG34-312, vol. 13

48 Grand Jury Reports, 28 Jan. 1824, 15 Mar. 1824, ibid. On the issue of convict labour in Upper Canada, see B. Palmer 'Kingston Mechanics and the Rise of the Penitentiary, 1833–1836' *Histoire sociale/Social History* 13 (1980) 7–32.

49 General Statement of Prisoners Confined in the County Bridewell since its Establishment till the Present Date (February 1822) PANS RG7, series B, vol. 5

50 Grand Jury Reports, 15 Dec. 1829, PANS RG34-312, vol. 13

51 See R. Baehre 'Pauper Emigration to Upper Canada in the 1830s' *Histoire sociale/Social History* 28 (1981) 364–5

52 *Blue Books* (Nova Scotia) 1832, PANS RG2, vol. 45

53 Grand Jury Reports, 15 Mar. 1833, PANS RG34-312, vol. 13

54 *JHA* 1841, app. 22, 102–3

55 List of prisoners in Bridewell, 1 Apr. 1839, Board of Works, PANS RG7, series B, vol. 5

56 Grand Jury Reports, 11 Mar. 1828; 15 Dec. 1829; 14 June 1830; 15 Mar. 1832; 17 Dec. 1833, PANS RG34-312, vol. 13

57 J.M. Beck 'A Fool for a Client: The Trial of Joseph Howe' in P.A. Buckner and D. Frank, eds *The Acadiensis Reader: Volume One* (Fredericton: Acadiensis Press 1985) 229
58 Grand Jury Reports, 8 Dec. 1832; 23 Apr. 1834, PANS RG34-312, vol. 13
59 Grand Jury Reports, 13 Dec. 1834, ibid.; Beck 'Trial of Joseph Howe'
60 *Acadian Recorder* 25 Feb. and 4 Mar. 1837
61 *JHA* 1839, app. 81, 155
62 Beck 'Trial of Joseph Howe' 229
63 Weekly Return of County Bridewell, 14 Mar. 1836, PANS RG34-312, series J4; Extracts from Presentment of Grand Jury, December Sessions, 1835, JHA 1836, app. 75
64 *JHA* 1838, app. 18, 70–71; 1839, app. 18, 12–13
65 *JHA* app. 81, 155
66 *Novascotian* 3 May 1838; *Acadian Recorder* 23 Feb. 1839
67 *JHA* 1836, app. 75
68 Glenelg to Lieutenant-Governor, 28 Nov. 1835, ibid. 1836, app. 65, 138; 1831–4, app. 75
69 *Blue Books* (Nova Scotia) PANS RG2, vols 44–47
70 *JHA* 1838, app. 18, 70–1
71 For a different interpretation, see K. Pryke 'Poor Relief and Health Care in Halifax, 1827–1849' in W. Mitchinson and J.D. McGinnis, eds *Essays in the History of Canadian Medicine* (Toronto: McClelland and Stewart 1988) 51–2. This trend was also evident in Upper Canada: see R. Baehre 'Paupers and Poor Relief in Upper Canada' *Historical Papers/Communications Historiques* (1981) 57–80.
72 *JHA* 1839–40, app. 18; 1841, app. 169, 182; SNS 1840, c. 41; Committee on the Penitentiary, *JHA* 1844, app. 65, 154–5
73 *JHA* 1842, app. 22; 1843, app. 100
74 *JHA* 1844, app. 65
75 Report of the Commissioners of the Provincial Penitentiary: A Return of Work and Labour executed and performed by the Convicts at the Provincial Penitentiary between the 1st January and 31st December, 1845; *JHA* 1846, app. 17, 60
76 Return of Criminal Trials in the Province for 1850, 1851, & 1852, PANS RG7, series B, vol. 5.
77 The military was permitted to avail itself of any prison at the cost of 6d per day per prisoner.
78 Fifth Annual Report of the Inspector of Penitentiaries, 1880, Daily Average of Prisoners in Halifax Penitentiary, from 1st January 1872 till 30th June 1880: Canada *Sessional Papers* 1881, app. 65. See also Convict Register, Halifax Penitentiary, 1873–80, PANS Misc. P–Penitentiaries, reel 3

79 Statement of Prisoners received during the Year ending 30th June 1880. Race, Country, Religion, Education, Age, Civil Condition, Crime, Length of Sentence: Canada *Sessional Papers* 1881, app. 65.
80 Taylor 'Kingston Penitentiary'
81 R.C. MacLeod, ed. *Lawful Authority: Readings in the History of Criminal Justice in Canada* (Toronto: Copp Clark 1988) 220. On moral architecture and the lunatic asylum, see T. Brown 'Architecture as Therapy' *Archivaria* 10 (1980) 199–223.
82 *JHA* 1845, app. 73, 207; SNS 1845, c. 42. On the micro-physics of power and panopticism see Foucault *Discipline and Punish* 170–228 and Ignatieff *A Just Measure of Pain* 77–8, 109–13. Detailed accounts are provided in A.G. Hess, ed. *Reports of the Prison Discipline Society* (Montclair, NJ: Patterson Smith 1972) and O.J. Lewis, ed. *The Development of American Prisons and Prison Customs, 1776–1845* (Montclair, NJ: Patterson Smith, 1967).
83 SNS 1845, c. 43
84 A statement of their occupational designations and wages is included in A Return of Work and Labour, supra note 75.
85 Board of Commissioners, 16 April 1852, ibid.
86 Report of the Commissioners of the Provincial Penitentiary, *JHA* 1845, app. 47, 142–55
87 Rules and Regulations for the Government of the Provincial Penitentiary of Nova Scotia, ibid. 147
88 Convicts, ibid. There is little doubt that strenuous efforts were made to effect this system. See Monthly Commissioners Visiting Report Book, 1845 to 1852, PANS RG1, vol. 418.
89 P. O'Neill *A Seaport Legacy* (Erin, Ont.: Musson 1976) 561; Stanley to Falkland, 30 Nov. 1844, *JHA* 1845, app. 36, 108
90 Report of the Commissioners of the Penitentiary for 1846, PANS RG7, series B, vol. 5.
91 Report of the Commissioners of the Provincial Penitentiary, *JHA* 1847, app. 27, 125
92 Carpenter to James B. Uniacke, 26 Jan. 1846, PANS RG7, series B, vol. 5. See also Penitentiary, *JHA* 1853, app. 31, 321.
93 See Return of Works performed by the prisoners confined in the Provincial Penitentiary during the year 1847, PANS RG7, series B, vol. 5.
94 Report of the Chairman of the Board of Works, Penitentiary, *JHA* 1853, app. 31, 320
95 *JHA* 1854, app. 18, 154
96 Report of Penitentiary Committee, *JHA* 1861, app. 37, 7. For a comparison of penitentiary with total provincial expenditures, see Board of Works Report, *JHA* 1865, app. 4.

97 See Fifth Annual Report of the Director of Penitentiaries, 1872, no. 75, 18; Board of Works Report, *JHA* 1862, app. 12, 8–10; Board of Works Report (c), *JHA* 1865, app. 8, 1–3; Report of the Directors of Penitentiaries, Canada *Sessional Papers* 1873, no. 42, 18–19; Board of Works Report, Penitentiary, *JHA* 1853, app. 31, 321; and Report of Committee on Penitentiary, *JHA* 1863, app. 35, 3.

98 Report of Penitentiary Committee, *JHA* 1862, app. 52, 2

99 Board of Works Report, ibid. app. 12

100 The Committee appointed to consider the Petition of the court of General Sessions, *JHA* 1845, app. 69, 199

101 Committee on Accounts of the Provincial Penitentiary, *JHA* 1851, app. 70, 378; Report of Penitentiary Committee, *JHA* 1853, app. 54, 378

102 *JHA* 1846, app. 17

103 Board of Works Report, *JHA* 1862, app. 12, 10; Report of Penitentiary Committee, *JHA* 1863, app. 35, 3–4

104 Board of Works Report, Penitentiary, *JHA* 1853, app. 31, 321; Report of Penitentiary Committee, *JHA* 1864, app. 45; R.J. Black to the Chairman of Board of Works, 31 Dec. 1858, *JHA* 1859, app. 12, 172

105 Fifth Annual Report of the Inspectors of Penitentiaries, Canada *Sessional Papers* 1881, no. 65, 93

106 Report of Penitentiary Committee, *JHA* 1852, app. 70, 382. The Crofton, or Irish, system called for convicts to be put into solitary confinement for up to nine months after their arrival as a reminder that they were being punished. It also employed a marks system that rewarded inmates with minor privileges for showing industry and good conduct. See M. Carpenter, ed. *Reformatory Prison Discipline as Developed by the Hon. Sir Walter Crofton in the Irish Convict Prisons* (Montclair, NJ: Patterson Smith 1967).

107 Carpenter to the Commissioners of the Provincial Penitentiary, 30 May 1846, PANS RG7, series B, vol. 5

108 Report of Penitentiary Committee, *JHA* 1852, app. 77, 382–3

109 Board of Works Report, Penitentiary, *JHA* 1853, app. 31, 322

110 Report of Committee on the Penitentiary, *JHA* 1862, app. 52, 2

111 Report of Committee on the Penitentiary, *JHA* 1865, app. 46, 1–3; Main features to be attended to, ibid. 2; Changes Recommended to be Carried Out at the Provincial Penitentiary, by the Committee for Improving the State of Prison Discipline and Management, ibid. 1

112 In the case of Kingston this was in part a response to penitentiary promoters who argued that economic considerations, such as the benefits that derived from convict labour, should be considered the primary benefits from the penitentiary system. See Canada *Sessional Papers* 1865, no. 14, 74; 1866, no. 6, 16–17; and 1868, no. 40, 6.

113 *JHA* 1866, app. 59
114 Sixth Annual Report of the Board of Inspectors of Asylums, Prisons etc for the Year 1866, Canada *Sessional Papers* 1867–8, no. 40.
115 First Annual Report of the Directors of Penitentiaries (1868), Canada *Sessional Papers* 1870, no. 5, 7–8. This crackdown came as officials began to express renewed concern about the effectiveness of penitentiary discipline after a series of American and European prison riots.
116 SC 1868, c. 75
117 Third Annual Report of the Directors of Penitentiaries, Canada *Sessional Papers* 1871, no. 60, 67; Fourth Annual Report of the Directors of Penitentiaries, Canada *Sessional Papers* 1872, no. 27, 73
118 Fifth Annual Report of the Directors of Penitentiaries, Canada *Sessional Papers* 1873, no. 75, 10
119 Ibid.
120 Sixth Annual Report of the Directors of Penitentiaries, Canada *Sessional Papers* 1874, no. 42, 19; First Annual Report of the Inspector of Penitentiaries (1875), Canada *Sessional Papers* 1876, no. 87, 22; Second Annual Report of the Inspector of Penitentiaries (1876), Canada *Sessional Papers* 1877, no. 15, 19
121 See Number and Description of Punishments inflicted in the Halifax Penitentiary for the Six Months ended 30th June 1877, in Third Annual Report of the Inspector of Penitentiaries (1877), Canada *Sessional Papers* 1878, no. 12, 120.
122 SC 1868, c. 75; Senate Debates 1867–8, 282–3
123 *Morning Herald* 16 July 1880
124 Warden's Daily Report, 14 and 16 July 1880, Canada *Sessional Papers* 1881, no. 65
125 Report of the Commissioners of the Provincial Penitentiary, *JHA* 1845, app. 47, 144
126 Report of the Commission appointed to enquire into the Management of Several Public Institutions Receiving Provincial Aid, *JHA* 1857–8, app. 136, 26
127 Sixth Annual Report of the Inspector of Penitentiaries (1881), Canada *Sessional Papers* 1882, no. 12
128 W.A. Calder 'The Way of the Transgressor Is Hard: Punishment in Canada's Federal Penitentiary System, 1867–1899' paper presented at annual meeting of Canadian Historical Association, 1978
129 H. Whitaker to W. Evans, 20 Dec. 1879, PANS RG34–312, series J, vol. 11

7

'Raised in Rockhead. Died in the Poor House': Female Petty Criminals in Halifax, 1864–1890

B. JANE PRICE

This essay is a contribution to the growing literature on the history of the female offender. Much of the recent work done in this area has dealt with prostitution[1] or with other aspects of the criminal law that particularly concerned women.[2] I wish to look at a broader range of offences – the petty crimes that resulted in incarceration in the city prison.[3] My focus is Halifax in the late nineteenth-century; in that period the city witnessed industrialization, urban and population growth, and the adjustment of municipal institutions in response to those changes.[4] Victorian Halifax had its own female criminal class, a caste of women who were repeatedly convicted of petty offences. They were poor, and vagrancy laws criminalized their poverty; they 'chose' prostitution because few jobs were open to them and those that were paid desperately low wages. The social milieu of these outcasts had little in common with the polite amusements of their betters and was apt to involve drinking and public rowdiness, both of which were also subject to the sanctions of the criminal law.

My examination of the female petty criminal is derived primarily from the prison records and newspaper accounts; it begins with a brief look at the criminal law and the courts that enforced that law. The major part of my study is built upon statistical analyses of the reasons for incarceration and of the demographic profiles of those incarcerated. I have also looked at the socio-economic backgrounds, the living conditions, and the social milieux of these women, and asked what their lives were like and why they committed the offences that saw them incarcerated. This essay is not about broader societal responses to women's crime. The impact of the later nineteenth-century social reform movement in that area undoubtedly merits study; indeed, it should receive a treatment by itself. For the present I wish to carry out the more modest but necessary task of laying the groundwork for such a study.

THE COURTS AND THE LAW

The offenders studied here appeared at the lowest levels of the criminal court system. Before 1867 they turned up in the Halifax Police Court, which met daily and was presided over by the mayor of Halifax or, in his absence, by one of the city's aldermen. the court dealt with all matters 'appertaining to the office of justice of the peace, necessary for the apprehension, committal, conviction and punishment of criminal offenders.' Above the Police Court stood the City Court, which was presided over by the mayor, one alderman, and the city recorder. The City Court exercised a broad criminal jurisdiction that extended to the non-jury trials of all criminal offences 'committed within the city or on the harbour' except 'charges of treason, homicide, burglary or arson.'[5]

In 1867, after attacks on its procedures and allegations of bias, the Police Court was abolished and replaced by the Stipendiary Magistrate's Court, which was presided over by a legally trained judge with security of tenure. For the first nineteen years after the position was established, Halifax's magistrate was Henry Pryor, a five-time mayor of the city and a former member of the House of Assembly.[6] In his courtroom Halifax's petty delinquents saw the law in action. No doubt some of the women examined in this study eventually found themselves in higher courts charged with more serious offences for which the penalty was incarceration in the provincial penitentiary rather than in the city prison at Rockhead.[7] But as long as their offences remained relatively minor they went to Pryor's court and faced a summary trial.

The substantive criminal law dealing with prostitution, vagrancy, drunkenness, profanity, assault, and larceny, the most common offences for which women were incarcerated, was the result of regulation by several different levels of government. The residents of Victorian Halifax were subject to the received common law, to a regime of municipal by-laws and ordinances, to the statute law of the colony (later the province), and, after 1867, to the federal criminal law.

Prostitution per se was not illegal, so the authorities had to apprehend prostitutes on other grounds.[8] Before Confederation, Halifax prostitutes were convicted under provincial vagrancy or public morals legislation, or under the public nuisance provisions of the City Charter.[9] The Vagrant Act of 1851 outlined three categories of offenders: beggars, idle and wandering persons lacking visible means of support, and paupers returning to a place from which they had previously been removed. The public morals legislation was aimed at keepers of bawdy-houses, who could be fined five pounds, imprisoned for a month, or both. It was probably easier for the authorities to apprehend the prostitutes themselves under the public nuisance provision of the City Charter. That section identified eleven categories of offenders, which gave police a wide discretion to remove undesirable characters from the streets (prostitutes generally being labelled 'lewd characters').

In 1869 the dominion government enacted a Vagrancy Act. Its definition of 'vagrants' was more expansive and included 'all common prostitutes, or nightwalkers wandering in the fields ... not giving a satisfactory account of themselves.' The provision relieved the courts of the need to label a prostitute a lewd character or a vagabond before convicting her. The same broad definition of 'vagrant' was used in the 1886 act that replaced the original statute, although it was expanded somewhat to include 'inmates' of brothels. The vagrancy section of the 1892 Criminal Code included both 'common prostitutes' and 'inmates' in its definition of 'vagrant.'[10] These statutory provisions reflected the perception that the sex trade should not merely be regulated, as it had been under the British Contagious Diseases Acts, but stamped out, and its victims 'saved.'[11] Another legal means by which the menace of prostitution could be attacked was a provincial statute that made keeping a brothel an offence.[12] Of all these enactments the municipal law seems to have been used most frequently. Many vagrants were sentenced to one year in Rockhead, and a sentence of that length could be imposed only under the City Charter. Originally, the federal legislation provided for a maximum penalty of only two months' imprisonment (increased to six months in 1874).[13]

The statutory regime pertaining to drunkenness was less elaborate. Under provincial legislation drunkenness alone, unaccompanied by any other illegal conduct, could trigger legal sanctions. The penalty was a maximum fine of four dollars, a considerable sum for the poor of the late nineteenth century, and imprisonment for those unable to pay. Under the City Charter a 'habitual drunkard' or an offender who was 'drunk and disorderly' could be sent to Rockhead for up to ten days. Drunks could also be apprehended under the federal vagrancy legislation for 'causing a disturbance in the streets or highways by ... being drunk.'

The penalty was substantially harsher – a maximum of two months' imprisonment in 1869 (increased to six months in 1874).[14]

Obscene language was not expressly mentioned in the City Charter's public-nuisance provision. It is conceivable that it could have been read into one of the other eleven categories of offences listed, although it seems more likely that those convicted of profanity were charged under provincial public morals legislation. Penalties for profanity were monetary: forty cents for a first offence, eighty cents for a second, etc.; two- to twelve-hour jail terms were imposed on those who could not pay.[15] The federal vagrancy legislation also contained a prohibition against causing a disturbance by swearing; again, the penalty was originally two months and later six.

The statutory regime under which women were convicted of larceny was not so straightforward. The Nova Scotia legislation provided a maximum penalty of seven years' imprisonment for petty larceny. The provision was repealed in 1869; larceny was subsequently dealt with by federal statute law, which listed numerous offences ranging from oyster-dredging to stealing 'to the value of two dollars any woollen, linen, hempen or cotton yarn.'[16] The minimum penalty for simple larceny was two years, but the offenders imprisoned in Rockhead during this period received much less. The sixty-day sentence that Elizabeth Riley served in December 1890 was typical.[17] It seems likely that before 1869 petty larcenists were convicted under the Nova Scotia act, and that they were charged with the common law offence of petty larceny thereafter.

A similar confusion comes in examining the laws on assault. Jurisdiction over cases of assault was granted to the City Court by the 1864 charter, but none of the acts governing the stipendiary magistrate expressly referred to assault, and it does not appear to have been covered by the charter's public-nuisance provision. Assault is mentioned in Nova Scotia legislation only in the context of assault on a police officer.[18] From 1869 a federal statute listed a wide variety of assaults. The relevant provision for the offenders studied here was probably section 43: 'Where any person unlawfully assaults or beats another person, any Justice of the Peace, upon complaint by or on behalf of the party aggrieved, praying him to proceed summarily on the complaint, may hear and determine such offence.' The maximum penalty was two months' imprisonment and a fine of twenty dollars plus costs. Substantially the same provisions were incorporated into the 1886 consolidation and the first Criminal Code of 1892.[19] We are left without a clear idea of how offenders convicted of assault were found to be legally liable until the introduction of the 1869 federal act; the common law probably operated to fill the gap left by statutes.

The law affecting petty criminals was a confusing and often contradictory, mélange of provincial, federal, and municipal legislation and the common law. Although this maze of regulation may appear confusing, those who used the system understood which activities should be punished and which should not, and common offences were disposed of with considerable dispatch and minimal concern for the legal niceties. Convicting authorities did not bother to state which law was being applied; offences were described by reference to the defendant's actions alone, unaccompanied by any mention of statutory provisions. It is possible that men like Henry Pryor did not care whether the precise elements of the offence were made out. When James March was convicted of being under the influence but let off with a warning in July 1879, for example, one Halifax newspaper noted that 'how much was not stated, and it was a very important question how far a man may be "legally" under the influence.'[20] In May 1886 Pryor's successor Robert Motton dismissed the case against a person charged with being under the influence of liquor and standing on a street corner on the ground that 'no offense against the law was noted in the summons.'[21] Yet the records of the Stipendiary Magistrates' Court under Pryor reveal numerous examples of convictions on precisely that charge.[22] Those who ran the city's courts believed that they had the authority to control prostitutes, drunks, vagrants, persons using obscene language, and those who committed larceny or assault. The fact of that authority was enough, and its precise source did not concern them a great deal; the operation of the courts was marked by paternalism rather than proceduralism.

PATTERNS OF INCARCERATION

The offences that resulted in imprisonment can usefully be divided into seven categories: prostitution, vagrancy, larceny, assault, drunkenness, nuisance, and miscellaneous offences. Those charged with prostitution were keepers, lewd characters, inmates of a bawdy house, and, less frequently, strumpets, night-walkers, and common prostitutes. There were legal grounds to convict prostitutes as vagrants; I have distinguished the two because not all female vagrants were convicted for prostitution. Included in the 'nuisance' category are the offence of using profane language and 'disorderly' offences, such as fighting in the streets. 'Miscellaneous' offences encompass everything from cruelty to animals and

TABLE 1
Chronology of Incarcerations by Sex

Year	Male	Female	Total	Female (percentage)
1864	259	180	439	41.0
1865	302	212	514	41.2
1866	305	224	529	42.3
1867	244	189	433	43.6
1868	345	175	520	33.6
1869	365	134	499	26.8
1870	335	207	542	38.1
1871	349	160	509	31.4
1872	410	175	585	29.9
1873	362	160	522	30.6
1874	367	149	516	28.8
1875	398	126	524	24.0
1876	468	152	620	24.5
1877	416	112	528	21.2
1878	439	131	570	22.9
1879	405	130	535	24.2
1880	393	137	530	25.8
1881	267	120	387	31.0
1882	298	114	412	27.6
1883	215	117	332	35.2
1884	216	86	302	28.4
1885	257	111	368	30.1
1886	221	86	307	28.0
1887	162	69	231	29.8
1888	164	77	241	31.9
1889	218	105	323	32.5
1890	259	97	356	27.2
TOTAL	8,439	3,735	12,174	30.7

interfering with the watch to neglecting children and contempt of court. The incarceration figures represent every offence recorded in the registers, even if one woman committed more than one crime on a single occasion; therefore, the number of offences is considerably higher than the number of offenders. The tables that accompany this section were compiled from the city prison registers.[23]

Crimes committed by women were a significant part of the later nineteenth-century carceral landscape (see table 1). Although this finding is no longer the startling revelation that it might have been ten or fifteen years ago, it is none the less noteworthy.[24] The relatively high incidence of imprisonment of women in Halifax also contrasts with the still powerful myth of the law-abiding Canadian past.[25] Women were imprisoned predominantly for moral offences, and they were imprisoned much less frequently than men: some 30 per cent of the more than twelve thousand people committed to prison were women! That figure accords with other studies; indeed, markedly lower numbers of female criminals as opposed to male criminals have been accepted as the norm by criminologists since the earliest days of the discipline.[26] The ratio shown here is some 10 per cent higher than the 21.2 per cent identified by J.M. Beattie in his study of eighteenth-century England, a difference probably explained by his inclusion of all criminal offences, serious and petty. Women are less inclined than men to commit offences such as murder and robbery. André Lachance identifies roughly the same ratio as Beattie.[27] Studies of female criminality in the nineteenth century suggest a ratio closer to 30 per cent: Victor Gattrell and David Hadden identify a high of 25.6 per cent in nineteenth-century Britain, and David Jones estimates 30 per cent.[28] Modern studies suggest a significantly lower crime rate among women than that ascertained here. Again, this variation may result from the inclusion of all varieties of offences in the studies.[29]

Why did women commit fewer offences than men? The historian's standard answer is that women's social roles made them less likely to commit criminal offences. As wives and mothers they lived in the private sphere, where they had fewer opportunities to offend. Moreover, they were trained by society to conduct themselves in a fashion that could not incorporate any criminal deviance. This explanation is less convincing for petty offences, however. The women who appear in the pages of the prison registers, particularly the chronic offenders, belonged to the underclass of Victorian Halifax. They lived in a community of outcasts. They were part of the 'dangerous class' in which women were not as well socialized in the roles of wives and mothers or as restricted to the private sphere as their 'betters.' Many of them were working women, forced to make their own way and unable to live their lives in seclusion. None the less, women's separate role reduced their crime directly, since the women of outcast Halifax were still wives and mothers, however removed their experience of those roles was from that of their betters. Patriarchy probably also operated indirectly, because its tendency to idealize women as maternal and for the most part docile creatures would have resulted in lower prosecution rates.[30]

Overall, the years between 1864 and 1890 witnessed a decline in the level of female criminality. This decline is most apparent in the later 1880s,

TABLE 2
Incarcerations by Sex

Offence	Male	Female	Female (percentage)
Drunkenness	4,288	1,722	28.6
Prostitution-related	89	505	85.0
Vagrancy	662	738	47.2
Assault	822	130	13.6
Larceny	1,224	246	16.7
Nuisance	677	402	37.2
Miscellaneous	602	68	10.1

and corresponds with a similar fall in imprisonment statistics for men. Several explanations suggest themselves. First, the 1880s saw very little population growth in comparison with previous decades. Crime levels in urban centres often rise as the population grows. In 1861 Halifax had a population of 25,026. By 1871 that figure had increased to 29,582, and by 1881 to 36,100; but the 1880s saw only a small rise to 38,556.[31] Perhaps crime rates fell as the population stabilized. Second, lower crime rates could be the result of the economic prosperity of the 1880s,[32] or of the reduced demand for prostitutes' services caused by a decline in troop levels, although the latter explanation does not account for the fact that the number of incarcerations of men also dropped off in the 1880s. It is possible that the police may have not so readily arrested wrongdoers, or, since these figures are based on incarcerations, that the courts may have been more lenient in their sentencing practices. A new stipendiary magistrate, Robert Motton, was appointed after Henry Pryor retired in 1886; Motton had a reputation as a harsher man than his predecessor. The evidence is inconclusive on all of these questions, and further research is needed with respect to court records, comparisons with serious crime, and the patterns of criminality following the decline in the 1880s.

Most of the women imprisoned were guilty of prostitution, vagrancy, nuisance, or drunkenness (see table 2). It is tempting to see this emphasis on morals offences as a conscious rejection by working-class women of respectable society's sexual and social mores. Their crimes may have been a form of rebellion against a society that offered them so little, but it is difficult to interpret them solely in a political sense; they probably were a reflection of their life-styles and social interaction, and a means of economic survival.

Prostitution-related incarcerations on average accounted for 13.5 per

TABLE 3
Major Offences for Which Women Were Imprisoned

Year	Prostitution	Vagrancy	Drunkenness
1864	25 (13.8)	59 (32.7)	70 (38.8)
1865	33 (15.5)	49 (23.1)	107 (50.4)
1866	36 (16.0)	57 (25.4)	89 (39.7)
1867	42 (22.2)	53 (28.0)	39 (20.6)
1868	17 (9.7)	40 (22.8)	75 (42.8)
1869	6 (4.4)	22 (16.4)	67 (50.0)
1870	27 (13.0)	26 (12.5)	106 (51.2)
1871	36 (22.5)	14 (8.7)	91 (56.8)
1872	49 (28.0)	21 (12.0)	73 (41.7)
1873	21 (13.1)	31 (19.3)	65 (40.6)
1874	17 (11.4)	38 (25.5)	71 (47.6)
1875	12 (9.5)	26 (20.6)	64 (50.7)
1876	21 (13.8)	21 (13.8)	70 (46.0)
1877	21 (18.7)	19 (16.9)	53 (47.3)
1878	23 (17.5)	29 (22.1)	58 (44.2)
1879	18 (13.8)	37 (28.4)	42 (32.3)
1880	14 (10.2)	26 (18.9)	63 (45.9)
1881	6 (5.0)	11 (9.1)	64 (53.3)
1882	6 (5.2)	5 (4.4)	81 (71.0)
1883	16 (13.6)	16 (13.6)	65 (55.5)
1884	4 (4.6)	9 (10.4)	51 (59.3)
1885	17 (15.3)	6 (5.4)	67 (60.3)
1886	13 (15.1)	6 (6.9)	44 (51.1)
1887	9 (13.0)	3 (4.3)	33 (47.8)
1888	10 (12.9)	8 (10.3)	25 (32.4)
1889	4 (3.8)	15 (14.2)	44 (41.9)
1890	2 (2.0)	15 (15.4)	45 (46.3)
TOTAL	505 (13.5)	662 (17.7)	1,722 (46.1)

cent of all female incarcerations, although rates altered considerably over time, and after 1880 there was a sustained falling off. In 1890 only one woman, Mary Ann Tolliver, an eighteen-year-old black, was imprisoned for actually being a prostitute (see tables 3 and 4). It is impossible to be sure how many of the female vagrants were imprisoned for prostitution. The charge of vagrancy, which was legally available for the purpose, was used throughout this period for apprehending prostitutes. Kate Mackenzie, seventeen, and her sister Ellen, nineteen, were brought up by their father for 'leading dissolute lives' and living in a 'disreputable house.' Pryor apparently 'could do no more but send them up as vagrants for a year.'[33] Mary Cahill went up eight times for prostitution and vagrancy

TABLE 4
Minor Offences for Which Women Were Imprisoned

Year	Assault	Larceny	Nuisance	Miscellaneous	Percentage of annual total
1864	1	12	13	0	14.4
1865	2	10	6	5	10.8
1866	1	16	22	3	18.7
1867	7	17	26	5	29.1
1868	9	11	19	4	24.5
1869	6	16	14	3	29.1
1870	10	12	22	4	23.1
1871	4	11	3	1	11.8
1872	10	10	10	2	18.2
1873	4	19	18	2	26.8
1874	5	12	4	2	15.4
1875	6	7	10	1	19.0
1876	3	15	21	1	26.3
1877	8	5	5	1	16.9
1878	3	9	8	1	16.0
1879	2	13	18	0	25.3
1880	9	12	10	3	24.8
1881	6	5	23	5	32.5
1882	1	7	13	1	19.2
1883	2	3	14	1	17.0
1884	1	6	13	2	25.5
1885	4	2	8	7	18.9
1886	6	4	13	0	26.7
1887	4	4	15	1	34.7
1888	3	4	24	3	44.1
1889	9	1	25	7	40.0
1890	4	3	25	3	36.0
TOTAL	130	246	402	68	22.6

offences during these years – three times for vagrancy, three times for lewd conduct, and once as the keeper and once as an inmate of a bawdy-house. Catherine Dryden numbered five vagrancy and five prostitution-related convictions among her total of nineteen, and the careers of Margaret Chandler and Sarah Fischer display a similar record of imprisonments for both vagrancy and prostitution. This pattern of charges was common in other jurisdictions.[34]

Not all female vagrants were prostitutes. Jim Phillips's study of vagrants in Halifax elsewhere in this volume demonstrates that many of them were imprisoned for poverty, homelessness, and begging. There is no way to ascertain precisely how many vagrants were arrested as prostitutes, but an approximate figure can be obtained by assuming that the percentage of female vagrants in excess of the average of 30 per cent was made up of vagrants imprisoned for prostitution. This means that approximately 340 incarcerations could be added to the prostitution-related category, increasing the total to 849, or 22.6 per cent of all crimes committed by women. Regardless of whether prostitution-related imprisonments actually constituted a little more or a little less than 22 per cent, the figures are dramatically lower than the 63 to 87 per cent given by Constance Backhouse for the city of Toronto between 1846 and 1890. Backhouse includes convictions for drunkenness in the 'possible prostitution' category, however; if these are excluded the Toronto figure is approximately 17 per cent, lower than that for Halifax. Margaret Langdon's study of Calgary shows that between 1914 and 1941 prostitution offences constituted approximately 60 per cent of all convictions of women, a much larger figure.

There are two principal hypotheses that might explain these differences. Toronto was more industrialized than either Halifax in the nineteenth century or Calgary in the first half of the twentieth century. Perhaps as women found themselves able to obtain alternative employment prostitution became less attractive. Margaret Langdon has argued that this is precisely what took place in Calgary as job opportunities for women increased.[36] An alternative explanation might be that prosecution levels varied significantly. That is, Torontonians were more accepting of the social evil, more willing to leave prostitutes' activities largely unrestricted by the criminal law. But Halifax, a port town and a military garrison, was the kind of community in which the prostitute would be accepted as a necessary evil, a means of keeping the sailors and soldiers from invading the territory of the respectable folk; and Calgary, particularly in the early years of the twentieth century, experienced massive population growth, and was a frontier city that might be expected to tolerate the reality of prostitution.[37] Different methods of compiling statistics may be partially responsible for the discrepancy, and nineteenth-century prison records may be inaccurate or incomplete; but neither explanation accounts for such wide variations. One conclusion that can be drawn, however, is that prostitution offences constituted a very significant proportion of the total number of crimes committed by women in the century between 1840 and 1940 in these three Canadian cities.

A clear trend in the prostitution and vagrancy figures for Halifax was the sustained decline of both categories in the 1880s. This corresponded with an upswing in the Halifax economy; after the severe depression of the 1870s, the following decade witnessed unprecedented growth. Industrial output in Nova Scotia increased by 66 per cent, a growth rate higher than that of all other eastern Canadian provinces. Women's employment also increased in this period. In 1871 women comprised 22 per cent of the industrial work-force. In 1891 the proportion of women employees in the industrial sector had risen to 32 per cent; the largest industrial employers of women were tailors and clothiers' establishments.[38] The relationship between economic prosperity and prostitution and vagrancy offences by women suggests that at least those two types of crime were, to a large extent, economically motivated. Other studies lead to the same conclusion. Jim Phillips's study of vagrancy in Halifax elsewhere in this volume demonstrates a substantial correspondence between vagrancy convictions and the performance of the local economy. Langdon argues that the incidence of female criminality in Calgary, and in particular the frequency of prostitution offences, tended to decrease as women found greater economic opportunity outside the home.[39]

Drunkenness-related offences were consistently the most common ones for which women were imprisoned (see table 3). The number of drunkenness offences declined somewhat between the 1860s and the 1880s: the most occurred in 1865, the fewest in 1888. These figures suggest that the abuse of alcohol was not simply a man's offence, and that drunkenness among women was a serious problem in Victorian Halifax. Public drunkenness and the disorderly conduct that resulted from it were common. The transient sailors and soldiers were well known for their drinking and rowdy conduct, which took place primarily in the roughest areas of the city, and they were joined in these activities by a rump of the local female population.

Assault and larceny convictions constituted a small component of crimes committed by women (see table 4). Assaults were generally of a minor nature; their perpetrators were moved to physical violence by anger, frustration, or drunkenness. Women were often the victims of assault. For example, Mary Grant was charged with assault and battery on a Mrs Burroughs in 1878. Mary Byers, a black woman, teamed up with David Byers to beat Mary Ann Thomas. When an unnamed woman broke into a liquor shop and was discovered, she attacked both the proprietress and a pane of glass.[40] These types of incidents represented the violent undercurrent in most of the women's lives, although reports of assaults by women are greatly outnumbered by reports of women, especially wives, as victims.

Female larcenists were also few, and their thefts were often surreptitious. A girl named Purcell stole seven dollars from her father's drawer; others took clothing, or easily saleable items such as watches, or money from brothel clients.[41] Sarah Beals was convicted in June 1888 and May 1889 of picking pockets. The historical relationship between the economy and property crime has been the subject of intense, if inconclusive, debate, even in instances where statistics are plentiful.[42] Here the gross totals for larceny are too small to draw significant conclusions about why such crimes were committed by women. But conviction patterns do reveal a gradual though not a completely consistent decline in the level of larceny, so that by the late 1880s many fewer women were being imprisoned for the offence than had been the case in the 1860s. If larceny is seen as an offence motivated largely by economic deprivation, it makes sense that its occurrence would decrease as the level of economic prosperity increased. Indeed, the rarity of the offence is more significant than changing incarceration patterns. In any event, if economic need turned women to crime, prostitution was a better option.

Of the other offences for which women were imprisoned, most of the nuisance convictions involved profanity, a rather smaller number disorderly conduct. The rise in the later 1880s is the result of the authorities' practice of adding 'profane' to many drunkenness charges where previously they had been content to cite the major offence alone. Female offenders in the miscellaneous category included primarily those who contravened the licensing laws, those who 'interfered with the watch,' and a few who neglected their children.

DEMOGRAPHIC PROFILE

The petty female criminals of Victorian Halifax were a youthful group. The average age was just under thirty, with few fluctuations of more than two to three years each way in any given year (see table 5).[43] The youngest offender was seven-year-old Mary Miller, who was convicted of larceny along with Anne Miller (presumably her mother) in September 1870. Mother and daughter served sixty days in Rockhead. Flora Ann Beckett was the oldest offender: when she was convicted of drunkenness and profanity in April 1880 she claimed that she was ninety years of age. Both the overall picture of youthfulness and the broad age range identified here correspond with American and other Canadian studies. Calgary's female offenders typically fell between the ages of twenty and thirty, and Constance Backhouse's examination of nineteenth-century Toronto

TABLE 5
Average Age of Female Criminal Population

1864	28	1873	20	1882	32
1865	27.5	1874	28	1883	31
1866	29	1875	28	1884	30
1867	27	1876	30	1885	31
1868	27	1877	31	1886	30
1869	36	1878	30	1887	27
1870	32	1879	32	1888	31
1871	32	1880	32	1889	28
1872	31	1881	31	1890	28

TABLE 6
Religious Affiliation of Female Criminals
(percentages)

	Census of 1881	Prison register (average)
Roman Catholic	41	55
Protestant*	44	45
Other and unrecorded	15	

*Census includes only persons born in Nova Scotia

prostitution suggests that offenders were youthful, although there were some aberrations in this pattern.[44]

Catholics were overrepresented within the population of offenders (see table 6). Jim Phillips reports a similar high proportion of Catholics in his examination of vagrancy elsewhere in this volume, and attributes this to the Catholics' low economic status.[45] If one accepts that offences such as vagrancy and prostitution were often closely related to poverty, then disproportionate numbers of Catholics would be present among the convicted.

The overwhelming majority of Halifax's female criminals were at least first-generation Canadians (see table 7). An overall average of 83 per cent of those imprisoned were Canadian-born, a figure that corresponds almost exactly with the ratio in the Halifax population as a whole. The only exception to this pattern was the Irish female offender. At a time when 6 per cent of Halifax's population claimed to be of Irish birth, twice that number of female offenders were Irish-born. Toronto also had a disproportionately high number of Irish offenders.[46] It is possible that this

TABLE 7
Place of origin of female criminal population

	Census of 1881 (percentages)	Prison registers (average)
Halifax	na*	32
Nova Scotia	77	36
Maritimes	5	11
Canada	1	1
Ireland	6	12
Scotland	2	1
England	5	5
United States	na	1
Other	na	1

*Census includes only persons born in Nova Scotia

high figure is inaccurate, the result of a stereotyping of the female offender, or at least the prostitute, as a 'fallen' Irish Catholic. In 1858 William Sanger published a major study which suggested that the prostitutes of New York city were commonly of Irish Catholic derivation.[47] This suggestion, added to Haligonians' long experience with Catholics as an impoverished group, might well have invited such stereotyping. Xenophobia also played its part; it would have been easier for Haligonians to continue to think of their city as a respectable, decent town if they painted the female offender as a foreigner.[48]

The Catholic Irish excepted, there was a close correspondence between the proportion of immigrant offenders and the proportion of immigrants in the population generally. This pattern differs markedly from those revealed in studies of Toronto prostitution between 1840 and 1914; both Constance Backhouse and Lori Rotenberg found that immigrant women were strikingly overrepresented in convictions.[49] This difference resulted from the fact that nearly 70 per cent of the convicted female offenders were immigrants, in the sense that they came from outside the city. Immigration from other nations was not a significant factor in Halifax's growth during this period, although transatlantic migration had played its role in earlier decades. From the early 1860s the city's growth was fuelled by a rural–urban migration: Maritimers came to Halifax from rural communities or other smaller cities, and often moved west or south after only a brief stay.[50] In Halifax the counterpart of Toronto's foreign offender was the woman who had migrated from somewhere else in the Maritimes. The distance, in terms of life-style and experiences, between Halifax and a small rural community in the Maritimes was almost as great as that between the old world and the new, so that Rotenberg's description of the female immigrant in Toronto as physically and psychologically vulnerable is probably equally applicable to the Maritime immigrant new to Halifax.[51] Rural women did not possess the wherewithal to move easily from a small, closed community to the 'fast track' of the city, especially if they were poor, unskilled, and without an urban family network.

Native women, referred to in the court records as 'squaws,' appeared very infrequently; in any year they represented no more than 1 per cent of female offenders. Of the charges laid against native women, many involved two chronic recidivists, Mary Gooley and Mary Paul. The former appears thirty-two times in the prison registers, the latter ten times; most of their convictions were for drunkenness. A further eighteen incarcerations were imposed on three other female members of the Gooley family. Unfortunately, the census gives no information about the proportion of the Halifax population that was of native origin, so I cannot say with certainty whether this 1 per cent was disproportionately representative.

A better picture can be drawn of black female criminals. In 1881 blacks totalled approximately 3 per cent of the city's population, but throughout this period they accounted for approximately 20 per cent of all incarcerated women: the highest figure was 36 per cent in 1867, the lowest 3 per cent in 1881. It seems likely that the later figures are artificially low. The records for the 1880s contain less detailed information, and often do not mention race, even though many of those imprisoned in the 1880s were black.[52]

Whatever the precise figure for the proportion of black incarcerations, their disproportionate representation suggests two things. First, economic alternatives open to black women were even fewer than those available to white women, so that they found themselves 'getting by' as petty criminals. Second, police and court practices in Halifax were discriminatory. The *Morning Journal* was not hesitant in proclaiming its disdain for an 'ugly black' brothel-keeper who appeared in court.[53] On other occasions the newspapers poked malicious fun at the black community. Betsy Johnson was a 'colored demsel' who, having 'left Governor Campbell's retreat after 90 days service,' went 'on a new howl' and consequently 'was requested to retreat again for 90 days.'[54] Discriminatory attitudes and practices were not unique to Halifax. Racism was a feature of the working of the Calgary courts in the early twentieth century; although few black prostitutes appeared in court, those who did were treated more harshly than white offenders. Indeed, Michael Cross has argued that

TABLE 8
Recidivism

Times incarcerated	Number of persons	Incarcerations	Percentage of total incarcerations
1	593	593	20.5
2	151	302	10.5
3	54	162	5.6
4	40	160	5.5
5	15	75	2.6
6	22	132	4.6
7–10	24	283	9.8
11–14	25	309	10.7
15–19	13	212	7.3
20–24	6	136	4.7
25–29	2	56	1.9
30–34	7	225	7.8
35–39	2	71	2.5
40–45	4	170	5.9
TOTAL	958	2,886	100

discrimination in this era operated to subject disproportionately the actions of all minority groups to criminal sanctions.[55]

RECIDIVISM AND THE LIFE EXPERIENCE OF THE CHRONIC OFFENDER

The personal information available on female petty offenders also offers insights into the extent of recidivism among the female criminal population.[56] I have consulted a variety of other sources to determine how the repeat offenders lived and what drew them into the ranks of the petty criminals.

The 593 one-time offenders incarcerated in Rockhead represent 61.8 per cent of all the women whose names appear in the records, but only 20.5 per cent of all incarcerations (see table 8).[57] Women who were imprisoned twenty times or more – 21, or a mere 2 per cent – accounted for approximately the same number of incarcerations, 22.8 per cent. If a significant recidivist is defined as someone who went to prison more than five times in this twenty-six-year period, the category embraces 105 women (10.9 per cent) and 1,594 incarcerations (55.2 per cent). Petty criminality among women was thus relatively highly concentrated. These are minimal figures for recidivism, for they do not take into account prison sentences given to these women before and after the period under study.

The life histories of some of the women feature nearly continuous imprisonment. Most of the ones who were put inside numerous times were convicted for drunkenness and vagrancy. Hannah Baker went up eleven times for drunkenness and nine times for vagrancy among her total of twenty-three incarcerations. Annie Weston's forty-five sentences include nineteen for drunkenness and seventeen for vagrancy. The same pattern is evident in the careers of other notable recidivists – Ellen Winstanley (who was jailed twenty-one times between 1874 and 1882), Catherine White (thirty-three times), and Margaret Howard (forty times, twenty-three of them for drunkenness).[58]

The hundred or so women who visited Rockhead at least half a dozen times during this period were part of the city's criminal underclass – men and women who moved to and fro between minor crime on the streets and incarceration either in Rockhead as criminals or in the poor asylum as paupers. They were the 'dangerous class' that so unnerved respectable society.[59] Living within their own subculture, they eked out a living on the margins of society and somehow survived. The city's middle class was intensely aware of this outcast community; in their repeated references to the 'old offenders' the press made it clear that such individuals were fundamentally different from the majority of industrious citizens who made up the ranks of the socially respectable.[60] At best the chronic offender was treated with disdain; at worst she was viewed with outright hostility. A report of one of Mary Barry's many convictions is typical; the *Morning Chronicle*, after noting that Barry was convicted of vagrancy 'yet again,' pointed out that 'her husband is now in the Poor House and some of her children [are] in prison for criminal offences.'[61] Occasionally some sympathy was shown to females sentenced to imprisonment, but compassion typically was reserved for prostitutes convicted for the first or second time who claimed they had been led from the path of virtue by evil influences.[62] In other respects concern was manifested in efforts to reform inmates through prison discipline and labour, which was stressed especially from the mid-1880s.[63] Those efforts were rarely successful, and most of the female recidivists were caught, served time, and returned again to the subculture of the Halifax underclass.

Life within that subculture was harsh. Halifax's seamy district was crowded with brothels and legal and illegal grog shops, and arrest patterns reveal that the neighbourhood was home, or at least the centre of activity, for the recidivist.[64] The area was bounded by Albemarle, Barrack, and City streets, just to the east of Citadel Hill, the highest point in Halifax and the centre of the military garrison. According to one nineteenth-century historian of the city, 'No person of character ventured to reside there; nearly all the buildings were occupied as brothels for sailors and soldiers. The streets of this part of town presented continually the disgusting sight of abandoned females of the lowest class in a state of drunkenness, bare-headed, without shoes and in the most filthy and abominable conditions.'[65] Citadel Hill was also the site of the town clock. A monument to regularity and regimental discipline, the clock stood as a 'forlorn symbol,' an unwitting beacon guiding the curious to the brothel district.[66]

The streets were mostly unpaved, and during spring and summer the dust would sometimes blow for two and three days at a time. The homes were overcrowded, poorly ventilated, and without an adequate water supply. The Reverend Mr Hill, rector of St Paul's, described the conditions in the area in 1866:

> The streets are made a receptacle ... for all the dirt that may be brought out of an overcrowded house. Go where you will through Barrack, Albermarle and Grafton Streets, you will see slatternly women and half grown girls emptying all sorts of vessels with every species of foulness into the gutter ... vegetable matter such as potato peelings, cabbage leaves, turnips, onions, in various stages of putrefaction form little heaps here and there. Dead dogs, cats and rats abound by way of variety, some disembowelled, some with brains bashed out ... A damp cloudy day succeeded by a bright and cloudless one is the proper day for a walk through one of these streets. The vapour literally ascends in clouds ... and one goes home with the temptation ... to resort to rum.[67]

Not a week passed without drunken altercations and charges of assault. Halifax's ever-changing population of soldiers and sailors was famous for its capacity to drink and cause trouble. In one incident in 1863 a group of soldiers literally tore apart the Blue Bell tavern on Barrack Street because they were angered that one of their party had been assaulted in the house earlier in the day. After the soldiers were finished, the building was a 'complete wreck.' In another fracas in 1880, dubbed the 'Hollis Street outrage,' a group of soldiers went on a 'rampage,' breaking glass and damaging other property. On many occasions the military authorities attempted to declare these areas out of bounds to their men, but the frequency of trouble attests to the failure of such policies.[68]

Female recidivists were frequently the victims of male aggression. Prostitution was a dangerous business. In 1874, for example, Mary Slattery resisted the advances of a man named John Kelly, who retaliated by setting her clothes on fire; she died of burns and shock. Twenty-nine years of age when she died, Mary had thirty-one convictions on her record. Eighteen-year-old Mary O'Brien was luckier; she survived a stabbing by a potential client in 1884.[69]

The courts offered little deterrence to male aggression. When Mary Ford charged her father with assault in 1872, he defended himself successfully by claiming that she had sustained her injuries by falling down the stairs. Later the same year she charged her husband with assault after he had twice stabbed her in the head. He was sent to Rockhead for forty days.[70] When fifteen-year-old Sarah Potter accused a man of assaulting her, he was arrested; the investigation apparently revealed that she had 'been a party to arranging the arrangement,' and she was remanded and her assailant discharged.[71] Not untypical was the treatment afforded John Palmer, charged in July 1879 with assaulting Laura Donahue. The case was dismissed 'as it was shown that she was one of a number of females frequenting the Province Building and pestering officials for money.'[72] In what was described as 'An Amusing Case,' John Roan was arraigned for assaulting Mary Killum and let go when 'the evidence showed that it was six of one and half a dozen of another.'[73]

In view of their environment it is not surprising that Halifax's female recidivists were frequently ill. It was not uncommon for female offenders to be sent from Rockhead to the poor asylum before serving out their sentence because they were ill; for part of this period the poor-house operated in conjunction with the city hospital.[74] The causes of this ill health were various – squalid living conditions, venereal diseases, and induced abortions. Little information is available about the incidence of sexually transmitted diseases among the prostitute population, perhaps because venereal disease was not a concern of Canadian social reformers before 1914,[75] but there were certainly enough carriers to pass on the diseases. In 1882, for example, 379 men were admitted to the military hospital in Halifax with venereal diseases.[76] Many of Halifax's recidivists also suffered from alcohol abuse. Mary Barry's record is typical; she was imprisoned twenty three times between July 1865 and June 1872, seventeen times for drunkenness. To a great extent the women's social lives, and often their working lives (for many worked in taverns and brothels), involved drinking to excess.[77]

The documents provide little evidence of the way in which these women earned their livings apart from criminal activity. They lived in an era where employment options for women were largely restricted to domestic service and the needle trades. Recidivists were not respectable enough for domestic service even if they had wanted the work; and if they did get a job in the needle trades they did not earn a living wage, particularly if they were supporting children.[78] Judith Fingard suggests that many of the prostitutes of Victorian Halifax were barmaids or maidservants who prostituted themselves to supplement their wages.[79] Her conclusion is supported by this study, for many of the recidivists were charged with prostitution offences as well as drunkenness and other crimes. Halifax's prostitutes wandered in and out of the sex trade as necessity demanded.

Halifax's female petty criminals were an impoverished group, struggling desperately to make ends meet. When they failed they went to Rockhead as vagrants or were sent to the poor asylum. Often the magistrate gave them an option of paying a fine rather than serving time, but it was rarely taken up. Margaret Howard's case is typical: she was given the choice on fifteen occasions but was only once able to pay the four dollars. The lives of these women seem to have met the description of a city missionary who lived among them: 'Raised in Rockhead. Died in the Poor House.'[80] Repeated institutionalization was their lot; Anne Weston, a frequent offender, once was sentenced to sixty days on the very day of her release. Two weeks earlier she had appeared in court charged with being drunk and incapable; she was 'remanded till it could be seen what to do with her.'[81]

For all the misery of their lives, the women did enjoy some control over their interaction with the authorities. The small police force, the constant figure of the magistrate during most of these years, and a familiarity with prison regimes enabled them to understand the criminal justice system and sometimes bend it to their needs.[82] They were not afraid to go to the police or the magistrate and ask to be sent to Rockhead or to use the court to resolve their squabbles. Dora Ford, for example, was 'given in charge by her son for creating a disturbance in his house' in 1864.[83] Julia Donovan was an offender of some notoriety in Halifax. On one occasion in 1865 her sentence for brothel-keeping was mysteriously commuted, resulting in allegations of impropriety and influence-peddling.[84] Donovan also used the Police Court for her own purposes. In 1863 she charged Ellen Bond with causing a disturbance in Donovan's home at two o'clock in the morning. The *Morning Chronicle* described the incident and reported that 'the charge against the Bond girl was not substantiated.'[85] The resort by some of the most notorious recidivists to the Police Court to resolve their own conflicts suggests that to some extent they accepted the legitimacy of that institution and the law it wielded.[86] This is surprising, given that the same people were so often before the court as defendants.

The system did operate mercifully on occasion. Margaret Howard, for example, was imprisoned for drunkenness in both April and May 1866. On 18 May she was released by order of the court, which is surprising in that it was her fourth conviction that year. She repaid this clemency by assaulting a police officer five weeks later. Not only was it common practice for sentences to be commuted, but it was also the norm for offenders to be released from Rockhead long before a sentence had expired. Some were let out to fill a 'situation,' others were released on promises that they would leave Halifax. Mary Slattery, for example, was released in November 1866 after serving two-thirds of her sentence on a charge of vagrancy, and was 'sent by steamer to Antigonish.' Others were let out early with no explanation. Margaret Howard was sentenced on four separate occasions to one year's imprisonment for vagrancy. The longest period she served was six months. The law as these women experienced it was personal, flexible, and sometimes lenient.

Another positive aspect of the women's lives was community. Halifax's petty offenders 'lived together, drank together, worked together, went to court and jail together.'[87] Through their association over the years they formed friendships and a sense of camaraderie. In their community they found work, shelter, and personal support from each other. They also escaped the constricting mores of Victorian womanhood. Although their prostitution was much more an economic act than an expression of sexuality, these offenders do not conform to the contemporary image of women. They were not docile and passive, nor were they unfamiliar or unable to deal with the rougher side of life. They lived on that rougher side.

Within their subculture the varieties of conduct in which women could engage with impunity were far broader than elsewhere. Morals were freer in the underclass, and the community was more tolerant than other subcultures. Prostitution, drunkenness, and profanity were condoned as normal and necessary parts of life. Racism appears not to have been as divisive a force as it was in the rest of society. Black and white women accepted each other with relative ease, and developed friendships, or at least a high degree of mutual tolerance, through their continual interaction. In their mischievous moments Halifax's chronic recidivists must have felt a certain pleasure when they reflected upon the sheer horror they inspired among the ultra-respectable. When Mary Francis and Mary Pendergast escaped from the 'Women's Home' in September 1880 the *Acadian Recorder* reported that they 'swore in a way that suggested they must have been saving up bad language for some time.'[88] Perhaps they were swearing in frustration at being caught, but their cursing was also for the benefit of those who apprehended them: what better way had these two women to voice their feelings and at the same time ensure that they would offend?

What made these women petty criminals? Contemporary explanations cited some combination of moral turpitude, intemperance, and indolence. Vagrants, drunks, thieves, and prostitutes were presumed to have fallen from the path of respectability primarily because of their own moral failings. One newspaper suggested a toughening of the prison regime on the grounds that it was preferred to the poor-house by the indolent.[89] Another warned of women who were 'drunkers and suckers' and who went about 'inventing and retailing lies' to obtain just enough money to 'waste upon their lusts.'[90] The most frequent explanation offered was drink. Reform groups and newspapers harped on this theme.[91] Their attitudes were typified in a report of a special committee appointed to investigate the prison in 1872, which lamented that few recidivists found stable employment, and concluded that they could have done so 'but for their intemperate habits.'[92]

Historians have posited two other explanations – poverty and pathology. Poverty is most often cited,[93] but a number of analyses speculate that personal and social problems[94] or a sense of rebellion[95] also drove women to crime, and especially to prostitution. But for most female offenders, prostitutes and others, poverty was always present, a common factor that brought a degree of communal unity to their way of life. The life experience of the recidivists, always difficult, was often desperate. Living at the edge of society, ostracized by the respectable, they lacked the resources to look after themselves. Some of these women, such as Mary Slattery, were literally born into the business.[96] Others may have had more choices, but they still existed within a society that offered women precious little in the way of employment alternatives. No doubt a variety of factors influenced these women each time they committed an offence, but it seems clear that poverty created their environment and shaped their existence. It was the destitution of Halifax's female recidivists that gained them entrance to the poor asylum. It was that same destitution that led them to commit the offences for which they were sent to Rockhead.

CONCLUSION

The petty crimes committed by women in late Victorian Halifax were similar in number and type to those that occurred in other jurisdictions. Women were always distinctly in the minority among criminal offenders, and their crimes were overwhelmingly morals offences, not crimes against persons or property. The women were a young, poor, and powerless segment of society. They existed in the nether world of Halifax's slums and brothels, a world notable for its dirt, disease, and degradation.

Many questions remain. What place did female criminals occupy in the pantheon of Victorian social reform ideology? What efforts were made to reform this segment of society instead of merely imprisoning it? Was the female petty offender somehow more reprehensible in society's eyes than the male? The answers to these and other questions will tell us a great deal more about the criminals themselves and about the society in which they lived. In particular, they will reveal much about that society's patriarchal impulses, for female offenders presented a substantial challenge to prevailing assumptions about the nature of women and their role in society. For that reason one might expect a sense of urgency to have invested movements for reform and rehabilitation. Certainly the group portrait presented here of the women who spent time in the city prison reveals that they bore little resemblance to the idealized contemporary picture of feminine domesticity and subservience.

NOTES

1 There are a host of these by now. The best British and American studies include R. Rosen *The Lost Sisterhood* (Baltimore: Johns Hopkins University Press 1982); J. Walkowitz *Prostitutes in Victorian Society: Women, Class and the State* (New York: Cambridge University Press 1980); F. Finnegan *Poverty and Prostitution: A Study of Victorian Prostitutes in York* (Cambridge: Cambridge University Press 1970). For Canada see J. Bedford 'Prostitution in Calgary, 1905–1914' *Alberta History* 25 (1981) 1–19; C. Backhouse 'Nineteenth-Century Prostitution Laws: Reflections of a Discriminatory Society' *Social History–Histoire Sociale* 18 (1986) 387–432; J.P. McLaren 'Chasing the Social Evil: Moral Fervour and the Evolution of Canada's Prostitution Laws, 1867–1917' *Canadian Journal of Law and Society* 1 (1986) 125–65; idem 'White Slavers: The Reform of Canada's Prostitution Laws and Patterns of Enforcement, 1900–1920' *Criminal Justice History* 8 (1987) 53–120; D. Nilsen 'The Social Evil: Prostitution in Vancouver, 1900–1920' in B. Lathan et al., eds *In Her Own Right* (Victoria: Camosun College 1980); L. Rotenberg 'The Wayward Worker: Toronto's Prostitutes at the Turn of the Century' in J. Acton et al., eds *Women at Work: Ontario 1850–1930* (Toronto: Canadian Women's Educational Press 1974).

2 I am referring here to such offences as abortion, infanticide, rape, petit

treason, and spousal assault. The best examples of this work include P.C. Hoffer and N.E.H. Hull *Murdering Mothers: Infanticide in England and New England, 1558–1803* (New York: New York University Press 1981); N. Tomes 'A Torrent of Abuse: Crimes of Violence Between Working Class Men and Women in London, 1840–1875' *Journal of Social History* 11 (1978) 328–45; C. Backhouse 'Desperate Women and Compassionate Courts: Infanticide in Nineteenth-Century Canada' *University of Toronto Law Journal* 34 (1984) 447–78; and idem 'Nineteenth-Century Canadian Rape Law, 1800–1892' in D. Flaherty, ed. *Essays in the History of Canadian Law* vol. 2 (Toronto: The Osgoode Society 1983).

3 General studies of female crime are much rarer than specific-offence studies. The best include J.M. Beattie 'The Criminality of Women in Eighteenth-Century England' *Journal of Social History* 8 (1975) 80–116; A. Lachance 'Women and Crime in Canada in the Early Eighteenth Century, 1712–1759' in L.A. Knafla, ed. *Crime and Criminal Justice in Europe and Canada* (Waterloo, Ont: Wilfrid Laurier University Press 1981); and M. Langdon 'Female Crime in Calgary, 1914–1940' in L.A. Knafla, ed. *Law and Justice in a New Land: Essays in Western Canadian Legal History* (Toronto: Carswell 1986). For a general review see N.E. Hull 'The Certain Wages of Sin: Sentence and Punishment of Felons in Colonial Massachusetts' in D.K. Weisberg, ed. *Women and the Law: A Socio-Historical Perspective* (Cambridge: Harvard University Press 1982); idem *Female Felons: Women and Serious Crime in Colonial Massachusetts* (Chicago: University of Illinois Press 1987).

4 This period was also selected because the prison records are largely complete from 1864.

5 SNS 1864, c. 81, s. 130. For an account of the development of the city's courts see P.V. Girard 'The Rise and Fall of Urban Justice in Halifax, 1815–1886' *Nova Scotia Historical Review* 8(2) (1988), 57–71.

6 SNS 1867, c. 82; SNS 1870, c. 37. For Pryor see P.V. Girard 'Henry Pryor' *DCB* vol. 12.

7 Rockhead Prison was opened in 1860 and located on the hill that rises above the Bedford Basin. See T. Raddall *Halifax: Warden of the North* (Toronto: McClelland and Stewart 1977) 189.

8 It was not an offence at common law. See Coke *Institutes of the Laws of England: Part III* (1798) 204 and *R.* v. *Pierson* (1705) 2 Ld Ray. 1179, 92 ER 291.

9 See RSNS 1851, c. 104, s. 2, c. 158, s. 3 and c. 1, s. 9; SNS 1855, c. 14; RSNS 1864, c. 81, s. 134; RSNS 1891, c. 58, s. 171.

10 SC 1869, c. 28; RSC 1886, c. 57, s. 8; H.E. Taschereau *The Criminal Code of the Dominion of Canada* (Toronto: Carswell 1893) 140–2

11 Backhouse 'Prostitution Laws' 387–8; McLaren 'Chasing the Social Evil' 152. Contagious Diseases Acts were introduced in Britain and Ontario in the 1860s to 'protect' the health of soldiers. They permitted prostitutes to be detained after an affidavit had been sworn before a justice of the peace to the effect that they were suffering from a venereal disease. Although they were aimed precisely at port and garrison cities such as Halifax, the acts were never passed in Nova Scotia.

12 RSNS 1864, c. 160, ss. 3 and 4. The keeping of a bawdy-house was also a common law offence.

13 By SC 1874, c. 28

14 RSNS 1864, c. 160, s. 1 and c. 81, s. 134; SC 1869, c. 28; SC 1874, c. 28

15 RSNS 1864, c. 160, s. 7

16 RSNS 1864, c. 167, s. 11; SC 1869, c. 21

17 PANS RG35–102, series 18B, Prison Registers 1864–73 (vol. 2) and 1873–1890 (vol. 3). Unless otherwise specified, references to individual offenders can be located by month and year in these records.

18 RSNS 1851, c. 1, s. 87; RSNS 1864, c. 81, s. 130, and c. 163, s. 1

19 SC 1869, c. 29, s. 43; RSC 1886, c. 162, ss. 34 and 36; Taschereau *Criminal Code* 140–2

20 *Acadian Recorder* 8 July 1879

21 Ibid. 15 May 1886

22 See PANS RG42, Magistrates' Courts Records, passim. For discussions of similar themes elsewhere see P. Craven 'Law and Ideology: The Toronto Police Court 1850–1880' in Flaherty *Essays in the History of Canadian Law* vol. 2; G.H. Homel 'Denison's Law: Criminal Justice and the Police Court in Toronto, 1877–1921' *Ontario History* 73 (1981) 171–86; and G. Marquis 'The Contours of Canadian Urban Justice, 1830–1875' *Urban History Review* 15(3) (1987) 269–73. Homel describes Denison's method (at 173): 'He did not attempt to understand most cases in any detail, and was not interested in the legal points pertaining to them. His goal was to render justice – and quickly. Usually a moment or two sufficed. It was not uncommon for Denison to deal with 250 cases in 180 minutes.'

23 All of the tables were compiled from the Prison Registers in PANS RG35–102, series 18B, vols 2 and 3. I am grateful to Jim Phillips for his assistance in compiling these statistical breakdowns. The records are complete except for three months in 1881 and another three months in 1882. I have filled the gaps by providing an average for the missing months on the basis of the rest of the year.

24 As recently as 1977 Carol Smart could still lament the assumption that the numbers of female criminals were too insignificant to merit serious study

by criminologists: see *Women, Crime and Criminology: A Feminist Critique* (London: Routledge and Kegan Paul 1977) 2.

25 For a general discussion see T.L. Chapman 'The Measurement of Crime in Nineteenth-Century Canada: Some Methodological and Philosophical Problems' in Knafla *Crime and Criminal Justice*. For particular studies that disprove the 'peaceful past' myth, see T. Thorner 'The Not So Peaceful Kingdom: Crime and Criminal Justice in Frontier Calgary' in A.W. Rasporich and H.C. Klassen, eds *Frontier Calgary: Town, City and Region, 1875–1914* (Calgary: McClelland and Stewart 1979); J. Weaver 'Crime, Public Order and Repression: The Gore District in Upheaval, 1831–1851' *Ontario History* 78 (1986) 175–207.

26 Cesar Lombroso acknowledged that women commit fewer crimes then men. He tried to explain criminality among women by suggesting that women who commit crimes are atavistic: *The Female Offender* (1892; reprinted Littleton, Col.: Rothman 1980). Pollack is virtually the only criminologist who has disputed the idea of relatively very low crime rates among women. In an analysis that is only slightly less misogynistic than Lombroso's, he suggests that women are dramatically underrepresented because the type of crime women commit tends not to be reported, and because the double standard in the legal system often bars arrest and conviction. Underlying his analysis is a perception of women as crafty, cunning, and secretive. See *The Criminality of Women* (New York: Barnes 1950). For a general review see S. Gavigan 'Women's Crime and Feminist Critiques: A Review of the Literature' *Canadian Criminal Forum* 5 (1982) 40.

27 Beattie 'Criminality of Women' 97; Lachance 'Women and Crime' 213. See also R.J. Simon *Women and Crime* (Lexington, Mass.: Lexington Books 1975) 107–8 and Langdon 'Female Crime' 295.

28 V.C. Gattrell and D. Hadden 'Criminal Statistics and Their Interpretation' in E.A. Wrigley, ed. *Nineteenth-Century Society* (Cambridge: Cambridge University Press 1972) 7

29 Simon *Women and Crime* 108 suggests that one in nine convicted offenders is female. Also see J. Fox and T. Hartnagel 'Changing Female Roles and Female Crime in Canada' in R. Silverman et al., eds *Crime in Canadian Society* (Toronto: Butterworths 1980) for a discussion of current conflicting evidence.

30 In late Victorian Halifax, as now, there was more than one vision of femininity and female sexuality. What I am suggesting here is that the dominant culture operated from a vision of womanhood that saw the female role as one of mother, wife, and care-giver, and offered few opportunities for women to cast off their submissive role. For a discussion of this ideal of femininity

see N.E.S. Griffiths *Penelope's Web* (Oxford: Clarendon Press 1976) 158–67. For a Nova Scotia example see J. Smith 'Social Purity' in R. Cook and W. Mitchison, eds *The Proper Sphere: Women's Place in Canadian Society* (Toronto: McClelland and Stewart 1986) 230.

31 Canada *Censuses of Canada, 1608–1876* (Ottawa: Queen's Printer 1878); Canada *Census of Canada 1890–1891* (Ottawa: MacLean, Roger 1891)

32 As seems to have been the case in twentieth-century Calgary: see Langdon 'Female Crime' 310.

33 *Acadian Recorder* 5 July 1879

34 Backhouse 'Prostitution Laws'; McLaren 'Chasing the Social Evil.' Information on these individuals is from my biographical index compiled from the Prison Registers.

35 Backhouse 'Prostitution Laws' 397–8; Langdon 'Female Crime' 310

36 Langdon 'Female Crime' 307

37 For discussion of this attitude in Calgary see Bedford 'Prostitution in Calgary' 3 and J. Gray *Red Lights on the Prairies* (Toronto: Macmillan 1971) 104–54.

38 See T.W. Acheson 'The National Policy and the Industrialization of the Maritimes, 1880–1910' in D. Frank and P. Buckner, eds *The Acadiensis Reader: Volume Two* (Fredericton: Acadiensis Press 1985); L.D. McCann 'Staples and the New Industrialism in the Growth of Pre-Confederation Halifax' *Acadiensis* 8 (1979) 47–79; I.G. McKay 'The Working Class of Metropolitan Halifax, 1850–1889' (Honours thesis, Dalhousie University 1975) 9–39.

39 Langdon 'Female Crime' 306–7

40 *Acadian Recorder* 17 July 1878 and 18 Oct. 1882; *Halifax Herald* 3 Sept. 1879. See also the case of Ellen MacLeod, 'drunk and disorderly and attempting to assault persons': *Acadian Recorder* 2 Dec. 1879.

41 *Acadian Recorder* 24 Dec. 1884, 22 Dec. 1879, and 22 Dec. 1886; *Herald* 15 Jan. 1884; *Citizen* 3 June 1876. See the discussion of this and the contemporary ballad warning of the 'Women of Barrack Street' in J. Fingard *Jack in Port: Sailortowns of Eastern Canada* (Toronto: McClelland and Stewart 1982) 135–6.

42 See the introduction to J.M. Beattie *Crime and the Courts in England 1660–1800* (Princeton: Princeton University Press 1986).

43 Accused persons did not always give their correct age, so these records should be used with caution when dealing with any one individual. But with a comprehensive statistical study such as this, I am confident of the accuracy of the general conclusions presented.

44 Langdon 'Female Crime' 303 and 306; Bedford 'Prostitution in Calgary' 8;

Backhouse 'Prostitution Laws' 397 and 402. For similar findings for Britain and the United States, see Rosen *Lost Sisterhood* 143; A.M. Butler *Daughters of Joy, Sisters of Mercy: Prostitutes in the American West, 1865–1900* (Urbana: University of Illinois Press 1985) 15; and Walkowitz *Prostitutes in Victorian Society* 18–19. One clearly biased observer estimated that the prostitute's career lasted 'a short five years before drugs and disease do their deadly issue': Rev. J.G. Shearer 'The Canadian Crusade' in E.A. Bell, ed. *Fighting the Traffic in Young Girls* (Chicago 1910) 335. But some scholars have suggested rather longer careers for prostitutes; see Finnegan *Poverty and Prostitution* 29–30 and Rotenberg 'Toronto Prostitutes' 145.

45 Backhouse finds a relatively even split between Catholics and Protestants in Toronto: 'Prostitution Laws' 400.

46 Ibid. tables 4 and 5

47 W. Sanger *History of Prostitution: Its Extent, Cause and Effects throughout the World* (New York: Harper 1869)

48 See the discussion of xenophobic attitudes towards prostitutes in nineteenth-century America in Rosen *Lost Sisterhood* 8–10. In the American west the tendency was to overplay the Chinese involvement: see Butler *Daughters of Joy* 4 and 6–7.

49 Backhouse 'Prostitution Laws' 399; Rotenberg 'Toronto Prostitutes' 38–9. In Calgary the majority of prostitutes were 'foreign' in that they come from outside Alberta. Calgary in the early twentieth century was a very young city growing rapidly from immigration: see Bedford 'Prostitution in Calgary' 8.

50 A. Brookes 'Out Migration from the Maritime Provinces, 1860–1900: Some Preliminary Considerations', in *Acadiensis Reader Two* 41

51 Rotenberg 'Toronto Prostitutes' 38

52 Judith Fingard suggests that 40 per cent of the prostitutes in Halifax were black. Her estimate is based on a variety of sources, but not on imprisonment statistics, and she is discussing only one offence. See 'Jailbirds in Mid-Victorian Halifax' in T.G. Barnes et al., eds *Law in a Colonial Society: The Nova Scotia Experience* (Toronto: Carswell 1984).

53 2 Mar. 1855

54 *Citizen* 9 Feb. 1878

55 Bedford 'Prostitution in Calgary' 10; M.S. Cross 'Violence and Authority: The Case of Bytown' in D. Bercuson, ed. *Law and Society in Canada in Historical Perspective* (Calgary: University of Calgary Press 1979) 6

56 It was not always possible to be sure that the same name meant the same person. But by cross-referring to the personal characteristics recorded I

was able to establish identity in many cases. If any doubt remained, I counted more than one person; therefore these figures are, if anything, an underestimate of the numbers of recidivists.

57 The total given in table 8 for female offences is lower than that given in table 1. For the purposes of a recidivism study based on number of occasions incarcerated I counted only the more serious offence when more than one was listed on the same occasion.

58 Information on these individuals is from the Prison Registers, passim.

59 The phrase 'dangerous class' is used in E. Monkkonen *The Dangerous Classes: Crime and Poverty in Columbus, Ohio* (Cambridge: Harvard University Press 1975). See also its contemporary use in *Presbyterian Witness* 2 May 1863.

60 For examples, see *Morning Chronicle* 10 and 15 Jan. and 13 Aug. 1864; *Herald* 30 Sept. 1880; and *Acadian Recorder* 24 Jan. 1880 and 18 May 1889.

61 15 Jan. 1864. For similar descriptions see *Acadian Recorder* 18 May 1867; 24 Jan. 1880; and 27 July 1883; *British Colonist* 9 Aug. 1868; and *Presbyterian Witness* 20 Nov. 1869.

62 See, for example, reports entitled 'A Sad Case' *Herald* 5 Oct. 1880 and 'A Girl's Sad Story' *Acadian Recorder* 18 May 1889.

63 Women's prison labour consisted of knitting and sewing under the supervision of the assistant matron. The products of these labours were used for prisoners and, when possible, sold to private buyers: City Prison Report, City of Halifax *Annual Reports* 1871–2, 1881–2, 1883–4, and 1886–7. There were frequent complaints that the tasks of the females incarcerated in Rockhead were not rigorous enough. Their labours, it was lamented, neither reformed their morals nor came close to covering 'the expense of their maintenance.' An increase in prison discipline came in the 1880s, when the prison governor and his wife, the prison matron, took it upon themselves to tighten things up. They admitted that there had been problems but insisted that through their efforts a much stricter regime had been established. Part of this tightening up involved the firing of some officers, and the change in staff was apparently 'attended with advantage' as the 'industry of the prisoners depends largely upon the vigilance of the keepers': *Annual Reports* 1865–6 and 1886–7.

64 G. Nicholls *Halifax: Sins and Sorrows* Halifax: Protestant City Missionary Society 1862) 25. The Halifax papers frequently recorded details of arrests, indicating that they took place in this district. See *Morning Chronicle* 10 Feb. 1863; *Herald* 5 Oct. 1880; and *Acadian Recorder* 1 May 1889.

65 T.B. Akins *History of Halifax City* (Belleville, Ont. 1895) 158. See also Fingard 'Jailbirds' 82; *Morning Chronicle* 16 Apr. 1863 and 12 May 1870; *Acadian*

Recorder 5 Nov. 1878, 5, 20, and 30 Dec. 1884, 18 May 1888; *Herald* 12 June 1880; and P. Blakely *Glimpses of Halifax, 1867–1890* (Halifax: Public Archives of Nova Scotia 1949) 13–15.

66 McKay 'Working Class' 1

67 *British Colonist* 26 Apr. 1866, cited in P.B. Waite *The Man from Halifax: Sir John Thompson, Prime Minister* (Toronto: University of Toronto Press 1985) 5–6. See also the description of conditions in this area by the Reverend J. Grierson in *Report of the Halifax City Missionary Society* (Halifax 1867) and *McAlpine's Halifax Dictionary* (1871–2) 47, which describes Barrack Street as a 'collection of old wooden buildings, the resort of the depraved.'

68 *Morning Chronicle* 16 Apr. and 28 Aug. 1863. This happened on other occasions also: see ibid. 25 Apr. 1873 and 12 May 1870. For soldiers' and sailors' drunkenness and disorder, see Fingard *Jack in Port* 82–140.

69 Fingard 'Jailbirds' 94; *Acadian Recorder* 15 Dec. 1884

70 Fingard 'Jailbirds' 99–100

71 *Acadian Recorder* 3 July 1878

72 Ibid. 16 July 1879

73 Ibid. 8 Sept. 1879. For similar incidents see ibid. 4 and 29 Aug. and 5 Dec. 1879, and 24 Dec. 1884, and *Morning Chronicle* 21 Jan. 1873 and 22 Dec. 1874.

74 G. Andrews 'The Establishment of Institutional Care in Halifax in the Mid-Nineteenth Century' (Honours Thesis, Dalhousie University 1974) 55–72

75 J.D. McGinnis and S. Buckley 'Venereal Disease and Public Health Reform in Canada' *Canadian Historical Review* 58 (1983) 337

76 J. Fingard 'The Social Evil in Mid-Victorian Halifax' (unpublished) 5

77 This same pattern of alcohol abuse has been identified as prevalent by virtually all of the historians who have considered prostitution in the Victorian era: see Finnegan *Poverty and Prostitution* 29–30; Rosen *Lost Sisterhood* 75; and Rotenberg 'Toronto Prostitutes' 49.

78 L. Lever 'Women in Industry in Halifax, 1871–1891' (unpublished). For a discussion of domestic service in this era see G. Leslie 'Domestic Service in Canada, 1880–1920' in Acton et al. *Women at Work* 71. For women's pay in Toronto, see Rotenberg 'Toronto Prostitutes' 45–50.

79 Fingard 'Social Evil' 11–15

80 North End City Mission *Report* 1896–7, 25, cited in Fingard 'Jailbirds' 88

81 *Acadian Recorder* 13 July and 1 Aug. 1879

82 The police force was small – 33 in 1864, 49 in the mid-1870s, and 40 to 44 throughout the 1880s. (See the essay by Jim Phillips elsewhere in this volume.)

83 *Morning Chronicle* 24 Jan. 1864. See also the discussion of petty criminals' use of the court in Fingard 'Jailbirds' 100–1.

84 See *Unionist and Halifax Journal,* 22 Sept., 11 and 23 Oct., 4 and 13 Nov., and 11 and 13 Dec. 1865.
85 *Morning Chronicle* 7 Feb. 1863
86 Fingard 'Jailbirds' passim
87 Fingard 'Social Evil in Halifax' 22
88 25 Sept. 1880
89 *Acadian Recorder* 11 Dec. 1867
90 *Presbyterian Witness* 20 Nov. 1864
91 See, for example, *Acadian Recorder* 8 Dec. 1884; *Novascotian* 18 Mar. 1867; *Presbyterian Witness* 2 May 1863
92 *Annual Report* 1872–3, 55
93 Langdon 'Female Crime' 303; Backhouse 'Prostitution Laws' 404; Fingard 'Social Evil' 4–5; Finnegan *Poverty and Prostitution* 19; Rotenberg 'Toronto Prostitutes' 48; Rosen *Lost Sisterhood* 147; Butler *Daughters of Joy* 2–4
94 Fingard seems to suggest this: see 'Jailbirds' 101.
95 Walkowitz suggests that in a society where there were 'few avenues of revolt open to a working class girl' who was not prepared to accept the 'absolute level of subordination and acquiescence' demanded of her, prostitution represented a form of revolt. Likewise, Rosen points to 'contempt for other occupational options,' and Nilsen argues that prostitution resulted from the urban environment's lessening social control on rural girls. See Walkowitz *Prostitutes in Victorian Society* 18 and 21; Rosen *Lost Sisterhood* 147; Nilsen 'Social Evil' 216.
96 Fingard 'Jailbirds' 86

8

Divorce in Nova Scotia, 1750–1890

KIMBERLEY SMITH MAYNARD

On 15 May 1750, a year after the founding of Halifax, the governor and council of Nova Scotia considered the petition of Lieutenant William Williams complaining of the conduct of his wife Amy during his absence. He claimed that he could produce proof of her adultery with Thomas Thomas, and demanded a divorce. Council decided that it could deal with the matter, even though divorce jurisdiction in England resided primarily in the ecclesiastical courts. Peter May, Ann May, and Adam Glen attested to Amy's guilt, and the council unanimously agreed to grant a divorce. The secretary was ordered to have an instrument of divorce drawn up by 'persons conversant in the Spiritual Courts,' and Williams was granted the right to remarry. Amy's 'infamous conduct' denied her the same privilege during her husband's lifetime, and she was ordered to quit the province within ten days.[1]

The *Williams* case was the first judicial divorce granted in Nova Scotia, and some 150 to 200 more followed it until 1890. Historians have been surprisingly slow to exploit this unique archive of domestic disharmony. Although the records are erratic before 1890, sixty petitions survive, upon which this paper is based.[2] I have selected the terminal date of 1890 because the records are virtually complete thereafter, allowing a more precise and sensitive probing of the data than is possible for the earlier period.

DIVORCE LAW IN NOVA SCOTIA

The *Williams* case shows that as early as 1750 the divorce law in Nova Scotia differed from that in England, which was administered largely by the Church of England as part of its jurisdiction over the sacrament of marriage.[3] Bishops' courts applied canon law, under which two kinds of divorce were available. Divorce *a vinculo matrimonii* (from the bond of matrimony) was given on the grounds that some original defect – non-consummation because of physical incompetence, insanity at the time of marriage, consanguinity within the degrees prohibited, or affinity (relationship by marriage) – voided the marriage from the outset; we would refer to this today as an annulment. The parties could remarry, since the first marriage was treated as if it had not occurred, but children of the earlier 'annulled' marriage were rendered illegitimate. Divorce *a mensa et thoro* (from bed and board) could be given on the grounds of adultery, cruelty, or sodomy. This decree merely freed the spouses from the obligation to cohabit, and did not permit remarriage. The husband retained his common law rights over his wife's property; the wife could be granted alimony and retain her dower rights only if she was not the adulterous party.

An absolute divorce could be obtained only by a private act of Parliament dissolving the marriage. This practice began in the late seventeenth century to circumvent the stringency of canon law, and some 325 such divorces were granted before 1857, when the Matrimonial Causes Act instituted judicial divorce. By the eighteenth century two prerequisites to a private act were established: a decree of divorce *a mensa et thoro* from the ecclesiastical court, and a 'verdict at law,' or award of damages, in an action for criminal conversation brought by the husband against the adulterer. These requirements were formalized by standing orders in Parliament in 1798. The majority of successful suits were brought by husbands; in only four cases was a wife successful, and in each of those the grounds included bigamy or incest in addition to adultery.[4]

Divorce in England before 1857 was always considered to be a costly affair, and thus restricted to the wealthy and well-born. Recent research, however, has challenged the estimates of six hundred to eight hundred pounds given by the 1853 Royal Commission to Inquire into the Law of Divorce (the Campbell Commission); it is now thought that those figures are as much as double the real cost.[5] It has also been suggested that the damages obtained in criminal conversation awards, 'commonly high ... must easily have paid for the rest of the proceedings.'[6] Even so, one writer has estimated that two-thirds of all divorces obtained between 1750 and 1857 were procured by the 'upper classes,' with perhaps 14 percent attributable to the 'lower classes.'[7]

The *Williams* decision was certainly not in tune with English law. The court granted a judicial divorce *a vinculo matrimonii* when the facts warranted no more than a divorce *a mensa et thoro*, unless the petitioner applied to Parliament. Nova Scotia law also differed from English law in that it did not demand the successful prosecution of a 'crim. con.' action as a prerequisite.[8] This departure from English practice no doubt encouraged further petitions. Mrs Ruth Wheeler obtained a divorce from the bed and board of her husband of 1752, although there is no record of the grounds on which the divorce was granted. The husband was ordered to 'allow her such a maintenance as his circumstances may admit of.'[9] A few months later Eliza Fairbanks appeared before the council complaining of her husband's 'abusive treatment,' but it was he who was granted a separation from bed and board on the basis of allegations of her 'base, wicked and unfaithful' conduct contained in his answer and defence.[10] He was obligated to return her clothes, give her five guineas for a passage to England, and maintain her until departure. This and the *Williams* case seem to be the only ones in which recourse to transportation for adulterous wives was endorsed. The result in a third case, in which a wife petitioned for relief in 1757 because her husband had 'broken his marriage contract with her' by committing adultery, treating her with great cruelty, and deserting her without maintenance is not known.[11]

In 1758 the Nova Scotia Assembly was established, and it quickly enacted statutes covering many aspects of the colony's life. Thomas Barnes has pointed out that rarely were these laws 'slavish copyings of the English books,'[12] and this holds true also for divorce law. The first divorce statute stipulated that 'all matters relating to marriage and divorce shall be heard and determined by the Governor, or Commander-in-Chief for the time being, and His Majesty's Council of this Province.'[13] Divorces could be granted for impotence, marriage to a kindred person within the prohibited degrees, adultery, and 'wilful desertion and withholding necessary maintenance for three years together.' The act did not distinguish between male and female petitioners, nor did it identify the type of divorce to be granted in particular circumstances. However, all divorces granted after 1758 were absolute; no decrees of divorce from bed and board appear again, although one was sought in 1835 and another in 1873.[14] Nova Scotia divorce law was therefore different from English law in a variety of ways. In particular, it gave jurisdiction to grant absolute divorces to a Court of Marriage and Divorce (governor and council) rather than to Parliament, and it allowed wives an absolute divorce for husbands' cruelty alone, which was not possible in England until the passage of the 1923 Matrimonial Causes Act.[15] Legislative divorces were expressly prohibited in the colonies by an imperial edict of November 1773. One such divorce, however, was passed by the Assembly and approved by London in 1835.[16]

The distinctiveness of Nova Scotia law became apparent in 1761 when London disallowed part of the 1758 act on the ground that it was inconsistent with English law. The offending clause allowed divorce for wilful desertion and for the withholding of maintenance for three years. The act was amended in 1761, and the amendment was approved by the Lords of Trade in March 1763.[17] The retention of adultery as grounds for divorce *a vinculo* did not arouse London's ire; nor, curiously, did the addition of cruelty and precontract as causes for divorce in the 1761 act. Apart from the removal of this last ground in 1866, the substance of divorce law throughout the nineteenth century remained that of the 1761 act.[18]

There were several subsequent attempts to alter the law, all of which foundered because of local or imperial opposition. In 1816 Brenton Halliburton introduced a bill in the Legislative Council which gave the governor in council a discretion to grant a separation from bed and board, following the practice of the English ecclesiastical courts, where a petitioner sought a divorce *a vinculo*. The Assembly concurred, but the act ran into heavy resistance in London and was eventually disallowed.[19] At first glance this may seem paradoxical: why should the Colonial Office have disapproved of an act that in effect permitted greater scope for the observance of English practice? A perusal of the objections raised in London illustrates the high degree of confusion that existed in the metropolis about the state of Nova Scotia divorce law, and also shows the importance imperial authorities placed on uniformity of marriage laws.

The report on the 1816 act was written by James Stephen Jr, who acted as legal counsel to the Colonial Office from 1813 until his resignation in 1847. Upon the basis of his reports the secretary of state for war and the colonies would advise the king in council whether particular colonial acts should be disallowed, specially confirmed, or 'left to their operation.'[20] Stephen was an extremely able lawyer who eventually developed a formidable expertise in colonial law, but he never understood divorce law in Nova Scotia. In part this was a problem of sources; he stated in his 1816 report that he was unable to obtain a copy of the 1758 act, and he appears not to have been aware of the 1761 act. His objection was not to the new discretion vested in the governor in council to grant divorce *a mensa et thoro*, but to the fact that divorces *a vinculo* could be granted at all by that body. Stephen rightly observed that the governor's instructions forbade him to assent to any private act of divorce, and argued that the governor should therefore not be allowed to delegate such power to a judicial tribunal. In addition, since there was no court in England that could grant a divorce *a vinculo*, 'there seems no sufficient reason why so high and important an authority should be confided to any Court in the Province of Nova Scotia.' But exactly such an authority had been confided in the governor in council in 1758 and confirmed by London in 1763, making Stephen's observations irrelevant. Only his last objection to the act had some merit: he queried the advisability of making divorces on grounds of adultery and cruelty retrospective in their operation; to do so, he said, would have the effect of bastardizing children born subsequent to the adultery or cruelty. Although the act can be interpreted that way, it is doubtful whether such an effect was intended, and in any case the objection could have been dealt with by amendment rather than the drastic remedy of disallowance. In fact, Stephen recommended simply that assent be withheld until copies of the earlier legislation could be sent. It is unclear whether the governor complied, but in the end the act was disallowed. The Colonial Office had shot itself in the foot as a result of Stephen's confusion.[21]

Stephen's analysis of the 1816 act rested mainly on legal factors. He noted in passing that 'very obvious reasons of policy' required any colonial power over divorce to rest with the legislature rather than with the courts; conveniently, however, the 1773 edict had already blocked legislative divorce. In fact, London took a dim view of colonial innovations in marriage and divorce law. Stephen's superior, Herman Merivale, regarded the law of marriage as 'really too important and almost too Imperial in its character to allow such enactments to pass without full examination,' and would have preferred a universal law.[22] In most other areas of the law Britain did not regard colonial uniformity as essential, and often encouraged local experimentation on the assumption that English law was not always appropriate. The overriding importance of the family in society, however, meant that the status of marriage should not be altered by any power except the Parliament of Westminster. In New Brunswick there had been a long debate between local and imperial authorities before an act permitting judicial divorce was finally approved in 1791. Nova Scotia had slipped through the cracks of the colonial review system in the eighteenth century, and its divorce process continued to plague imperial authorities in the nineteenth.

An attempt to broaden further the scope of divorce grounds was made in 1834, when it was proposed that the definition of cruelty be expanded to include 'wilful and continued desertion and absence of the Husband from the Province and his withholding necessary maintenance from the wife continually for the Term of Seven Years.' The bill also would have eliminated the procedural requirement that the husband be served personally with notice of the action. It was again proposed in actions on these grounds to give the court a discretion in deciding whether the decree would be absolute or for separation from bed and board only.[23] The impetus for the reform may have been the case of Anne Kidston, who had married Richard Kidston in 1811 but had lived apart from him since 1819 because of his 'brutal cruelty.' She could not sue for divorce because her husband had left the province and could not be found to be served. Her family connections explain why she was the only successful applicant for a legislative divorce in Nova Scotia. A kinswoman of the wife of Chief Justice Sampson Blowers, Kidston married William Hill, a former solicitor general and a recent appointee to the Supreme Court, soon after the private bill passed in March 1834. The general bill failed to become law. After being passed by the Assembly, it was amended by the council to give the court the power to order alimony and reasonable costs to the wife in such circumstances. For some reason – no record of the debate exists – the Assembly thought that the measure went too far and rejected it.[24]

The arrival on James Stephen's desk in London of the private act granting Anne Kidston her divorce led to another imbroglio. Stephen was by now aware of the legislation under which divorces could be granted, but asserted that it had remained a dead letter and that no law granting a divorce had been passed by any British colony during his tenure as legal adviser to the Colonial Office. Once again he seems to have confused legislative divorce with judicial divorce. Although it may have been true that no private divorce acts had been passed in the empire since 1773, Nova Scotia had been granting judicial divorces for eighty-five years, New Brunswick for more than forty. The law was hardly a dead letter, though Stephen had no way of knowing this since the governor did not inform London when divorce decrees were granted. Although the governor had disobeyed his instructions in giving his assent to the Kidston divorce, Stephen did not limit himself to that objection; he went into the whole question of divorce policy, albeit with some reluctance. He thought it a 'very momentous subject.' He was aware that attitudes to divorce were changing and he wished to ensure that the Colonial Office authorities kept this fact in mind, but in the final analysis he doubted whether any circumstances in colonial life could justify the 'Sacrifice of any of the great permanent Maxims of political Society.' In a more political vein, he alerted the Colonial Office to the possibility that colonies such as Nova Scotia could become 'divorce havens' for British subjects. Had the Kidstons been married in England, subsequently acquired a Nova Scotia domicile, and been divorced there, the effect of such actions in England would be 'a question of perfect Novelty.' He thought that if either party should remarry in England the Nova Scotia divorce would not be a bar to a bigamy prosecution there, and any children of the second 'marriage' would be regarded as illegitimate.[25]

Lord Aberdeen reiterated Stephen's objections in a testy letter to Lieutenant-Governor Sir Colin Campbell, who referred it to Chief Justice Brenton Halliburton for reply.[26] Halliburton's letter is remarkable for its calm, confident, magisterial tone. He admitted that it was 'not surprising that that Act ... should have elicited a reaction in London,' but he thought 'his Lordship [would] ... be induced to take a different view of it when he learned the peculiar state of the Law relating to Divorce in Nova Scotia.' In his long account of the relevant legislation and its application he at last gave London a clear description of local law. The origins of the legislation he ascribed to New England sentiment; the law there was 'more lax than in England.' Halliburton found it ironic that only the week before Aberdeen's dispatch arrived, the governor in council had dissolved the marriage of Charlotte and George Hynes on the ground of cruelty, an action that would elicit no reaction from London because it was judicial rather than legislative in form.

As to the merits of the Kidston case, Halliburton gave a sophisticated and ingenious argument, too complex to detail here, which seems to have carried the day in London, since the act was confirmed. A minute in Stephen's reports states merely that the governor was to be 'cautioned against assenting to any similar Act in future.' Halliburton's account of Nova Scotia law may have persuaded James Stephen to adopt a more liberal view of colonial divorce laws. While he was equivocal about an 1833 Prince Edward Island act modelled on Nova Scotia's legislation, he reported favourably to Lord Glenelg on a second PEI act in 1835, which he said was 'not only an unobjectionable, but a very salutary measure' supported by 'sufficient colonial precedents.'[27]

It is likely that the differences between the English law and the Nova Scotia law were primarily the result of the New England influence in the young colony, as Halliburton suggested. Puritan colonies such as Massachusetts were the first common law jurisdictions to make divorce possible through the secular courts; their law was based on the civil law theory of marriage as a contract that could be breached by such offences as adultery, great cruelty, or desertion without maintenance. The New England colonies avoided a clash with London on this issue by making divorce a matter for governor and council, not a question for the legislature; not until after the Revolution were the grounds for divorce in Massachusetts codified. Chief Justice Jonathan Belcher, the drafter of most of Nova Scotia's early statutes, was from Massachusetts, as were many of the early settlers, and it is reasonable to suppose that this New England influence was instrumental in the framing of a divorce law different from that of the mother country.[28]

The firmness with which the Nova Scotia authorities maintained their divorce law in spite of imperial displeasure on at least three occasions (1761, 1816, and 1835) suggests, however, that additional explanations are necessary. It has recently been suggested that the scarcity of women in the early years of the British North American colonies and the desire of their governments to encourage population growth operated in favour of more liberal, 'gender-neutral' divorce laws.[29] In Nova Scotia, a 1789 bill proposed to tax all bachelors between the ages of twenty-five and sixty possessed of more than ten pounds per annum. The act, said to be for 'better promoting ... the propagation of the human species in Wedlock in this infant Province,' did not survive first reading; nevertheless, it is indicative of an anxiety about the population question.[30] Beamish Murdoch argued strongly that the reception of various eighteenth-century English acts restricting marriage would be inconsistent with the needs of a young colony in which 'no checks should be placed on the increase of population.'[31] This reasoning would equally justify more relaxed divorce laws, though in his comments on divorce Murdoch prefers to cite Milton's 'most ably and beautifully elucidated' essay as sufficient justification for the enlightened state of the Nova Scotia law.[32]

In the end Milton probably did contribute more than Malthus to Nova Scotia's defence of its divorce law. In England the Anglican hierarchy was the main bastion of anti-divorce sentiment; in the New World Dissenters' ideas about divorce travelled with New England settlers and loyalists to Nova Scotia in the eighteenth century. No doubt Bishop Inglis and his son and successor staunchly defended certain Anglican privileges, such as the exclusive right of Anglicans to marry by licence; but the fact of a religiously heterogeneous population with a decided minority of Anglicans suggested moderation to Anglican political leaders such as Haliburton, even as it encouraged a certain irenicism on the part of the religious authorities.[33]

Nova Scotia's divorce law differed not only from England's, but also from that of other British North American colonies. In New Brunswick the governor and council constituted the Divorce Court; grounds for divorce included frigidity and impotence, adultery, and consanguinity within the degrees prohibited by the English statute of 1541. In 1835 Prince Edward Island also gave divorce jurisdiction to the governor and council; acceptable grounds were the same as New Brunswick's, though the island saw only one divorce before Confederation. West of Ontario the law was that of the English Matrimonial Causes Act of 1857, which gave a husband the right to divorce on grounds of adultery alone but required a wife to prove adultery and some other aggravated ground, such as incest or bigamy. In Roman Catholic Quebec marriage was dissoluble in principle only on death; separation from bed and board could be obtained by a husband if his wife committed adultery, but a wife only if the husband introduced his 'concubine' into the family home. In Quebec and Ontario, however, legislative divorce was permitted.[34] When compared with their sister colonies, Nova Scotia and New Brunswick appear to have been the 'divorce capitals' of nineteenth-century Canada.[35] We must not label divorce in Nova Scotia as 'liberal,' however, until its operation in practice has been examined and compared with that of other jurisdictions.

THE OPERATION OF THE DIVORCE LAWS

Gaps in the records do not permit an analysis of fluctuations in divorce rates in Nova Scotia. Nevertheless, by any standards divorce was not an integral part of the relations between the sexes. According to the 1881 census, the ratio of divorced to married persons in Canada was 1 to 10,222; Nova Scotia and New Brunswick were at the upper end of the scale with ratios of 1 to 2,608 and 1 to 2,350 respectively. Ontario and Quebec brought up the rear with ratios of 1 to 32,580 and 1 to 62,334 respectively. Although Nova Scotia was a relatively liberal province in this regard, divorced persons were still rare throughout the nineteenth century.[36]

Low divorce rates in Nova Scotia did not necessarily mean that the colony enjoyed harmonious relations between the sexes, and other explanations can be offered for the relative infrequency with which people resorted to the divorce court. There were both social and legal barriers to divorce. The petitions studied here show that divorce was sought only in extreme circumstances that put the health or reputation of the petitioner in jeopardy; this suggests a fear of societal disapproval for seeking divorce on less serious grounds. The legal barriers were both substantive and procedural. The deserted wife in particular was disadvantaged if her husband had left the jurisdiction or could not be found; the common law recognized the wife's domicile as that of her husband during the subsistence of a valid marriage, and the wife could petition only in the foreign jurisdiction, which might not recognize divorce at all.[37]

Until 1841, at least, the procedures for obtaining a divorce could be costly and cumbersome, and must have served to repel many would-be divorcees. Beamish Murdoch noted 'strong objection[s] against this court [that is, the governor and council sitting as a Court of Marriage and Divorce] in the want of regular terms or stated sittings, and it has happened that no court could be assembled for many months ... because it required the presence in town of a majority of the members of the council, as well as that of his excellency the governor ... in [whose] absence it cannot act.'[38] Judges were excluded from the executive council in 1838, and in 1841 the governor was authorized to appoint as vice-president of the court one of the judges of the Supreme Court who, along with two members of the executive council, would constitute a quorum. In 1865 the judge in equity was appointed vice-president, and in 1866 he was made the sole judge of the newly named Court for Divorce and Matrimonial Causes, where he was to sit as judge ordinary. An appeal to the Supreme Court would be heard by three judges; in 1886 the Supreme Court in banco became the appeal court.[39]

It would be inaccurate to describe the divorce process as dilatory or unduly lengthy, however, even before 1841. In view of the need to copy documents by hand and the slowness of travel, a divorce could often be had surprisingly quickly, even for parties outside Halifax. Charlotte Hynes filed her divorce petition, or libel, on 13 June 1834, and her final decree of divorce issued on 30 March 1835, less than ten months later. She resided in Halifax but had left her husband George in Lunenburg, where documents had to be served on him and witnesses examined. William Hamilton of Brookfield, Colchester County, was even more fortunate; he received his decree just over four months after he filed his libel in March 1850. This suit too was undefended, but that fact alone did not guarantee an expeditious proceeding. In a case very similar to Hamilton's, Hector McLean of East Pictou sought a divorce from his wife Sarah on the ground of adultery, but it took almost three years for his decree to issue. There appeared to be some problem with examining the witnesses in Pictou; this, rather than any flaw in the legal process itself, accounted for a large part of the delay. The absence or illness of key witnesses could stall the proceedings for months.[40]

The procedure in divorce cases remained fairly constant during the period under review, and resembled that used in Chancery. The 1837 case of *Hicks* v. *Hicks* provides an excellent description of the process. The plaintiff, called the promovent, launched the action by filing a libel with the court. This document contained a detailed list of allegations to which the defendant wife, or 'impugnant,' was permitted to respond. It was then served personally on the wife on 24 January 1837, together with a citation to appear before the court. It was not usual for impugnants to do so; only one-third of the cases in which this information is recorded (fourteen of forty-three) were contested. The promovent invariably had an attorney, or advocate, and might have a separate proctor, or proxy, upon whom documents could be served. William Hicks employed John Whidden; no one appeared for his wife, who was duly found in contumacy after the lapse of the specified period. It later became the practice in uncontested cases for the court to appoint a 'watching counsel' who would appear for the absent party; his function was mainly to ensure that the parties were not conniving to obtain a consensual divorce, and his fees were paid by the petitioner.[41]

The next step was to appoint commissioners to take the written depositions of witnesses, whether they lived in Halifax, elsewhere in the province, or outside the jurisdiction. William Hicks resided in Digby, as did the witnesses he wished to call, and this decentralized process would have been convenient for him. Only at the very beginning of the period, when the procedure under the governor and council was quite fluid, and at the very end, after the 1889 appointment of Wallace Graham as judge in equity, did the court hear *viva voce* evidence from witnesses, although the statutes of 1841 and 1866 allowed such evidence to be taken if the court directed. In the eighteenth century the witnesses seem to have given their evidence in simple narrative form, but later a set of interrogatories was administered, containing standard questions and others agreed upon by counsel and tailored to the particular case. The interrogatories detailed the alleged misconduct of the impugnant and asked the witnesses to confirm it. The divorcing parties were not permitted to testify on their own behalf until 1855.[42] In the *Hicks* case adultery was proved on the evidence of eleven witnesses, and William was granted a divorce on 30 November, ten months after the initial application. The average length of proceedings was a little shorter, about nine and a half months.[43]

Although court proceedings of this length and complexity could be expensive, costs decreased over time. Especially after 1841 the door was open to the middle class and eventually to the working class. As early as 1759 court fees alone for a divorce action came to about £50.[44] Until the

1841 reforms, much of the expense resulted from the fees for the governor and his councillors, set at £1 per person for each day of the hearing. Lewis Davis, a surgeon, received a divorce in 1798 from his wife Margaret, but not before the governor and six councillors had listened to legal argument for two days. This cost him £14, together with £3 10s for the impress of the great seal on his decree, £4 9s for the court clerk's fees, and £2 19s for filing costs. Davis was lucky; the governor and councillors waived their fees at the instance of Dr John Halliburton, sometime legislative councillor, surgeon of the Naval Hospital, and probably Davis's professional colleague.[45] Lucy Etter, divorced in 1826, was not so fortunate: the councillor's fees of £20, along with additional court costs of £14 8s, were recorded as fully paid in February 1827. It is not clear, however, whether Lucy or her ex-husband paid them.[46]

In 1850 a statute set court costs at £1 per day, in addition to the fees for filing, drawing documents, etc.; the latter costs were the same as they were in an ordinary case in Chancery.[47] Nevertheless, legal fees doubtless came to much more than the bare court fee, and at least four complainants could not afford to petition until they had accumulated the capital (which in one case took seven years).[48] Data on costs were available in only thirteen cases: they ranged from $30.68 (court costs alone) in 1887 to $315.20 (court costs and legal fees) in 1890. Court costs at mid-century ranged from £36 in the *Hicks* case to £49 in *McLean*, an uncontested 1849 case, to £58 17s in *Thomas*, a contested 1841 case. Later in the century a refundable hundred-dollar deposit accompanied an application to guarantee that court expenses would be paid; earlier, the deposit had been lower. In 1875 Norah Ormond had to borrow her deposit from a friend, and in 1890 William Taylor's employer thought he would have done very well to have saved the deposit over a three-year period from his $30-per-month salary as a clerk in a Yarmouth dry-goods store.

An analysis of the social backgrounds of petitioners for divorce reveals that over 70 per cent of the petitioners came from outside Halifax; this suggests that proximity to the capital and courts was not a significant factor in encouraging suits.[49] Halifax was overrepresented, but not greatly so, and to some extent this overrepresentation can be accounted for by the fact that no petitioners came from the Catholic counties of Richmond, Guysborough, Inverness, Antigonish, and Victoria. The fact that the court never left Halifax (except at the very end of the period) was compensated for by procedures that did not require oral testimony; thus rural petitioners appear not to have been put at any significant disadvantage because of geography.

It is perhaps surprising, given the figures for English divorces, that 30

TABLE 1
Petitions Filed, by Cause, 1750–1890

Ground	Male petitioner	Female petitioner	Total[1]
Adultery	27[2]	14	41
Cruelty		9	9
Cruelty and adultery		5	5
Impotence		2[3]	2
TOTAL	27	30	57

1 Cause not ascertainable for three petitions
2 Represents 26 individuals (one man petitioned twice)
3 One petition alleging cruelty and duress in addition to impotence is included here and not under 'cruelty.'

petitioners were female and 27 male (see table 1). The Nova Scotia pattern was similar to that of Massachusetts, where between 1692 and 1786 122 wives and 101 husbands filed for divorce. Nancy Cott attributes this preponderance of female petitioners to the 'powerful reasons [that] urged unhappy wives to sue for divorce – reasons that did not so affect husbands.' These included the need for abused wives to seek legal protection and women's difficulty in achieving economic self-sufficiency in the absence of a husband. The latter would impel a deserted wife to seek either the freedom to remarry or the legal status of a single woman, without which she could not carry on a business or control her property.[50] These explanations are unnecessary for Nova Scotia, where the preponderance of female petitioners is not statistically significant; but women were no less economically vulnerable in Nova Scotia than in Massachusetts. Elizabeth Pollard, who petitioned the governor in council in 1777 for a decree of alimony, feared that she would become a burden on the parish because her husband was about to leave the province.[51] Women deserted by their husbands could not afford to wait for a divorce before finding a new male partner. Hector McLean left to work in the United States for three years shortly after his wife Sarah gave birth to their sixth child. On his return he found that Sarah had been married to someone else by the priest in Antigonish and borne her new 'husband' a child.[52] In such cases it would have been useless for the wife to petition for divorce (had she been able to prove adultery, for example) since her own adultery probably would have been raised as a bar to relief.

The relatively small sample makes it hazardous to speculate about why the figures differ from those in Massachusetts. Cott's own sample is small,

TABLE 2
Divorces by Cause: Petitions Filed, 1750–1890[1]

Ground	Petitions filed by men		Petitions filed by women		Total	
	Made	Granted	Made	Granted	Made	Granted
Adultery	21	16	13	12	34	28
Cruelty	0	0	7	4	7	4
Adultery and cruelty	0	0	2	1[2]	2	1
Impotence	0	0	1	1	1	1
TOTAL	21	16	23	18	44	34[3]

1 The figures are based on 44 petitions in which cause and outcome are definitely known.
2 Granted on the ground of cruelty alone
3 Of the 10 listed here as not granted, 3 were discontinued and 7 were refused.

and she tends to make heavy weather of a 20 per cent variation in the rate of petitioning. The experiences of both jurisdictions appear quite similar when they are compared with England, and suggest that if a legal regime does not directly discriminate against women, women will apply for divorce at least as often as men. While one might expect women's relative inability to bear the costs of an action to decrease their petitioning rate, female promovents could expect to get an order for costs against their husbands if successful, and probably even if unsuccessful.

An analysis of the grounds on which divorce was sought illustrates Cott's point that physical abuse by husbands was an important motive in impelling women to seek divorce. The cases involving cruelty are examined in detail later, but for now it is sufficient to note that men and women sought divorce on different grounds. Men invariably alleged adultery alone; women did so in just over half the cases. I have analysed causes of divorce on the basis of two different sources of data, but the breakdown of causes by sex of petitioner shows similar results. Over 40 per cent of the decrees obtained by women between 1868 and 1888 (eleven of twenty-seven) alleged cruelty, alone or in combination with adultery (see table 3).[53] Forty-six per cent of all petitions filed by women alleged cruelty (see table 1).

The erstwhile families who applied to the divorce court represented a wide range of occupations; the majority were decidedly middle-class, but the very wealthy also were represented.[54] Of the 47 identifiable male occupations, there were 7 farmers, 6 merchants, 5 'mariners,' 3 members each of the medical profession and military, 2 barristers, 1 shipwright,

TABLE 3
Divorces by Cause:
Decrees Granted, 1868–88

Ground	Male petitioner	Female petitioner	Total
Adultery	23	15	38
Cruelty		7	7
Adultery and cruelty		4	4
Impotence		1	
TOTAL	23	27	50

and 1 'gentleman.' Not all men were comfortably off. John Thomas, disowned and disinherited by his family after marrying (at age seventeen) a woman twice his age, spent seven years saving money from his meagre teaching salary for his divorce.[55] William Taylor's difficulties have already been mentioned. There were also several artisanal or service occupations: an actor, a painter, a blacksmith, a mason, a sometime butcher, a felt-maker, and a brothel-keeper. The occupational findings for men are similar to those for Massachusetts.[56] Women's occupations appear much less frequently in the records, although in the 1880s there is a sudden blossoming: a telegraph operator, a teacher, a cashier in a government department, a dressmaker, and a woman who managed a farm inherited from her previous husband. Norah Ormond worked as a domestic servant in the 1870s after parting company with her merchant husband, and there are a few earlier references to women who inherited wealth from husbands or parents. Women alleged in almost formulaic fashion that they had been the sole support of themselves and their children since cohabitation ceased, but for the most part they did not reveal how they earned their livings. Certainly, very few men seem to have supported their wives or children after a separation.

The overwhelming majority of petitioners were Protestants. Only two were positively identified as Catholic, although more than a quarter of Nova Scotia's population was Catholic by 1881.[57] Obviously, the church's position deterred applications for divorce; one of the two Catholic petitions came from a woman who cited as cause her husband's impotence, which was a ground of nullity under canon law.[58] Various Protestant denominations were represented – Methodists and Baptists (six each), Presbyterians (five), and Lutherans (one).[59] While 47 per cent of petitioners reported that their marriages had been solemnized by Anglican clergy, it is impossible to determine how many of these couples were in fact

Anglican. During the first half of the period, Anglican clergy routinely presided at the weddings of non-Anglican Protestants.

Adultery was by far the most common ground for divorce petitions (see tables 1 and 2). In every instance in which a husband applied, adultery was cited; sixteen of twenty-one male petitioners, or 76 per cent, were successful on this ground. This figure is almost certainly inflated, however, because of the likelihood that the number of petitions refused is underrepresented in the pre-1866 files.

The petitions that failed did so for lack of credible evidence. In all cases in which a decree was granted to a husband, evidence was forthcoming not only of a wife's adultery but also of desertion and a common law relationship with another man.[60] These changes usually occurred when the husband was away working. Among the women, thirteen cited adultery by itself and two cited adultery combined with cruelty. Of these fifteen cases, six fit into the classic pattern of adultery, desertion, and cohabitation with another, and two combined adultery and desertion; the rest do not provide enough information to categorize them.[61] The courts may have been more sympathetic to female victims of adulterous behaviour. Of thirteen petitions filed by women on the ground of adultery alone, twelve (92 per cent) succeeded; once again, this figure is probably inflated. It is likely that the success rate for colonial Massachusetts (65 per cent for women, 72 per cent for men) is closer to the real figure for Nova Scotia.[62]

What is notable about both New World jurisdictions is that they do not seem to have adopted the blatant double standard seen in England, where a wife's adultery generally brought the husband a divorce but a husband's adultery did not free his wife. Cott attributes this to an American rejection of British 'corruption' after the revolution, and a consequent reaction against loose standards of marital fidelity, irrespective of the sex of the offender. This explanation is more persuasive, of course, for the United States than for a loyal British colony, but the similarities between Massachusetts and Nova Scotia are striking and may well have been the result of New England immigration, the prevalence of Dissenters, and the differing attitudes towards women that emerged on the colonial frontier.

The *Dixon* case typifies the pattern of male-plaintiff divorces on the ground of adultery. The parties were married in May 1883 in Halifax and lived together for three years, except when George Dixon was at sea on the government schooner *Acadia*. In 1886 George found out that his wife had kept company with soldiers during his absence, and, 'becoming satisfied that his wife was unfaithful,' he urged the forces' chaplain to encourage her 'to lead a moral life.' This seems to have done no good, for when George left again for a total of three years in 1889 she went back to her old ways, had a child by another man, and set up housekeeping with him. George's petition was found to have been sufficiently proved.[63] In such cases the court castigated the wife for her conduct; words such as 'infamous,' 'indiscreet,' 'immoral,' and even 'criminal' were used, and it appears that the social stigma of being married to a woman who was living in sin led men to apply to the court. The adultery as such was not the problem; it was the continued and open nature of the offence, particularly for men who had been away for a time and then returned to live in the same community. John Thomas, a teacher from Blandford, Lunenburg County, asserted in his libel that his wife's scandalous conduct was too much to bear: 'I did not feel comfortable in my mind being called a married man when the one I formerly married lived in adultery with another.' He wanted a divorce 'to stop the talk if possible of other tongues.'[64]

Thomas's wife, like Dixon's, allegedly consorted with soldiers; indeed, military paramours appeared frequently in the male-plaintiff cases. Mrs Denoon, whose husband later became a judge of the Inferior Court of Common Pleas, was found to have committed adultery with Colonel Fraser. Peter Kemble discovered his wife's liaison with Ensign John LeBreton of the Newfoundland Fencible Regiment of Foot after the 'ladies of Sydney ceased to visit [her].' He forgave her, but drew the line when he discovered her with Captain Brown of the Royal Welsh Fusiliers after the family's removal to Halifax.[65] Such liaisons were not fortuitous: the military formed an important stratum in provincial society, especially in Halifax.

The adultery cases involving female petitioners reflect equally scandalous behaviour. They suggest that for many women 'community shock' provided the motivation for a resort to the court. In one such case George Robertson, a prominent Annapolis lawyer, had had 'carnal knowledge' of Jane McGuire, Louisa Clements, Betsy Brooks, Margaret Hawkes, and 'others.' Robertson's neighbours apparently took an avid interest in his activities; Hugh Murray, a tinsmith, stopped Robertson on the street and chided him for his doings. George Lewis knew Robertson was 'after women,' and watched him. His testimony that he saw a woman enter Robertson's office at sunrise (and his account of what he saw when he peeped through the window) was very helpful to Laleah Robertson when she sued for divorce in 1869 after only one year of marriage.[66] Adultery was a serious affront to the moral economy of small-town life, and zealously repudiated by the community. That zeal also provided the witnesses necessary for the successful prosecution of divorce suits.

The other 'community shock' cases involved acts of adultery that resulted in the termination of two marriages in Newport, Hants County. Frederick Robarts, who had been married eighteen years, committed adultery with Mary Mosher, who had been married to Major Mosher for twenty-seven years, and both Mrs Robarts and Mr Mosher obtained divorces on the same day after witnesses gave firsthand reports of seeing their spouses engaged in sexual intercourse.[67] Two further cases illustrate the extreme circumstances in which wives sought to terminate their marriages. George Jamieson deserted his wife Marion and their three children after seven years of marriage. He impregnated the children's nurse and abandoned her, and their unfortunate child eventually died in the Infants' Home in Halifax. In such circumstances Marion Jamieson was compelled to dissociate herself legally from her 'drunken brute' of a husband.[68] Captain Lamarchand Carey impregnated his maid (twice) and often proclaimed to all and sundry that he 'would go sleep with a black whore.' Patricia Carey no doubt often regretted her adolescent Gretna Green marriage as she sought, probably unsuccessfully, to end it.[69] A situation had to be particularly scandalous and sordid before middle-class wives sought their freedom but also the public shame of the divorce court.[70]

If cases of adultery were relatively straightforward as long as the evidence was clear, those involving cruelty were not. The law was uncertain and contested during much of this period, and although it supposedly became clearer in the 1870s, that clarity appears to be have been ignored by the courts. Unfortunately, key pieces of evidence are missing.[71] Despite the gaps in the record, however, the subject deserves close analysis because of Nova Scotia's unique position in the patchwork of colonial and early Canadian divorce law. Not surprisingly, all petitions alleging cruelty came from wives, although in theory men could sue for divorce on this ground. The figures tell us little about the success rate. A relatively high proportion of decrees (40 per cent) was granted on the ground of cruelty between 1868 and 1888 (see table 3), but we do not know how many petitions alleging cruelty were filed in that period. Only five out of nine petitions were successful in cases where the outcome is definitely known (see table 2). This small sample may not be representative, however. One fact that tends to suggest a higher success rate is that lawyers kept advising clients to allege cruelty in relatively large numbers; presumably, they would not have done so had they believed the chance of success to be 50 per cent or less. Many of the lawyers employed by women in cruelty cases were among the leading lights of the bar; the Uniackes, Beamish Murdoch, William Young, S.G.W. Archibald, and Benjamin Russell all appear in the records. If this investigation seems inconclusive, one thing is certain: Nova Scotia judges in the nineteenth century were more receptive to pleas of cruelty than their Massachusetts counterparts in the eighteenth. Cott found that of twenty-three women who filed petitions, not one was given a divorce on the ground of cruelty alone.[72]

In part this lack of success was due to evidentiary problems; it was also the case, however, that the Nova Scotia divorce court construed 'cruelty' very strictly. The successful petitions give some idea of the extreme degree of physical violence required to establish cruelty in the eyes of the law. A neighbour of Charlotte Hynes in Lunenburg deposed that she had often heard George Hynes say that he would 'never rest till he washed his hands in [his wife's] blood.' On one occasion she saw him chasing Charlotte with an open razor, saying he would cut her throat. After fifteen years of beatings and woundings, Charlotte finally returned to her father in Halifax, as he had often implored her to do. The father seems to have been the couple's principal support during the marriage; George virtually ceased to ply his trade as a butcher after the marriage, having 'addicted himself to idleness and drinking.'[73] Minnie Lovitt, aged seventeen when she married the son of one of Nova Scotia's wealthiest men in 1883, was often forced to flee to her parents' home to escape her husband William's violent rages. He would beat her and threaten her with weapons, and on one occasion he threw a plate of hot porridge at her head. Once he sought her at her parents' home, knocked her to the floor, and attempted to drag her bodily from the house while she clung to the newel-post; a week later she suffered a miscarriage which she and the court attributed to this altercation.[74]

Yet the degree of cruelty involved in the unsuccessful petitions was generally no less significant than that involved in the successful ones. This pattern suggests two things: a general judicial insensitivity to domestic violence, and a tendency on the judges' part to respond to factors other than the violence itself. This judicial insensitivity probably represented general societal attitudes to domestic violence. The complaints of abused wives were not well received by the criminal courts, for example. Of seventeen husbands brought before the stipendiary magistrate in Halifax during the 1870s for threatening their wives, only two were fined.[75] In these criminal cases the women often were accused of initiating or provoking the violence, and the same attitude appears to have informed divorce proceedings lodged on the ground of cruelty. Lydia MacAlpine's husband George defended his cruelty by saying that she had provoked him, despite the fact that over a five-year period he threatened to break a plate over her head, pushed her into the wood-box, struck her, knocked her down, kicked her, beat her with a stick until she was black and blue, threw a stove-hook at her head, punched her in the face, and pushed her down the stairs. When she could finally take no more she left the home and moved in with a friend. George claimed that 'any force or violence used ... was necessarily used by him in self-defence and in protecting himself from the attacks of the petitioner.' Lydia discontinued the action and returned to the family farm, which she owned. Perhaps George mended his ways when he was faced with a loss of livelihood, but both Lydia's long suffering and her decision to abandon the petition testify to the difficulties women in her position faced.[76]

The other unsuccessful cases reveal similar patterns. Richard Myrer allegedly beat his wife over a period of twenty years; on one occasion he knocked out two of her teeth. He argued provocation, and claimed that he used 'no more force than necessary to protect himself.' Helen Myrer alleged adultery as well as cruelty, but failed on both grounds. The court concluded that the acts of cruelty were not such as to place her 'in a continual state of fear' such that she 'apprehended serious danger to her person or health' and that the acts were 'never complained of until the story of the adultery reached the ears of Mrs Myrer.' Mr Justice Graham's approach to the cruelty question illustrates the double messages the court sent to women. He was troubled by the fact that the incidents of violence alleged in her petition dated from several years earlier, and suggested that she should have immediately sued for divorce if the incidents truly disturbed her.[77] Other judgments preach the virtues of wifely submission and obedience, reminding the wife of her duty to accommodate and forgive her husband.

How was this lack of sympathy for battered wives justified in law? Before 1886 the Court of Marriage and Divorce gave only formulaic reasons when granting decrees, and none for refusing them. In the post-1866 Court of Divorce and Matrimonial Causes the judges tended to give written reasons for judgment.[78] The most important post-1866 decision was that in *Anne DesBrisay* v. *Charles M. DesBrisay* (1873). According to the petitioner, her husband, a Dartmouth physician, was addicted to opium, used cruel and threatening language, drugged and hit her, refused to allow her visitors, did not give her money for clothes, and threatened to commit her to the insane asylum. She claimed that her health had deteriorated substantially as a result. The Judge Ordinary, Joseph W. Ritchie, was not impressed:

> The law of this province, having gone beyond that of England in authorizing this Court to decree a marriage to be null and void for cruelty, it becomes of the greatest importance to consider the nature and character of the cruelty which is to have such extensive operation.
>
> The legislature never could have intended that the relationship of husband and wife ... should be severed, unless for causes of the gravest character; and where the intervention of this Court is invoked on the ground of cruelty of a husband, it is bound ... to have it clearly established here that the cruelty complained of has been so aggravated as to render it impossible that the Duties of the married life could be discharged, and the complaining party must make it appear, not only that she has not brought her troubles on herself by provocation or other misconduct, but that she has exhausted all the means in her power by her conciliatory conduct to render a more kindly feeling in her husband toward her ... It is the duty of the courts to keep the rule extremely strict.[79]

Ironically, the greater liberality of the law was partly responsible for this attitude: Ritchie noted that had it been possible to grant only a divorce *a mensa et thoro* for cruelty the wife might have succeeded, but a previous decision had declared that the statutes did not authorize it. Since the court could grant only an absolute divorce, said Ritchie, a stricter standard of proof was required. In support of his conclusion he invoked the nearly century-old case of *Evans* v. *Evans*, along with an American case cited in J.F. MacQueen's treatise on divorce.[80]

There was some shift in judicial attitudes towards the end of the century, undoubtedly related to the growing influence of the anti-cruelty movement of the 1870s and 1880s.[81] In the United States, the strength of the movement was illustrated graphically (and ironically) by campaigns in a dozen states after 1876 to institute public whipping as a penalty for wife-beating.[82] A current of opinion in Nova Scotia favoured such developments: the *Acadian Recorder* agreed with the Nova Scotia Society for the Prevention of Cruelty (NSSPC) that 'the "cat" is the proper punishment for cases such as this.'[83] The primary agent of the anti-cruelty campaign in Nova Scotia was the NSSPC, which was incorporated in 1876 to deal with cases of cruelty to animals. Its concerns soon broadened, however, and under its secretary, the indefatigable John Naylor, its investigation of instances of cruelty to women and children mushroomed in the 1880s: in 1879 13 cases were investigated; by 1888 the number had grown to 170 involving women and 354 involving children.[84] The NSSPC was virtually unique in North America in explicitly including women as well as children in its mandate.[85] The NSSPC actively prosecuted wife-battering, and in flagrant cases sometimes agreed to withdraw charges if the husband would sign a separation agreement providing for maintenance of the wife and children.[86] This procedure took place 'in the shadow of the law'; the stipendiary magistrate had no jurisdiction to grant judicial separations or to force parties to sign separation agreements. Although the NSSPC was an all-male organization concerned with reforming the morals of the poor and the working class, it did provide some support to women seeking protection and maintenance from abusive husbands, and was actively sought out by those women.

These new sentiments had percolated only slowly into the Court of Divorce and Matrimonial Causes by 1890. It is ironic that one of the moving spirits behind the NSSPC was J.W. Ritchie, the author of the decision in *DesBrisay* which virtually defined cruelty out of divorce law. One of Ritchie's successors, however, followed *DesBrisay* in *Jeffery* v. *Jeffery* (1889), with the greatest reluctance. Wallace Graham, who succeeded Alexander James on the latter's death in 1889, found that Anna Jeffery had been 'inhumanly treated' by her husband, a Lunenburg mason, during their twenty-odd years of marriage. But for *DesBrisay*, he said, he would have granted a judicial separation. Graham urged her to amend her petition to include specifically a prayer for judicial separation, and to appeal to the Supreme Court to review the whole question de novo. Graham also criticized MacQueen, and indirectly Ritchie, for making his statement on cruelty without providing references to the state statutes in issue, 'few if any [of which] are as lax as the Nova Scotia Act in respect to a divorce on the ground of cruelty.' He cautioned against using the older English cases, and encouraged Nova Scotia judges to look to local circumstances when interpreting the 1761 legislation.[87] Anna Jeffery appears not to have taken up the invitation to appeal the decision. She had received an order for costs against her husband, but a year later her counsel had 'not recovered one cent of [his] costs.' No doubt Anna had difficulty persuading him to launch an appeal on her behalf.[88]

Only a year before *Jeffery* Mr Justice James had granted a divorce to Minnie Lovitt on the ground of cruelty. Why did Minnie succeed where Anna Jeffery failed? It is true that Minnie was found to have suffered a miscarriage as a result of her husband's brutality, but the degree of violence endured by Anna appears to have been even more severe. Social class is an obvious distinguishing factor in the cases of Anna Jeffery and Minnie Lovitt, but does not survive generalization to other cases. Anne Kidston, another successful divorcee, was from an élite family, but Charlotte Hynes probably was not. Anne (Falconer) DesBrisay, an unsuccessful petitioner, was the daughter of a wealthy distiller and had married into an eminent professional family. Class was an important factor in judicial perceptions of both men and women, with later Victorian society tending to define middle-class women as delicate and in need of protection, class could cut both ways in the divorce court. Only poor or working-class men were assumed to be rough, coarse, and brutal; middle-class men were expected to adhere to strict standards of proper Christian conduct, to be manly and above all gentle with women.[89] To convince a man from the privileged segment of society that one of his peers had contravened this code of behaviour was a difficult task.

The most obvious characteristic distinguishing successful from unsuccessful petitioners is the absence of children: none of the successful petitioners had children and all of the unsuccessful petitioners had at least one. Anna Jeffery had four, two of whom were still minors; Helen Myrer had eleven, three of whom were minors. A second factor was the length of the marriages: the briefer the period of cohabitation, the more likely the wives were to succeed. Minnie Lovitt had spent five years with her husband; Anne Kidston had been married eight years before being deserted, and Margaret Adams six before filing for divorce. Charlotte Hynes does not fit the pattern, with fifteen years of marriage, nor does Anne DesBrisay, who was married for four years (but she had a child). Contrast this with Anna Jeffery's twenty-one years of marriage, or Helen Myrer's thirty-seven. Admittedly, there are problems with using such a small sample, but it does seem that the divorce court did not believe that severe physical cruelty entitled women to a dissolution of marriage. If a woman had put up with the abuse for many years, she was probably assumed to be able to endure it; consequently, it was not 'impossible' for her to continue in the relationship. In cases where children were involved, the judges felt strongly that families should be kept intact, even with an abusive father. Conversely, if a woman left the marriage relatively early and no children were involved, the normal reluctance of the court to respond to allegations of domestic violence was lessened.

While Nova Scotia divorce law articulated a standard of equality between the sexes where adultery was concerned, and observed it in practice, the law of cruelty revealed a strong patriarchal attitude. In England by 1869 'the requirement for violence was no longer necessary to substantiate a charge of cruelty' for the purposes of judicial separation; [90] but in Nova Scotia the judiciary refused to recognize all but the most extreme physical violence as necessarily providing a justification for divorce. There are suggestions in the cases that the judges regarded adultery as more serious than cruelty. That perception may correspond to an implicit public-private distinction that formed part of their world-view. Adultery was a matter of public morality, an offence affecting the community as well as the parties involved. The eighteenth-century petitions often speak of the 'crime of adultery,' and adultery remained a criminal offence until well into the nineteenth century. The contractarian view of marriage which the New Englanders brought with them to Nova Scotia reinforced the idea that the husband's adultery was as much an affront to public morals as the wife's. It is probably in this set of ideas about marriage and sexuality that we should locate the partial 'gender-neutrality' of Massachusetts and Nova Scotia divorce law, rather than in any concern over 'British corruption.'

Cruelty, in contrast, was a matter of private, not public, concern; it was 'painful to have these quarrels brought into Court,' lamented the Judge Ordinary in the *Myrer* case. The idea that the domestic arena is an extra-legal sphere is not unique to the nineteenth century, but the cruelty cases illustrate just how devastating the consequences of this view could be for women. The merest slap between strangers was actionable, but anything short of attempted murder on the domestic front was invisible in the eyes of the law. This reluctance to police the level of domestic violence seems to have been rooted in the idea that the husband was entitled to exercise a moderate degree of violence in disciplining his wife. Comments about 'legitimate anger' made as late as 1890 have an Old Testament ring: 'I am satisfied,' said Wallace Graham, '[that] there was irritating conduct on the one hand and anger on the other.' Where this 'droit de correction' ended and impermissible violence began, no judge was prepared to delineate precisely: such delicate calculations were best left to the husband.[91]

In the end, we are left with a paradox. If the law really was applied as strictly as it was articulated in *DesBrisay* and *Jeffery* and *Myrer*, why were eleven divorces granted on the ground of cruelty, alone or in combination with adultery, in the twenty years after Confederation? Cruelty cases represented 40 per cent of all divorces granted during those decades, and the figure seems much higher than one would expect. Extensive newspaper and biographical research has not revealed much useful information about the parties, leaving us with only the decrees themselves. It is not inconceivable that, on average, a woman alleged every other year before a court in Nova Scotia that her husband had battered her almost to death. It seems likely that the law was more flexible in practice than in theory, as suggested above. What is striking is the refusal of wives to accept domestic violence as legitimate, and their willingness to use legal process to end it, even when the outcome of that process was far from certain.[92]

Finally, the one divorce granted for impotence should be noted. The case was one of only two that involved Catholics.[93] The Bishop of Arichat had declared the marriage of Norah and William O'Connell of North Sydney null and void, but Norah waited six years before applying for a civil divorce, not realizing that the law still considered her married. She was successful on the ground that the marriage had never been consummated owning to 'the malformation and impotence' of her husband's 'organs of generation,' a condition 'wholly uncurable by art or skill.' Norah had no difficulty in proving her case; a doctor confirmed that she was still a virgin.

No analysis of the operation of divorce in Nova Scotia can afford to ignore the fact that some couples, unable or unwilling to apply to the court, chose to divorce themselves. Social historians have noted the importance of 'self-divorce' for the lower classes in Europe and the United States,[94] and examples can be found in the Nova Scotia records. Cases of bigamy in particular indicate that folk mores allowed a spouse to consider herself divorced after a long period of desertion.[95] The traditional practice of effecting divorce through 'wife sale' also occurred on occasion. Very common in Britain, it continued in Nova Scotia as late as 1889, when a sailor returned home from a voyage to find his wife living with another man. At first outraged, he soon became more reasonable and agreed to formalize the transfer of his wife and children for forty dollars.[96] These dealings, of course, went far beyond mere desertion by one party, which was even more common,[97] and involved agreements between the parties to separate and a community acceptance of their action. At times the practice met with the approval of the local élite. In 1794 Major John Cunningham, a magistrate with the authority to perform marriages in Sydney, pronounced William Roby and Jane Measure divorced, and then married Jane to another man. The honeymoon was short-lived, ending when a complaint reached the Sessions Court at Guysborough, and the magistrate was chastised for acting 'contrary to law and morality.'[98]

Today divorce proceedings are generally concerned less with the divorce itself and much more with arrangements for children and financial settlements. In the eighteenth and nineteenth centuries this was not the case. Seventy-five per cent of the couples involved had either no

TABLE 4
Children of Divorced Couples, 1750–1890*

Children	Petitions
0	15
1	15
2	3
3	2
4	1
5	1
more than 5	3

*Forty-one of the petitions provide information on this subject, representing 40 couples

children or just one child. Those figures are comparable to those for the United States, where 50 per cent of divorces were granted to childless couples.[99] Large families did not often divorce, presumably because two or more children provided one more obstacle to the difficulties faced by divorcees (see table 4). Contrast these statistics with those for the nineteenth-century United States, where 33 per cent of women bore seven or more children, and only 9 per cent of those born between 1846 and 1855 had just one child.[100] Generally, the children appear to have stayed with the mother after the divorce, except when the husband brought a suit alleging adultery. The evidence is scanty before 1866 because custody was a separate legal issue and rarely figured in divorce proceedings; the patterns in custody awards after 1866 are dealt with in Rebecca Veinott's essay elsewhere in this volume.

A similar 'hands-off' approach was taken to alimony. Although the court was empowered to allow costs to either party and alimony to the wife, as late as 1887 judges maintained that alimony was a separate matter. One judge commented, 'I wish it were in my power to grant a Decree for permanent alimony,' and lamented that it was not, unless the wife brought a separate proceeding.[101] None the less, awards of permanent alimony were occasionally made, as were awards of alimony *pendente lite*.[102]

CONCLUSION

Despite the relative liberality of its laws, Nova Scotia saw few divorces in the eighteenth and nineteenth centuries. One significant constraint was that imposed by societal attitudes; provincial society prided itself that it did not encourage marriages to break up, and newspapers sneered at the nation to the south, where it was so easy to obtain a divorce. Stories about the Indiana doctor who got divorced 'because his wife was subject to epilepsy' and who then remarried and 'adopted his first wife as a daughter,' or about a man from California 'who sued for a divorce because, during his absence from home, his wife wrote him to the effect that the longer he stayed away the better she liked him' no doubt provided amusement and confirmed the picture of a frivolous, divorce-happy society that Nova Scotians did not wish to emulate.[103] As Constance Backhouse has said, it was 'commonplace in the late nineteenth century for Canadians to congratulate themselves on the sanctity of their marital affairs,' to the point where J.A. Gemmill could unblushingly assert that Canadians showed 'a cleaner record than that of any other progressive people on the face of the earth.'[104] The equation of infrequent divorce with domestic harmony may be ridiculed today as hypocrisy, but it seems to have been taken seriously at the time.

While Nova Scotians demonstrated the same smugness about local virtue as other Canadians, their judicial divorce mechanism set them apart from the non-Maritime Canadian provinces, where the more cumbersome legislative divorce was the norm. The competition between the two procedures was eventually resolved in favour of the 'Maritime model,' and it appears that the Nova Scotia example was an important factor in the eventual liberalization of Canadian divorce law. When the British Columbia Supreme Court was called upon to consider the applicability of English divorce legislation in that province, the fact that Nova Scotia and New Brunswick ('England's more practical colonies') had had judicial divorce for over a century led Gray J to conclude that the English act was not unsuitable for local conditions.[105] J.M. Beck has noted a strong effort on the part of influential Nova Scotians to liberalize federal divorce law in the early twentieth century; Robert Borden and W.S. Fielding proposed bills in 1918 and 1919 that would have instituted judicial divorce across Canada.[106] It is true that there were many other social factors at work creating a demand for more liberal divorce laws in twentieth-century Canada; but in view of the disrepute into which the American and English solutions had fallen, one should not underestimate the importance of the Maritime model of divorce in the eventual translation of that demand into law. The men and women who created Nova Scotia's divorce apparatus in the eighteenth century would no doubt have been surprised at its durability.

NOTES

1 Executive Council Minutes, 15 May 1750, PANS RG1, vol. 209, 57–8. C.J. Townshend *Historical Account of the Courts of Judicature in Nova Scotia* (Toronto: Carswell 1900) states (at 17) that '[t]he mode in which the Court ... exercised their powers on this occasion was subsequently disapproved of by the Home authorities', but it is not clear whether he is suggesting that the divorce itself was disallowed. There is no record of its disallowance, and the court continued to exercise its jurisdiction repeatedly in the 1750s, an odd practice if the first attempt had been struck down. He may be referring to the disallowance of part of the 1758 statute which put the council's power on a legislative footing: see below, note 17 and accompanying text.

2 Before 1811 divorce petitions are contained in the Executive Council Minutes, and thereafter in the records of the Halifax County Supreme Court. There are, however, a few in the papers of Sir William Young, PANS MG2, vol. 765 (hereinafter Young Papers). These sixty petitions were all that could be discovered, although a nineteenth-century source reports a total of fifty-two divorces granted between 1868 and 1888 alone: J.A. Gemmill *The Practice of the Parliament of Canada upon Bills of Divorce* (Toronto: Carswell 1889) 257. The records of the court disappeared about 1880, and T.B. Akins was only partially successful in tracing them: see T.B. Akins Papers, PANS MG1, vol. 8, no. 13, Akins to Alexander James, 8 Mar. 1887; no. 14, Akins to C. McCraigen, 8 Mar. 1887.

While it is not possible to establish precisely how many divorces were sought in the period studied, the petitions that have survived are quite likely a significant sample of the whole, and reasonably representative. The sample of sixty will be treated as representative for the purposes of this study for all characteristics except temporal distribution. It is likely that the procedural reforms of 1866 stimulated an increase in divorce petitions, and that the number of petitions prior to that date was much smaller. The figure mentioned in the text (150 to 200) was arrived at by accepting Gemmill's figure and adding to it an estimated one divorce per year from 1750 to 1867. These records are unique in Canada, as New Brunswick and Prince Edward Island, which also provided for judicial divorce from an early date, granted almost none – apparently only one in Prince Edward Island before 1867 and four in New Brunswick before 1860: Public Legal Information Services *Manners, Morals and Mayhem: A Look at the First 200 Years of Law and Society in New Brunswick* (Fredericton: PLIS 1985) 51. The pace quickened considerably after 1860 in New Brunswick: 121 petitions survive for the period from 1860 to 1900: Angela Crandall 'Divorce in Nineteenth-Century New Brunswick: A Social Dilemma' paper presented at the Atlantic Law and History Workshop, 20–21 Oct. 1989.

3 For English divorce law see A. Horstman *Victorian Divorce* (New York: St Martin's Press 1985); C.E.P. Davies 'Matrimonial Relief in English Law' in R.H. Graveson and F.R. Crane, eds *A Century of Family Law* (London: Sweet and Maxwell 1957); L. Holcombe *Wives and Property: Married Women's Property Law in Nineteenth-Century England* (Toronto: University of Toronto Press 1983) 93–109. For Canada see Gemmill *Bills of Divorce*; R.R. Evans *The Law and Practice Relating to Divorce and Other Matrimonial Causes* (Calgary and Montreal: Burroughs 1923); and W.K. Power *The Law and Practice Relating to Divorce and other Matrimonial Causes in Canada* (Calgary: Burroughs 1948).

4 S. Wolfram 'Divorce in England 1700–1857' *Oxford Journal of Legal Studies* 5 (1985) 155

5 Ibid.; S. Anderson 'Legislative Divorce: Law for the Aristocracy?' in G. Rubin and D. Sugarman, eds *Law, Economy and Society: Essays in the History of English Law, 1750–1914* (Abingdon: Professional Books 1984) argues that the cost was less than £475 for about one-half of pre-1857 petitioners.

6 Wolfram 'Divorce in England' 167. This assumes that the damages will be paid once awarded, and ignores the fact that such actions were not guaranteed to succeed, which might inhibit plaintiffs from bringing them because of the consequent liability for costs.

7 Ibid. 165. The institution of judicial divorce in 1857 did bring an increase in the number of divorces; but for a variety of reasons, particularly the law's obsession with collusion and the continued high expense of bringing a case before the one divorce court in London, divorces remained relatively inaccessible to the less well off. See G. Savage 'The Operation of the 1857 Divorce Act, 1860–1910: A Research Note' *Journal of Social History* 16 (1983) 103–10.

8 In only one case, *Hicks* v. *Hicks* (1837) (cited infra note 41) was there mention of such a previous action by the husband. Hicks had recovered £27 10s damages plus £36 in costs from the adulterer for 'trespass' to his wife.

9 Executive Council Minutes, 29 May 1752, PANS RG1, vol. 209, 149, 160

10 Ibid. 9 July 1752, 163

11 Ibid. 19 Feb. 1757, vol. 210, 279

12 T.G. Barnes 'As Near as May Be Agreeable to the Laws of This Kingdom: Legal Birthright and Legal Baggage at Chebucto, 1749' in P.B. Waite et al., eds *Law in a Colonial Society* (Toronto: Carswell 1984) 15, 17

13 SNS 1758, c. 17. The court also heard cases dealing with matrimonial matters other than divorce. In 1759 the council was called upon to decide an action in jactitation of marriage, an ancient form of proceeding in which the plaintiff seeks an order restraining the defendant from claiming publicly, contrary to fact, that he or she is married to the plaintiff. Eva Catherine Roussin complained that Caspar Strauch persisted in claiming that they had married on board the vessel that had brought them to Nova Scotia in 1752. The governor, Chief Justice Belcher, and several councillors heard *viva voce* evidence over two days, as well as argument from the parties' counsel, William Nesbitt and Daniel Wood, before deciding that Strauch had not proved the fact of marriage to their satisfaction: PANS RG39, series D, vol. 1A, file 2. In 1777 the court was seised of a petition for alimony unaccompanied by a request for divorce or separation from bed and board: *Elizabeth Pollard* v. *John Pollard* ibid. file 5.

14 Respectively, *John Meagher* v. *Mary Ann Meagher* (1835) PANS RG39, series D, vol. 1A, file 16; *Anne DesBrisay* v. *Charles M. DesBrisay* (1873) ibid. vol. 1, file 2. Counsel in the latter case sought and received permission to amend the petition to request a divorce *a vinculo* when apprised of the judge's opinion that he had no jurisdiction to grant a judicial separation. (Records of cases after 1811 not in the Young Papers are hereinafter identified by date, volume, and file number only.) Annulments as such have never been granted in Nova Scotia. In cases of impotence or consanguinity the decree was called a 'double decree,' 'namely, a decree which was both a decree of divorce and a declaration that the marriage was "null and void" ': *R* v. *R* (1976) 18 NSR (2d) 662, at 667, per MacKeigan CJNS. I am grateful to Alastair Bissett-Johnson for providing this reference.

15 13 & 14 Geo. V, c. 19 (UK)

16 L.W. Labaree *Royal Instructions to British Colonial Governors, 1670–1776* 2 vols (New York: Octagon Books 1967) vol. 1, 154–5. On the background to the prohibition, see E.B. Russell *The Review of American Colonial Legislation by the King in Council* (1935; reprinted New York: Appleton Century Croft 1976) 171–3. The legislative divorce was An Act to Dissolve the Marriage of Anne Kidston with Richard Kidston, SNS 1834, c. 44. Joseph Fairbanks, who had obtained a divorce *a mensa et thoro* in 1752, subsequently remarried and had issue, then sought a legislative confirmation that he was fully divorced in order to regularize the second marriage. The Assembly, of which he was a member, passed a private bill, but the council rejected it: *JHA* 19 Sept. 1760. A similar bill passed both houses in 1762, but Lieutenant-Governor Jonathan Belcher refused his assent because the bill 'appeared contrary to His Majesty's instructions and to good policy and order':

Belcher to Lords of Trade, 2 July 1762, PANS CO 217, vol. 19, L-94, L-99–102. The second 'wife,' Lydia Blagden or Blackden, continued to be regarded as his legal wife, but matters never had to be clarified, since Fairbanks survived Lydia and all their issue.

17 SNS 1761, c. 8; J. Munro *Acts of the Privy Council of England, Colonial Series; Volume 4, 1745–1766* (London: HMSO 1911) 558

18 Precontract was defined in volume 2 of Murdoch's *Epitome* as 'the subsistence of a former contract of marriage undissolved, which has been valid in all its circumstances, although not solemnized by the rites of religion.' The ecclesiastical courts in England could force the parties to such a contract to celebrate their marriage in the proper way (*in facie ecclesiae*), which would render the later purported marriage by one of them liable to dissolution: R.H. Helmholz *Marriage Litigation in Medieval England* (Cambridge: Cambridge University Press 1974) chapter 2. The absence of a system of ecclesiastical courts in the Canadian colonies meant that this ground of divorce was irrelevant in Nova Scotia; none of the divorce petitions I studied was based on precontract. Presumably, it was added in 1761 to give the appearance of making Nova Scotia law conform to English law at a time when the imperial authorities regarded this as important. It was removed by SNS 1866, c. 13.

19 SNS 1816, c. 7

20 D.B. Swinfen *Imperial Control of Colonial Legislation 1813–1865* (Oxford: Clarendon Press 1970) 11–31

21 Law Officer's Reports on Colonial Acts 1814–18, NA CO 323/40, Stephen to Bathurst, 11 Sept. 1816. There was later some doubt whether the Act had been disallowed, as the 1851 Revised Statutes purported to repeal it (see RSNS 1851, c. 170), which suggests it was still in force at mid-century. The attorney general in his 1859 *Report on the State of Divorce in Nova Scotia*, however, believed with Murdoch (*Epitome* vol. 2, 23) that the act had been disallowed. See PANS RG2, vol. 1, no. 63.

22 Swinfen *Imperial Control* 70

23 Unpassed Bills, 1834–5, PANS RG5, series U, vol. 12

24 For the passage of the bill see *JHA* 1834, 561, 569–70, 579–80, and 585. Both the failure of the bill on these grounds and the absence of newspaper reports of any debates are difficult to explain, but at this time council and Assembly were locked in acrimonious discussions about the method of selection of executive councillors, and the divorce bill may have been a casualty of this larger issue: see *Novascotian* 19 and 26 Feb., 5 and 13 Mar. 1834. Kidston and Hall were married in Gloucester, Massachusetts, on 3 Feb. 1835: *Acadian Recorder* 7 Feb. 1835.

25 Law Officers' Reports on Colonial Acts 1834, PAC CO323/50, Stephen to G. Spring Rice, 5 Nov. 1834

26 Colonial Office Original Correspondence, NA CO217/158, Aberdeen to Campbell, 4 Feb. 1835. Halliburton's reply is appended thereto, and can also be found in draft form in PANS RG1, vol. 240, no. 143.

27 Law Officers' Reports on Colonial Acts 1834, NA CO217/50, Stephen to Stanley, 11 Feb. 1834; CO 323/52, Stephen to Glenelg, 8 Feb. 1836. The Assembly never again passed a private divorce act, but parties continued to petition in the hope that it would do so – Russell Caldwell in 1844 (*JHA* 1844), John A. Barry in 1852 (*JHA* 1852), and Mary Hierlihy in 1851 (*JHA* 1851) and 1853. The last petition was addressed to the Legislative Council: PANS RG5, series P, vol. 13, no. 95.

28 On American colonial divorce law see N.F. Cott 'Divorce and the Changing Status of Women in Eighteenth-Century Massachusetts' *William and Mary Quarterly* 33 (1976), especially 588–91, and Roderick Phillips *Putting Asunder: A History of Divorce in Western Society* (Cambridge: Cambridge University Press 1988) chapter 4. Beamish Murdoch saw the relationship between colonial divorce law and the civil law tradition, noting that the 'civil law of Rome has a greater share in the composition of our laws than it has in those of the mother country,' and that as a result 'marriage is not shackled by arbitrary legislation': *Epitome* vol. 2, 35–6. For Belcher see Townshend *History of the Courts* 43–9. On New England immigration to Nova Scotia see C.B. Fergusson 'Pre-revolutionary Settlements in Nova Scotia' *Collections* 37 (1970) 5–22; E.C. Wright *Planters and Pioneers: Nova Scotia, 1749–1755* (Wolfville, NS 1978); and Barnes 'As Near as May Be Agreeable.'

29 Constance Backhouse 'Pure Patriarchy: Nineteenth-Century Canadian Marriage' *McGill Law Journal* 31 (1986) 284, citing D.K. Weisburg 'Under Great Temptations Here: Women and Divorce Law in Puritan Massachusetts' in Weisburg, ed. *Women and the Law: A Social Historical Perspective* vol. 2 (Cambridge, Mass.: Schenkman 1982) 117–28

30 PANS RG1, vol. 302, no. 2

31 Ibid. vol. 2, 14–15

32 Murdoch was referring to John Milton *The Doctrine and Discipline of Divorce* (1643), in Don M. Wolfe, ed. *Complete Prose Works of John Milton* vol. 2 (New Haven: Yale University Press 1959).

33 On marriage licences, see S. Buggey 'Churchmen and Dissenters: Religious Toleration in Nova Scotia 1758–1835' (MA thesis, Dalhousie University 1981) 10–14, 112–31. Anglicans made up 23.5 per cent of the population in 1829; the proportion fell to 13.5 per cent by 1881. Whereas the Dissenters stressed marriage as a civil contract and permitted divorce, Anglican theol-

ogy maintained the status-based indissolubilist view of marriage, inherited from Roman Catholicism: Phillips *Putting Asunder* chapter 3. The lieutenant governor of New Brunswick, writing to Lord Sydney with regard to a proposed Marriage Act in that province, 'did not approve of holding up marriage so openly in the light of a merely civil contract': T. Carleton to Lord Sydney, 31 July 1789; New Brunswick Museum, file 67. I thank D.G. Bell for bringing this correspondence to my attention.

34 See Backhouse 'Pure Patriarchy' 269–70; Gemmill *Practice upon Bills of Divorce*, 37; Power *The Law and Practice relating to Divorce* 8–9; Civil Code of Lower Canada, 1866, articles 187, 188. In Quebec spouses could also demand separation from bed and board on the ground of 'outrage, ill-usage or grievous insult committed by one toward the other' (article 189). Not until 1954 was the double standard relating to adultery removed.

35 The divorce laws of Nova Scotia and New Brunswick continued in force until 1968 by virtue of section 129 of the British North America Act, which allowed all laws of Canada, Nova Scotia, or New Brunswick to stay operative unless repealed by the competent authority. The Nova Scotia act of 1761, as amended in the nineteenth century, was reproduced as an appendix to each edition of the Revised Statutes of Nova Scotia up to and including the 1954 edition. It was eventually supplemented by the federal Divorce Jurisdiction Act, 1930, SC 1930, c. 15, which allowed a married woman who had been deserted for two years to apply for a divorce.

36 Gemmill *Practice upon Bills of Divorce* 257. The 1901 census records 91 divorced persons in Nova Scotia and a married population of 152,485, for a ratio of about 1 to 1,650. On the historical incidence of divorce in Canada, see R. Pike 'Legal Access and the Incidence of Divorce in Canada: A Sociohistorical Analysis' *Canadian Review of Sociology and Anthropology* 12 (1975) 115.

37 In fact this seems to have been less of a barrier than one might expect, given the frequency with which men deserted their wives and moved to foreign parts. It is not mentioned in some cases where it clearly could have been, such as *Jane Rafuse* v. *Robert Rafuse* (1885) vol. 1 [no file number], where the husband had settled in Massachusetts and started a new family. It may have been the stumbling-block in some cases where the result is unknown but it is likely that no decree was granted, such as *Patricia Carey* v. *Lamarchand Carey* (1842) Young Papers. The explanation for *Rafuse* may be simply that the suit was undefended, and the court would not raise such defences on its own initiative.

38 *Epitome* vol. 4, 97. T.C. Haliburton noted that a majority vote by a quorum of councillors sufficed for a valid decree even if the governor did not concur:

An Historical and Statistical Account of Nova Scotia vol. 1 (Halifax: Joseph Howe 1829) 292.

39 SNS 1841, c. 13; SNS 1865, c. 1, s. 10; SNS 1866, c. 13; SNS 1886, c. 49. The 1866 act adopted the name and structure of the new court from the English Matrimonial Causes Act of 1857, and endowed its judge with most of the powers possessed by his English homologue.

40 *Charlotte Hynes* v. *George Hynes* (1835); *William Hamilton* v. *Martha Hamilton* (1850); *Hector McLean* v. *Sarah McLean* (1849) Young Papers

41 *William Hicks* v. *Lydia Hicks* (1837) vol. 1, file A2. The first watching counsel to be noted in the records was Beamish Murdoch, who appeared for the absent wife in *McLean* (1849).

42 SNS 1855, c. 9, s. 2. Spouses were still neither competent nor compellable to give evidence with regard to adultery, but they could henceforth do so in cases of cruelty. Before 1855, a wife had to produce witnesses to establish a case of cruelty. The 1866 Divorce and Matrimonial Causes Act was careful to specify that spouses could give evidence regarding cruelty where the petition coupled adultery and cruelty.

43 Derived from twenty-five petitions where sufficient information was recorded to calculate the time.

44 Executive Council Minutes, PANS RG1, vol. 211, 85, 142

45 *Lewis Davis* v. *Margaret Davis* (1797) vol. 1A, file 9

46 *Lucy Etter* v. *Benjamin Etter* (1826) vol. 1A, file 15

47 SNS 1850, c. 21

48 See *John Thomas* v. *Elizabeth Thomas* (1841) vol. 1, file B; *George Dixon* v. *Mary Dixon* (1890) vol. 1, file 21 (seven-year wait, husband 'unable for want of means to petition at an earlier date' because he was 'a poor man in straitened financial circumstances and in receipt only of a very small salary as a clerk in a store'); *William Taylor* v. *Kate Taylor* (1890) vol. 1, file 25; *Norah Ormond (O'Connell)* v. *William O'Connell* (1875) vol. 1, file 3.

49 This calculation is based on the parties' place of marriage, which is given in 53 of the petitions. Most petitioners still resided in the same area. Of the 53, 38 were from outside Halifax. Compare this finding with Savage's work on the English Act; she found that the location of the court in London gave a distinct advantage to London-based couples: Savage 'Operation of the 1857 Divorce Act' 104–5.

50 Cott 'Divorce in Massachusetts' 587, 595. For a discussion of women's property rights at common law see Holcombe *Wives and Property* 18–29.

51 *Elizabeth Pollard* v. *John Pollard* (1777) vol. 1A, file 5

52 *Hector McLean* v. *Sarah McLean* Young Papers

53 Table 3 is based on data different from those mentioned in note 2. PANS

RG39, series D, vol. 2 contains a document that purports to be a list of all divorces granted between 1868 and 1888, together with a notation of the ground(s) on which they were awarded. The document seems to have been drawn up by a court official and appears to be authoritative. The total number of divorces recorded in it (52) agrees with both Gemmill's 1889 figure (see note 2 supra) and the 1901 Census of Canada. It is likely that the document was prepared as a result of Gemmill's query and that a copy was subsequently forwarded to the Dominion Bureau of Statistics. One would expect that in instances where adultery and cruelty were listed as causes the divorce was granted on both grounds, but this is not absolutely clear. I have assumed the causes to be accurate for the purposes of creating table 3.

54 Both of the sons of Yarmouth shipowner William D. Lovitt, whom the *Novascotian* (6 Jan. 1894) thought was 'probably the wealthiest man in Nova Scotia' at his death in 1894 were divorced by their wives for cruelty: William Lovitt, his father's 'confidential clerk,' was divorced by his wife Minnie in 1888, and Dr Israel Lovitt's marriage to Bessie (Beveridge) ended in 1895. See PANS RG39, series D, vol. 2, file 42, and Rebecca Veinott's essay elsewhere in this volume.

55 *John Thomas* v. *Elizabeth Thomas* (1841) vol. 1, file B

56 Cott 'Divorce in Massachusetts' 588

57 Canada *Census of Canada 1880–1881* (Ottawa: MacLean, Roger 1881)

58 *Norah O'Connell* v. *William O'Connell* (1875) vol. 1, file 3

59 Religious affiliation has been determined for thirty-six petitioners by the denomination of the church in which the parties were married.

60 See the following cases: Memorial of Henry Potter, Executive Council Minutes, 9 Apr. 1764, PANS RG1, vol. 188, 450; *Hugh Denoon* v. *Jack [sic] Denoon* (1811) vol. 1, file A1; *Jacob Allen* v. *Mary Allen* (1849) vol. 1, file E; *Hector McLean* v. *Sarah McLean* (1847) Young Papers; *William Hamilton* v. *Martha Hamilton* (1850) ibid.; *Richard Upham* v. *Lucy Upham* (1875) vol. 1, file 4; *Charles Graham* v. *Evelyn Graham* (1880) vol. 1, file 6; *John Leonard* v. *Annie Leonard* (1884) vol. 1, file 10; *Charles Gaudet* v. *Catherine Gaudet* (1887) vol. 1, file 11; *George Dixon* v. *Mary Dixon* (1890) vol. 1, file 21; *Major Mosher* v. *Mary Mosher* (1890) vol. 1, file 24; *William Taylor* v. *Kate Taylor* (1890) vol. 1, file 25.

61 *Sarah Nauffts* v. *Alexander Nauffts* (1882) vol. 1, file 8; *Evalina Archibald* v. *Melville Archibald* (1888) vol. 1, file 26; *Eleanor Tollemache* v. *Hon. John D. Tollemache* (1881) vol. 1, file 7; *Maggie Daley* v. *Jeremiah Daley* (1889) vol. 1, file 15; *Marion Jamieson* v. *George Jamieson* (1887) vol. 1, file 12; *Jane Rafuse* v. *Robert Rafuse* (1885) vol. 1 [no file number]

62 Cott 'Divorce in Massachusetts' 599. In contrast, petitions based on grounds other than adultery had a success rate of only 47 per cent (women) and 50 per cent (men). Cott defined 'successful' petitions as including those requesting annulments or separation from bed and board.

63 *George Dixon* v. *Mary Dixon* (1890) vol. 1, file 21

64 *John Thomas* v. *Elizabeth Thomas* (1841) vol. 1, file B. Evidence regarding this anxiety over public knowledge of spousal infidelity can be found outside the divorce files. Donald MacKenzie of Malagawatch complained to the Legislative Council in 1835 that the local magistrate would do nothing to silence Lauchlan MacLean, who was allegedly spreading rumours that he had slept with MacKenzie's wife: PANS RG5, series GP, vol. 1, no. 65. Adultery was made a crime by SNS 1759, c. 17, s. 9, which also provided for an action in damages 'by any of the parties aggrieved.' The provision remained in force at least until Confederation.

65 *Hugh Denoon* v. *Jack Denoon* (1811) vol. 1, file A1; *Peter Kemble* v. *Elizabeth Kemble* (1809) vol. 1A, file 11

66 *Laleah Robertson* v. *George Robertson* (1869) vol. 1, file 1

67 *Ruby Robarts* v. *Frederick Robarts* (1889) vol. 1, file 20; *Major Mosher* v. *Mary Mosher* (1890) vol. 1, file 24

68 *Marion Jamieson* v. *George Jamieson* (1887) vol. 1, file 12

69 *Patricia Carey* v. *Lamarchand Carey* (1842) Young Papers

70 See also *Jane Rafuse* v. *Robert Rafuse* (1885) vol. 1 [no file number]

71 Of the eleven decrees issued on the grounds of cruelty or cruelty and adultery between 1868 and 1888, we have reasons for judgment in only one. Reasons have survived, however, in the three post-1866 cases where decrees based on allegations of cruelty (*DesBrisay*, 1873 and *Jeffery*, 1889), or cruelty and adultery (*Myrer*, 1890) were refused. No files involving cruelty from the 1850s or 1860s have survived and we do not know the outcome of two cases from the 1840s, but there is ample information about two successful petitions in the 1830s. The several petitions alleging cruelty in the eighteenth century provide little information.

72 Cott 'Divorce in Massachusetts' 608. On matrimonial cruelty in nineteenth-century English jurisprudence, see A.J. Hammerton 'Victorian Marriage and the Law of Matrimonial Cruelty,' paper presented at the Law and History Conference, LaTrobe University, Bundoora, Victoria, May 1987. It is there argued that Divorce Court judges in England adopted increasingly flexible interpretations of the law of cruelty through the nineteenth century, departing from the rigid standards inherited from the ecclesiastical courts. Given the small number of surviving cases in Nova Scotia, it is difficult to discern any long-term trend in judicial attitudes towards

matrimonial cruelty. For the twentieth-century experience see J.G. Snell 'Marital Cruelty: Women and the Nova Scotia Divorce Court 1900–1939' *Acadiensis* 18 (1988) 3.

73 *Charlotte Hynes* v. *George Hynes* (1835) Young Papers

74 *Minnie Lovitt* v. *William Lovitt* (1888) vol. 1, file 13

75 The figure is based on newspaper research and not on court records, which do not survive in this period. See M. Himmelman 'For Whom the Bell Tolls: A Quantitative Sketch of Marriage Patterns, Halifax, 1871–1881' (Honours thesis, Dalhousie University 1979) 12. Richard Grainger was brought before the stipendiary magistrate in Halifax in January 1873 'for the dozenth time' on a charge of assaulting his wife. He had 'obtained quite a notoriety in police circles on that charge' and his wife had 'become famous for her forgiving disposition, which has invariably led her to intercede for her husband after having him arrested.' On this occasion Grainger was remanded because his wife was too ill from her latest beating to give evidence against him: *Morning Chronicle* 21 Jan. 1873. Another shocking incident involved Christopher McLean, who was sentenced to ninety days in prison or a twenty-dollar fine for beating his wife with a shovel: ibid. 22 Dec. 1874. Backhouse ('Pure Patriarchy' 295–312) also finds a judicial insensitivity to battered wives in her examination of alimony petitions from wives who alleged cruelty, although most of her examples date from the 1850s and 1860s.

76 *Lydia MacAlpine* v. *George MacAlpine* (1889) vol. 1, file 17. In one sense, however, Lydia was lucky. Before the passage of the Married Women's Property Act, SNS 1884, c. 12, she would not have found it so easy to reclaim her farm and manage it on her own.

77 *Helen Myrer* v. *Richard Myrer* (1890) vol. 1, file 23

78 Divorce cases only began to appear in the law reports in the twentieth century; the first was *Cesale* v. *Cesale* (1920) 54 NSR 91. Newspaper reports were erratic and often unhelpful. For example, the *Unionist and Halifax Journal* of 11 Apr. 1866 gives a bare mention of two decrees granted on the ground of adultery, stating only the names of the parties and sex of the petitioner. These two cases do not survive in the files at PANS, and have not been included in my calculations. *Jamieson* was one of the few cases that attracted any significant interest on the part of the press: see Rebecca Veinott's essay elsewhere in this volume.

79 *Anne DesBrisay* v. *Charles M. DesBrisay* (1873) vol. 1, file 2. A similar attitude marked the deliberations of the New Brunswick courts. In the leading case of *Hunter* v. *Hunter*, (1863) 10 NBR 593, at 602, the court admitted that 'there may have been something, perhaps a good deal, to put up with;

yet balancing advantages with disadvantages, there was not more than in the ordinary circumstances of life, many women are called on to endure.' Benjamin Russell, an eminent lawyer called to the Nova Scotia bench in 1904, called *DesBrisay* 'the *locus classicus* here on the question of Divorce' and gave a rather different version of the facts in his *Autobiography* (Halifax: Royal Print and Litho 1932) 119. As counsel for Dr DesBrisay, he naturally omits any reference to his alleged cruelty, but says that Anne 'with the help, and probably at the instigation of her very able and muscular sister, compel[led] the doctor to jump out through the window and take refuge for a time in my father's house, covered with wounds and blood.' This incident is nowhere referred to in the evidence, which renders its authenticity suspect as it clearly would have been favourable to Dr DesBrisay. Russell does confirm that DesBrisay had a clear financial motive for resisting the divorce, as Anne's father was a well-to-do distiller who had built and furnished a house for the newly wed couple. His main interest in recounting this story is to show that 'however unpleasant for the parties concerned,' it was 'a godsend for me at the beginning of my career as a lawyer.' It should also be noted that Ritchie's wife was related to the DesBrisay family; her grandmother and Dr DesBrisay's grandmother were sisters, the daughters of Rev. Mather Byles. See A.W.H. Eaton 'Genealogy of the Byles Family' PANS MG100, vol. 115, no. 20C.

80 J.F. MacQueen *A Practical Treatise on the Appellate Jurisdiction ... together with the Practice on Parliamentary Divorce* (London 1842). The continued existence of divorce *a mensa et thoro* remained a vexed question in Nova Scotia. The explanatory note to the 1761 act stated that adultery and cruelty were 'proper causes for temporary separation a Mensa and Thoro, yet they do not affect the validity of the Marriage,' yet the disallowed 1816 act had purported to authorize the court to grant either a divorce *a mensa et thoro* or a divorce *a vinculo matrimonii* where adultery or cruelty was alleged. The enactments that remained in force until 1841 did not mention the lesser divorce explicitly, leading Murdoch to wonder if it might have been 'tacitly abrogated' (*Epitome* vol. 2, 30; vol. 4, 101). In 1841 a new act empowered the court to declare 'by definitive sentence *or otherwise*, the Marriage ... to be absolutely null and void' (emphasis added), and specifically forbade 'any person who may be divorced from Bed and Board only to marry again': SNS 1841, c. 13. The former clause was repeated when the act was included in the 1851 revision, but the latter was not: RSNS 1851, c. 128, s. 4. Faced with these conflicting directions, the courts continued to grant only divorces *a vinculo*. The position was clearer in New Brunswick, where the 1791 statute (31 Geo. III, c. 5) clearly gave the governor in council

full power to determine all matrimonial causes, including 'Divorce, as well from the bond of Matrimony, as divorce, and separation from bed and board, and alimony' (section 5). *Hunter*, for example, involved a petition for judicial separation.

81 For a recent overview, see L. Gordon *Heroes of Their Own Lives: The Politics and History of Family Violence, Boston 1880–1960* (New York: Viking 1988). A more concrete reason for Graham's apparent sympathy to abused wives may be that he began to hear oral evidence during his tenure in the courts, as in *Dixon*. It is not clear whether he heard oral testimony in *Myrer*. Previously only written evidence had been submitted, which would not have generated the same emotional impact. In order to expedite the new process Graham was prepared to hold court outside of Halifax, something that had not been done since the 1750s. *Innes* v. *Innes* (1889) vol. 1, for example, was heard in Liverpool.

82 E. Pleck 'The Whipping Post for Wife Beaters, 1876–1906' in L.P. Moch and G.D. Stark, eds *Essays on the Family and Historical Change* (Arlington: Texas A & M University Press 1983) 127–49

83 9 Dec. 1892

84 SNS 1877, c. 87; *Halifax Herald* 8 Mar. 1889. On the NSSPC see W.M. Ross 'Child Rescue: The Nova Scotia Society for the Prevention of Cruelty, 1880–1920' (MA thesis, Dalhousie University 1975) and J. Fingard *The Dark Side of Life in Victorian Halifax* (Porters Lake, NS: Pottersfield Press 1989) chapter 8.

85 Fingard *Dark Side*; Gordon *Heroes* 253

86 *Evening Mail* 4 Sept. 1884, 15 Apr. 1891; PANS MG 20, vol. 516, no. 9 (journal of NSSPC agent John Naylor for 1889)

87 Graham finally took on the task of law reform personally. In *Woodend* v. *Woodend* (1909) PANS RG 39, series D, vol. 9, file B-82, he established that a 'lesser' degree of cruelty would suffice for a judicial separation, leaving the 'higher' standard intact for total divorces. See also *Jones* v. *Jones* (1947) 20 MPR 213.

88 *Anna Jeffery* v. *Charles Jeffery* (1889) vol. 1, file 16. This was not the first time the legal system had failed Anna. She had tried to get a magistrate to bind over her husband to keep the peace, but the action failed when her brother refused to put up security for costs. Another petitioner, Hannah Cupples, also sought this protection after a severe beating, and followed it up with her divorce petition a week later. A widow of substance who had remarried, Hannah had more options than Anna and could use the legal system to better effect: *Hannah Elizabeth Cupples* v. *Samuel Cupples* (1838) Young Papers.

89 C. Smith-Rosenberg *Disorderly Conduct: Visions of Gender in Victorian America* (New York: Knopf 1985) 92

90 Hammerton 'Victorian Marriage' 13

91 It is impossible to say whether this judicial attitude reflected any societal consensus. Gordon *Heroes* 255 suggests that wife-beating was not generally accepted as a marital right by 1870.

92 Snell 'Women and the Divorce Court' brings this out very clearly for the post-1900 period.

93 *Norah Ormond (O'Connell)* v. *William O'Connell* (1875) vol. 1, file 3. Another petition alleged impotence (*Young* 1763, vol. 1A), but since the husband deserted his bride the day after the marriage it would have been difficult to prove.

94 See O.W.G. Mueller 'Inquiry into the State of a Divorceless Society' *Pittsburgh Law Review* 18 (1957) 572–3; Samuel P. Menefee *Wives for Sale* (Oxford: Blackwell 1981); K. O'Donovan 'Wife Sale and Desertion as Alternatives to Judicial Marriage Dissolution' in M. Eekelaar and S. Katz, eds *The Resolution of Family Conflict: Comparative Legal Perspectives* (Toronto: Butterworths 1984). The most famous literary example is Michael Henchman's sale of his wife in Thomas Hardy's *The Mayor of Casterbridge.*

95 See *R.* v. *Debay* (1872–5) 3 NSR 540 (SC in banco); *R.* v. *Penaul* (1915) 49 NSR 391 (SC in banco)

96 *Daily Echo* 2 Nov. 1889, cited in Himmelman 'Halifax Marriage Patterns' 8. See also *Novascotian* 24 Feb. 1862. This practice was prevalent for at least a century, and was not greatly altered by the passage of the new divorce law in 1857: see Mueller 'Divorceless Society' 567–8.

97 See *Acadian Recorder* 20 May 1806.

98 R.A. MacDonald 'The Life of Major John Cunningham of Sydney County' PANS MG1, vol. 2472

99 O'Neill *Divorce in the Progressive Era* 24

100 Ibid. 461

101 *Marion Jamieson* v. *George Jamieson* (1887) vol. 1, file 12. It is difficult to understand how judges justified this, since the 1866 act clearly stated that 'on any decree for dissolution of marriage' the court could order the husband to pay alimony, and that it should have the same powers as the English Court of Divorce and Matrimonial Causes in this regard.

102 *Ruby Robarts* v. *Frederick Robarts* (1889) vol. 1, file 20; *Rachel Reid* v. *William Reid* (1882) PANS RG39, series D, vol. 2 (possibly obtained in separate action); *Valentine Bernardi* v. *Anna Bernardi* (1819) vol. 1A, file 14; *DesBrisay* v. *DesBrisay* (1873) vol. 1, file 2. On alimony generally, see Rebecca Veinott 'The Changing Legal Status of Women in Nova Scotia 1860–1920' (MA thesis, Dalhousie University 1989) chapter 4.

103 *Novascotian* 2 Dec. 1867; *Morning Chronicle* 16 Jan. 1873. Another story doubtless intended both to amuse and to warn the readers was one about a divorced man in Osago, Iowa, whose young second wife left him on the afternoon of their marriage because 'she was persuaded that his divorce was fraudulent' and because 'she had changed her mind and didn't love him as much as she thought she did': *Morning Chronicle* 17 Dec. 1874.
104 Backhouse 'Pure Patriarchy' 264, 265
105 *M., falsely called S* v. *S* (1877) 1 BCR 25
106 J.M. Beck 'The Canadian Parliament and Divorce' *Canadian Journal of Economics and Political Science* 123 (1957) 297

9

Child Custody and Divorce: A Nova Scotia Study, 1866–1910

REBECCA VEINOTT

Nova Scotia child-custody law underwent profound changes during the nineteenth century. At common law women enjoyed no legal rights whatsoever to their children during marriage. The common law position had its roots in the doctrine of the unity of husband and wife.[1] The husband was the legal head of the household, and his authority could not be undermined because, it was argued, to give women power in the family would lead to marital discord. Although the home was considered woman's 'proper sphere,' she had no legal authority even in that restricted realm. The hand that rocked the cradle did not rule the nursery, let alone rest of the world.

The common law position was gradually eroded during the nineteenth century. Legislative initiatives were first undertaken in 1866 to give divorcing women the right to apply for custody of their children. By the end of the nineteenth century, women were given essentially equal rights to child custody.

In this essay I will explore the evolution and operation of custody law in Nova Scotia from 1866 to 1910.[2] I have based this study on the surviving records of all the divorce actions involving children during those years.[3] Because I have not relied only upon reported decisions, I hope to provide insight into many of the questions raised by Constance Backhouse in her study of child custody in Canada.[4] How many divorces occurred in Nova Scotia during the period? What were the circumstances in which divorce and custody proceedings arose? What were the outcomes of custody litigation at the lower court level? Which parent was more likely to retain de facto custody of the children upon marital breakdown?

The changing social conditions that gave rise to legislative innovation in this area are also explored. Particular emphasis is placed upon the combined effect of the ideology of separate spheres, feminism, and the child protection movement in securing legislation that gave mothers rights to their children. In this context the interactions between maternal feminists and opponents of women's rights is highlighted. Despite their differences, these two groups shared the belief that women's parental role was a crucial one that required legislative support.

At the case level I hope to provide insight into the effects of divorce and judicial separation on women and children. Divorce was economically devastating for women in an age when very few married women were paid labourers.[5] The educational, cultural, and legal barriers that prevented women from obtaining remunerative work were only beginning to be removed during the last half of the nineteenth century, and only a handful of the women studied here were able to achieve economic independence after the breakdown of their marriages.[6] Consequently, the task of being a single parent was especially formidable. Indeed, it was difficult for both men and women to combine the earning of a livelihood with the domestic responsibilities of child-rearing. Many custodial mothers and fathers resorted to placing their children with relatives.

THE EVOLUTION OF CHILD-CUSTODY LAW IN NOVA SCOTIA, 1866–1892

Child-custody law in Nova Scotia during the nineteenth century evolved through three stages. Initially, child custody was governed by the common law, as it was in Britain. In 1866, with the creation of the Court of Divorce and Matrimonial Causes, the law in Nova Scotia was changed to mirror that set out in the English Matrimonial Causes Act of 1857.[7] Finally, in 1893, new legislation greatly eroded the common law precepts of fathers' rights.

The common law position with respect to child custody was succinctly expressed by Erna Reiss: 'Over children during minority born in lawful wedlock the father had an absolute control ... This right held good not merely against a third person but also against the mother of his children.'[8] A father could determine his child's religion, choose its educational path, and even deprive it of its mother's care and presence if he chose. A wife had no legal recourse. Only in extreme cases, in which a father's conduct was clearly harmful to his child, could the Court of Chancery intervene to act in loco parentis. In such cases, however, the law was concerned with protecting the child, not with recognizing a mother's rights. As Reiss states, 'the law afforded no means by which the mother's wishes could be considered, and no court could grant her even access to her children as a matter of right.'[9] Even in death a father did not lose his dominion. He could by will appoint a guardian of his choice; the mother had no say in the matter. The mother's position as 'guardian of the hearth' did not extend to the children who surrounded it.

The common law reflected a complex constellation of cultural values, economic relationships, and scientific beliefs. Marriage was above all a property relationship. Wives were effectively their husbands' chattels. Indeed, married women were legal nonentities. A woman's very identity was subsumed in that of her husband, whose name she took upon marriage. She could not sue or be sued, nor could she enter into contracts.[10] A married woman could not even control her own property, for upon marriage all her property came under the control of her husband.[11] The corollary of the destruction of a woman's legal personality upon marriage was that her husband became her legal representative and her moral guardian. A husband was legally responsible for any debts his wife had incurred, any contracts she had made, and any torts she had committed before her marriage. He was also, of course, responsible for all of her actions during marriage. In addition, husbands were legally required to support their families, although there was no effective legal mechanism compelling them to do so.[12]

Since married women could not control property, it is not surprising that they had no legal right to custody of their children, who could contribute greatly to the family economy. In both the rural and urban preindustrial economies children were crucial to household production, and during the transition to industrialism their wages were important to the maintenance of the family. The father exercised absolute control over the children and their earning power; he was entitled to the earnings of his children, and he was empowered to bind them out as apprentices.[13]

Apart from economic considerations, there was also thought to be a scientific basis for denying women rights to their children. Early scientific opinion held that a mother's role in procreation was greatly inferior to that of the father. In this view, the father alone was capable of originating a new life. The mother merely sustained the child, first as a 'germ' or embryo and later as an infant.[14] It naturally followed that a mother should have no claim on the children in the event of marital breakdown.

Legislative initiatives that undermined fathers' rights were not taken until the mid-nineteenth century. These innovations had their roots in changing conceptions of childhood and the woman's role within the family. With the rise of industrialism the home gradually lost its place as the centre of production; instead, it became a haven from the rigours of life in an increasingly complex urban world. While men went out to work, married women stayed at home. Women's economic role in the family diminished and the concept of women as the 'guardians of the hearth' began to emerge as their domestic responsibilities centred increasingly on their children. The exclusion of women from public life (which, it was thought, would protect them from the rigours of the harsh world beyond the home) infused women with new power. Their very insulation from the moral vicissitudes of urban industrial life gave rise to the view that women were men's moral superiors. Thus the image of women as weak creatures (in both a physical and a moral sense) was gradually supplanted by the domestic ideal of womanhood. Women came to be seen as the moral pillars of society, whose influence within the home (and eventually in the public sphere) could ameliorate many social evils.[15] This dramatic change in attitudes set the stage for legislation that would confer upon women the right to custody of their children in certain circumstances.

The common law with respect to child custody was altered in Britain with the passage of the Custody of Infants Act of 1839 ('Serjeant Talfourd's Act').[16] This legislation came about largely through the efforts of one woman, Caroline Norton. Deprived of access to her children by her husband, whose cruelty had forced her from the home, Norton used her literary skills, influential friends, and political connections to campaign successfully against the injustice of the common law. The act empowered the Court of Chancery to grant women access to their infant children; furthermore, it enabled the court to grant a mother custody of children under seven years of age. The act had serious drawbacks. It did not give women guardianship rights; it merely gave them the right to apply to have the Court of Chancery grant custody or access at its discretion.[17] Despite its flaws, however, the act was a crucial first step.

The Matrimonial Causes Act of 1857 further extended judicial authority over custody in Britain; it gave the English Court for Divorce and Matrimonial Causes was given discretionary authority to make orders with respect to child custody. The provisions of this legislation were adopted in Nova Scotia in 1866 through section 10 of An Act to amend the Laws relating to Divorce and Matrimonial Causes: 'The court shall have the same powers with respect of or as incidental to divorce and Matrimonial

TABLE 1
Results of Cases by Sex of Petitioner, 1866–1893

	Total suits	Children involved	Custody requested	Custody awarded
Female petitioner	21	11	9	2
Male petitioner	18	9	1	1
TOTAL	39	20	10	3

causes and the custody, maintenance and education of children as are possessed by the Court for divorce and Matrimonial Causes in England, except as enlarged or abridged or altered or modified by this act, and the act hereby amended.'[18] This was the first legislation in Nova Scotia to temper the common law rights of fathers.

Historians have noted that the English divorce legislation did not immediately result in any widespread radical change on a practical level. Allen Horstman has put forward one reason the English legislation did not mark a turning-point in women's custody rights:

> [C]hildren attracted little attention in divorce. In 1871, 40 per cent of the suits involved childless couples, a marked contrast with the rest of Victorian society. Moreover, the structure of divorces meant children had been disposed of before the proceeding – wives who eloped with lovers and husbands who deserted mates had left their children also. Adding to this the presence of servants to help care for children and strong legal presumptions about who got custody at what age meant fights between parents rarely involved the divorce court in the matter of the children.[19]

Horstman's comments with respect to the low number of divorcing couples with children and the infrequency with which child-custody issues came before the court appears to be valid for Nova Scotia (see table 1). Of the thirty-nine divorce cases for which records exist there were no children or no mention of children in nineteen.[20] It appears that custody was not in issue in an additional ten cases. Thus, the divorce court's power to award custody upon the granting of a decree for the dissolution of the marriage did not touch the majority of mothers and their children.

Although custody was not a paramount feature of most of the cases that came before the divorce court during the period, it was important in one-quarter of the cases. However, as Susan Maidment has pointed out, the judicial discretion given to the English Court for Divorce and Matrimonial Causes did not bring about a new era in the history of women's rights with respect to their children in that country: '[T]he judges throughout this period [1857–85] interpreted their powers restrictively, and upheld the father's common law rights and punished an erring mother.'[21] This observation seems to apply to Nova Scotia; the Nova Scotia court was not quick to recognize the new rights given to mothers, and awarded custody to only two of nine women who requested it between 1866 and 1893.

That the 1866 legislation answered a need in the province is evidenced by the fact that in the first post-1866 case for which records survive, *Laleah Robertson* v. *George Robertson* (1869), the petitioner requested custody of her young son.[22] Laleah Robertson's husband George, a prominent Annapolis County barrister, was accused of having committed adultery with Elizabeth Mott, a married woman, and numerous other women. He was further accused of having visited a house of ill fame. In a judgment delivered 9 April 1870 Sir William Young bemoaned the fact that Nova Scotia law went further than English law and permitted a wife to divorce her husband for adultery alone. He saw his duty, however, and granted the divorce. As to custody, he said, 'It [the child] is but eighteen months old and no court would permit it to be separated from its mother.' However, he concluded that a custody order could only be made on a petition subsequent to the final decree.[23] Whether Laleah Robertson ever presented such an application is unknown; nothing further appears in the file. The case demonstrates that judicial attitudes towards a mothers' right to custody, at least where infants of tender years were concerned, could be favourable. This appears to be a more liberal approach than that taken by the English Court in *Cartlidge* v. *Cartlidge* (1862), where the father of a seven-month-old infant was allowed to retain custody pending the suit 'on the grounds that the court must exercise its discretion under the Matrimonial Causes Act 1857, s. 35, in accordance with the common law right of the father; to displace this, the mother must show "more than the mere natural desire of the mother to have custody of the child." '[24] An important distinction between the two cases, of course, is that in the *Robertson* case the father was found guilty of adultery, whereas in the *Cartlidge* case the suit was pending. This difference may not have been decisive, however. Although English courts might deny adulterous fathers custody, they would not do so if the man was not continuing in his immorality.[25]

The 1873 case of *Anne DesBrisay* v. *Charles M. DesBrisay* highlights one deficiency of the 1866 legislation – it only operated upon divorce.[26] Anne brought her case on the ground of cruelty, and alleged that her husband was intemperate, used opium, beat her, and had threatened her life. The one child of the marriage was with Anne at the time the action was brought; she asked for permanent custody, claiming that Charles would abuse the child and that he had threatened to dash its brains out. Anne further alleged that Charles had threatened to drive her mad and thereby procure both her property and the child. A trust fund that had been set up for the benefit of Anne, her husband, and their children seems to have been a complicating factor. Anne's testimony indicates that she believed Charles wanted to get access to the trust fund through the child; thus, along with child custody went the protection of her property.

Anne was able to produce a number of witnesses to support her side of the story. Her husband, however, contested the action and asked that his right to custody be upheld. He was a Dartmouth doctor, and his testimony carried some authority. Furthermore, he produced witnesses to refute many of the charges made against him. In the end the court did not know whom to believe. In the final judgment the court said that 'to dissolve the marriage on the evidence produced in this case is out of the question,' and the petition was denied. In the meantime Charles had succeeded in regaining custody of the child through an action for habeas corpus.[27] Presumably the child remained with him after the failure of the suit.

The assertions Anne made at the trial with respect to her husband's treatment of their child highlight the inadequacy of the child-custody law of 1866 with respect to child welfare. If a child was being abused, the Court of Divorce and Matrimonial Causes could deprive the parent of custody only if the circumstances were such that a divorce could be granted.[28]

The first known occasion on which the Nova Scotia court awarded custody to the mother in accordance with the 1866 legislation occurred in 1882. In *Rachel Amelia Reid* v. *William Reid* the court awarded not only custody but also a permanent alimony of $150 per annum and child support of $100 per annum for each of two children until they reached the age of twenty-one. Unfortunately, no records of the divorce case itself survive. What is known of the case is gleaned from an 1892 action to recover arrears in alimony and support payments totalling $4,427.17.[29] Given that Rachel was entitled to $350 per annum over ten years, and allowing for reasonable interest payments, it appears that no alimony or child support was ever paid. One can only speculate about the economic hardships faced by Rachel and her children.

The 1887 case of *Marion Jamieson* v. *George Jamieson* (1887) is the first case in which the court awarded custody to the mother for which a full record survives.[30] Marion sued for divorce on the ground of adultery, and specifically requested custody of her children. The background of the case suggests that it may have been a concern for the welfare of her children that prompted Marion to sue for divorce in the first place. George Jamieson was a Halifax trader who married Marion Locke on 15 June 1876. Although George physically abused Marion and used profane language in front of their three children, the marriage was stable until 1881. It was then that Marion discovered that Rebecca Ross, the children's nurse, was pregnant with George's child. George refused to send Rebecca away, and Marion left him, taking the children with her. She returned to her home town of Lockeport and started a new life. Fortunately, Marion possessed skills that enabled her to earn a living. She obtained work as a telegraph operator, for which she made $240 per annum, and she taught music. She also earned money by writing. However, her economic resources were insufficient to support the family. Two of the children had to be farmed out to relatives: one boy stayed with his maternal grandmother, another with this great-aunt. George contributed a total of ten dollars to the support of his children after Marion left.

If Marion escaped from George relatively unscathed, Rebecca Ross was not so lucky. At first it appeared that George was determined to take responsibility for Rebecca's situation. George took Rebecca to the town of Hubbards, where he represented himself as Mr Ross and secured lodging for her at his expense. After their child was born, however, he brought her and the baby back to Halifax, where he abandoned them in the streets. Rebecca was forced to go to the poor-house, and their child subsequently died in the Infants' Home.

George suffered severe personal and financial difficulties after the breakdown of his marriage. He lost his job during the domestic upheaval and also began to drink heavily. Perhaps in an effort to restore some measure of stability to his life, George began to seek access to his children. Marion agreed that he could see them so long as he was sober. He failed to oblige. When he was denied access to his children, George threatened to take legal action if they were not returned to him. Marion refused to restore them to his custody, stating that he was living in adultery with a housekeeper who, she claimed, was a former prostitute. In July 1882 he applied for a writ of habeas corpus. In Marion's view, he had brought the action in order to force her to live with him again. Evidence presented at the hearing portrayed George as 'intemperate, immoral and untruthful' and 'totally unfit to have the care, custody and education of his children.'

Marion was described as 'a woman of excellent moral character and in every way qualified for the proper bringing up of her children.' Considering the weight of testimony against George and the testimony in favour of Marion, it is not surprising that George was unsuccessful in his efforts to regain custody of his children through legal action.

It was against this background that Marion finally instituted divorce proceedings, which George contested. He denied that he had committed adultery, accused her of the same, and asked that the court give custody of the children to him. He also instituted proceedings to be granted access to the children during the interim. As he put it, 'I love my children exceedingly and have always been invariably kind and affectionate to them, and intend that I will continue so to do.' The judge ordinary, Alexander James, denied the request pending the trial of the suit on its merits. After the facts of the case had been fully disclosed, James expressed his relief that he had not been deceived by George's empty expressions of love for his children: '[I]t now appears that he has not only shown no kindness to them nor to their excellent mother but has endeavoured in every way in his power to disturb their peace and happiness.'

During the trial George chose to represent himself, probably because he could not afford legal counsel. This decision had unfortunate results for him. His lack of legal knowledge and his constant objections, coupled with an excessively deferential demeanour before the court, made for a spectacle which the Halifax press could not resist.[31] Although George had the good sense not to be present when Rebecca Ross gave her testimony, he cross-examined many other witnesses who were scathing in their criticism of his character. When he asked witnesses if they could honestly say he was intemperate and unfit to have the custody of his children, he was answered with a resounding yes. The fact that witnesses looked him in the eye while testifying against him only added weight to their testimony and made George appear ridiculous. Most of the witnesses who testified against him were his business associates and acquaintances. Witnesses were specifically asked whether they had children themselves and whether they felt that George Jamieson was a fit person to have the care and custody of his children. Only two of numerous witnesses gave favourable testimony. Both stated that they had not known George to be intemperate; neither commented on his fitness to care for his children. Another had some reservations about condemning him altogether: Thomas Jenkins stated that George probably could look after his family 'provided he kept sober and took care of himself.' The rest were unanimous in their feeling that he was unfit to have custody.

Ultimately, the evidence weighed against George. The judge granted

Marion full control and custody of the children until they were fourteen, saying that George was 'an unfit person to have the care and custody of his children.' He also stated that Marion and her children were entitled to the fullest protection of the court at all times against any interference by their father.[32] George said he would appeal, but no record of an appeal exists.

The *Jamieson* case shows that the Nova Scotia court was willing to override the father's common law right to custody when the situation warranted. It would be wrong to make too much of the decision, however. The circumstances of the case were extreme, and the evidence was almost entirely one-sided. But the message was plain: the Nova Scotia court was willing to grant custody to mothers even when the children were not of tender years.

Six other custody applications were brought between 1866 and 1893: the court refused to grant a divorce in two cases; one case was discontinued; in one case it is unknown whether the court made a custody award; and in one case the court did not address the custody issue in the final decree.[33] In *John Leonard* v. *Annie Sophia Leonard* (1884) the male petitioner who requested custody was successful in his suit and received custody of his daughter.[34] The decision in favour of awarding custody to an innocent father when the mother was found guilty of adultery was in keeping with English decisions of the time. Although adulterous husbands might be forgiven their indiscretions if they departed from their immoral ways, fallen women presumably were irredeemable.[35] This view remained paramount in the 1893 custody legislation, which expressly forbade courts to give custody to adulterous mothers.

Despite the Nova Scotia court's authority to make custody orders, male petitioners still retained a distinct advantage. They did not need a court decision to legalize their rights over their children. Their entitlement to custody was essentially a rebuttable presumption, and their custody rights were truly rights. Mothers acquired 'rights' only at the pleasure of the court.

THE EVOLUTION OF CUSTODY LAW, 1893–1910

In 1893 the law with respect to child custody underwent a radical change when An Act Respecting the Custody of Infants was passed.[36] In essence, this legislation abrogated the father's common law right to custody. It permitted mothers to apply to the Supreme Court or any judge thereof for access to or custody of their children. Its provisions were applicable to the Court for Divorce and Matrimonial Causes in so far as the judge ordinary of the Divorce Court was a judge of the Supreme Court. The paramount consideration in future custody decisions was to be child welfare, not parental rights. (The specific provisions of the act are discussed in detail below.)

By 1893 women's organizations were becoming a major force across the country, and women's legal disabilities in all areas of life were being hotly debated in provincial legislatures. During the 1870s and 1880s most of the provinces had passed married women's property acts, and women's suffrage was receiving serious attention in the legislatures. In Nova Scotia a married women's property act had been passed in 1884, and unmarried women and widows had won the municipal vote in 1887.[37] During the 1890s the question of women's suffrage was almost constantly before the House of Assembly. This was largely the result of the efforts of the Women's Christian Temperance Union, which campaigned avidly for the right of women to vote. In the view of the WCTU it was time that women's staunch moral influence was extended beyond the boundaries of the home. Given the social dislocation caused by rapid industrial expansion and the growth of urban centres, it was not only the family that had to be mothered, it was society as a whole. Furthermore, the injustices women suffered as the result of male vice, and of intemperance in particular, were no longer seen as trials that had to be endured. It was felt that by extending women's influence beyond the home and into the public sphere many of these social evils could be eradicated.

The emergence of maternal feminism at the end of the nineteenth century coincided with new perceptions of childhood. As Neil Sutherland has said, '[a] child's need for firm but loving family care, the central importance of his mother ensuring he received it, and her concern that his tender, plant-like nature not be menaced in an inappropriate environment – these were the important dimensions of the relationship between parents and children as urban, middle-class Canadians saw them towards the end of the nineteenth century.'[38] This changing attitude was evidenced by a rise in child welfare activities at both the private and the governmental levels. Winifred Ross has explored the rise of the Nova Scotia Society for the Prevention of Cruelty, which began to campaign for governmental protection of abused children as early as 1879, and which was legally empowered to intervene on behalf of abused children in a quasi-public capacity in 1880.[39] This legislation was followed in 1882 with the passage of An Act to Prevent and Punish Wrongs to Children, which permitted Nova Scotia courts to take children from parents or others having custody of them if the custodian had been

> convicted before any court or magistrate with having assaulted, beaten, ill used, abandoned or treated said child with habitual cruelty and neglect, or said child is suffered to grow up without salutary parental control, or in circumstances exposing him or her to lead an idle and dissolute life, and the court or magistrate before whom such conviction is had, deems it desirable for the welfare of such child that the person so convicted should be deprived of custody thereafter, such court or magistrate may commit such child to an orphan asylum, charitable or other institution, or make such other disposition thereof as now is or hereafter may be provided by law in cases of vagrant, truant, disorderly, pauper or destitute children.[40]

This was followed in 1884 with the passage of An Act to Enable Agents of the Society and Others to Remove Children from Persons who are Neglecting or Abusing them.[41] These acts saw the beginning of a trend towards active state intervention in the rearing of children, a trend that encompassed compulsory school attendance acts (to ensure that children were equipped with the basic skills required to function in an increasingly complex industrialized society), factories acts (to protect young children from the physical and moral perils of factory work), and acts relating to juvenile delinquency and neglected children.[42]

The 1893 legislation formed a part of the reformulation of the state's power in the domestic sphere. The state was moving away from its passive role as conservator of the father's authority in the family towards a more active role as the arbiter of familial disputes. The rhetoric of child welfare, though sincere, masked the underlying reality of the emerging industrial economy in Nova Scotia. The value of children to a capitalist state was comparable to their previous value to the family economy. They were future workers, and their welfare could no longer be entrusted solely to their parents. The state required broad powers of intervention to ensure that children were raised 'properly.'[43] Nova Scotia's activity in the area of child custody followed the lead of England and Ontario; those two jurisdictions had progressed further towards industrialization, and Nova Scotia often looked to them for leadership in legislative matters during this period.

It was in this climate that two bills respecting the custody of infants came before the House of Assembly in 1893. The fact that two bills were introduced during the same session indicates the growing interest in and support for such a measure. The first was introduced by Barclay Webster, a Harvard-educated lawyer and a supporter of women's suffrage; the second was introduced by the attorney general, J.W. Longley, the arch-enemy of women's political rights, whose lengthy diatribes were heard during the women's suffrage debates. Longley's views on custody were consistent with his approach to women's political rights: he believed women were entitled to custody rights because child-rearing lay within women's proper and natural sphere. Longley stated his views with respect to child custody during the suffrage debates of the same year:

> Only recently he [Longley] had introduced an act into the legislature dealing with the care and custody of infants, and giving wives, in the event of separation from their husbands, much larger control and power over their children than had previously been conferred upon them. The proposition embodied in the bill before the house was really a proposition which involved the question whether the gentler sex should be unsexed or whether women should continue to exercise the functions which nature had imposed upon them with no unfaltering voice. The proposition meant that women, in the course of time, would be expected to regard the duties assumed by them in wedlock, the care and nourishment of children, the protecting of children from harm until they reach maturity, as secondary duties to be subordinated to her political duties as a voter and legislator. The bill therefore was an initial step of a movement which would, if successful, result in the entire revolution of society.[44]

Longley had no reservations about extending to women rights that would increase their ability to fulfil their role as mothers, but he was vociferously opposed to extending to them any rights that might interfere with that role.[45]

Longley's stance as an opponent of women's suffrage but a supporter of women's rights in the family was not unique. Another important jurist and legislator also shared this viewpoint. Sir William Young, who heard the 1869 *Robertson* case, in which he favoured the mother for custody, was also opposed to women's suffrage. In his decision in *McGregor* v. *Patterson* (1862) Young railed against the concept of women's political rights.[46] Like Longley, Young believed ardently in women's proper sphere. Anything that might detract from their role as wives and mothers was to be guarded against.

The desire of reformers to promote women's equality, combined with the desire of conservatives to extend to women those rights that were in keeping with their proper sphere, made women's custody rights one area in which both groups could come close to agreement. Even so, there were important differences of opinion about how far their rights should extend, which probably accounts for the fact that two separate bills on the subject of child custody were introduced. Unfortunately, neither of the two original bills has survived, and their provisions remain a mystery. None the less, it may not be inappropriate to surmise that Webster's bill may have taken a more liberal approach to child custody than Longley's in view of their respective positions concerning women's rights. In any event, the two bills were consolidated by the law amendments committee, and it was the consolidated bill that passed into law in 1893.[47]

The hybrid bill that became law contained only six sections, but it altered forever the legal status of mothers and children. The Supreme Court was now free to make orders entitling any mother who so requested access to or custody of her children. According to section 2 of the act, '[i]n making such an [access or custody] order the court or judge shall have regard to the welfare of such infant or infants, and to the conduct or circumstances of the parents, and to the wishes as well of the mother as of the father.'[48] No longer were women second-class parents, at least in legal theory. Custody decisions were to be based primarily on concern for the welfare of the child. Parents were to be equally considered, with two important provisos: first, women had to apply to the court for custody or access but fathers did not; second, no mother against whom adultery had been proved was to have custody. In practice, however, there was virtually no discrimination in the divorce court's custody awards. In every case but one between 1893 and 1910 custody was denied to adulterous fathers as firmly as it was denied to adulterous mothers. The legislation also remedied two other important injustices. Section 3 provided that on the death of the father the mother was to be the guardian of any children, either alone or jointly with any other guardian who may have been appointed. The same section enabled the mother to appoint a guardian by will. Section 6 provided that separation agreements between husbands and wives were no longer to be held invalid by reason only of the father's agreement to give up custody of his children.[49]

The application of the 1893 act, dependent as it was on judicial interpretation, owed much to the attitudes of Wallace Graham, who occupied the position of judge ordinary of the Divorce Court from 1889 to 1915, when he became chief justice of the Supreme Court of Nova Scotia. Born at Antigonish in 1848, Graham was relatively young when he ascended to the bench, and his youth may have ensured his receptivity to new ideas

TABLE 2
Results of Cases by Sex of Petitioner, 1893–1910

	Children involved	Custody sought[1]	Custody awarded[2]	Custody not addressed	Other[3]
Female petitioner	41	27	28	5	8[4]
Male petitioner	31	18	23[4]	2	8

1 The court awarded custody in some cases in which it was not specifically requested.
2 This column includes one case in which custody was awarded first to the mother and later to the father.
3 This category comprises all cases in which there was no known court decision with respect to custody, including those for which the result is unknown, those in which the court refused to grant the divorce, those that required further application for custody, and those that were discontinued.
4 This includes the one case in which the mother was the petitioner and custody went to the father, despite the fact that the mother was successful in her divorce suit.

about women. Graham, a Baptist, was educated at Acadia University. Graham's long tenure on the bench served to keep judicial attitudes largely constant during the period from 1893 to 1910.[50]

The purposive approach Graham adopted in applying the 1893 legislation stands in striking contrast to the situation that prevailed under the 1866 act. Records are extant for 126 divorce actions heard by the court between 1893 and 1910.[51] Fifty-nine of the suits were brought by women, and 67 were brought by men. There were no minor children involved in 46 of the suits. In an additional 8 cases there was no mention of children. In the remaining 72 cases there were minor children of the marriage at the time of the divorce action. Women comprised the majority of petitioners in cases in which children were involved (see table 2), although men comprised the majority of petitioners overall. This pattern suggests that perhaps the presence of children was a factor in a woman's decision to seek an official dissolution of her marriage. This hypothesis is borne out to some extent by the fact that men requested custody less frequently than women, though not markedly less: men requested custody in 18 of 31 cases (approximately 59 per cent), while women requested custody in 27 of 41 cases (approximately 68 per cent). The figures may be accounted for by two factors. First, one would expect that men would be more confident of their rights to their children because they had always enjoyed such rights. Furthermore, those rights were not in dispute in the absence of a court ruling awarding the mother custody (an unlikely eventuality where the wife was the guilty party). Women would be more likely to seek a court order awarding them custody. They, unlike their husbands, would want proof of their legal guardianship of their children. Second, husbands were perhaps less inclined to seek custody. It was difficult for men to combine the demands of job and family, particularly in a culture that saw child-rearing as women's work. Furthermore, men may have wanted to get on with their lives without the burden of raising children from a failed marriage.

The first post-1893 case in which we know the mother was successful in her custody application is the 1895 case of *Bessie Agnes Lovitt* v. *Israel Melbourne Lovitt*.[52] The circumstances of the *Lovitt* case, like those of the *Jamieson* case, were extreme. Bessie brought her action on the ground of cruelty. Her husband, a doctor, was the son of one of the wealthiest men in Nova Scotia. They had four children, a daughter aged seven, a son aged five, and twin sons aged four. Initially, the marriage was stable; but Israel's severe alcoholism and violent conduct, which began six years after their marriage in 1887, eventually forced Bessie to seek a divorce. This was a case in which the best interests of the child must have played some role in the court's decision to award custody to the mother. Apart from the numerous beatings to which Israel subjected Bessie, he also slapped and whipped the children, and at one point attempted to force them down a steep flight of stairs. His abusive behaviour towards his family was a scandal in Yarmouth.[53] A number of people tried to intervene to help Bessie; one even got the police to patrol the area near her house in case she needed aid. All of the witnesses agreed that continuing to live with Israel would put Bessie's health and perhaps even her life in danger. Wallace Graham awarded Bessie entire custody and control of the children.

The *Lovitt* case set the pattern for all custody actions undertaken after 1893. Of a total of 35 cases involving children which resulted in a decree and in which the mother was the petitioner, the mother received custody in 28. Of the remaining 7 cases, custody was not addressed in the decree in 5, custody went to the father in 1, and the mother was given leave to apply for custody in 1. By the time of the court's decision in the 1909 case of *Jemima Gilchrist Woodend* v. *Robert John Woodend*, Wallace Graham could state that the court had established the practice of awarding custody to the successful petitioner.[54]

One case is out of keeping with the general trend of the court's decisions after the 1893 act. In *Myrtie Power* v. *George G. Power* (1901), custody went to the father, who was guilty of adultery with a family servant.[55] The wife, who had requested custody of the seven-year-old child, was granted reasonable access. No indication of the reason for favouring the father for custody in this case is evident from the file. However, Wallace Graham's comments in an earlier case in the same year, *Jeanette Josephine Baker* v. *Judson Baker*, may provide illumination.[56] In that case Graham expressed reservations about depriving a father of custody. The *Baker* case was also brought on the grounds of adultery. In his reasons for judgment Graham expressed reluctance about separating a father from all of his children and imposing on him the burden of supporting them in another establishment 'when he could keep them so much more cheaply and easily at his house.' However, he went on to say that Judson Baker had a 'very deep feeling of enmity towards this petitioner and that he cannot help talking about it.' He concluded that Baker was not a fit person to have custody of the children. In *Baker* the best interests of the child once again played a role, for Graham went on to say that he was 'not satisfied that [the father's] home kept by a housekeeper is as good a place for [the children] as the home their mother keeps.' Here we have the first reference to the 'circumstances of the parents' criterion listed in the 1893 legislation. The final result was that Jeanette was awarded custody and her husband was awarded reasonable access. The doubts about depriving a father of custody expressed in the *Baker* case and the decision in *Power* may be seen as the last bastion of resistance to the new order instituted by the 1893 legislation.

Nova Scotia appears to have been egalitarian in its approach to custody awards in comparison with other Canadian jurisdictions at the turn of the century. Its practice may well have been affected by the nature of the provincial divorce law, which Kimberley Smith Maynard has shown to be 'gender-neutral' de facto as well as de jure where adultery was concerned. The long tradition of penalizing both male and female adulterers through divorce must have influenced the judges in their decision to apply the 'gender-specific' provision of the 1893 act in a 'gender-neutral' way. While this approach appears to have mirrored that of England, which also ceased to discriminate against mothers during the latter part of the nineteenth century,[57] the trend in the rest of Canada was different. A brief study of New Brunswick custody decisions indicates that that province clung steadfastly to the common law concept of father's rights well into the twentieth century, despite the enactment of legislation designed to give mothers greater rights to custody of their children.[58] Furthermore, Backhouse has shown that other Canadian jurisdictions were not actively implementing the 'mothers' legislation' at the turn of the century.[59] Her study ends at 1899, however, and further research is necessary to determine whether any Canadian provinces followed the Nova Scotia pattern and began vigorously applying the legislation.

It is important to note, however, that the Nova Scotia court did not adopt a full-fledged 'maternal presumption' as American jurisdictions did in the early twentieth century.[60] Although common law paternal rights were at last laid to rest, the Nova Scotia court did not swing to the opposite pole. It seemed to be inclined towards the view that the best interests of the child were served by placing the child with the innocent party, rather than concluding that it was always in a child's best interests to be with its mother. An important consideration that probably weighed upon the court in this regard was that the guilty party (whether male or female) was frequently absent and had little interest in gaining custody of the children. Often the adulterers had begun new families with their paramours.[61] In awarding custody to the innocent party, the court was often merely giving the force of law to the status quo. In twenty-nine cases the records identify the party who had de facto custody; in twenty-seven of those cases legal custody was awarded to the de facto custodian.

In considering the best interests of the child, the court apparently thought it important, where the situation warranted it, not to deprive the child of the presence of both parents. In nine cases the court awarded reasonable access to the parent who was denied custody. This may have been a method of preserving paternal rights to some extent, for six of the cases involved men who were guilty of adultery or cruelty. Furthermore, two of the cases involved decrees for judicial separation, indicating that the court may have been reluctant to deprive a father of access when the situation did not warrant an absolute divorce.

The main criterion for awarding reasonable access was that the 'guilty' parent have exhibited some active interest in continuing a relationship with the child. Such an interest was evident in eight of nine instances in which reasonable access was granted. The remaining case involved a decree for judicial separation.[62]

Two of the cases in which reasonable access was awarded are worthy of particular note; they demonstrate the purposive approach Wallace Graham adopted in applying the 1893 legislation. In *George Fairfax* v. *Hannah Fairfax* (1901), the mother had taken the child with her when she left her husband, but the husband had managed to get the child back.[63] In keeping with the practice of the court, George was granted custody when he successfully sued Hannah for a divorce on the ground of adultery. However, the court awarded Hannah reasonable access in spite of the fact that she was living with her paramour. The 1893 legislation barred adulterous mothers from gaining custody of their children, although the prohibition was not extended to reasonable access. If the court had wished to take a restrictive view of the legislation, it might have considered the mother's living arrangements and chosen not to allow her to see her child because of her continuing adultery. Instead, it chose to give more weight to the desire of the mother to have access to her child. The emphasis the court placed on child welfare is highlighted by its action in *Harriet Norton* v. *Charles Norton* (1902).[64] Custody had originally gone to Harriet when she obtained a divorce on the grounds of adultery. Charles was given reasonable access. The order was reversed in 1908 on Charles's application; he stated that his son had grown up 'without salutary parental control and is exposed by [his mother's] neglect to a mode of life which has a tendency to lead the said son to pursue a life of idleness and vice.' In keeping with the doctrine of the best interests of the child, the court awarded the father custody and the mother reasonable access in the hopes that Charles would be able to discipline the boy.

The Nova Scotia court under Wallace Graham could be creative in applying its legislative mandate. In one case the desirability of maintaining contact between the child and both parents led Graham to devise an innovation: the parents were to have joint custody pending the final decree.[65] In the *Woodend* case, the parties were engaged in a heated custody battle. Jemima Woodend stated that her main reason 'in bringing [the divorce] action was to obtain the lawful custody of the ... child.' Extensive testimony on the issue of interim custody revealed that both parties were fit parents. Jemima was portrayed as a good housekeeper and mother. Robert was said to be a model parent who spent an hour each day instructing his four-year-old daughter in religion. Graham chose not to deprive either party of the child before the case was tried on its merits. Instead, he ordered that the child stay with its mother one week and the father the next until a final decree was issued. Both parties were barred from taking the child out of the jurisdiction.[66] Upon his decision to grant a judicial separation, Graham followed his now stated policy of awarding custody to the successful petitioner (the mother), and awarded the father reasonable access.

One topic that deserves consideration in the light of the Nova Scotia court's mandate to consider the circumstances of the parents in making its custody awards is the economic situations of the women who received custody. Although the legislation did not define the factors to be considered in determining 'circumstances,' one might expect financial status to have been a relevant category. Indeed, one would expect that women's

TABLE 3
Occupations of Parties

Surname	Husband	Wife
Boutilier (1899)	Unemployed	Domestic servant
Burns (1901)	Blacksmith	Domestic servant
Norton (1902)	Liquor dealer	Nurse
Davis (1903)	In prison[1]	Nurse
McNutt (1904)	Farmer	Unknown (had been a teacher)
Croke (1905)	Unknown	Woollen-mill worker
Baker (1907)	Clerk	Doctor
McNutt (1909)	In prison[2]	Domestic servant
Woodend (1909)	Machinist	Milliner

1 Lewis Davis was serving a four-year sentence in Massachusetts for passing counterfeit money.
2 Morton Ross McNutt was serving a twenty-year sentence in Dorchester, New Brunswick, for attempted murder. He had shot his wife Mary Ellen three times and had also shot her mother.

growing economic role in Western Europe and North America may have been a factor in leading legislatures and courts to allow mothers to have custody of their children.[67] Although the Nova Scotia court appears to have looked favourably upon women who worked outside the home, it did not make financial status a priority in its custody determinations.[68]

Custody was awarded to the mother in twenty-eight cases between 1893 and 1910; women are known to have had an independent means of support in only nine of those cases (see table 3). Two were nurses, three were domestic servants, one worked at an unspecified job, one was a milliner, one worked in a woollen mill, and one was a medical doctor. It is likely that, with the exception of the doctor, none of the women earned more than a subsistence wage. Of the husbands who were employed, several earned as much as or more than their wives. Yet the court did not discriminate against the women in these cases in favour of the more affluent parent. It appears that as far as the welfare of the child was concerned, moral considerations took precedence over financial ones. This is seen most clearly when one looks at the women who had no independent source of income. Of the remaining nineteen women who were granted custody, twelve appear not to have worked or to have had any means of support; six were supported by a parent or parents; and one stated that she had made unspecified arrangements to support herself and the children. Unfortunately, the financial circumstances of the women's parents are not known, though it seems likely that few were particularly affluent, if their sons-in-laws' jobs can be used as indicators of their social class. Two may have been from middle- to upper-class backgrounds: Sophie Fraser's husband was a merchant and Asaphine Griffin's was an engineer. Four, however, probably were from a working-class background: Kate Stafford's husband was a tailor, Mabel Morrison's husband was a blacksmith, Mary Ellen McNutt's husband was a labourer, and Flora Munro's husband was a miner.[69]

What actually happened to the children on marital breakdown? Which parent was most likely to retain de facto custody before any court action? Although most files contain no information on this question, a sufficiently large sample does indicate that in the majority of cases children stayed with their mothers. It is possible to identify the person who had custody of the children on the commencement of the action in sixty-one cases decided between 1866 and 1910: the children were with the mother in forty-five, and with the father in fifteen. In one case the couple had divided the two children between them. This confirms what one would suspect in view of prevailing social and economic conditions. It also shows just how out of step with reality the notion of paternal rights was. The burden of child-rearing fell predominantly on the shoulders of women, and yet before 1893 women rarely had any legal rights in their children.

What child-care arrangements were made for the children of divorcing or separating couples? Did the children stay with the parent to whom custody was awarded? Most of the files do not answer these questions specifically. However, a number of cases indicate that children were placed with various family members or in boarding-schools.[70] One might expect to find that men were more likely to make alternative care arrangements for their children because of the demands of work outside the home. Although the data are incomplete, the cases for which records exist indicate that this was indeed the case. A total of six men and four women placed children with relatives or in boarding school in the small sample for which such information is available.[71] The lower number of women is probably accounted for by the fact that many of the women went home to their parents, bringing their children with them. If those women chose to seek outside employment they probably relied upon their own mothers to care for the children.[72] This option was not resorted to by men. It seems clear that the economic and social conditions of the late nineteenth and early twentieth centuries made it difficult for both men and women to function as single parents.

The emotional upheaval that children of divorcing parents experienced must have been greatly exacerbated by the family fragmentation that often accompanied marital breakdown. Children not only lost regular contact with one parent, they often had little contact with their brothers and sisters. In at least one case the custodial parent was not a daily part of the child's life.[73] The experience of Jeanette Baker's children and Charles McDonald's children were probably not uncommon. Jeanette's four children were divided between her two sisters: two daughters aged five and twelve lived with one sister, and a daughter aged fourteen and a son aged ten lived with another sister. Charles McDonald placed one son with his mother-in-law and the other son with his sister; he cared for his daughter himself.[74] One can only speculate upon how warmly these children were welcomed into the homes and families of relatives and the difficulties they faced in adjusting to their new situations.

CONCLUSION

Changes in attitudes about the roles of women and children in society were primary factors in the emergence of mothers' rights legislation at the end of the nineteenth century. That legislation, in practice, gave women equal rights to custody of their children in Nova Scotia. Those who advocated greater rights for women in the public sphere were staunch supporters of their rights in the home, while those who espoused a 'domestic ideal' of womanhood could find no fault with enabling them to become 'guardians of the hearth' in a legal as well as a moral sense. Maternal feminism not only advanced women to their place at the electoral polls, in public office, in the schools, and in the work-force; it also won for them, for the first time, legal rights within what many considered their 'proper sphere.' An emerging consciousness of childhood as a crucial time in physiological and psychological development also played a role in effecting a change in the state's approach to custody. No longer would the state function merely as a passive enforcer of a father's property rights in his children. The reliance of a capitalist state on a healthy and productive citizenry necessitated broad powers of intervention to ensure that children were well cared for. The mothers' legislation formed a part of a series of laws tending in that direction.

By the end of 1910 Nova Scotia custody law had evolved to a point at which mothers were afforded equal status with fathers. Although the 1866 legislation which first gave the Court of Divorce and Matrimonial Causes power to make custody decisions was seldom used, it marked the beginning of a path that led to equality between parents. After the enactment of the 1893 mothers' legislation the court regularly made custody awards. Despite the fact that women were discriminated against in the legislation itself in so far as it required that adulterous mothers be denied custody, in practice women were treated equally. The court routinely awarded custody to the innocent party in a divorce proceeding, and adulterous fathers were denied custody.

It must be stressed, however, that the 1893 legislation operated only when court proceedings were initiated. In the absence of a court order, the father still remained the natural guardian of his children. Furthermore, there was opposition to the new system as late as 1921. In that year the Nova Scotia Supreme Court was called on to overturn a decision of Chisholm J, who had denied a mother custody of her infant child because the father 'had not forfeited his paramount right at "common law to the custody of his child."' In *In Re Boyd* Harris CJ said,

> It is, I think, with deference to the learned judge who heard the application, not a correct statement of the law to say that the common law right which the father had to the custody of a child continues unless forfeited.
>
> The paramount right which the father had at common law has been seriously affected by the statutes which have been passed for the relief of mothers of children ... and, as I understand these statutes, as much regard has now to be paid by the courts to the wishes of the mother as to those of the father.[75]

Custody was restored to the mother, and the egalitarian approach to custody adopted at the end of the nineteenth century remained intact.

Despite some lingering opposition to mothers' rights, and despite the legislation's drawbacks, the gains women and children made in the nineteenth and early twentieth centuries were remarkable. Yet in one sense the legal change only mirrored reality. Although fathers had always enjoyed rights in their children, the children most often stayed with their mothers upon separation or divorce. The legal implementation of mothers' rights at last accorded women the legal rights that corresponded with the responsibilities they incurred as their children's primary caregivers.

NOTES

1 William Blackstone *Commentaries on the Laws of England* vol. 1 (Oxford: Clarendon Press 1775) 442

2 An end-date of 1910 was chosen because it allows for a comprehensive study of the 1893 'mothers' legislation,' and because the beginning of the First World War in 1914 marked the start of a period of dramatic change in Canadian domestic life.

3 This study is limited to an examination of custody in the context of divorce and judicial separation. Custody issues arising in the context of private separation agreements have not been addressed because a sufficiently large data base does not exist. The emerging role of the state in removing children from 'unfit' parents is a related but separate issue and must be addressed in another study.

4 Constance Backhouse 'Shifting Patterns in Nineteenth-Century Canadian Custody Law' in D.H. Flaherty, ed. *Essays in the History of Canadian Law* vol. 1 (Toronto: The Osgoode Society 1981) 240

5 For an account of the number of married women working in Nova Scotia during the period from 1880 to 1910, see S. Meyers's forthcoming MA thesis (St Mary's University). See also Kimberley Smith Maynard's paper elsewhere in this volume on the economic impact of divorce on women.

6 Of the 165 women involved in divorce actions between 1866 and 1910, only 19 can be identified as professional or skilled workers. Of the women professionals, all but one were 'ghettoized' in the low-paid, low-status 'women's' professions of teaching and nursing. One woman had broken through into a male-dominated occupation: Annie Rose Baker had obtained a medical degree in the United States and was practising in South Dakota at the time of her divorce. See *Annie Rose Baker* v. *John Carleton Baker* (1906) Supreme Court Records, PANS RG 39, series D, vol. 7, file B-48. (Records of cases are identified hereinafter by date, volume, and file number only.) Twenty-six divorcing women were employed in unskilled jobs. Of these, fourteen were domestic servants.

7 20 & 21 Vict., c. 85

8 E. Reiss *The Rights and Duties of Englishwomen: A Study in Law and Public Opinion* (London: Sherratt 1939) 15–16

9 Ibid. 17

10 E. Tulloch *We the Undersigned: A Historical Overview of New Brunswick Women's Political and Legal Status 1784–1984* (Moncton: New Brunswick Advisory Council on the Status of Women 1985) 84

11 L. Holcombe *Wives and Property: Reform of the Married Women's Property Law in Nineteenth-Century England* (Toronto: University of Toronto Press 1983) 25

12 Ibid 25–30, 30–33

13 Beamish Murdoch *Epitome of the Laws of Nova Scotia* vol. 2, 35

14 See F.E. Hoggan, MD 'The Position of the Mother in the Family in Its Legal

and Scientific Aspects' in S. Groag Bell and K.M. Offen, eds *Women the Family and Freedom: The Debate in Documents* vol. 2 (Stanford: Stanford University Press 1983) 191. See also M. Nowak *Eve's Rib: A Revolutionary New View of Female Sex Roles* (New York: St Martin's Press 1980) 83.

15 See J. Demos 'Images of the American Family: Then and Now' in V. Tufte and B. Myerhoff, eds *Changing Images of the Family* (New Haven: Yale University Press 1979) 49–55; C. Lasch *Haven in a Heartless World: The Family Besieged* (New York: Basic Books 1977) 4–8; C. Hall 'The Early Formation of Victorian Domestic Ideology' in S. Burman, ed. *Fit Work For Women* (New York: St Martin's Press 1979) 29; B. Berg *The Remembered Gate: Origins of American Feminism, The Woman and the City, 1800–1860* (New York: Oxford University Press 1981) 77–8, 153, 181–4, 197; N. Cott *The Bonds of Womanhood: 'Woman's Sphere' in New England, 1780–1835* (New Haven: Yale University Press 1977) 64

16 2 & 3 Vict., c. 54

17 Reiss *Rights and Duties* 2, 96

18 SNS 1866, c. 13

19 A. Horstman *Victorian Divorce* (New York: St Martin's Press 1985) 104

20 Between 1868 and 1893 sixty-five divorces were granted in Nova Scotia. No divorces were granted in 1874, and between one and five divorces were granted in each of the other years. Thus, although the divorce court records at PANS (which contain thirty-nine files) are far from complete, I believe that they are sufficiently comprehensive to enable me to conclude that the surviving records are representative of the divorcing population in general. Kimberley Smith Maynard has determined that nearly 40 per cent of Nova Scotian couples divorcing between 1750 and 1890 were childless: see her essay elsewhere in this volume.

21 S. Maidment *Child Custody and Divorce* (London: Croom, Helm 1984) 120

22 *Laleah Robertson* v. *George Robertson* (1869) vol. 1, file 1.

23 Ibid. Young's assertion that a petition subsequent to the final decree was required was based on his reading of 22 & 23 Vict., c. 61, s. 4, which amended the 1857 English legislation. This section was very poorly drafted and it is debatable whether Young interpreted it correctly. Two factors suggest that he may not have done so. First, it should be noted that Young was not the judge ordinary of the Divorce Court, but was substituting for J.W. Johnston when he heard the *Robertson* case, and he may not have been familiar with Divorce Court practice. Second, the court did not continue to require a petition subsequent to the final decree. In *John Leonard* v. *Annie Sophia Leonard* (1884) vol. 1, file 9, the custody award was contained within the decree itself.

24 Quoted in Maidment *Custody* 120

25 Ibid. 120, 121

26 *Anne DesBrisay* v. *Charles M. DesBrisay* (1873) vol. 1, file 2

27 Benjamin Russell, the lawyer who represented Charles in this action, states that Charles was successful in a habeas corpus action to have the child restored to his custody. However, we do not know for certain that this was the final word on the matter. See B. Russell *Autobiography of Benjamin Russell* (Halifax: Royal Print & Litho 1932) 119.

28 The 1866 act did not abolish the traditional powers of the Court of Chancery with respect to the protection of abused children, powers that would have been exercised by the Supreme Court after the abolition of Chancery in Nova Scotia in 1855. Thus there was some relief available for children of abusive parents outside of the jurisdiction of the divorce court: SNS 1855, c. 23.

29 *Rachel Amelia Reid* v. *William Reid* (1892) vol. 2, file 33A

30 (1887) vol. 1, file 12, part 2

31 Ibid. The press reported that 'at every sentence ... [George] would interrupt Mr MacCoy [Marion's counsel] and the Judge would rebuke him. The meekness of Moses was nothing to the way he received a reprimand, as with bowed head and quivering lip he showed his deference to the awful majesty of the law. (clipping, *Evening Mail* 22 July 1887).

32 Ibid.; see final decree in file.

33 The two cases in which divorces were denied were *Anna Jeffery* v. *Charles Jeffery* (1889) vol. 1, file 16, and *Helen Myrer* v. *Richard Myrer* (1890) vol. 1, file 23. The action that was discontinued was *Ada Curry* v. *Frederick Curry* (1889) vol. 1, file 141/2. It is unknown whether the court made a custody order in *Mary Rebecca Inness* v. *Edwin Inness* (1890) vol. 1, file 22. Custody was not addressed in the decree in *Ruby Robarts* v. *Frederick Robarts* (1890) vol. 1, file 20.

34 *John Leonard* v. *Annie Sophia Leonard* (1884) vol. 1, file 9

35 Maidment *Custody* 120

36 SNS 1893, c. 11

37 SNS 1884, c. 12, SNS 1887, c. 28. The 1887 act also provided that married women who held property under the Married Women's Property Act could vote, although it was extremely restrictive: only those married women whose husbands were not qualified to vote could cast their ballots.

38 Neil Sutherland *Children in English-Canadian Society: Framing the Twentieth-Century Consensus* (Toronto: University of Toronto Press 1976) 20. For an excellent discussion of changing attitudes to childhood in Nova Scotia during the mid-nineteenth century, see J. Guildford ' "I Often Run in the Streets of Halifax": Middle Class Attitudes towards Children in Halifax, 1850–1870' (unpublished).

39 SNS 1880, c. 68. See W. Ross 'Child Rescue: The Nova Scotia Society for the Prevention of Cruelty, 1880–1920' (MA thesis, Dalhousie University 1975).

40 SNS 1882, c. 18

41 SNS 1884, c. 95

42 For a discussion of compulsory school legislation in Nova Scotia see J. Carroll 'Public School Education in Nova Scotia, 1870–1935' (MA thesis, Dalhousie University 1950). Nova Scotia enacted laws for the protection of children working in factories beginning in 1895. See SNS 1895, c. 17 and SNS 1901, c. 1. In 1912 the office of provincial superintendent of neglected and dependent children was established and the law respecting juvenile offenders was amended and consolidated: see SNS 1912, c. 4.

43 For a discussion of the rise of state intervention in the family in the United States, see Stephen J. Morse 'The Family in Transition: From Traditional Families to Individual Liberty' in Tufte and Myerhoff *Changing Images* 340–1. See also S. Tiffin *In Whose Best Interest? Child Welfare Reform in the Progressive Era* (Connecticut: Greenwood Press 1982) 33 and Lasch *Haven* 12–21.

44 *DHA* 10 Apr. 1893, 204

45 Longley's views are of particular importance as he sometimes replaced Judge Wallace Graham, the judge ordinary of the Court for Divorce and Matrimonial Causes, from 1889 to 1915.

46 *McGregor* v. *Patterson* (1862) was an action in replevin to recover cattle and goods that had been seized by the defendant, a constable, because McGregor had failed to pay a school rate that had been levied on the ratepayers of the Big Island school district. One of the issues was whether the assessment was legal in light of the fact that the votes of four women had been excluded. On this point Young stated, 'There is no doubt that the words "ratable inhabitants" will comprehend both sexes, and that the property of women is ratable, who ought, therefore, it may be said, to have a right ... to vote at all meetings for the support of the poor and of schools. But if this doctrine prevail, women may be called upon by the same rule to fill many offices for which their domestic duties, their retiring modesty, and the delicacy of their sex, wholly unfit them.' He held that the assessment was legal. See 1 Old. 217.

47 A thorough search of PANS RG5, series U, which contains the unpassed bills of the House of Assembly, failed to turn up either of the original bills. For the consolidation of the two bills see *DHA* 1893, 158.

48 SNS 1893, c. 11

49 Ibid. This tension between the supporters of women's rights and those who insisted upon separate spheres for men and women also manifested itself during later attempts to reform the law with respect to rights in children. In 1896, when Albert Hemeon, the foremost champion of women's rights in

the legislature, introduced a bill to amend the legislation concerning guardians and wards in an effort to give greater rights to mothers, it failed to pass. An 1899 amendment to the 1893 legislation also met with opposition. One member of the Legislative Council, the Hon. Mr Francheville, referred to the amendment giving the Supreme Court power to review custody awards made before 1893 as 'vicious legislation' and expressed his fear that 'throughout the province it would be productive of litigation and expense. Despite his reservations, however, the bill passed into law. Clearly, although the vast majority of legislators supported greater rights for women with respect to their children, there was no consensus as to how far the legal reform should go. See An Act to amend Chapter 96, Revised Statutes, Fifth Series, 'Of Guardians and Wards' in PANS RG5, series U, vol. 30. See also *DHA* 30 Jan. 1896, 70–1, *DLC* 1899, 64, and SNS 1899, c. 46.

50 The information regarding the life of Wallace Graham is taken from *Macmillan Dictionary of Canadian Biography* 4th ed. (Toronto: Macmillan 1978) 309 and *Canadian Men and Women of the Time: A Handbook of Canadian Biography of Living Characters* 2d ed. (Toronto: William Briggs 1912) 466.

51 I believe that the records for the period 1893–1910 are nearly complete. A comparison with lists of cases before the court, which were drawn up by the registrar and which covered the period 1893–1908, turned up only one case for which records do not survive – *Florence A. McMullen* v. *Frank A. McMullen* (1902 or 1904). See the folder marked 'miscellaneous' in RG 39, series D, vol. 3 for the lists.

52 *Bessie Agnes Lovitt* v. *Israel Melbourne Lovitt* (1895) vol. 2, file 42. Israel was the brother of William Lovitt, also divorced by his wife for cruelty: see Kimberley Smith Maynard's paper elsewhere in this volume.

53 Ibid. See evidence of George H. Randall, 29 Mar. 1895.

54 *Jemima Gilchrist Woodend* v. *Robert John Woodend* (1909) vol. 9, file B-82

55 *Myrtie Power* v. *George G. Power* (1901) vol. 4, file B-3

56 *Jeanette Josephine Baker* v. *Judson Baker* (1901) vol. 4, file B-4

57 Maidment *Custody* 99

58 See *Manners, Morals and Mayhem: A Look at the First 200 Years of Law and Society in New Brunswick* (Fredericton: Public Legal Information Services 1985) 55–7 and Tulloch *We the Undersigned* 86, 87.

59 Backhouse *Canadian Custody Law* 212

60 For a discussion of the emergence of the maternal presumption in the United States see J.A. Stiles 'Nineteenth-Century Child Custody Reform: Maternal Authority and the Development of the "Best Interests of the Child" Standard' in *Probate Law Journal* 6(5) (1984) 5–32; J. Einhorn 'Child Custody in Historical Perspective: A Study of Changing Social Perceptions

of Divorce and Child Custody in Anglo-American Law' in *Behavioural Sciences and the Law* 4, no. 1 (1986) 119–35; and M. Grossberg *Governing the Hearth: Law and the Family in Nineteenth-Century America* (Chapel Hill: University of North Carolina Press 1985) 253.

61 Twenty-five of a total of 126 respondents in divorce actions occurring between 1893 and 1910 are known to have been involved in continuing relationships with their paramours at the time of the action.

62 *Jeanette Josephine Baker* v. *Judson Baker* (1901) vol. 4, file B-4; *Myrtie Power* v. *George G. Power* (1901) vol. 4, file B-3; *George Fairfax* v. *Hannah Fairfax* (1901) vol. 4, file B-6; *Harriet Norton* v. *Charles Alexander Norton* (1902) vol. 8, file B-63; *Mary Jane Rogers* v. *Benjamin Rogers* (1907) vol. 8, file B-55; *Frank D. Burris* v. *Florence Elizabeth Burris* (1909) vol. 9, file B-74; *Jemima Gilchrist Woodend* v. *Robert John Woodend* (1909) vol. 9, file B-82. The case in which a continuing interest in the child was not evident was *Nettie Grace Conrod* v. *Harold Leslie Conrod* (1910) vol. 10, file B-93. The *Norton* case has been counted twice in the category of reasonable access. Originally, the mother was granted custody and the father was awarded reasonable access, but this state of affairs was reversed in 1908 on the application of the father.

63 *George Fairfax* v. *Hannah Fairfax* (1901) vol. 4, file B-6

64 *Harriet Norton* v. *Charles Alexander Norton* (1902) vol. 8, file B-63

65 *Jemima Gilchrist Woodend* v. *Robert John Woodend* (1909) vol. 9, file B-82. Joint custody had never been proposed by the Nova Scotia court before this decision.

66 Ibid. Affidavits of Mabel McPherson, Robert J. Murray, and James Wood; testimony of Isabella Alcoin; Order for custody 27 Apr. 1909.

67 The expanding role of women in the paid labour force during the nineteenth century has been addressed in a number of studies. For a study of working women in Nova Scotia during the period between 1880 and 1910, see S. Myers, supra note 5. In the United States, the percentage of women in the labour force rose from 4.6 per cent in 1800 to 18.3 per cent in 1900. See W.E. Brownlee and M.M. Brownlee *Women in the American Economy: A Documentary History, 1675–1929* (New Haven: Yale University Press 1976) 3. Lee Holcombe provides statistical information on the rise of the participation of middle-class women in the work force in England and Wales from 1861 to 1911. According to her figures, the number of women working in a variety of middle-class jobs rose by 307 per cent during that period: *Victorian Ladies at Work: Middle-Class Working Women in England and Wales 1850–1914* (Newton Abbot: David and Charles 1973) 203–17.

68 Despite the importance of economic factors in creating an acceptable home environment, the favourable attitude of the court towards working

women is somewhat surprising in the light of the ideal of womanhood that was pervasive during the nineteenth and early twentieth centuries. Although it is seldom overtly stated, one senses from reading the files that the court admired women who were able to support their families. Such admiration was expressed in *Jamieson*, where Judge Alexander James stated, '[Marion] has by her own labour supported [her children] without aid from [George] and in all respects is worthy of the highest commendation.' See *Marion Jamieson* v. *George Jamieson* (1887) vol. 1, file 12, part 2. The fact that women often stressed their self-reliance in their petitions indicates that lawyers expected the court to respond favourably to women who worked to support their families. However, this should not be overemphasized. It is likely that in large part the court was reacting out of sympathy for the women's plight in having to work.

69 *Sophie Fraser* v. *Charles Fraser* (1901) vol. 4, file B-8; *C. Asaphine Griffin* v. *Michael Griffin* (1907) vol. 8, file B-54; *Kate Stafford* v. *William Stafford* (1899) vol. 3, file 60; *Mabel Gertrude Morrison* v. *Roderick Herbert Morrison* (1906) vol. 7, file B-44; *Mary Ellen McNutt* v. *Morton Ross McNutt* (1909) vol. 8, file B-61; *Flora Trerice Munro* v. *Albert Ernest Munro* (1910) vol. 9, file B-85

70 Annie Ross Baker placed a child in boarding-school. It is impossible to tell, however, whether this was the result of difficulties she encountered in fulfilling her role as a single parent or whether it was done simply to further the children's education. See *Annie Rose Baker* v. *John Carleton Baker* (1907) vol. 7, file B-48.

71 *Marion Jamieson* v. *George Jamieson* (1887) vol. 1, file 12, part 2; *Jeanette Josephine Baker* v. *Judson Baker* (1901) vol. 4, file B-4; *Agnes McNutt* v. *Benjamin McNutt* (1904) vol. 8, file B-61; *Annie Rose Baker* v. *John Carleton Baker* (1907) vol. 7, file B-48; *Charles Brown* v. *Rosa Ellen Brown* (1901) vol. 4, file B-1; *Charles McDonald* v. *Barbara McDonald* (1903) vol. 5, file B-18; *William Reagh* v. *Ethel Reagh* (1909) vol. 9, file B-77; *Frank D. Burris* v. *Florence Elizabeth Burris* (1909) vol. 9, file B-74; *Clifford McLellan* v. *Nettie McLellan* (1910) vol. 10, file B-91; *Leonard Brown* v. *Laura Alice Brown* (1910) vol. 10, file B-92

72 Six women who received custody returned to their parents' home. For case citations see note 69 above.

73 *Leonard Brown* v. *Laura Alice Brown* (1910) vol. 10, file B-92

74 *Jeanette Josephine Baker* v. *Judson Baker* (1901) vol. 4, file B-4; *Charles McDonald* v. *Barbara McDonald* (1903) vol. 5, file B-18

75 54 NSR 490. It should be noted that the parties involved in *Boyd* had not divorced. The mother had petitioned the Supreme Court for custody of her child when she and her husband experienced marital difficulties.

10

The Mines Arbitration Act, 1888: Compulsory Arbitration in Context

MARGARET E. McCALLUM

Since the Second World War, legislation in most Canadian jurisdictions has compelled employers and unionized employees to settle their grievances through arbitration. No matter which provisions of the collective agreement are being violated, employees are prohibited from striking and employers from locking out their employees while the agreement is in effect. Strikes or lock-outs are legal only when the collective agreement has expired, and then only as a last resort, after the parties have exhausted the conciliation and mediation process specified in the applicable labour legislation. Although most collective agreements are signed without resort to a strike or lock-out, organized labour regards the possibility of a strike as essential to the bargaining process. In labour's mind there is a clear distinction between grievance arbitration, in which the arbitrator interprets and applies an existing collective agreement, and interest arbitration, in which the arbitrator writes the agreement. Legislation imposing interest arbitration in place of strikes meets what resistance the labour movement can muster. Even unions that voluntarily submit some of their bargaining issues to binding arbitration face criticism from their members and colleagues in the labour movement.[1]

In the late nineteenth century labour leaders actively sought legislation to facilitate or compel the arbitration of disputes about wages and conditions of employment. The Canadian Labor Union, a central Canadian labour federation organized in Toronto in 1873, made aid to locked-out or striking workers contingent on their having first 'endeavoured by arbitration to settle [the] difficulty.' Motions approving the use of arbitration in place of strikes were passed at the last annual CLU convention in 1877 and at the conventions of the CLU's successor, the Trades and Labor Congress of Canada. In 1898 the TLC included compulsory arbitration of labour disputes in its 'platform of principles.' The Knights of Labor, an American union that began organizing in Canada in 1881, called for legislation providing for arbitration between employers and employed and a means for enforcing the decision of the arbitrators.[2]

Labour historians often dismiss efforts to force employers to submit to arbitration as fruitless distractions from collective bargaining and/or the class struggle. But the proponents of compulsory arbitration, considered in the nineteenth-century legal context, deserve more sympathy. In this essay I will examine Canada's first compulsory arbitration legislation, the Mines Arbitration Act of 1888, passed by the Nova Scotia government at the request of the Provincial Workmen's Association (PWA), the union representing the province's coal miners.[3]

Canadian law in the nineteenth century did not provide a regulatory framework for compulsory collective bargaining, with penalties for unfair labour practices, failure to bargain in good faith or discrimination against union members. In 1864, Nova Scotia passed An Act Relating to the Combination of Workmen, which protected union members from criminal prosecution for meeting with others to discuss or to establish wage rates or hours of work, but prohibited attempts by employees to enforce rates or hours. Workers convicted of interfering by force or otherwise with employers' rights to set wages and hours, or to hire whomever they wished, faced up to twelve months' imprisonment at hard labour. The act also made it an offence to compel a person to join a union, or to force him to demand the wages or hours established by the union. Despite these restrictions on union activity, the Nova Scotia legislature also passed legislation incorporating several unions.[4]

In 1872 the Nova Scotia legislation was superseded by the federal Trade Unions Act, introduced by the prime minister, Sir John A. Macdonald, during the Toronto printers' strike. Despite Macdonald's claim to be the friend of the working man, this legislation did not change the legal position of trade unions; rather, it reiterated the common law doctrine that the purposes of a trade union were not to be deemed unlawful merely because they were in restraint of trade.[5] Concurrently with the Trade Unions Act the federal government enacted the Criminal Law Amendment Act, which imposed criminal sanctions for picketing. As with the Nova Scotia legislation, unions could establish wage rates or hours of work, but could not compel employers to discuss or accept them. Even picketing 'merely to obtain or communicate information' was prohibited, except from 1876 to 1892.[6]

Picketing was illegal, but striking was not in itself a criminal offence. Under civil law, striking workers were considered to have breached their individual contracts of employment, and employers had no obligation to rehire them. In Ontario, Quebec, and Prince Edward Island, however, master and servant legislation also made it a criminal offence for an individual to leave his employment without permission. The conflict between the federal and provincial laws was resolved in 1877, again following a celebrated strike, with passage of the Breaches of Contract Act. This legislation repealed the offending sections of the provincial master and servant acts, and created penalties for specified breaches of contract, applicable in every province. A worker was liable to a fine of up to one hundred dollars or three months' imprisonment for, inter alia, 'wilfully and maliciously' breaking any contract made by him if the probable consequences of his action included danger to life or to valuable property.[7] This definition would include a strike in a coal mine involving maintenance workers, known as an 'all-out' or '100 per cent' strike, since the mine was likely to be damaged by the ensuing accumulation of water and gas.

Despite the legal impediments to union activity, Nova Scotia's coal miners successfully established a union in 1879 during a strike provoked by successive wage cuts at the Springhill mine in Cumberland County. During the strike Robert Drummond, one of the coal company's surface employees, wrote an anonymous letter to a Halifax newspaper supporting the workers' claim that the wage cuts were not justified. When officials of the Springhill Mining Company learned the identity of the letter-writer, he was fired. The new union, the Provincial Workmen's Association, elected Drummond to the position of grand secretary, and paid him forty dollars a month to work as a full-time organizer and publicist. Drummond, a Scottish Presbyterian immigrant, infused the new union with his own ideas on self-help, temperance, and social mobility. While he was the grand secretary of the PWA he also served for a time as a justice of the peace, and used both positions to promote opposition to the liquor trade. Drummond retired from leadership of the PWA in 1898; three years later he was appointed to the provincial Legislative Council by the Liberal government. Drummond's influence in the PWA is reflected in the union's constitution, which he drafted, and in its motto, 'Unity, Equity, and Progress.'[8] Members declared, 'In taking a firm stand against the ofttimes dishonest impositions of our employers, let not ourselves be unreasonable in our demands. If equity be the base of all our actions, then we may say to "capital" – "Give the laborer his hire," and fearlessly demand an honest wage for honest work.'[9] To ensure that the union did not find itself supporting unreasonable demands, no strike aid was to be given unless the strike had been approved by the PWA grand council.[10] It was an approved strike in 1887 that moved the Nova Scotia government to introduce compulsory arbitration legislation.

In general, the state in capitalist society serves the interests of capital through the promotion of capital accumulation and preservation of the existing order. Although the state attempts to maintain the appearance of neutrality during a strike, it often intervenes on behalf of the employer under the guise of maintaining public order. In strikes in the Nova Scotia coalfields, both levels of government were willing to send in the army or special police in order to protect strike-breakers and to maintain continued coal production. The state did not acknowledge that miners had any property interest in their jobs, and so the miners' actions to prevent strike-breakers from replacing them were viewed as a threat to public order, freedom of contract, and private property.

But in resorting to force the Nova Scotia government was not acting simply as a coercive agent for the coal companies: it had its own economic interest in minimizing work stoppages in the coal industry. Royalties from coal were a significant source of provincial revenue, and the coal companies' position as monopsonistic purchasers of labour created heavy relief burdens for municipalities (and hence for the province) in any lengthy work stoppage. To use Ian McKay's apt metaphor, the Nova Scotia government's relationship to the coal industry was that of a shareholder interested in dividends. If arbitration legislation would reduce work stoppages in the coal industry, it would benefit the government as well as the miners who had requested it.[11]

The government was also interested in labour support at the polls. Nova Scotia was governed in 1887 by the Liberals under W.S. Fielding. Fielding had been premier since 1884; he succeeded W.T. Pipes, who had regained the government benches for the Liberals in 1882, defeating Nova Scotia's first Conservative government since Confederation. The *Trades Journal*, founded by Drummond to report on PWA activities, supported the Conservatives at the federal level, arguing that the National Policy had led to increased coal production in the province. Despite this support for their rivals, the Liberals under Fielding responded favourably to PWA demands for tougher mine safety regulations and better enforcement of existing laws. In 1883, after considerable pressure from the PWA, the Liberals appointed two deputy mine inspectors, one a former member of the union executive.[12]

In the provincial election of 1886, encouraged by legislation that enfranchised many coal miners, the PWA decided to run candidates in Cape Breton, Pictou, and Cumberland counties. Pictou County was a multimember constituency, electing three representatives to the provincial legislature. Drummond ran in Pictou on a Labour-Liberal ticket; both the Liberals and the conservatives had offered to back him, but Drummond said that the Liberals had promised him his independence. He was defeated, but his support for the Liberals may have contributed to the victory of a running-mate, Jeffrey McColl, a shipbuilder and businessman, and the first Liberal MLA from Pictou since Confederation.[13] In the following years, Drummond was one of the people Fielding consulted about appointments to office and nominations for provincial and federal elections.[14]

With McColl in the Assembly and Fielding cultivating Drummond, the PWA could expect sympathetic attention from the government. The extent of that sympathy was soon to be tested. In mid-December 1886 the Acadia Coal Company announced a substantial wage reduction for underground workers at its Albion Mine in Stellarton, Pictou County. The reductions provoked a strike by miners organized in the PWA Fidelity Lodge, who argued that they already were receiving starvation wages. In mid-January Fidelity Lodge offered to submit the matter to arbitration, but the company declined unless the men first accepted part of the proposed reduction. The men stayed out. At the end of January they were joined by miners at the Acadia mine in Westville and the Vale mine in Thorburn, both operated by the Acadia Company.[15] In all, between nine hundred and a thousand men were on strike. Dealers were unable to honour their contracts for coal, manufacturers shut down because of the lack of fuel, and the port of Halifax suffered a loss of trade.[16] In elaborating on the Grand Council's reasons for giving its approval to the strike, Drummond emphasized that the men had no alternative:

> To prevent misapprehension, it may here distinctly be stated that the members of Council are not ... advocates of strikes, as a means of settlement of disputes, so long as a more peaceable method was available. At the same time, they are not ... afraid to face the music when the alternative was an ignominious and unconditional surrender. The Council unhesitatingly admits that strikes are bad ... and yet ... there are some things which are far worse than even a strike, and

one of these is for workmen tamely and meekly to submit to imposition, injustice and fraud without murmur, and without complaining; without a protest or without a struggle, allow a soul-less corporation, possessed, if it be, with brute force, to drive them to the wall and pen them there. It is bad to strike and be pinched with hunger, but many times worse to submit to be plucked by grasping capitalists, without a fight for fair treatment. It is bad to strike and lose the hard wrought earnings carefully laid by for sickness or age, but far worse to surrender that liberty and those privileges which our fathers, and ourselves, fought hard to secure.[17]

The strike was an inauspicious beginning for the recently reorganized Acadia Coal Company, which had been formed by the merger of three Pictou County coal operators – Acadia, the Halifax Company, and the Vale Coal, Iron and Manufacturing Company. The Halifax Company was a subsidiary of a British industrial–mining complex owned by Sir George Elliott, a former coal miner. Sir Hugh Montague Allan inherited the majority interest in the other companies from his father, Sir Hugh Allan, the Montreal financier and shipping magnate. Sir Hugh, with some New York associates, had incorporated the Acadia Company in 1865, and subsequently had invested heavily in the Vale company, formed in 1872 by Joseph B. Moore, also of Montreal. Suspicions of stock-watering have usually accompanied corporate reorganizations in the Nova Scotia coalfields; the Acadia merger was no exception. Like the miners at Cape Breton in the 1920s, the miners at the Albion mine may have resisted the wage reduction partly because they suspected that it had more to do with paying dividends than with meeting the competition on coal prices.[18]

Despite the sympathy strikes, the Acadia Company refused to retract the wage reduction. In mid-February, the miners again suggested arbitration. This time they offered to start with a one-half-cent reduction from the maximum rates; the company had initially proposed ten- and five-cent reductions. Again, the company responded with a condition: that the men deposit fourteen days' pay with the company, to be forfeited if they did not abide by the arbitrator's decision. The men refused, arguing that the company would provoke a work stoppage over a non-wage issue and then claim the deposit as forfeit.[19] The matter was still unresolved when the legislature met in March 1887; in the speech from the throne the government expressed its hope for an early and amicable adjustment of the dispute. At a meeting in April between the premier and a delegation from the PWA (the Acadia Company declined to attend) the union urged the government to introduce a compulsory arbitration bill, a measure that had been discussed at the PWA Grand Council meeting earlier in the month.[20]

As early as 1881 Robert Drummond had observed in the *Trades Journal* that it was mine operators, not trade-union leaders, who opposed settling disputes by arbitration. In his report to the grand council in the spring of 1886, he looked forward to the day when capital would recognize labour's right to be heard on matters affecting it. Once capital accepted labour's right to take disputes to arbitration, rather than tamely submitting to unilateral management decisions, strikes would be obsolete. In arguing the merits of arbitration, Drummond referred to the British practice of tying wages to changes in the price of coal and to Pennsylvania legislation that provided for voluntary arbitration of industrial disputes.[21] Drummond did not mention Ontario's Trades Arbitration Act of 1873, which had been enacted by Oliver Mowat's Liberal government as part of a pre-election package designed to counter the Conservative appeal for the working man's vote.[22]

Nova Scotia did not turn to Great Britain or Ontario for a model for the arbitration bill introduced in the legislature on 20 April 1887. The bill prohibited strikes and lock-outs before a dispute had been submitted to the commissioner of mines, who investigated and, if necessary, referred the matter to a board of arbitration. Upon the joint application of the employer and employees the matter could go directly to arbitration. An arbitration board was to have five members; two were to be appointed with each request for arbitration by the parties to the dispute, and the remaining three were to be government appointees. A decision issued by an arbitration board would be binding on the parties; unlike boards established under the Ontario legislation, the Nova Scotia boards could establish wage rates. The arbitration bill incorporated the condition for arbitration suggested by the Acadia management; employers were permitted to hold back fourteen days' pay from the first wages due each employee, which would be forfeited if the employee failed to comply with an arbitration decision. If the employer did not comply, the government could cancel its coal lease.[23]

Attorney General J.W. Longley compared the Mines Arbitration Bill to legislation introduced by the Gladstone government in England in 1881 creating a government commission to determine the rent for agricultural land. Just as the land commission adjusted rents according to the prices received for agricultural products, the arbitrators would adjust wages according to the price of coal. In Longley's view, matters of contract were not immune from government interference so long as the interference went no further than was demanded in the interests of society. Premier Fielding based the government's right to intervene on Crown ownership of the coal. Since numerous strikes deprived the public treasury of royalties, the government, as custodian of the public interest, was entitled to intervene to ensure the continuous and efficient operation of the mines. The bill passed third reading in the elected Legislative Assembly with some minor amendments.[24] Hearings on the bill, at which the coal operators, according to Drummond, were assisted by 'innumerable lawyers,' delayed its passage until the last day of the session, giving the appointed Legislative Council good reason to kill the bill by deferring its consideration for three months on the ground that more time was needed for discussion.[25] The *Morning Herald*, a partisan Conservative paper, observed that 'the mock heroics indulged in by the government about "grappling" with the labour question, resulted in what they have always intended they should result in – namely, nothing.'[26]

For the PWA the bill's introduction and defeat provided an excellent opportunity to observe that the striking miners were acting responsibly and deserved the support of the community. In praising the bill in the *Trades Journal*, Drummond emphasized that it had been introduced at the suggestion of the PWA and over the opposition of a majority of the managers. As described by Drummond, the bill provided a means of ascertaining 'who has the right side of the story' so that public opinion would be aroused against those in the wrong.[27] 'The public profess to have a horror of strikes and lockouts, and have been in the habit of blaming the men whenever a suspension of work occurred,' but the Acadia strike and the fate of the arbitration bill made it clear that the coal operators, 'while professing to be in favor of arbitration are opposed to it, as they are to everything, however just, which takes from them the absolute right of dictating to their workmen what wages they must take, and how many hours they must labor. That is the secret of their opposition to the bill. They are afraid to be compelled to deal fairly and honestly by their workmen.'[28]

Hoping to invoke public sympathy for the men in their battle against a large corporation, Drummond argued that 'monopolists have no right to grind their employees to a powder without interference or protest from the people.'[29] He welcomed the introduction of the arbitration bill, even without its passage, as a partial recognition of this principle:

> The fight over the bill has not been ... without its substantial victories. ... We have forced parliament to discuss the principle of the state stepping in and declaring

its right to interfere in disputes as to wages between employers and employed, and have carried the measure in the lower house. ... We have intimated, in emphatic tones, to the capitalist to set about putting his house in order, and ... by the reasonableness of the offer to submit to arbitration, and the declaration of aversion to strikes as a means of settling differences, we have won the public opinion of the province to our side.[30]

The Acadia strikers went back to work in mid-May 1887, having secured few of their demands, and the Acadia Company refused to re-employ thirty active unionists.[31] A new arbitration bill was promised in the speech from the throne at the 1888 legislative session, and was introduced the following week. Again, employers could retain fourteen days' wages from each employee, but only on receipt of notice of an arbitration request, not when the employee began work. Employees who struck before requesting arbitration forfeited fourteen days' pay to their employer; employers who illegally locked out their employees were liable to them for an equivalent amount. The government, however, would no longer have the power to cancel a coal company's lease for non-compliance with an arbitration order, the provision of the earlier bill that had most alarmed the coal operators.[32] The operators may have hinted that if it remained they would appeal to the federal government to disallow the legislation. This would not have been an idle threat; in 1889 the federal government disallowed New Brunswick legislation annulling certain mining leases on the ground that such an invasion of the rights of property imperilled the credit of the whole nation.[33]

While the arbitration bill was being debated in the legislature, the federal Royal Commission on the Relations of Labor and Capital was holding hearings throughout the province. Arbitration was included in its list of subjects for investigation. Nova Scotia coal miners who were asked about arbitration said that they favoured it, having arbitrated disputes satisfactorily in the past. Some praised the pending legislation, and criticized the Acadia Company for its refusal to arbitrate the wage dispute the year before. On his appearance before the commission, H.S. Poole, the general manager of the Acadia Company, claimed that he could not remember whether the men had requested arbitration or whether the company had refused. Although he approved of arbitration 'broadly speaking,' he would not be specific. R.H. Brown, manager of the General Mining Association at Sydney Mines, was less reticent. Acknowledging that he had protested against the 1887 bill, which he considered the work of the PWA, he argued that compulsory arbitration legislation 'would make agitation a livelihood to some persons.' Drummond testified to the PWA support for arbitration, emphasizing that the coal companies would not submit a dispute to arbitration unless forced to do so. He said that the PWA was content with the elimination of the clause allowing cancellation of coal leases, and noted that Poole had withdrawn his objection to the bill when that provision was removed.[34]

The coal operators relied on the members of Legislative Council rather than on the Assembly to respond to their remaining objections to the bill. William H. Owen, the member for Lunenburg, stated that he had received a memorial signed by a large number of mine operators in the province. These operators warned that the proposed arbitration bill would prevent further investment of capital in the province's mines, and might prompt the withdrawal of money already invested. Passage of the bill would be a breach of faith on the part of the legislature, because it would unilaterally change the terms of the coal operators' leases. To permit a board of arbitrators to examine a coal company's books 'was an extraordinary and unjustifiable provision, and contrary to business principles.' M.H. Goudge, the member for Windsor and a past director of the Mineral Exploration and Mining Association of Nova Scotia, had opposed the 1887 bill, but had since been informed by a 'representative of a large mine in the east' that the mine operators did not think it necessary to defeat the new bill. He suggested two amendments, which were accepted. One provided that of the five arbitrators the government should appoint two, not three: the two appointed by the parties would appoint the fifth. His other amendment attempted to guarantee the confidentiality of company books examined during an arbitration. Two other Legislative Council amendments ensured that no person in the employ of a rival company would have access to a company's books, and that any monetary award made against a coal company would rank in priority behind previously registered mortgages and judgments. In the original bill, awards took priority over everything but the government's claim for royalties. Although the mines arbitration bill applied only to the coal industry, the council members may have feared its effect on the province's gold-mining boom. Even with the amendments, it passed the council only with the Speaker's deciding vote.[35]

The *Pictou News* had predicted that the 1887 bill would be useless except as proof of the old saw about leading a horse to water.[36] This scepticism was borne out in 1889, when the PWA attempted to arbitrate a dispute at the Springhill mine. In April, Pioneer Lodge complained of wage reductions and dismissals at Springhill in violation of an agreement between the union and the mine operator, the Cumberland Railway and Coal Company. The agreement had been put in writing and signed by management and the union in 1885, after lengthy negotiations and discussion. In return for accepting a wage reduction, the men were assured that they would have steady work five days a week, that all coal mined would be loaded before the end of each shift, and that no new men would be hired so long as the existing work force could meet all production requirements.[37]

Ian McKay has characterized 1889 as a watershed year in labour relations in the Springhill mine. The assumption of active management by J.R. Cowans, the company's general manager and principal shareholder, consolidated and accelerated the change from paternalism to autocracy that had begun the year before. Cowans was an advocate of scientific management: he imposed detailed supervision and a structure of rewards and punishment to secure maximum efficiency. In a marked departure from previous practice, dismissals were not negotiated, work sites in the mine were assigned without consultation, and union members were discriminated against in hiring.[38]

In 1889 dismissals and wage reductions were the first salvos in a decade-long campaign that ended in the elimination of Pioneer Lodge. Rather than walking out in protest, the men decided to apply for arbitration under the Mines Arbitration Act. The statement of the issues in the *Trades Journal* shows that they were aware of what was at stake:

> Some two months ago, the Cumberland Coal and Railway company inaugurated a cheese paring policy in regard to the wages of some of their employees. No general reduction was attempted. ... The managing director – or whatever his title may be – had too much upper province cuteness for that. He thought to steal on the men singly and unawares ... and annihilate the army by popping them off one by one. He ordered a reduction in wages of a shiftman or two, a carpenter or two, with an odd carter and laborer thrown in. ... The men affected demurred to the reduction, and their demurring was sustained by their fellow workmen.[39]

On receipt of the man's application for arbitration, the commissioner of mines summoned the parties before him to determine whether the matter required reference to an arbitration board. The two lawyers for the company argued that the commissioner had no jurisdiction to proceed, because the documents had been signed by the Pioneer Lodge master workman and secretary, not by a majority of the employees. William Hall, the colliery manager, said that the company did not recognize Pioneer Lodge as representing a majority of the men, and refused to say whether the company had granted such recognition in the past. The company lawyers threatened to apply to the provincial Supreme Court for a writ of prohibition to stop the proceedings, with costs to be levied against the PWA. Pioneer Lodge collected 703 signatures on a letter reiterating the complaints against the company and requesting arbitration. At the end of June the commissioner again summoned both parties to give evidence, but the company declined to attend. The commissioner ordered the appointment of an arbitration board, whereupon the company obtained a Supreme Court writ of certiorari setting aside the commissioner's decision on the ground that the company had not received the requisite notice of the proceedings. (The commissioner had communicated with the Springhill office, not with the company's registered agent.) Notwithstanding its objections to the proceedings, the company had retained a fortnight's pay from every worker.[40]

Although the coal miners presented themselves as having 'the right side of the story', and being denied the opportunity to present it, the company was not castigated in the press for its obstructionism. As Drummond commented to the grand council in October 1899,

> '[t]he cry, for a long time, has been for some rational way of settling disputes between masters and men. The public, generally, in the past have inclined to the opinion that a spirit of rashness and restlessness in the men was the motive power of many strikes. Here, however, we see a readiness on the part of the workmen ... to try the new and peaceable way, and lo! the employer will have none of it, while the press, so loud in condemnation of strikes, so ready to blame workingmen, has precious little to say, has very few and feeble words of condemnation for the manager.'[41]

In its effort to break the union the Cumberland Company began hiring newly arrived British immigrants to replace PWA supports in violation of its 1885 agreement. In June 1890 the grand council sanctioned a strike. When the strike began on 23 June, the maintenance workers remained on the job, ensuring that the mine did not fill with water. In mid-August, with no settlement in sight, the miners increased the pressure by launching the PWA's first '100 per cent' strike, leaving no one to operate the mine's pumps. Faced with the possibility of irreparable damage to the mine, and the loss of future royalties, Premier Fielding and Edward Gilpin, the inspector of mines, intervened to assist the parties in reaching a settlement. The strike ended in August 1890; most of the men's demands were met.[42] Meanwhile, the PWA legislative committee lobbied the government for amendments to the Mines Arbitration Act. In the 1890 session the government responded with a new act remedying some of the defects revealed during the Springhill dispute, and making it unlawful for a mine operator to reduce wages during a labour dispute. Provision was made for appealing an arbitration decision to the provincial Supreme Court, but certiorari proceedings were prohibited.[43]

Despite the failure to secure arbitration in 1889–90, Drummond cited the Mines Arbitration Act as evidence that the general public and even the mine operators recognized that workers were entitled to a say in what they were paid. Because they were reasonable and demanded only what was just, they preferred to assert their views through arbitration; but if the employer refused, they would strike.[44] 'Corporations may have no souls but they have pockets; and at times only an appeal to the pocket can secure success.'[45] In 1892 the PWA began proceedings to arbitrate a rate reduction in the Victoria mines in Cape Breton, but was able to secure the miners' demands before the arbitration board had met. Even in Springhill some non-wage matters were resolved through arbitration, although the Arbitration Act did not end strikes there. From June 1890 to December 1911 Springhill endured twenty-eight strikes.[46]

The arbitration process proved unsatisfactory for the miners in a wage dispute in 1900 with the Dominion Coal Company, a huge company organized by the Boston financier H.M. Whitney in 1893. In response to an autumn increase in the price of coal from two dollars to three dollars per ton, the miners asked for a 10 per cent increase in wages, and the mechanics for an increase of fifty cents a day for themselves and twenty-five cents for their helpers. The company refused, and a arbitration board was appointed. The miners chose the Catholic archdeacon of Cape Breton as their representative, and the coal company chose H.S. Poole. The government appointed Wallace Graham, a Supreme Court judge, and Drummond, who had retired as PWA grand secretary in 1898 and since 1891 had been a member of the Legislative Council. When the parties' nominees failed to agree on a fifth board member, the government appointed Angus G. Macdonald. After hearing evidence from both sides, the arbitration board upheld the company's position. The board accepted the company's arguments that it had already granted an increase in May 1900, and that it did not benefit from the increased price of coal because much of its production was sold under long-term contracts at low prices.[47] In its report of the board's decision the *Labour Gazette* does not indicate whether the board considered the fact that these long-term contracts had been negotiated at below-market prices with the New England Gas and

Coke company, also owned by Whitney.[48] Subsequent *Labour Gazette* reports of disputes in the coal industry in Nova Scotia contain no references to the Mines Arbitration Act.

In 1900 the federal government entered the field of labour relations with the Conciliation Act, modelled on English legislation of 1896. The act provided for registration of boards to which employers and employees could voluntarily submit their disputes. In practice, however, the act gave William Lyon Mackenzie King, an ambitious civil servant in the Labour Department, an opportunity to intervene in labour disputes. In 1903 the federal government passed the Railway Labour Disputes Act, which provided for the compulsory investigation of labour disputes on the railways. Both acts were superseded in 1907 by the Industrial Disputes Investigation Act (IDIA), which required employers and employees in mining, transportation, communications or public utilities to submit their disputes to a tripartite board before they could legally commence a strike or lock-out. The board could make recommendations, but could not issue a binding order.[49]

Despite the use of the IDIA in the Nova Scotia coalfields, the provincial Assembly continued to experiment with arbitration legislation. In 1903 it passed a Conciliation Act modelled on the federal legislation of 1900. The Mines Arbitration Act remained on the provincial statute-books, with minor amendments, until 1925 when both it and the Conciliation Act were repealed by the new Industrial Peace Act, modelled on the IDIA. Unless the parties agreed otherwise, the decisions of boards established under the act were not binding. The Industrial Peace Act also provided for an arbitration commission that could make binding decisions; that provision, however, was not proclaimed in force.[50] In the same year the Privy Council ruled that the IDIA was ultra vires the federal government. A revised IDIA, limited to industries within the federal jurisdiction, enabled provinces to pass complementary legislation to bring their labour force under the federal legislation. Nova Scotia did so in 1926, and at the same time repealed its Industrial Peace Act. There were no more provincial experiments with compulsory arbitration for private sector workers until July 1971, when the government enacted the Construction Projects Labour-Management Relations Act at the behest of Michelin Tires (Canada) Limited.[51]

When the Mines Arbitration Act was first introduced, Drummond predicted that 'to be able to say that the legislature of little Nova Scotia was the first to enact a compulsory arbitration act will be the proud boast, or we are mistaken, of future generations.' He was mistaken; the act was not copied in other jurisdictions. When British Columbia and Ontario introduced arbitration legislation in the 1890s, they looked to New South Wales, not Nova Scotia, for their model. Neither province compelled employers or employees to submit their disputes to arbitration; if they did so voluntarily, the arbitration decision was binding only if the parties so agreed.[52]

In 1902, at its Berlin Convention, the TLC abandoned its support for compulsory arbitration. The decision was one of several that brought the TLC under the direct control of the American Federation of Labor, an American trade union central led by Samuel Gompers, who was an implacable opponent of any state intervention in the employment relationship. The PWA had not affiliated with the TLC, and after the Berlin Convention it was no longer eligible for affiliation, since it competed with an existing AFL union, the United Mine Workers of America. Beginning in 1906, the UMWA challenged the PWA for the right to represent the workers in Nova Scotia's coal mines. The coal companies preferred the increasingly conservative PWA to its aggressive rival, and used the IDIA to harass and defeat the UMWA and its supporters. By 1919, when the UMWA succeeded in completely routing the PWA, state-imposed arbitration had been discredited as an effective tactic by which labour could gain either union recognition or the union standard in wages and working conditions.[53]

Why had the PWA been unable to make more use of the Mines Arbitration Act in settling disputes with the mine operators? Without effective sanctions against a recalcitrant company, or an administrative apparatus to enforce the legislation, coal companies could avoid arbitrations with impunity. As Drummond and labour leaders after him learned, public opinion did not always rally behind the party in the right; and even when it did, it availed little against a 'soul-less corporation.' The PWA members initially supported arbitration because they expected it would be less costly than going on strike. The mine operators, by using the courts to resist arbitration, could make that alternative just as costly. The fear of forfeiting fourteen days' wages was a powerful incentive not to invoke the arbitration legislation, as was the lack of protection against dismissal or discriminatory treatment because of union activity. Given the inherent conservatism of the judiciary, the operators could anticipate considerable success in fighting any arbitration application in the courts. Even the strongest privative clause cannot preserve the decisions of a statutory body if a judge is determined to review them.[54]

The government did try to make the arbitration legislation work, amending it in 1890 in the light of the previous year's unsatisfactory experience. But despite the power the state derived from its ownership of the mines, there were definite limits to the extent to which it would use that power against the mine operators. With its interest in maintaining public order and the flow of coal royalties to the provincial treasury, the state was willing to support labour demands that promised peace and production in the coalfields – up to the point at which the demands provoked threats from the mine operators to invest their capital somewhere else. The only effective sanction against the coal companies – cancellation of their leases – was eliminated from the Mines Arbitration Bill before it became law; since its application would have defeated the state's goal of increased coal production, it was unlikely to have been used in any event.[55]

Even the most carefully drafted and draconian legislation would be of limited assistance in forcing an unwilling employer to submit to arbitration and abide by an award not in its favour. As Drummond recognized, arbitration was viable only if the employer already accepted that the union had sufficient strength and legitimacy to limit some management prerogatives. Otherwise, even if the union secured a favourable decision, it would eventually have to strike to enforce it.[56]

The PWA, in asking for arbitration to determine what wage levels the industry could afford, was starting from untenable assumptions. Drummond argued that if the operators provided evidence that wage cuts were necessitated by the state of trade, the coal miners would accept the cuts without striking. If the new rates were less than a living wage, the men would look for other work.[57] But Drummond underestimated the facility with which a coal company with manufacturing and transportation subsidiaries could arrange its books to conceal any profit from its mining operations. He also ignored the vulnerability of the wage-earner in the highly competitive soft-coal industry, in which wages often comprised 60 per cent of production costs. Coal-mine operators, faced with the need to cut costs, had several options. They could adopt mining techniques that produced a higher coal extraction rate, or they could bring all the mines in a single coalfield under one management, so that pit-heads, roads, shafts, levels, and ventilation, pumping, and power systems could all be planned for maximum efficiency and duplication could be avoided in non-productive work. The Nova Scotia coal industry used both of these expedients in the late nineteenth century, particularly after the creation of Dominion Coal. It also used the most obvious and immediate cost-cutting option, wage reductions.[58] But strike after strike belied Drummond's assurances that coal miners would move on to other mines or other jobs if the mines could not pay a living wage. In the face of the miners' commitment to their communities and way of life, the industry in the twentieth century looked to government subsidies to permit Nova Scotia coal, brought from deep, gassy mines or from under the ocean floor, to compete with American coal mined under much less difficult conditions.[59]

Although the Mines Arbitration Act proved of little help to Drummond in his efforts to reduce the number of strikes in the coal industry, its passage furthered a larger goal – improving the public image of coal miners. In his reports to the PWA Grand Council and in his articles in the *Trades Journal*, Drummond linked union organization with sobriety, responsibility, and respectability. In assessing the union's first ten years, Drummond rejoiced that '[i]n large degree our society has educated to orderliness, to method, to industry. Socially it has given workmen a big lift. One may still meet with a drunken and disorderly miner, but the PWA has rendered meaningless the word "rough" and "drunken" as applied to miners, as a class.'[60]

In his promotion of arbitration and his expression of regret at being forced into a strike, Drummond was able to draw a sharp distinction between the reasonable and responsible conduct of the miners and the ruthless aggression of the soulless corporations intent on destroying the people's liberty. Such populist rhetoric had a wide appeal in the late nineteenth century, and could reasonably be expected to arouse sympathy for the coal miners in their struggle against large companies controlled by capitalists from outside the province.[61] In the context of the readiness to strike if necessary, the PWA's enthusiasm for arbitration reflected an astute assessment of how best to develop a reputation for orderliness and responsibility that would stand the union in good stead during any labour dispute.

NOTES

1 P. Weiler *Reconcilable Differences: New Directions in Canadian Labour Law* (Toronto: Carswell 1980) 67, 90–1. Since Weiler wrote, Saskatchewan has joined the rest of Canada in prohibiting strikes and lock-outs during the term of a collective agreement. See SS 1983, c. 81. H.J. Glasbeek 'Compulsory Arbitration in Canada' in J.J. Loewenberg et al. *Compulsory Arbitration: An International Comparison* (Lexington, Mass.: Lexington Books 1976) 71–2 states that in Ontario in 1970–3, 11 per cent of collective agreement settle-

ments were reached after work stoppages. An agreement to refer non-monetary contract issues to binding arbitration was repudiated by members of the Public Service Alliance of Canada at their 1985 convention. Opponents of the pact said union leaders had died for the right to strike: see *Globe and Mail* 19 June 1985.

2 L.E. Wismer, ed. *Proceedings of the Canadian Labor Union, 1873–1877* (Ottawa: Trades and Labor Congress 1951) 24, 77, 85–7; *Proceedings of the Trades and Labor Congress of Canada, 1883–1898* (1883) 37; (1886) 30–1; (1887) 50; (1888) 9, 13, 16, 21; (1889) 22; (1890) 30; (1891) 23; (1892) 11, 16, 25; (1893) 12; (1894) 5, 6, 8; (1895) 8, 22; (1897) 7, 21; (1898) 31; G.S. Kealey, ed. *Canada Investigates Industrialism: The Royal Commission on the Relations of Labor and Capital, 1889* (Toronto: University of Toronto Press 1973) 164; E. Forsey 'Canadian Labour and Compulsory Arbitration 1877–1902' *Canadian Labour* 10 (1965) 21–2, 44

3 For a careful and sympathetic account of the PWA, see Ian McKay 'The Provincial Workmen's Association: A Brief Survey of Several Problems of Interpretation' in W.J.C. Cherwinski and G.S. Kealey, eds *Lectures in Canadian Labour and Working Class History* (St John's: New Hogtown Press 1985) 127–34 and ' "By Wisdom, Wile or War:" The Provincial Workmen's Association and the Struggle for Working-Class Independence in Nova Scotia, 1879–87' *Labour/Le Travail* 18 (1986) 13–62.

As Ian McKay has noted, that the PWA favoured compulsory arbitration is often taken as evidence of its conservatism. See also E. Forsey *Economic and Social Aspects of the Nova Scotia Coal Industry* (Toronto: St Martin's House 1926) 17; S. Reilly 'The Provincial Workmen's Association of Nova Scotia, 1879–1898' (MA thesis, Dalhousie University 1979) 96. G.S. Kealey and B. Palmer *Dreaming of What Might Be: The Knights of Labor in Ontario 1880–1900* (Cambridge: Cambridge University Press 1982) 96 acknowledge that the Knights' preference for arbitration was ' not always a collaborationist stance of surrender but an approach to class relations understandable given the limited experience available to late-ninteenth-century labor reformers.'

4 SNS1864, c. 11; C.B. Fergusson *The Labour Movement in Nova Scotia Before Confederation* (Halifax: Public Archives of Nova Scotia 1964) 24–8; K. Pryke 'Labour and Politics: Nova Scotia at Confederation' *Histoire Sociale/Social History* 6 (1970) 35, 37–8

5 SC 1872, c. 30; P. Craven 'Workers' Conspiracies in Toronto, 1854–72' *Labour/Le Travail* 14 (Fall 1980) 49, 86–70; M. Chartrand 'The First Canadian Trade Union Legislation: An Historical Perspective' *Ottawa Law Review* 16 (1984) 272–82. There are several good accounts of the Toronto printers' strike; see G. Kealey *Toronto Workers Respond to Industrial Capitalism 1867–1892*

(Toronto: University of Toronto Press 1980) 132–7, and 368 note 9, which gives references to other accounts.

6 SC 1872, c. 31; amended SC 1876, c. 37, included in the 1886 Revised Statutes as c. 173, ss. 10–14. In 1892, in Canada's first consolidated Criminal Code (SC 1892, c. 29), sections 516–20 and 523–4 re-enacted the 1872 Criminal Law Amendment Act without the exemption for informational picketing that had been added in 1876. It was not until 1934 that this exemption was restored: SC 1934, c. 47, s. 12.

7 SC 1877, c. 35; D. Morton 'Taking On the Grand Trunk: The Locomotive Engineers' Strike of 1876–7' *Labour/Le Travailleur* 2 (1977) 5–34; for cases decided under the Ontario Master and Servant Act, see P. Craven 'The Law of Master and Servant in Mid-Nineteenth-Century Ontario' in D. Flaherty, ed. *Essays in the History of Canadian Law* vol. 1 (Toronto; The Osgoode Society 1981) 175–211.

8 E. Forsey *Trade Unions in Canada 1812–1902* (Toronto: University of Toronto Press 1982) 64–7, 348; Reilly 'Provincial Workmen's Association,' 31–4, 143, 157; McKay 'Provincial Workmen's Association' 128

9 Initiation ceremony of the PWA, PWA Papers Labour Canada Library, Hull, PQ

10 Constitution of the PWA, ibid.

11 Ian McKay 'Industry, Work and Community in the Cumberland Coalfields 1848–1927' (PHD thesis, Dalhousie University 1983) 182–7; McKay 'Wisdom, Wile or War; 44; L. Panitch 'The Role and Nature of the Canadian State' in L. Panitch, ed. *The Canadian State: Political Economy and Political Power* (Toronto: University of Toronto Press 1977) 3–27; Desmond Morton 'Aid to the Civil Power: The Canadian Militia in Support of Social Order, 1867–1914' *Canadian Historical Review* 51 (1970) 407–25; David Frank 'Coal Masters and Coal Miners: The 1922 Strike and the Roots of Class Conflict in the Cape Breton Coal Industry' (MA thesis, Dalhousie University 1974) gives the following figures for coal royalties as a percentage of the provincial budget (at 29 n 14): 1892, 21.3 per cent; 1896, 32.6 per cent; 1904, 49 per cent.

12 J.M. Beck *The Government of Nova Scotia* (Toronto 1957) 350–1; Reilly 'Provin cial Workmen's Association' 89; D. McLeod 'Colliers, Colliery Safety and Workplace Control: The Nova Scotian Experience, 1873–1910' Canadian Historical Association *Historical Papers 1983* 238–9, 245. Not all the reforms brought the results the union had wanted – for example, the requirement that Nova Scotia mine operators fill positions as overmen, underground managers, and miners with men who held a certificate from a provincial board of examiners. See McLeod 241–6, 251–2.

13 Minutes of the Grand Council of the PWA, Labour Canada Library, 9 Apr. 1886; An Act to Extend the Electoral Franchise, SNS 1885, c. 2; C.B. Fergusson *A Directory of the Members of the Legislative Assembly of Nova Scotia 1758–1958* (Halifax: Public Archives of Nova Scotia 1958) 453–4, 510

14 Reilly 'Provincial Workmen's Association' 98; PANS MG2, vol. 491, Fielding to Drummond, 1 Nov., 8 Nov. 1889; numerous other telegrams or letters to Drummond are copied into Fielding's letterbooks, but are now illegible.

15 Grand Council Minutes, 1 Apr. 1887

16 Reilly 'Provincial Workmen's Association' 62–3; W.S.A. Martin 'A Study of Legislation Designed to Foster Industrial Peace in the Common Law Jurisdictions of Canada' (PHD thesis, University of Toronto 1954) 3, 99–100

17 Grand Council Minutes, 1 Apr. 1887 (report of grand secretary)

18 J. Cameron *The Pictonian Colliers* (Kentville, NS: Kentville Publishing Co. 1979), 48–51, 71, 83; SNS 1886, c. 162; D. Frank 'Class Conflict in the Coal Industry: Cape Breton 1922' in G.S. Kealey and P. Warrian, ed *Essays in Canadian Working Class History* (Toronto: McClelland and Stewart 1976) 163, 169

19 Grand Council Minutes, 1 Apr. 1887. Coal miners' wages were based on their daily production, but the rate varied depending on the kind of work being done, the quality of the coal, and the difficulties peculiar to the workplace – for example, excessive water or a very narrow coal seam. See McKay 'Cumberland Coalfields' 729–39.

20 JHA 10 Mar. 1887; *Trades Journal* 27 Apr. 1887

21 *Trades Journal* 18 May 1881, 31 Jan. 1883; Grand Council Minutes, 9 Apr. 1886

22 SO 1873, c. 36; Martin 'Study of Legislation' 77–8, 83–4;

23 JHA 20 Apr. 1887; the Mines Arbitration Bill was printed in the *Trades Journal* 27 Apr. 1887. There is no evidence as to what precedents were used. The parallel to the later Industrial Disputes Investigation Act, drafted by William Lyon Mackenzie King, is striking. P. Craven, in his study of the IDIA (at 143), mentions the Mines Arbitration Act but does not cite it as a source of inspiration for King.

24 JHA 1887, 2 and 3 May; Martin 'Study of Legislation' 103–6; *Morning Herald* 2 and 3 May 1887

25 *Trades Journal* 11 May 1887; *Morning Herald* 3 May 1887

26 *Morning Herald* 4 May 1887

27 *Trades Journal* 4 May 1887

28 Ibid. 18 May 1887

29 Ibid. 4 May 1887

30 Ibid. 11 May 1887

31 Reilly 'Provincial Workmen's Association' 66

32 JHA 1888, 23 Feb., 2 Mar.; SNS 1888, c. 3
33 J.R. Mallory *Social Credit and the Federal Power in Canada* (Toronto: University of Toronto Press 1976) 17
34 Royal Commission on the Relations of Labor and Capital, 1889 (Nova Scotia) *Evidence* 273, 337, 343, 346, 350, 351, 364–5, 358, 361, 417, 366
35 *Morning Herald* 4, 10, 11, and 16 April 1888; Martin 'Study of Legislation' 11; J.A. Gemmill *Canadian Parliamentary Guide* (Ottawa: J. Durie 1889) 287–8; Beck *Government of Nova Scotia* 236–7 notes that when Pipe's victory in 1882 ushered in forty-three-years of Liberal rule, the power and prestige of the Legislative Council diminished dramatically and it seldom rejected government bills.
36 Quoted in *Trades Journal* 4 May 1887
37 Grand Council Minutes, 6 Apr. 1889; McKay 'Cumberland Coalfields' 12–25, 739–40; Copy of Agreement Made 9 April 1885 between the Cumberland Railway and Coal Company and Pioneer Lodge #1, PWA, PANS RG21, series A, vol. 13.
38 McKay 'Cumberland Coalfields' 745–52; scientific management is usually taken to be synonymous with 'Taylorism,' the management practices elaborated by Frederick Taylor in *Shop Management* (1903) and *Principles of Scientific Management* (1911). There were precursors to Taylorism in the efficiency drives of the late nineteenth century. See David A. Hounshell *From the American System to Mass Production 1880–1932* (Baltimore: John Hopkins University Press 1984) 249–50; Daniel Nelson *Managers and Workers* (Madison: University of Wisconsin Press 1975) 55–61.
39 *Trades Journal* 12 June 1889
40 Ibid. 19 June 1889, 3, 10, 17, and 31 July 1889; Correspondence and Documents Concerning the Arbitration Between the Cumberland Railway and Coal Company and Pioneer Lodge #1, PWA, PANS RG21, series A, vol. 13
41 Grand Council Minutes, 4 Oct. 1889
42 *Trades Journal* 16 Oct. 1889; Reilly 'Provincial Workmen's Association' 67–70; McKay 'Cumberland Coalfields' 760–1; McKay 'Wisdom, Wile or War' 49–52
43 SNS 1890, c. 7 and c. 8
44 Grand Council Minutes, 29 Sept. 1894, 5 Sept. 1895
45 Ibid. 29 Sept. 1894
46 Victoria Mines Arbitration, Springhill Arbitration, PANS RG21, series A, vol. 13; McKay 'Cumberland Coalfields' 746
47 *Labour Gazette* May 1901, 507–8; Reilly 'Provincial Workmen's Association' 99, 157
48 D. Schwartzman 'Mergers in the Nova Scotia Coalfields: A History of the

Dominion Coal Company 1893–1940' (PHD thesis, University of California 1953) 297; Craven *'Impartial Umpire'* 142–9; Forsey *Trade Unions* 501

49 Craven *'Impartial Umpire'* 194–5, 220–2, 230–1, 277–9, 287–8; SC 1907, c. 20

50 SNS 1903, c. 37, re-enacted RSNS 1923, c. 247; Mines Arbitration Act, SNS 1891, c. 31, re-enacted RSNS 1900, c. 21, amended SNS 1901, c. 30, re-enacted RSNS 1923, c. 248; Industrial Peace Act, SNS 1925, c. 1; *Labour Gazette* Nov. 1903, 412–13, May 1925, 455

51 F.R. Scott 'Federal Jurisdiction over Labour Relations – A New Look' *McGill Law Journal* 6 (1960) 157–9; SC 1925, c. 14; SNS 1926, c. 5; SNS 1971, c. 1; B. Langille 'The Michelin Amendment in Context' *Dalhousie Law Journal* 6 (1981) 526–8

52 *Trades Journal* 27 Apr. 1887; SBC 1893, c. 21; SBC 1894, c. 23; SO 1894, c. 42; Martin 'Study of Legislation' 120–1

53 R.H. Babcock *Gompers in Canada: A Study in American Continentalism before the First World War* (Toronto: University of Toronto Press 1974) 83–97; Craven *'Impartial Umpire'* 121–2, 142–9, 312–13, 316–17; Paul MacEwan *Miners and Steelworkers: Labour in Cape Breton* (Toronto: Samuel Stevens 1976) 19–46, 53–5; McKay 'Cumberland Coalfields' 792–6; Forsey 'Nova Scotia Coal Industry' 19–20, 23

54 Mallory *Social Credit* 30–5, 49 explains the Privy Council decisions on the division of powers within the British North America Act in terms of the conservatism of the judiciary. The law lords were not trying to expand provincial powers at the expense of the federal government, but were trying to curtail government intervention in the economy at whichever level it appeared. On the inefficacy of privative clauses, see J.M. Evans et al. *Administrative Law: Cases, Texts, and Materials* (Toronto: Emond-Montgomery 1984) 528–9.

55 Capitalists' threats to move their money elsewhere are an effective means of keeping state initiatives within the bounds considered acceptable by capital. See H. Collins *Marxism and Law* (London: Clarendon Press 1982), 49.

56 Grand Council Minutes, 9 Apr. 1886; in support of this argument, see Weiler *Reconcilable Differences* 33, 49–55, 64–8, 223–31. Weiler recommended compulsory arbitration for first contract disputes where the employer was stubbornly anti-union and not bargaining in good faith. Although such a provision was included in the labour code enacted in British Columbia after the New Democratic Party victory in 1972, it was used infrequently in Weiler's five years as chairperson of the British Columbia Labour Relations Board. In each instance the union was decertified once the first contract expired. Not strong enough initially to force the employer to the bargaining table, the union was unable to survive.

57 *Trades Journal* 4 May 1887

58 Schwartzman 'Mergers' 37–41, 102–12, 174–7; D. McLeod 'Miners, Mining Men and Mining Reform: Changing the Technology of Nova Scotian Gold Mines and Collieries: 1858–1910' (PHD thesis, University of Toronto 1981) 338–49

59 Because of the adverse physical conditions of the Nova Scotia coalfields, by 1926, when 55 per cent of Nova Scotia coal came from submarine mines, the cost of production per ton was double that in the United States: see R.J. Sacouman 'Underdevelopment and the Structural Origins of Antigonish Movement Co-operatives in Eastern Nova Scotia' in R.J. Brym and R.J. Sacouman, eds *Underdevelopment and Social Movements in Atlantic Canada* (Toronto: New Hogtown Press 1979), 113; F.W. Gray 'Mining Coal under the Sea in Nova Scotia' *Canadian Mining and Metallurgical Bulletin* 182 (June 1927) 638. Cameron *Pictonian Colliers* quotes a mining engineer with international experience who described mining conditions in Pictou County in 1937 as 'the most difficult found in any coal fields known to the writer' (at 296). For an excellent account of the coal miners' struggle to preserve their way of life, see D. Frank 'The Cape Breton Coal Miners, 1917–1926 '(PHD thesis, Dalhousie University 1980).

60 Grand Council Minutes, 4 Oct. 1889

61 In the United States, where populism found expression in a political party and presidential campaigns in 1892 and 1896, the term is more narrowly defined and its manifestations more widely studied than in Canada. I use the term here to mean the whole panoply of reform sentiment that differentiated between the 'interests' and the 'people.' See R. Hann *Farmers Confront Industrialism: Some Historical Perspectives on Ontario Agrarian Movements* 3d ed. (Toronto: New Hogtown Press 1975); Ramsay Cook *The Regenerators: Social Criticism in Late Victorian English Canada* (Toronto: University of Toronto Press 1985); idem 'Henry George and the Poverty of Canadian Progress' Canadian Historical Association *Historical Papers 1977* 142–57; idem 'Tillers and Toilers: The Rise and Fall of Populism in Canada in the 1890s' Canadian Historical Association *Historical Papers 1984* 1–20.

11

From Private Property to Public Resource: The Emergence of Administrative Control of Water in Nova Scotia

JENNIFER NEDELSKY

In 1919 Nova Scotia took charge of the management of its inland water resources in a radical and dramatic way. The Water Act of 1919 simply expropriated basic riparian rights by vesting in the province the 'sole and exclusive right to use, divert and appropriate any and all water.'[1] Water was transferred from private to public ownership without compensation or recourse to the courts.[2] In short, the government of Nova Scotia decided that water resources should no longer be conceived of as private property. Water was now a public resource to be managed by the government, not a private right to be defined and protected by the courts.

To understand this dramatic conceptual and institutional transformation we need to see it in the broad context of the emergence of the regulatory state.[3] The rise of regulation in the first half of the twentieth century was not just an expansion of governmental control but a shift in forms of control and ways of thinking about problems. The Water Act of 1919 is a particularly clear instance of the broader phenomenon: a sphere of activity that had been conceived of in terms of private rights – and thus handled by market transactions overseen, enforced, and adjudicated by the courts – became redefined as a matter of public interest involving the sorts of collective decisions only elected governments are suited to make or to delegate. Like the move to regulation generally, the Water Act reflected a sense of the inadequacy of the courts and the market as means of allocating resources, and a redefinition of the appropriate spheres of public and private decision-making.

In the years between 1880 and 1930 all the Canadian provinces experimented with various forms of regulatory control of natural resources, transportation, and utilities such as telephones, gas, and electricity.[4] But Nova Scotia's Water Act was atypical in its timing and scope. Ontario, for example, passed a series of acts governing water resources, but comprehensive regulatory control was not established until 1957.[5] In 1884 New Brunswick had the foresight to secure public control over some of its water resources by providing that in all future Crown grants a strip of land along certain named rivers should be reserved to the province.[6] This provision, which retained riparian rights for the province, was extended to all rivers and lakes in 1927.[7] But only Nova Scotia handled the widespread problem of competing uses of water by expropriating riparian rights. To understand Nova Scotia's response we need to see the problems it shared with other provinces in light of its particular history.

COMMON LAW AND CONFLICTING USES

In Nova Scotia the period between 1880 and 1920 was one of both important industrial development and disturbing economic decline. The bright hopes of the 1880s, during which Nova Scotia had one of the fastest rates of industrial growth in Canada,[8] gave way to unfavourable shifts in the national and international economies, the exodus of capital, and the loss of local control of manufacturing.[9] As Graeme Wynn puts it, 'By 1914, the [Atlantic] provinces were losing ground in the expanding continental Confederation. Their population grew at barely a fraction of the Canadian rate. Their traditional export industries languished. And they slipped further and further off the pace of manufacturing expansion.[10] Water was central both to the industrial expansion that did take place and to the hopes of stemming the decline. The industrial use of water presented Nova Scotia with conflicts to be resolved and an elusive promise of prosperity.

The productive uses of water were not always compatible with one another, and the courts were increasingly called upon to decide which use had the sanction of law. The cases reveal that the most frequent conflicts were caused by dams, which were used for irrigation, for power, for mills, for storing water to facilitate timber-floating. The dams flooded agricultural land, impeded the floating of timber, backed up water (thereby rendering upstream dams useless), and occasionally washed out, sweeping away the dams of downstream owners. The intensity of some of the conflicts is indicated not only by the fact that they ended up in court, but in stories of dams being torn down in irate and determined assertion of individual private rights.[11] There were also disputes over city water supplies, which drew off water that had been used for industrial purposes, and wharves, which were said to impede navigation.

In most cases the judges faced these new conflicts with only the traditional tools of the common law inherited from England. Riparian rights, the most important part of the common law of water, gave the rights of use, of access, and of flow to individuals whose property abutted water. The use of water, the protection against misuse, and the resolution of conflicting uses were essentially matters of private property rights to be defined and defended in the courts.[12] The legislature supplemented the common law by stipulating a right to float timber,[13] but the courts were the institution that primarily determined the legal uses of water.

In addition to riparian rights, the common law affecting water included prescriptive rights and easements, nuisance, and negligence. These basic concepts had been used and modified in U.S. courts to foster certain kinds of development.[14] In Nova Scotia, however, there is no clear pattern of the courts' trying to encourage or facilitate one use over another. In the decisions one finds no articulation of a policy of water allocation, or of which uses were most important or desirable. In fact, there is little indication that such factors were taken into account. The judges seem to have focused on the details of the particular legal issues before them rather than on the consequences of the decisions. Decisions on the use of Nova Scotia's water resources were made, for example, on the basis of whether a particular water use constituted a quasi-easement rather than on the basis of what would be best for economic development or water conservation. The closest the judges came to a policy of development was to show a certain reluctance to grant injunctions that would permanently shut down an industry. The unwillingness to forge new policy through modifications in the law thus meant that the judiciary implemented the policy implicit in the traditional common law of water rights.[15]

Part of this tacit 'policy' was an absolute regard for private property rights. All the common law doctrines relevant to conflicts over water use – riparian rights, trespass, and nuisance – provided for the strict protection of the individual property owner's rights. One could claim damages for unauthorized physical invasion of one's property whether any actual damage was done or not. Damages and an injunction could be granted for changes in the quantity or quality of the water that passed one's land without additional proof of injury. The same remedies were available for any interference with the reasonable enjoyment of one's property, which included freedom from foul odours. That the defendant had taken reasonable care in his or her activities was no defence to any of these actions.

In its strictest form, the doctrine of riparian rights accorded owners the right to the water flowing past their land undiminished in quantity or quality. Taken literally, this right would have virtually precluded any upstream industrial activity: most commercial uses would violate strict common law rights in some way – by flooding property, discharging effluent, landing logs on banks, or diverting or backing up water. The traditional property rights may thus be seen as having a built-in anti-developmental bias. But the doctrine of riparian rights was modified, first in the United States and then in England, by allowing for some interference with water flow if the defendant's use was 'reasonable,' and by adding the requirement of 'material' or 'sensible' injury.[16] These vague terms offered great potential for flexible interpretation. Nova Scotia courts, however, seem not to have been inclined to take advantage of the modifications. In at least one case where the flow of water had been diverted and diminished, the court held that such interference with riparian rights was illegal even without proof of injury.[17] However, the judge refused an injunction, saying that 'the way should be left open for a friendly adjustment ... between the two companies before invoking the last drastic remedy.'[18] The plaintiff, having won the suit, was now, of course, in a much better bargaining position.

One finds the same general protective approach to traditional property rights in cases involving early statutory interventions in water use. For example, in 1913 plaintiffs Miller and Thomson claimed damages for trespassing against the Halifax Power Company, whose act of incorporation granted it the power to divert water, to flood lands, and even to expropriate.[19] The court responded with the common law maxim that it is never presumed to be the intention of the legislature to infringe on private rights, and that those statutes which explicitly do so will be strictly construed. In this case the powers granted were both clear and broad, but the court found other grounds for protecting traditional rights. The expropriation was illegal because it interfered with the public right of flotation, and the governor in council did not have the power to authorize such an interference.

The possible exception to the courts' strict interpretation of riparian rights arose with respect to pollution. I found only two reported cases dealing with water quality rather than quantity, and in neither case were the courts particularly sympathetic to the complainant. In *McCann* v. *Pidgeon*, which was decided in 1901, the plaintiff alleged pollution of his stream by run-off from the defendant's cesspool. In denying the plaintiff any remedy the court clearly took into account the consequences of allowing such claims: 'It is extremely probable that this overflow ... or a portion of it, finally reached the stream, but to carry plaintiff's contention to its legitimate conclusion, no cesspools could be constructed anywhere, as the tendency of the overflow from them undoubtedly would be to pollute to a greater of less degree the streams and wells in their vicinity.'[20] I think there is little doubt that the doctrines of nuisance and riparian rights (the plaintiff sued in both alternatively) could have been interpreted to find such pollution an unlawful invasion of rights. But Mr Justice Ritchie was clearly not prepared to declare illegal a well-established, widespread, and probably necessary practice for the sake of a strict view of a right to pure water.

In the second case, *Ball* v. *The Sydney and Louisburg Railway Co.*, the plaintiff sued a railroad (always a risky proposition during this period) for polluting his stream.[21] The court did not find that there was no pollution, but found that it occurred, 'if at all,' only during rainstorms and was thus only a temporary and occasional inconvenience. At the trial a jury had awarded $250 in damages; the appeal court decided that there was no evidence on which the jury could appraise the damage, and ordered a new trial. Once again, it seems that it would have been possible for the court to have found the pollution illegal.

Judging from the small number of pollution cases and the courts' handling of them, there does not seem to have been a great deal of concern about water pollution.[22] This impression is confirmed by the reports of the officers who administered the Public Health Act.[23] From its inception in 1888 the Public Health Act contained various clauses empowering its officers to control the quality of the water. There is little indication that the public health officers devoted much time to exercising those powers; the yearly reports hardly mention the subject of water. One report, however, suggests why that might have been the case. Pollution, even where it existed, was not perceived as a problem: 'Our province is singularly well situated for the purpose of successful public health administration. Nearly every community is able to secure near at hand an abundant supply of water from an unpolluted source, so that maintenance of filtration or treatment plants is not required. *Practically every community discharges its sewage directly into tidal waters, rendering sewage treatment works unnecessary*. Thus we are saved the large expenditure which so commonly associates elsewhere with these two very essential services.'[24]

So far, we have seen a picture of a developing industrial economy that placed increasing demands on the water supply. Allocation, not pollution, was the primary concern, and decisions on this important issue were being made by the courts in accordance with traditional common law doctrines and values. To grasp the enormous importance of the courts as policy-makers in this area, we must remember that 90 per cent of the land in the province was privately owned. Nova Scotia had pursued a policy of trying to attract settlers by granting large tracts of land, and until 1910 these grants had not reserved for the province any water, river-beds, or lakes.[25] Nova Scotia thus found itself in the unique position of having let almost all its water resources pass out of the immediate control of the government and into the realm of common law property rights, which still bore traces of their pre-industrial origins.[26] It is against this background that we must view the long history of legislative intervention and intrusion on traditional private rights.

LEGISLATIVE DEVELOPMENT

The timber-floating laws were the first steps in the process of legislative development. In 1884 the first statute allowed a commission to remove obstructions from rivers and to enter upon private land.[27] Compensation was to be made to the owners, by arbitration if necessary. An amendment in 1899 provided for further incursions by giving not just the commission but all persons the right to float logs during freshets, to remove any obstruction, to build any necessary dam, and to have reasonable access to the banks to reclaim logs thrown up.[28] Instead of a provision for compensation, there was a limitation of liability to 'actual damage,' preventing the owner from recovering for simple trespass. Further, there was to be no liability for any except wilful discoloration or impurity of the water caused by floating, which would otherwise have been a violation of riparian rights. In addition, dams could be built to retain water necessary for running mills. But the final section stated that nothing in the act should 'be construed to authorize any damage to riparian proprietors or other parties by reason of backflowage thereof.'[29] Just one year later, in 1900, that provision was repealed; riparian owners' rights to compensation were limited in this instance as well to actual damage.[30] The legislature thus did not insist that riparian owners suffer uncompensated damage at the hands of timber-drivers and mill operators. But the land owners were not to be allowed to impede these important economic activities by standing on the absolute rights provided by the common law.

The legislature also decided that another industrial enterprise needed immunity from the citizens' power to demand their common law rights to reasonably clean air and water. As of 1916, any person desiring to carry on milling, mining, smelting, or refining could apply to the governor in council to be covered by the Act to Encourage and Promote Smelting and Refining in the Province of Nova Scotia.[31] Once covered, the company or person was required to carry out the operation with due care and to take 'such precautions as may be reasonably and commercially possible to prevent or minimize damages: No action for injunction or indictment shall lie at the suit of the crown or any private person or corporation.' As if that were not enough, the companies were to be protected against the possibility that an overly sympathetic jury might see to it that the damages were fully satisfactory: all questions arising under the act were to be tried without a jury.[32] This act is still in force in identical form.[33]

The courts' position on nuisance law may help to explain legislative limits on common law property rights. Courts in Ontario and Nova Scotia had generally allowed plaintiffs the strict protection of the traditional law of nuisance; the judges were considerably less willing than their English and American counterparts to modify this area of the law in order to foster industrial development.[34] Perhaps the legislation was introduced because there was a general concern that the courts were not willing to balance the economic importance of industry against the common law rights of individuals. The new legislation made sure that the courts did not shut down industries because of pollution. But, like the timber acts, the act to encourage smelting did not prevent the recovery of damages, although the requirement that only 'commercially possible' precautions be taken may have virtually precluded recovery.

The justification of the act in the House of Assembly linked the limitation of liability to the control the government could exercise over the location and selection of enterprises to be covered; the purpose of the act was 'to insure *bona fides* and that a proper location be selected before such enterprises be allowed to go on' and to 'relieve a company from liability to injunction after it received approval of the government.' It was also pointed out that such protection of industry was not novel, since some companies already had exemptions from injunctions in their charters.[35]

Both the Timber Act and the Smelting Act limited private suits and thus took certain decisions about water policy out of the hands of the courts. The same pattern was ultimately followed to a dramatic extent in the 1919 Water Act. But the chief reason for the passage of this act does not seem to have been that common law action had significantly hindered productive development of water; rather, the act grew out of a long controversy over the control and development of water power, which by 1914 had become a major issue in the Nova Scotia legislature.

The events that brought the issue to a head are part of a complicated and fascinating tale of early corporate mergers.[36] For present purposes, however, a bare outline is sufficient. The Nova Scotia Power and Pulp Company was granted a charter with immense powers to develop hydro power on the Gaspereau River. The company, which was owned by Montreal capitalists, wanted to take over the very successful Halifax Electric Tramway, which could absorb power from the development and provide close to half a million dollars to pay dividends and interest on the large number of stocks and bonds the owners planned to float. The takeover produced a bitter struggle, with the Halifax city council trying to retain municipal control of the tramway. In the end, the Montreal-based group succeeded. Incorporating as the Nova Scotia Tramway and Power Company, it made an estimated gross profit of over a million dollars in transfers of stocks and bonds. The Montrealers then sold controlling interests to a group of Americans in 1919 'for a further undisclosed profit.'[37]

All of this did nothing for the productive use of Nova Scotia waters. 'The ostensible purpose of the merger was to permit the development of hydroelectricity on the Gaspereau and the distribution of cheaper light and power within the city of Halifax. But nothing came of that ... the funds raised for that purpose were promptly channelled out of Nova Scotia.'[38] This experience was unfortunately typical of an emerging pattern: entrepreneurs from outside Nova Scotia bought control of local industry, maximized their profits instead of developing the industry, and ultimately took the capital out of Nova Scotia.[39]

The controversy over the merger and its aftermath brought renewed demands for public ownership and for a comprehensive water-power policy preferably through an agency modelled on the Ontario Hydro-Electric Commission.[40] Everyone agreed that cheaper power for manufacturing purposes was essential to make Nova Scotia's industries competitive, which was necessary if Nova Scotia's economic decline was to be halted. Water-power seemed the best hope. The disagreement was about whether the water-power should be developed by private enterprise or by the government. The Tories argued that there was no coherent policy, that there was insufficient information on Nova Scotia's resources, and that in the meantime water-power was passing piece by piece into the hands of private corporations, which were given 'vast and almost unlimited powers.'[41] The Liberal government resisted, arguing that Ontario was a special case because of Niagara Falls and that the government could not manage and develop Nova Scotia's many small sources of water-power. A few months later, however, the Liberals apparently agreed that ad hoc charters to private companies were not achieving the desired end and that some general policy was needed. A bill was introduced which set up the Nova Scotia Water Power Commission.[42]

It is clear from the preamble to the bill that the primary objective was the maximization of the productive use of water. Water-power was to be developed and rules made to 'reconcile the interests of agriculture, of industrial and lumbering pursuits, and of the forests, with respect for the rights of private property.' As it turned out, these interests were not all found to be compatible with traditional private property. The commission was instructed to advise whether the reconciliation would be best achieved by changes in the existing laws. The preamble also made clear that radical measures might be necessary: the commissioners were to 'consider and recommend rules for the expropriation of real property and riparian rights necessary for the establishment of factories and power plants.'[43] The basic priority of industrial development was clear. There were only a few, seemingly peripheral, references to conservation, and no mention of pollution as such – this despite the fact that in 1911 a federal commission had found pollution to be a serious and neglected problem.[44] The federal commission suggested that the apparent indifference resulted from a 'misapprehension': 'The statement has been made that Nova Scotia has a surplus of inland water, and from this it has been inferred that the conservation of this resource was therefore not a matter of pressing concern. The fact was lost sight of that, in a large portion of the Province, the depth of the soil is not great and, instead of the water being stored as underground water, it lies exposed on the surface of the earth.' The federal commission concluded that 'no effort should be spared to prevent the pollution of waters by the improper disposal of domestic sewage and industrial wastes.'[45] Although the Nova Scotia Water and Power Commission co-operated from the start with the Dominion Water Power Branch, there is little evidence that the federal concern with pollution changed the priorities of the provincial body.

With the assistance of a federal engineer, the Water Power Commission set about gathering extensive information on all the potential sources of water-power in the province. As part of their mandate the commissioners took note of conflicting water uses, particularly the relation of power development to lumbering and fishing. They reported that 'the practice, so prevalent in the past, of dumping sawdust and general saw-mill refuse in the natural harbours or stretches of river has no doubt caused serious injury to harbour facilities and the fishing industry. The fishing industry has further been hampered in some cases by lack of proper fishways in the lumbering dams.' For each of the rivers studied the commissioners listed the accommodations that would have to be made for logging and fishing. They even noted in one case that on Indian River 'certain interests having fishing rights have bitterly opposed any power scheme, on the grounds that it would spoil the fishery.' But their conclusion was not that power should not be developed; they merely noted that any case it would seem necessary to provide proper fishways in any dams built on these rivers.'[46] It seems clear that although fishing was always mentioned, industrial development was to take priority. The commission's first report optimistically concluded with what it saw as good news – Nova Scotia had sites well suited to industrial needs, and there was apparently a good opportunity for the development of an extensive pulp and paper industry.[47]

By 1918 the Water Power Commission was ready with its recommendations for law reform. The stated objectives of the resulting legislation were to encourage the most efficient development of water power, to protect the public from 'worthless power schemes,' 'ill designed plants and dams,' and 'monopolistic control,' and 'to in all ways have in view the fullest conservation of the water resources.'[48] The act seems to have been a response to the Nova Scotia Tramways fiasco, and in particular it seems to have been an effort to keep control of water resources within Nova Scotia. The commission presumably came to the plausible conclusion that the only way to ensure local control was to remove water from the realm of unregulated market transactions.

The act can be seen as a preliminary step towards the drastic action of the 1919 Water Act. The right to use all watercourses was vested in the Crown, except 'the right of every riparian proprietor to the use of water for domestic purposes' (section 5). This was a major exception, since 'domestic purposes' included the workings of railways or factories by steam (section 2). All grants were to be retroactively construed as having reserved to the Crown all watercourses and beds of all watercourses. In case there was any doubt left in the minds of judges that these provisions would fundamentally change existing riparian rights, it was further stated that 'the grant shall be construed accordingly, and not in accordance with the rules of the English Common Law' (section 5). There was also another exception to the expropriation power: the act did not apply to persons who, before the act, had developed water-power or used water for other purposes when they had a legal right to do so.[49] The commission could still exercise control over those users; it could require such water-power to be developed 'to the fullest possible extent or make other use of said water' (section 6(1)). The act also authorized the governor in council to make regulations governing the use, diversions, and damming of water, for the taking of Crown or private lands, and for the fixing of compensation to be paid to the owners of lands taken, used, or injuriously affected (section 8). This was a broad definition of what was compensable. The scope of the expropriation was especially large, however, since the powers could be transferred to private companies. The commissioners could grant authorized enterprises the power to 'take, acquire, and use the requisite lands, providing just compensation is paid' (section 9). There were, not surprisingly, no provisions for public hearings, but there was at least some requirement of public scrutiny: all regulations had to be laid before the legislature.

It is not clear whether the 1918 act was intended as an interim measure, but in the following year it was replaced by two new acts. The Power Commission Act was long and detailed; it covered all aspects of the development, sale, and transmission of power, and granted powers of expropriation extending to plants and machinery as well as land and water.[50] It was said to be modelled on the act that created the publicly owned Ontario Hydro-Electric Commission and thus to require a companion Water Act,[51] 'so that the commission idea might be made more applicable to the situation existing in the province.'[52] The Water Act, in the words of the *Halifax Herald*, 'declare[d] that the government of Nova Scotia has power to divert and appropriate any water at any time in any water course no matter by what grant.'[53] This description was accurate, except that section 2(b) of the Water Act excluded small rivulets or brooks unsuitable for milling, mechanical, or power purposes. This simple and sweeping act gave rise to a heated debate in the legislature, portions of which were reported in the local newspapers. The *Herald* headline read, 'A Bill before the Legislature That Takes from the Owners the Water Powers of Nova Scotia and Can Take Also Other Valuable Property.'

The real point of objection was not public ownership, but that there was no provision for compensation in the Water Act and no exception for investment in existing power developments. The attorney general, who introduced the bill, argued lamely that it was not an expropriation measure but simply a 'vesting bill,' and that it had to do only with unused waters.[54] This was clearly not the case, although those who had lawfully used water when the act was passed were to be 'entitled to be authorized by the Governor-in-Council to use such water.' That entitlement, however, was subject to 'such terms and conditions as the Governor-in-Council deems just.' This did not satisfy the critics in the House or the newspaper editorialists, but their dissatisfaction was apparently not widely or vocally shared. As the *Halifax Herald* put it, 'What is surprising is that those who now own the beds of rivers, many of them at a very heavy cost, and those who have mills and dams along rivers for their business are so VERY QUIET ... the mill owners and lumber men evidently say about protesting, "WHAT'S THE USE?" '[55]

Perhaps the reason for the lack of response was not apathy, but sympathy with a scheme that empowered the government to control the development of water resources in the interests of Nova Scotians. Unregulated market transactions had, after all, brought the Nova Scotia Tramways buy-out, which had hardly helped local entrepreneurs and which still left water-power undeveloped. The various competing interests may have decided that they were willing to forfeit their private property rights and take their chances with 'party government,' which they could at least lobby directly.[56] And there may have been a sense that it was appropriate to vest water rights in the province, since only the provincial government would have sufficient power to protect the people against 'worthless power schemes' and 'monopolistic control.' By 1919 it may have seemed clear that the combination of common law and private enterprise had not provided an adequate basis for developing Nova Scotia's water resources. If that development could best be furthered by a legal framework based on public control, then the loss of private rights to water was an acceptable price to pay. Or perhaps the general understanding was that it was appropriate for the legislature to redefine property rights when the members thought it was in the public interest. Most Nova Scotians may not have invested property rights with the sanctity the critics and the courts thought appropriate.[57]

EXCLUDING THE COURTS

If the legislature and the population at large were prepared to take an instrumental approach to traditional rights, the courts were not. They remained true to their common law tradition. In 1920 the courts heard two cases in which defendants had violated traditional property rights; both pleaded licence under the 1919 legislation and argued that the plaintiffs had no right to a remedy in court. In one case, *Cook* v. *Davison Lumber*, the court found that the defendant had no right to flood the plaintiff's land even though the dam in question was authorized under the Water Act. The court's position was the classic one: when legislation 'interferes with or takes away private rights of property [it] will, as a matter of course, be strictly construed.'[58] The second case, *Stanford* v. *Imperial Oil*, arose over conflicting licences.[59] Stanford's licence was granted under section 4(1) of the Water Act, which entitled those using the water when the act was passed to continue to do so. The licence of the defendant, Imperial Oil, was granted under section 4(2), which was 'subject to the provisions of s. 4(1).' In giving judgment for the plaintiff, the court deduced from this wording that '[i]t was evidently the intention of the legislature, while assuming control of water rights, to preserve as far as possible, the rights of all persons outstanding on the date of the act.'[60] In both cases the courts clearly stated that the plaintiffs' rights to a remedy at common law had been supplemented but not removed.

The legislature had good reason to worry that these cases would be typical of the courts' response to what they would see as the infringement of traditional common law rights and the usurpation of traditional judicial roles. In the related area of nuisance law, the Nova Scotia courts, like those of Ontario, showed a strong tendency to interpret and protect common law rights in the traditional fashion, with little scope for the overt balancing of rights against some conception of the public good. And Ontario had a history of legislation whose modifications of common law water rights were narrowly interpreted by the courts. The judiciary consistently displayed 'their continuing respect for established property rights.'[61]

The Nova Scotia legislature, like that of Ontario , felt no such constraints. In what seems to be characteristic Canadian fashion, the legislature perceived its role with respect to rights very differently from the courts.[62] The legislature responded immediately to the *Cook* and *Stanford* cases by ensuring that the judiciary's different perception would not intrude on the exclusive control of the cabinet and commissioners over water policy. The legislature removed the protection for previously vested rights which the plaintiff Stanford had relied on. Section 4(2) of the Water Act was amended to read 'notwithstanding provision for previous users, the Governor-in-Council may authorize any water use.' Moreover, compensation was available only at the discretion of the governor in Council, who could fix the amount or appoint a judge of the Supreme Court to do so. The courts were absolutely excluded: 'no action, process or proceeding whatsoever shall be commenced or issued in any court or before any tribunal by or against any person authorized by the Governor-in-Council to use such water course or any water therein conditionally or otherwise.'[63]

The Power Commission Act had already provided that no action could be brought against the commission without the consent of the attorney general,[64] but additional modifications were considered necessary. The original act had said that all matters of compensation would be dealt with in the manner prescribed by the Expropriation Act.[65] In 1920 the Power Commission Act set out its own provisions, leaving no terms to the discretion of a court. There was to be compensation only for damages 'beyond any advantage' the owner might derive from the enterprise.[66] Further, compensation could be settled in court, but only for incidental damage, not for the loss of water use itself: '[t]he court shall not allow compensation for the taking or injurious affecting by the commission of any water course, but the compensation for the same shall be fixed and determined by the Governor-in-Council.' This made sense, of course, since all water rights were now vested in the province. With the exception of such limited compensation suits, there was to be no other action in court in connection with any aspect of the commission's activities.[67] Finally, the 1920 act made it clear that power development was to have absolute priority: section 15(9) stated that regardless of any authorization under the Water Act, the governor in council could authorize exclusive use for the purposes of the Power Commission and no damages or compensation could be claimed except 'such amount, if any, as may be fixed and determined by the Governor-in-Council.' The language and intention of the legislation was clear; water resources were no longer to be treated as private property rights that citizens could protect in court. The government did not want its policy interfered with by common law notions of due process and vested rights.

The courts were not entirely willing to accept this ouster. They expressed their last major resistance in 1926 in the case of *Hanf* v. *Yarmouth Light and Power*.[68] The defendant's dam had flooded the plaintiff's meadow, and the defence offered was that the court had no jurisdiction by virtue of the 1920 amendment. The governor in council had not chosen to exercise his discretion to grant compensation. The trial judge decried the statute as obviously unjust and a 'sorry substitute for a man's common law rights,'[69] but reluctantly agreed that he had no jurisdiction to award damages for any time after authorization had been given under the Water Act. The appeal court judges, however, were more subtle and ingenious in their statutory interpretation. Mellish J found that the Water Act did vest all watercourses in the Crown 'with appalling directness,' but that the provisions of the act did not extend to the flooding of land, although the flooding was clearly the necessary result of the authorized dam. To accept the defendant's contention that no damage resulting from his licensed activities was redressable in court would, according to Harris be 'to confiscate private property and rights by implication, and to license defendant to commit wholesale acts of trespass without compensation; and it is clear, I think, that such an interpretation cannot be adopted by any court.'[70] The plaintiff was awarded nine hundred dollars in damages and an injunction.

This victory proved to be anomalous. Although the case was never overturned, it disappeared from sight for years. Citizens, their lawyers, and the judiciary apparently came to accept the legislative attempt to prevent individuals from using the courts to claim redress for the pollution or misuse of water. *Hanf* was not cited in the reported cases until the 1970s, when the Supreme Court of Nova Scotia once again showed a willingness to protect private claims to water.[71]

AFTERMATH AND IMPLICATIONS

The history of the Water Act of 1919 provides a glimpse into the pattern of economic development in Nova Scotia that formed the context of the act. The act is an unusual example of a common practice: the use of public resources to foster private development in the public interest. It is also an example of the ways in which a focus on economic development subsumes other values – in this case, water conservation and purity. Finally, the history of the Water Act invites a comparison of the advantages and disadvantages of the administrative system it established with those of the common law it displaced. The conclusion looks at each of these points in turn.

If the Nova Scotia Tramways episode was the impetus for the passage of the Water Act of 1919, it is worth noting that the offending company reaped the benefits to the move to public ownership and development: 'Far from viewing public enterprise as a threat, the private company's directors were delighted to purchase public power; it freed them from the need to raise at least $700,000 to expand capacity at a time when the company was not earning enough to pay the dividends on its stock ... the taxpayers of Nova Scotia underwrote the capital costs of a new generating station, because the government considered it necessary to supply the infrastructure in the hope of promoting economic development.'[72]

Once the provincial power commission began building a power station, the needs became reciprocal: the commission needed a customer for its power and entered into a long-term contract with Nova Scotia Tramways that created an intertwining of public and private enterprise.[73]

The focus on facilitating economic development that originally shaped the Water Act continued to be reflected in the legislation that governed Nova Scotia's water resources. Despite some startling experiences with water contamination (in Halifax, 'eels began slithering out of the taps in 1905'),[74] it was not until 1962 that water legislation in Nova Scotia shifted from a focus on facilitating development to a preventive approach to pollution control.[75]

It seems clear that the primary concern behind the Water Act of 1919 was not the institutional competence of the courts, but economic development, and the judgment that it would be best fostered by vesting water rights in the province rather than in individual property owners. But the transformation of water from a private to a public resource had important consequences for the allocation of decision-making power. Administrative control over water replaced not only private decision-making and exchange, but judicial control. Before the Water Act was passed, the courts determined what constituted legitimate use and transactions. The history of Nova Scotia water law thus offers insights into the role of the courts and the nature of the common law in Canada.

Even in recent history, long after the initial attempt to exclude them, the courts have continued to display their inclination to protect traditional private rights. In the early 1970s two parties successfully used the old exception of small rivulets or brooks to bring an action as riparian owners,[76] and the legislature once again responded by removing the exception.[77]

As amended, the Water Act covered 'water sources of almost every conceivable description.'[78] Nevertheless, the Supreme Court upheld a private action for damages for the pollution of ground water despite the defendant's argument that the plaintiff had no cause of action since all water rights are vested in the province. Sixty years after the Act was passed, the court still referred to it in disparaging terms and gave it the narrowest possible construction: '[I]t only proscribes proceedings against persons actually authorized by the Minister,' which the defendant was not.[79] The court concluded, 'It will be readily apparent that a very great number of persons in this province make continuous use of natural sources of water without specific authorization under the *Water Act* and, however far-reaching and heavy-handed the provincial statute may be, it is not reasonable to suppose that the legislature intended, in the absence of any Crown use or authorization, to assume the burden of redressing wrongs among private individuals *inter se* by cutting off ancient rights of private recourse against those who would pollute or contaminate a water supply of actual use.'[80] This decision in no way interfered with the government's exclusive power to authorize the use of water. But the court did acknowledge the fact of extensive unauthorized use, and claimed the power to protect traditional common law rights against unauthorized interference.

This focus on traditional private rights reflects the individualistic conception of rights that is basic to the common law. But in water law this individualism exists in a complex context that reveals the richness of common law concepts. In important respects, private rights in water were held subject both to the public interest (for example, navigation)[81] and to the private rights of other riparian owners. Water law is one of the few areas of property law that had built into it the famous Lockean proviso that there be 'enough and as good' left over for others.[82] The common law concept that rights to water were in many cases intrinsically both public and private provides a basis for preventing individuals from asserting rights in complete disregard of the general welfare, and for preventing large-scale enterprises from trampling on individual rights in the name of the public interest. In fact, neither intrusion has consistently been prevented in common law jurisdictions, although it is the former that is now commonly cited as a problem. It may be that in Canada, in contrast to the United States, a strict interpretation of riparian rights tended to give greater scope to individual rights than to the public welfare.[83]

The history of the Water Act gives us a sense of the complex relation between rights and policy, and between individual and collective values in Canadian common law. This history also points to the political function that self-proclaimed 'apolitical' courts can serve. First, although there are only a few cases involved, they fit the emerging picture of Canadian courts as vigilant protectors of traditional rights, with little inclination to modify those rights in accordance with some conception of public policy.[84] This disinclination distinguishes them in important ways from their American counterparts. It suggests that the reigning conception of judicial decision-making and perhaps the very meaning of 'rights' was different in the United States and Canada. But the protective stance towards traditional rights does not mean that Canadian judicial decisions were free of policy content. It means that the policies the courts in fact implemented were those embedded in the rules they applied; that is, they fostered old policy in the name of timeless rights. Despite the obvious disadvantages of this form of policy implementation (not least of which is the tacit denial of its existence), there are advantages to the courts that a stark instance of their exclusion, such as the Water Act, can help us to see.

The courts can provide a forum wherein the voices of the relatively powerless can be heard – if they can link their claims to traditional rights and if they can get over the financial hurdle of access to the courts. If these conditions are met, even a minority of one can make her claim heard in a public fashion. And with the courts' inclination to protect individual rights, she may prevail over powerful interests that would have swamped her in any other forum.

Of course, the common law and judicial practices do not exist in a vacuum, immune from power. They reflect (as well as shape) the allocation of power in society. But power makes itself felt very differently in the courts than in the legislature or in market transactions. For example, while basic terms of the common law such as property rights may reflect the power and importance of landed property in an earlier era, the courts – particularly Canadian courts – may be relatively indifferent to the economic power of the parties before them. They may even be relatively indifferent to widely shared notions of what 'economic progress' requires. Power is present in the terms of the common law and is given effect by judicial decisions, but the judicial implementation of power is different from that wielded in the overtly political contests of the legislature or the economic battles of the marketplace.

The Nova Scotia Water Act offers an opportunity, which I can only point to here, to compare the sources and effects of power under different structures of decision-making. The Water Act seems to have been a deliberate effort by the Assembly to take decisions affecting water resources out of the hands of private citizens, and more particularly to insulate those decisions from the forces of the market. The question the subsequent history invites us to answer is whether the interplay of competing sources of power in the political realm of the cabinet and commission worked to promote the interests of Nova Scotians better than the interplay in the market. Perhaps in the end those with effective power were very much the same in both arenas. If that was the case, then the Water Act may have brought few advantages and caused the loss of an alternative forum for citizens to assert private rights either to protect their own interests or to focus attention on the collective significance of those interests.

The significance of this loss is made clearer when we realize that the highly individualistic values of the common law turn out to overlap with important collective values, such as freedom from pollution. Private citizens' suits based on traditional riparian rights can be a means of challenging the balance between development and environmental degradation that the political channels have arrived at. The Water Act's exclusion of the courts thus reminds us of Willard Hurst's famous argument that the common law and the market provide for a decentralization of decision-making.[85] Even if one tempers his view with a recognition of the unequal power in those decisions, the basic insight remains.

Finally, the Water Act of 1919 reminds us of the possibility of the basic transformations even in very old values and institutions. In particular, it suggests a striking flexibility with respect to private property, and thus an important difference between the legal and political traditions of the United States and Canada. From an American perspective, the ease with which the Nova Scotia legislature accomplished the abolition of a whole class of private property rights is astonishing.[86] The history of the Water Act is a testimony both to the possibility of dramatic change and to the complicated consequences that flow from basic transformations in conceptual and institutional structures.

NOTES

This work was supported by the Institute for Resource and Environmental Studies, Dalhousie University. The legal training that formed the basis for this research was made possible through a Killam post-doctoral fellowship at the Faculty of Law, Dalhousie University, 1977–8.

1 SNS 1919, c. 5, s. 3. The only exception was 'small rivulets or brooks unsuitable for milling, mechanical or power purposes' in s. 2(b). Riparian rights are the rights of owners of property abutting water. The basic rights are the rights of access to the water, the right to use the water, the right to have the water remain undiminished in quantity and quality, and rights of accretion and drainage. All of these rights flow from ownership of the land, not from ownership of the water itself. Riparian rights do not entitle the landowner to own the water, but to use, enjoy, and benefit from it. Because of this special 'non-ownership' quality of riparian rights, it is not clear that they are completely eliminated by the provincial expropriation. Of course, the rights vested in the province to use, divert, and expropriate no longer belong to riparian owners, and riparian rights to quantity and quality cannot be asserted in the face of authorized use. (The 1920 amendment [SNS 1920, c. 75] prevented the bringing of an action against authorized users.) The extent to which riparian rights can be asserted as against unauthorized use still remains uncertain.

2 SNS 1920, c. 75
3 For a descriptive overview, see C.D. Baggeley *The Emergence of the Regulatory State in Canada, 1867–1939* Technical Report no. 15 (Ottawa: Economic Council of Canada 1981).
4 C. Armstrong and H.V. Nelles *Monopoly's Moment: The Organization and Regulation of Canadian Utilities, 1830–1930* (Toronto: University of Toronto Press 1986)
5 See J. Benedickson 'Private Rights and Public Purposes in the Lakes, Rivers, and Streams of Ontario 1870–1930' in D.H. Flaherty, ed. *Essays in the History of Canadian Law* vol. 2 (Toronto: The Osgoode Society 1983).
6 47 Vict., c. 7 (NB)
7 RSNB 1927, c. 30
8 'In the first years of [the National Policy's] operation the Maritimes experienced a dramatic growth in manufacturing potential, a growth often obscured by the stagnation of both the staple industries and population growth. ... This development was so significant that between 1881 and 1891 the industrial growth rate of Nova Scotia outstripped all other provinces in eastern Canada': T.W.Acheson 'The National Policy and the Industrialization of the Maritimes, 1880–1910' *Acadiensis* 1 (1972) 3.
9 See G. Wynn 'The Maritimes: The Geography of Fragmentation and Underdevelopment' in L.D. McCann, ed. *Heartland and Hinterland: A Geography of Canada* (Toronto: Prentice-Hall 1982), especially 168–78; Acheson 'National Policy'; and J.G. Reid *Six Crucial Decades: Times of Change in the History of the Maritimes* (Halifax: Nimbus Publishing 1987) chapter 6.
10 Wynn 'The Maritimes' 174
11 Such 'self-help' was legal in certain instances. There are old common law rules governing the circumstances in which one may 'abate a nuisance' oneself rather than having to seek recourse from the courts. See, for example, *Wood* v. *Esson* (1883) 9 SCR 239, in which the defendant removed the piles for an extension of a wharf that interfered with his ability to dock at his own neighbouring wharf. The builder of the piles brought action for trespass and failed, 'the Supreme Court of Canada holding that the piles constituted an obstruction to navigation causing special damages to the defendant': G.V. La Forest and Associates *Water Law in Canada: The Atlantic Provinces* (Ottawa: Information Canada 1973) 237.
12 The right of navigation was, however, a public right with which private rights could not interfere.
13 By SNS 1899, c. 19. The courts themselves undertook this addition in New Brunswick.
14 See M. Horwitz *The Transformation of American Law* (Cambridge: Harvard University Press 1977).

15 I have also found this to be the case in nuisance Law. The unwillingness to use the common law to forge new policy seems characteristic of the Canadian judiciary at the turn of the century: see Nedelsky 'Judicial Conservatism in an Age of Innovation: Comparative Perspectives on the Canadian Nuisance Law, 1880–1930' in D.H. Flaherty (ed.) *Essays in the History of Canadian Law* vol. 1 (Toronto: The Osgoode Society 1981).

16 J. Later 'The Common Law Background of the Riparian Doctrine' *Missouri Law Review* 28 (1963) 60

17 *Bras D'Or Lime Co.* v. *Dominion Iron and Steel Co.* (1911) 9 ELR 348

18 A strict insistence on the traditional definitions of common rights when damages were at stake, combined with a reluctance to grant injunctions, is consistent with my findings on nuisance law. Courts frequently granted stays of injunctions (sometimes with the option of requests for additional stays) and showed a willingness to consider the economic consequences of injunctions, which amounted to modifications of traditional rights. Of course, the courts did sometimes grant injunctions, but their stance towards injunctions did not as consistently reflect an unmodified insistence on protecting traditional rights. The famous *KVP* case is, of course, from a much later era: *KVP Co. Ltd* v. *McKie* [1949] SCR 698. See also Nedelsky 'Judicial Conservatism.'

19 *Miller* v. *Halifax Power Co.* (1913) 13 ELR 394. The defendant company claimed the right to expropriate under its act of incorporation: SNS 1911, c. 113.

20 (1901) 40 NSR 356, at 358

21 *Ball* v. *The Sydney and Louisbourg Railway Co.* (1913) 46 NSR 507, at 509

22 This is always somewhat risky. First, it is difficult to be certain that one has found all cases reported (even after consulting indexes, the *Canadian Abridgement*, and case references). More important, the cases reported are primarily appeal cases (only the appeal court had an official reporter), selected because they contained some significant point of law. It is difficult to know how representative the reported appeal decisions are of what was routinely taking place in trial courts.

23 SNS 1918, c. 9

24 Annual Report of the Public Health Officer, *JHA* 1917 (emphasis added)

25 The Crown Lands Act (SNS 1900, c. 4) allowed the governor in council to reserve lands for protecting and regulating water and for developing water-power. The governor in council could also lease Crown land for developing water-power and lease the privilege of placing dams or floating timber. But as was made absolutely clear in a 1915 written opinion of the deputy attorney general of Nova Scotia, '[t]hese provisions, of course, only apply to water rights appurtenant to lands held by the Crown': Report

of the Water Power Commission of Nova Scotia for the period ending 30, September 1916, *JHA* 1917.

26 In 1909, 1,448,100 acres remained ungranted in Nova Scotia. By comparison, in New Brunswick between 7,000,000 and 8,000,000 acres were still in the possession of the Crown. New Brunswick had made provision for reserving a strip along named rivers in 1884 (47 Vict., c. 7 (NB), which was extended to all rivers and lakes in 1927 (RSNB 1927, c. 30). This, of course, vested the corresponding riparian rights in the province: Leo G. Denis and Arthur V. White *The Water Powers of Canada* (Ottawa: The Mortimer Co. 1911).

27 RSNS 1884, c. 69

28 SNS 1899, c. 19, ss 1 and 3

29 Ibid. ss 3, 4, 5

30 SNS 1900, c. 33

31 SNS 1916, c. 1

32 Ibid. ss 4, 5, 6, 7

33 RSNS 1967, c. 283

34 See Nedelsky 'Judicial Conservatism'

35 *DHA* 1916, 94

36 This story is set out in detail in C. Armstrong and H.V. Nelles 'Getting Your Way in Nova Scotia: "Tweeking" Halifax, 1909–1917' *Acadiensis* 4 (1975) 105–31. The following account is based on this article.

37 Ibid. 108

38 Ibid.

39 See the references cited in notes 8 and 9 supra.

40 The Tories had first 'raised the question of investigating the sources of power in Nova Scotia and reserving them for the benefit of the people' in 1907. Report of the Nova Scotia Water Power Commission, *JHA* 1917, appendix 30.

41 *DHA* 3 March 1919

42 SNS 1914, c. 8

43 Ibid. ss 1(2), 1(5)

44 In particular, the commission found that 'the deposit of saw-dust, mill refuse, and crusher sand in harbours and inland waters of Nova Scotia is a fruitful source of pollution': *Water Powers of Canada* 197.

45 Quoted ibid. 195, 197

46 Report, *JHA* 1917, appendix 30, 24, 52

47 There was also an additional factor which the Water Power Commission did not take account of. The federal study had pointed out the potential effect on the tourist trade of indiscriminate use of lakes for storage for power or logging. The raised water destroys the shoreline vegetation and plea-

sure seekers are not attracted by a lake or river fringed with five or ten feet of dead and whitened shrubs': Denis and White *Water Powers of Canada* 200. The Nova Scotia Water Power Commission optimistically pointed out how easy it would be to use the many lakes for storage.

48 An Act Respecting Water Power, SNS 1918, c. 13

49 It should be noted that the word 'expropriation' was never used, and these powers were not governed by the Expropriation Act.

50 SNS 1919, c. 6

51 C. 5

52 Attorney General Armstrong, quoted in *Morning Chronicle* 26 Apr. 1919

53 28 Apr. 1919

54 *Morning Chronicle* 29 Apr. 1919. The official debates were not published after 1916; thus, newspapers are the main source for the debates.

55 28 Apr. 1919. Lumbermen were affected because the act declaring the public right to flotation (SNS 1899, c. 19) was repealed. Authorization for floating was now required, although the provisions with respect to liability for damage remained the same.

56 'Is it fair to put the lumbering operators in the power of party government? It might be disastrous': *Halifax Herald* 26 Apr. 1919.

57 See also the concluding paragraph of this essay and the accompanying note on property.

58 (1920) 53 NSR 375, at 378

59 (1920) 54 NSR 106

60 Ibid. at 109

61 See Benedickson 'Private Rights and Public Purposes' at 370–1.

62 See Benedickson's discussion of the role Oliver Mowat played as judge in protecting traditional rights and his arguments as premier in favour of legislation modifying those rights. R.C.B. Risk makes a similar comparison between Sir William R. Meredith's treatment on the bench of cases involving the 'fellow servant rule' and his advocacy of legislation to supplant that common law rule by some form of Workers' Compensation. ' "This Nuisance of Litigation": The Origins of Workers' compensation in Ontario' in Flaherty *Essays in the History of Canadian Law* vol. 2, 456.

63 SNS 1920, c. 75 s. 1(2)

64 SNS 1919, c. 6, s. 28

65 Ibid. s. 15

66 SNS 1920, c. 76, s. 12. Such 'offsetting' of damages by advantages was commonly done by the courts and legislatures in the United States. See Horwitz *Transformation of American Law* and H. Scheiber 'Property Law: Expropriation as Resource Allocation by Government, 1789–1810' in L.M.

Friedman and H.N. Scheiber, eds *American Law and the Constitutional Order* (Cambridge: Harvard University Press 1978).

67 SNS 1920, c. 76, ss 4, 29(a)

68 58 NSR 430

69 Ibid. 431

70 Ibid. 442, 443

71 *Lockwood* v. *Brentwood Park* (1970) 10 DLR (3d) 143; *George* v. *Floyd* (1972) 26 DLR (3d) 339

72 Nelles and Armstrong *Monopoly's Moment* 314

73 See ibid. 302: '[A]n agreement was worked out to sell the public hydroelectricity to Nova Scotia Tramways and Power. Extending over a 30-year period from 1922, this contract prohibited the city from entering into competition and permitted Nova Scotia Tramways and Power to charge whatever rates were necessary to earn an 8 percent return on its investment.'

74 'Apparently the creatures had managed to hurl themselves up and over the intake screens into the reservoirs. With commendable understatement and barely concealed pride, the city engineer reported: "All the eels taken out were large and a great many were washed out through the hydrants, numbers of them being caught in the street sprinkling carts."' Ibid. 31.

75 SNS 1962, c. 54. Even then, the provision that the minister might order any material not to be discharged was hedged with qualifications; if the discharge was approved by any other act, that took precedence. The prevention of pollution still took second place to the encouragement of smelting. Furthermore, the penalty provided for failure to comply with orders under the act was a maximum of $50.83 (section 8(3)) or in default of payment not more than twenty-five days' imprisonment.

76 *Lockwood* v. *Brentwood Park* supra note 71; *George* v. *Floyd* ibid.

77 SNS 1972, c. 58, s. 1(4). One of the judges had virtually recommended such a change.

78 *Corkum* v. *Lohnes* (1979) 38 NSR (2d) 417

79 Ibid. 425. This is in fact exactly what the statute says: RSNS 1967, c. 335, s. 3(1). The wording is identical to that in the original act.

80 *Corkum* v. *Lohnes* supra note 78, 425. Mr Justice Burchell also pointed out that the right to unpolluted groundwater was never a proprietary right, and thus arguably was not affected by the vesting of water rights in the province.

81 One of the classic texts on the public interest in water rights was *De Portibus Maris*, written circa 1670 by Lord Chief Justice Matthew Hale. Not all waterways were subject to the public interest, and in both the United States and Canada the redefinition of public waterways was an important adap-

tation of English common law to the requirements of North America. The defining characteristic came to be whether the waterway was navigable (as opposed to tidal, as it had been in England). See H. Scheiber 'The Road to Munn: Eminent Domain and the Concept of Public Purpose in the State Courts' in B. Bailyn and D. Fleming, eds *Law in American History* (Boston: Little, Brown 1971) on the important ways in which Hale's concept of the public interest was broadened into other areas of law.

82 The quotation comes from Locke's initial definition of property: 'For the labour being the unquestioned Property of the Labourer, no Man but he can have a right to what that is once joined to, at least where enough and as good is left in common for others': *The Second Treatise of Government* P. Laslett, ed. New York: Cambridge University Press 329. This initial limitation is, however, not ultimately part of Locke's conception of property. At common law there was also an exception to this limit on riparian rights – water could be used for domestic purposes even if there were not enough left over for others.

83 See, for example, the famous Ontario case of *KVP*, supra note 18, and compare Benedickson's references to a 'recurring tension between the evident desire of legislators to promote economic development and the reluctance of the judiciary to endorse interference with established proprietary interest': 'Private Rights and Public Purposes' 398.

84 New Brunswick might look somewhat different. At least in the area of water law, the courts there seemed more inclined to make modifications. American legal history suggests that the U.S. Courts have had a stronger inclination to incorporate issues of public policy directly into their common law definitions and determinations. The clearest (and most controversial) picture of this inclination emerges in Morton Horwitz's *Transformation of American Law*.

85 *Law and the Conditions of Freedom in the Nineteenth-Century United States* (Madison: University of Wisconsin Press 1956).

86 Carmen Baggeley offers an interesting commentary on the differences between the United States and Canada with regard to protection of property: 'In the absence of constitutional protection of rights and judicial review, the power of the legislature in Canada is almost unlimited. As a result, the concept of a business being "affected with a public interest," which formed the legal basis for government regulation in the United States, was unnecessary in Canada. As Christopher Armstrong and H.V. Nelles point out, the absence of constitutional protection for property, as provided in the United States by the Fourteenth Amendment, significantly altered the rules of the game in Canada. Early in this century, when the "due process of

law'' clause was being interpreted broadly, American businessmen were able to turn to the courts for protection. Canadian businessmen did not have this option; instead, they tried to play one level of government off against the other. Sometimes they succeeded, but more often than not they failed. In desperation, some Canadian businessmen began to discuss ways in which they might get the constitution amended. In 1911, B.E. Walker, President of the Bank of Commerce, even suggested pressure from abroad, ''... a complaint from those who represent capital in the United States would seem to be a most natural way in which to bring about consideration of the subject by the Government at Ottawa'' ': *Emergence of the Regulatory State*, supra note 3, 18. Of course, the Charter of Rights and Freedoms now provides for constitutional protection of rights and judicial review, but property is not included among those rights. See also my brief discussion of concerns about protecting property in 'Judicial Conservatism.'

Index

Aberdeen, Lord 170, 238
abintestacy 26
abortion 219
Acadia Coal Company 307, 308, 310, 311
Acadia mine 307
Acadians 10–35 passim, 65, 110; expulsion of 6, 13, 34; oath of allegiance and 13, 17, 20, 21, 25, 31, 33, 34; involvement in government in Annapolis regime 22; leadership among 30–1; self-government of 29; use of courts in Annapolis regime 18, 19, 20, 26–7, 28
Acadia University 52, 287
Act for the benefit and better protection of the rights of married women (NS 1855) 85
Act for the protection of married women (NS 1866) 92
Act for the Relief of Insolvent Debtors (NS 1763) 94
Act relating to the Combination of Workmen (NS 1864) 304
Act respecting the Custody of Infants (NS 1893) 282
Act to Enable Agents of the Society and Others to Remove Children from Persons who are Neglecting or Abusing them (NS 1884) 284
Act to Encourage and Promote Smelting and Refining in the Province of Nova Scotia (NS 1916) 332
Act to Prevent and Punish Wrongs to Children (NS 1882) 284
Adams, John 23, 24, 34
adultery: and divorce 232–58 passim
Albion mine 307, 308
alcohol: and female petty offenders 219, 222; and married women's property law 86, 91; violation of licensing laws 212
alimony 233, 257, 279
Allan, Sir Hugh 308

Allan, Sir Hugh Montague 308
Almon, Mather 86
Almon family 61
American Federation of Labor (AFL) 317
Amhurst, Lieutenant 28
Anglicans 50, 51, 52, 65, 179; and divorce 239, 246–7
Annapolis regime 10–35; Acadian involvement in government 22, 29; Acadian use of courts in 18, 19, 20, 26–7, 28; appeals in 15, 16; civil litigation in 18, 19, 22; conventional portrait of 13–14; council 15–35 passim; criminal cases in 18, 27, 28; government of 13, 16–35 passim; governors of 10–35 passim; indigenous population of 11; judicial structure of 16–35 passim; juridical failure in 34–5; justice in 33–5; land-granting practices in 25–6, 27, 28, 34; leadership among Acadians 30–1; procedure in courts 18; problems in administration 11, 17, 22–3, 28; Roman Catholic church in 30. *See also* Acadians
Annapolis River 14, 17
Annapolis Royal 11, 13, 15, 16, 17, 21, 32, 50, 248, 278
Antigonish (NS) 140, 221, 243, 244, 286
Appeal, Court of: Nova Scotia 43
apprentices 167, 275
apprenticeship, legal 52, 53, 55
arbitration 304–19 passim
Archibald, Adams G. 58, 60, 64
Archibald, Samuel G.W. 44, 46, 53, 54, 56, 57, 68, 171, 250
Armstrong, Lt-Gov. Lawrence 16, 17, 20, 22, 23, 24, 25, 26, 28, 29, 32, 34
arson 28, 164, 179, 180, 201
assault 164, 174, 179, 180, 201, 203–4; soldiers and 218; women and 211, 218–19
Assembly, House of (Nova Scotia) 15, 44, 46, 47, 52, 57, 62, 65; and bankruptcy and insolvency law 93, 96, 97, 98, 99, 101, 102, 103, 104, 105; and Chancery reform 107, 108, 109, 111; and child custody 283, 284–5; and divorce law 234–5; and labour law 310, 312, 316; and married women's property 89, 90, 91; and punishment 164, 170, 173, 174, 175, 176, 177, 184–7 passim; and resource regulation 326–44 passim; Speaker 57; and vagrancy 129
asylums 164, 178, 219, 220
attorney general: of England 58; of New Brunswick 60; of Nova Scotia 56, 57, 58, 59, 62, 188, 339
Auburn State Prison (NY) 180, 183, 185, 187, 191

Baker, Hannah 147, 217
Baker, Jeanette Josephine 289, 294
Baker, Judson 289
Ball v. *The Sydney and Louisburg Railway Co.* 330
bankruptcy and insolvency law: England 93, 94, 95, 96, 97, 98; New Brunswick 101; Nova Scotia 83, 92–106, 114, 115; United States 95, 96, 97, 98, 101
Baptists 179, 246
Barry, Mary 140, 217, 219
bastardy 29
Beals, Sarah 212
Beckett, Flora Ann 212
beggars. *See* vagrancy
Belcher, Chief Justice Jonathan 43–4, 48, 52, 53, 54, 56, 62, 65, 66, 239

Bell, Hugh 183
benefit of clergy 164, 165
Bentham, Jeremy 81, 180, 181
Bermuda 164, 170
bigamy 232, 256
Bishops' Courts (England) 233
Black, Dr Rufus 184
blacks 66, 168, 179, 222; and petty offences 208; and vagrancy 137, 141; assaults on 221; female petty offenders 215
Blanchard, Hiram 50, 90
Blandford (NS) 248
blasphemy 165
Bliss, Jonathan 60
Bliss, William Blowers 46, 47, 52, 53, 54, 55, 56, 60, 62–3, 67, 100, 113
Blowers, Sampson Salter 45–6, 48, 53, 56, 57, 58, 60, 61, 64, 67, 237
Board of Inspectors of Asylums and Prisons 188
Board of Trade (UK) 32, 62, 235
Board of Works 180, 183
Bond, Ellen 220
Borden, Robert 258
Boston 23, 24, 85, 315
Boudre, Peter 23
Bourg, Alexander 20
Bouthillier, Guy 50, 58
Boyle, Robert 140
Breaches of Contract Act (Can. 1877) 305
Brenton, James 46, 48, 53, 55, 56, 61, 65, 67
Breslay, Abbé René-Charles 30
bridewell (Halifax) 163, 166, 167, 168, 169, 173, 174–6, 177, 183, 184; changing roles of 168, 169, 191–2; conditions in 148–9, 167, 169
British Columbia 144, 317
Brookfield (NS) 214
Brookfield, Samuel 150
Brooks, Betsy 248
Brossard, Widow 26
brothels 202, 212, 218, 219
Brougham, Lord 107
Broussard, Jean 29
Broussard, Joseph 29
Brown, Captain 248
Brown, Councillor 104
Brown, R.H. 311
buggery 164, 165
Burke, Ann 142
Burroughs, Mrs 211
Byers, David 211
Byers, Mary 211

Cahill, Eliza 139
Cahill, Mary 208
Calgary 210, 211, 212, 215
Campbell, Sir Alexander 191
Campbell, Sir Colin 170, 176, 215, 238
Canada: economy and legal change 131; female petty offenders in 212; law reform in 81; vagrancy in 129–30
Canadian Labour Union (CLU) 303, 304
Canso (NS) 17, 23, 28
Cape Breton (NS) 11, 27, 50, 60, 168, 179, 307, 308, 315
capital offences 28, 164, 168, 171
capital punishment 27, 164, 170, 171–2
Carey, John 147
Carey, Capt. Lamarchand 249
Carey, Patricia 249
Carnarvon, Lord 186
Carpenter, George 182, 185
Carsal, Peter 27
Cartlidge v. *Cartlidge* 278
Catholics 29, 51, 57, 84, 179, 240, 243, 246, 256, 315; and vagrancy 136,

137, 142, 144; barred from office 15; female petty offenders 213–14; in Annapolis regime 29, 30; toleration of 15
Caulfeild, Thomas 11, 13, 17
Chancery, Court of: of England 19, 106, 107, 109, 276; of New Brunswick 110, 111; of Nova Scotia 44–5, 46, 86, 87, 89, 90, 106–13, 114, 242, 243, 275; of the United States 108, 109
Chancery Procedures Acts (UK 1852) 111
Chandler, E.B. 111
Chandler, Margaret 147, 208
charity 131; changing attitudes towards 149–50
Chebucto 10, 35
Chevreuil, Abbé Claude 30
Chignecto 11, 14, 21, 31, 34
child custody: in England 274, 276–7, 278, 282, 284; in New Brunswick 289; in Nova Scotia 257, 273–95 passim; in Ontario 284; in United States 290
children: and divorce 254; and vagrancy 136, 145; changing perceptions of 276, 283; neglect of 212; welfare of 283. *See also* child custody
cholera 174
Church of England 50, 51, 52, 65; and divorce 233
City Courts (Halifax) 129, 146, 184, 201, 203
Clements, Louisa 248
coal miners 303–19 passim
Cobequid (NS) 17, 31, 34
Cody, Pat 136, 139, 141
Colbert, John 136
Colchester County (NS) 241
Collier, John 44, 53, 56, 60, 65, 66
Colonial Office (UK) 46, 166, 169–70, 176, 235, 236, 237, 238
commercial law 115
Common Pleas, Court of: of Nova Scotia 44, 60, 61, 178, 248
concealment: of birth 166, 179; of sailors and soldiers 165
conciliation 304
Conciliation Act (Can. 1900) 316
Conciliation Act (NS 1903) 316
Confederation 44, 52, 57, 58, 63, 82, 85, 89, 92, 93, 163, 184, 192, 201, 256, 327
Conservative party: of Nova Scotia 58–9
constables 15, 19, 20, 32
Construction Projects Labour-Management Relations Act (NS 1971) 316
Contagious Diseases Acts (UK) 202
contempt 28
Cook v. *Davison Lumber* 337, 338
Cornwallis, Governor Edward 16, 27, 35, 43, 166
corporal punishment 164–6, 168, 170–1; branding 165, 171; flogging 28; in military prisons 168; mutilation 164, 171; pillory 20, 164, 165, 171; whipping 164, 165
Cosby, Major Alexander 20, 21, 22
Cotter, Garrett 148
counterfeiting 165, 180
courts martial 28, 168, 170
Coutume de Paris 28
Cowans, J.R. 313
crime: and vagrancy 144, 147; crime rates 206–7. *See also* criminal law; criminals
Criminal Code (1892) 202, 203

criminal conversation 233
criminal law: of Canada 201; of Nova Scotia 130, 164, 201
Criminal Law Amendment Act (Can. 1872) 304
criminals: changing views of 176–8, 179; felons 165; perceptions of 163–4, 166, 173, 174, 182
Crofton system 185, 191
cruelty: as grounds for divorce 223, 234, 235, 237, 238, 245, 250–2, 254, 255, 256
Cumberland County (NS) 87, 104, 305, 307
Cumberland Railway and Coal Company 313, 314
Cunningham, Major John 256
Currie, Lauchlin 58
Custody of Infants Act (UK 1839) 276

Dalhousie University 52, 53
Dartmouth (NS) 50, 145, 150, 279
Dartmouth Provincial Hospital for the Insane 183
Davis, Lewis 243
Davis, Margaret 243
debtors 59, 93, 94, 95, 177, 178; debtors' prison 92, 93, 94–5, 167, 169; legislation 8, 94; relief system 93–5 passim
Denoon, Mrs 248
Desbarres, Justice William Frederick 53, 56, 67, 98
DesBrisay, Anne 251, 253, 254, 255, 278–9
DesBrisay, Charles 251, 253, 278–9
Deschamps, Isaac 48, 53, 56, 60, 65, 66, 67
desertion: as grounds for divorce 234, 235, 237; of sailors 165
Devines, William 139
Dickey, Robert 61, 104
Digby (NS) 179, 242
Diminus, George 141
disallowance 235, 236, 311
Dissenters: attitudes to divorce 239, 247
divorce 232–58 passim, 273–95 passim; class and 245–6; confusion over law 235–8; costs of 242–3; different from English law 234–5, 238; *a mensa et thoro* 233, 234, 236, 251; *a vinculo matrimonii* 233, 234, 235, 236; rates 240; petitioners for 243–56; procedure 241–3; judicial divorce 232–58 passim; whipping 164, 165
Divorce and Matrimonial Causes Act (UK 1857) 91, 92, 233, 235, 240, 274, 276–8 passim
Divorce and Matrimonial Causes, Court of: of England 276, 277, 294; of Nova Scotia 63, 241, 253, 274, 279, 283
Dixon v. *Dixon* 247–8
Dodd, Edmund M. 53, 54, 56, 60, 64, 67
domestic service 140, 219
domestic violence 84, 211, 255; judicial insensitivity to 250. *See also* cruelty
Dominion Coal Company 315, 318
Dominion Water Power Branch 334
Donahue, Laura 219
Donovan, Julia 220
Dorchester penitentiary 163, 185, 189; escape from 147, 169
Doucett, Capt. John 17, 19, 20, 23, 32
Doull, John 150
dower 233

Downey, Henry 147
Drew, Thomas 142, 147
Drummond, Robert 305–19 passim
drunkenness 4, 132, 133, 141, 165, 201, 202–3, 204, 207; women and 210, 211, 217, 219, 220
Dryden, Catherine 209
Duman, Daniel 43
Dummer's War 20
Dunkin, Robert 188–9
Duport, John 46, 54, 56, 60, 66
dysentery 184

ecclesiastical courts 232, 235
economic conditions 82, 92–3, 108, 115, 174, 207, 211; and declining crime rates 210–11; and property crime 212; impact on attitudes to law in Canada 131; in England 83–4, 90, 115; in New Brunswick 89; in Nova Scotia 89–90, 97, 128, 131, 132–4, 138, 152, 166, 168, 207, 327; in the United States 84, 89, 90, 97, 115, 131
elections: of 1830 96; of 1859 58–9; of 1886 307
Elliott, Sir George 308
England 43, 44, 46, 47, 48, 49, 52, 55, 140, 168, 170; attitudes to criminals 176, 177; attitudes to punishment 172–3; attorney general 58; bankruptcy and insolvency law 93, 94, 95, 96, 115, 116; bar 55; Chancery reform 106, 107, 109, 111; child custody 274, 276–7, 278, 282, 284; criminality of women 206; divorce law 232, 233, 234, 235, 236, 243, 254–5; economy and legal change 83–4, 115; influence on judicial system of Nova Scotia 6, 7, 48, 84, 88, 92, 93, 101, 111, 129, 309, 316; law reform 80, 81, 82, 83; married women's property law 83, 84, 88, 92; penitentiary 173, 178, 186–7, 192; reformatory 166; resource regulation 328, 329, 332; vagrancy law 130, 132
epidemics: cholera 174; dysentery 184; typhoid 184
Episcopalians 51
equal partibility 26
equity 43, 44, 45, 59, 63, 83, 86, 106, 171; of redemption 26; reform in Nova Scotia 106–13. *See also* Chancery
Etter, Lucy 243
Evans v. *Evans* 251
Executive Council (NS) 43, 44, 57; and divorce 232; in Annapolis Royal 15–35 passim; pardons 165, 166, 170
Expropriation Act (NS) 339

Fairbanks, Justice Charles Rufus 44, 46, 51, 53, 54, 56, 64, 68, 98, 100
Fairbanks, Eliza 234
Fairfax, George 290
Fairfax, Hannah 290
Female Inebriate Home 147
female reformatory 139
Ferres, James 187
Fidelity Lodge 307
Field, David Dudley 88
Fielding, John 169
Fielding, W.S. 258, 306, 307, 310, 314
fines 28, 164–5
Finucane, Chief Justice Bryan 45, 51, 53, 56, 62, 64, 67
Fischer, Sarah 209
Fish, William 185–6
Flinn, John 189, 190
Flinn, William 142
Ford, Dora 220

Ford, Mary 219
Francis, Mary 221
Fraser, Colonel 248
Fraser, Sophie 293
Freeman, Johanna 142
Frivolous Arrests Bill (NS 1827) 96, 97
frontier: and law 210, 247; theory 33
Fuller, Harry 136
Fundy, Bay of 14, 21

Gaulin, Abbé Antoine 20
Gay Desenclaves, Abbé Jean-Baptiste de 30
General Court of Nova Scotia 18, 43
General Mining Association 311
George, Andrew 136
Gibbons, Susanna 60
Gibson, Barbara 140
Gilpin, Edward 314
Glen, Adam 232
Glenelg, Lord 170, 176, 238
Gompers, Samuel 317
Gooley, Mary 215
Gore, Annie 140
Goudge, M.H. 312
Gousile, Jacques 29
Graham, Sir Wallace 53, 54, 55, 56, 63, 66, 68, 242, 251, 253, 255, 286, 287, 288, 289, 290, 291, 315
Grand Falls (NS) 89
Grant, Mary 211
Griffin, Asaphine 293
Griffin, Martin 63
Grimké, Sarah M. 85
Guysborough County (NS) 243, 256

habeas corpus 15
Haliburton, Thomas C. 53, 54, 56, 60, 62, 64, 67, 82, 101, 105
Halifax 13, 15, 43, 48, 50, 80, 86, 98, 101, 106, 114, 134, 241, 243, 248, 307; charter of 129, 202, 203; city council 333; County of 57, 60; founding 10, 164, 232; female petty offenders 200–23 passim; merchants 90, 92, 98, 114, 175; political élite 48, 52, 175; relations with hinterland 174; urban underclass 4, 200, 206, 217; vagrancy 128–53 passim
Halifax Company 308
Halifax Electric Tramway 333
Halifax penitentiary 163, 164, 178, 201; architecture 178–9, 180; conditions in 184–5, 187–8; discipline in 180, 181, 182, 185, 189; inmates 179–80; maladministration of 185–6; regulation of 180–2, 185, 186, 187–9; segregation of inmates 183–4
Halifax Power Company 329
Hall, William 313
Halliburton, Brenton 45, 48, 53, 55, 56, 57, 58, 61, 62, 64, 67, 110, 113, 170, 235, 238, 239
Halliburton, Dr John 243
Halliburton, Margaret Inglis 61
Halliburton, Susannah 61
Hamilton, Dr Charles 91
Hamilton, George, Earl of Orkney 15
Hamilton, William 241
Hanf v. *Yarmouth Light and Power* 339, 340
Hants County (NS) 249
Harrington, Charles 108
Harrison, John 23
Harvard University 48, 53, 66, 285
Hawke, Ellen 140
Hawkes, Margaret 248
Henry, Hugh 52–3, 56, 66, 68
Henry, William Alexander 108
Hicks, William 242

Hicks v. *Hicks* 242, 243
Hill, Rev. Mr 218
Hill, William 56, 60, 64, 67, 171, 237
historiography of Maritimes 3, 6, 7
Holihan, Edward 136
Holihan, John 136
Horstman, Allen 227
hospitals 139, 140, 219, 243
House of Correction (Halifax) 129
How, Edward 22
Howard, Margaret 217, 220–1
Howe, Joseph 59, 82, 89, 98, 102, 104, 105, 106, 107, 108, 114, 115, 175
Hubbards (NS) 280
Hutchinson, Foster 53, 54, 56, 64, 67
Hynds, John 171
Hynes, Charlotte 238, 241, 250, 254
Hynes, George 238, 241, 250

illegitimacy 165
immigration 134, 144, 168, 169, 173, 214; and labour disputes 314; of female petty offenders 214–15
impotence: as grounds for divorce 234, 256
imprisonment 164, 165, 166; for debt 8, 89, 90, 92, 93, 94–5, 96, 101, 114, 167, 169; for drunkenness 132, 133, 141, 202–3, 211, 217
incest 165; as grounds for divorce 232, 234
indentured servants 165, 166
Indian River 335
Industrial Disputes Investigation Act (Can. 1907) 316, 317
industrialization 128, 133–4, 152, 200, 210, 211, 276, 283, 327
Industrial Peace Act (NS 1925) 316
infanticide 164, 166
Infants' Home 249, 280
Ingat, George 165
Inglis, Bishop Charles 61, 239
inheritance 21, 26, 84, 88
insane: asylum for 252; treatment of 166, 177
Insolvent Debtors Act (NS 1855) 99, 102
intestate estates 21
Inverness County (NS) 90, 243
Ireland 50, 51, 65
Irish 169, 179; and vagrancy 137, 144; female petty offenders 213–14
Isle Royal (NS) 11

jails. *See* prisons
James, Alexander 50, 53, 55, 56, 59, 66, 68, 253, 281
Jamieson v. *Jamieson* 249, 280–2, 288
Jeffery v. *Jeffery* 253, 254, 255
Jesuits 29
Johnson, Betsy 215
Johnston, Amelia Almon 61
Johnston, James W. 44, 45, 48, 53, 54, 55, 56, 57, 58, 59, 61, 64, 67, 104, 112
Jones, George 178
Jones, Robert 142
Judicature, Court of: of Annapolis regime 17, 18
judiciary 6; Annapolis Royal 14, 15; in Canada 42, 61; in England 43, 49, 51, 58; in Lower Canada 6; in Massachusetts 43, 49, 51, 55, 58; in New Brunswick 55; in Nova Scotia 45–79 passim, 108, 180, 249–58, 277–8; in Quebec 43, 47, 50, 58; in the United States 42–3, 49, 51, 58; in Upper Canada 6
jury: grand 28, 167, 168, 169, 171, 173, 174, 175, 178; petit 28, 172; trial by 15, 16, 27; in civil cases 330, 332

justices of the peace 14, 15, 17, 23, 32, 56, 57, 59, 129, 166, 167, 168, 169, 173, 175, 201, 203, 220, 256, 305; manuals for 53

Kelly, John 218
Kemble, Peter 248
Kidston, Ann 237, 254
Kidston, Richard 237
Killum, Henry 141
Killum, John 141
Killum, Martha 141, 142
Killum, Mary 142, 219
King, Thomas 107
King, William Lyon Mackenzie 8, 316
King George's War (1743–8) 2, 28, 33
Kings County 60
Kingston penitentiary 163, 173, 180, 181, 182, 187
Knights of Labor 304

La Goudalie, Abbé Charles de 30
labour relations 303–9 passim; in Britain 309; in the United States 309
land: escheat 21; grants in Annapolis regime 25–6, 27
law: conservatism of 6, 7, 80, 116; imperialism and 10–11, 13; innovation in 7; politics and 113; reform of 6, 7, 8, 80–113 passim, 116, 171
Lawrence, Charles 35
lawyers: and bankruptcy law reform 105; and Chancery reform 106; anti-lawyer sentiment 106, 111, 114–15; Dominion Bar Society 66; Free Trade in Law bill (1850) 114; in Annapolis regime 16; in divorce cases 249–50; in England 55; in Halifax 55; in New Brunswick 52; in Nova Scotia 52, 53, 54–5; notaries 19, 22, 34
LeBreton, John 248
Lee, John 171–2
legal history: of Canada 3, 5, 6, 7; of England 3, 5; of Nova Scotia 3–8, 116; of United States 3, 5, 8
Legislative Council (NS) 85, 87, 90, 99, 102, 103, 104, 113, 114, 305, 312
Le Loutre, Abbé Jean-Louis 29
Leonard, Annie Sophia 282
Leonard, John 282
Lewis, George 248
libel 115, 175
liberalism 116
Liberal party 305, 306, 307
limited liability 8, 115, 331, 332
liquor licensing 165, 204, 212
Little, Otis 59
Locke, John 342
Lockeport (NS) 280
Longley, J.W. 285, 286, 309
Lovitt, Bessie Agnes 288
Lovitt, Israel Melbourne 288
Lovitt, Minnie 250, 253, 254
Lovitt, William 250
loyalists 48, 239
Lunenburg (NS) 102, 241, 248, 250, 253, 312
Lutherans 179, 246

MacAlpine, George 251
MacAlpine, Lydia 251
McCann v. *Pidgeon* 329
McCarthy, Michael 135
McColl, Jeffrey 307
McCulloch, Thomas 82, 92–3
McCully, Jonathan 8, 50, 53, 56, 57, 58, 64, 67, 85, 86, 87, 88, 89, 91, 98, 99, 101, 102, 103, 104, 105, 114

McCutcheon, Thomas 82
MacDermott, James 142
Macdonald, Angus G. 315
McDonald, Charles 294
McDonald, Hugh 50, 51, 53, 56, 57, 68
MacDonald, James 47, 48, 53, 55, 56, 58, 61, 68
Macdonald, Sir John A. 57, 191, 304
McDonnell, John 141
MacGregor, George 188
McGregor v. *Patterson* 285
McGuire, Jane 248
Mackenzie, Ellen 208
Mackenzie, Kate 208
Mackenzie, Mary 139
McLean, Hector 241, 244
McLean, Sarah 241, 244
McMaster, James 136
McMillan, William 168
McNamara, Mary 147
McNutt, Mary Ellen 293
Macphail, Sir Andrew 100
MacQueen, J.F. 251, 253
magistrates. *See* justices of the peace; stipendiary magistrates
Mahony, Ann 139, 140
Mahony, John 139
Maidment, Susan 277–8
Maloney, Patrick 142
Mansfield, Lord 45
manslaughter 164, 165, 174, 179, 190
March, James 204
Maroons 11
marriage 5, 273, 275; unity of personality 83, 87, 90, 91, 275
Marriage and Divorce, Court of (NS) 235, 241, 251
Married Women's Property Act (NB 1851) 88, 89
Married Women's Property Act (NY 1848, 1849) 87, 89
Married Women's Property Acts (NS) 83–92 passim 114, 283
Married Women's Property Acts (UK 1870, 1882) 83
married women's property law: England 83, 84, 88, 90, 92; New Brunswick 88, 89, 114; Nova Scotia 7, 83–92, 114, 283; New York 87, 88, 89; United States 83, 84, 85, 90; Upper Canada 114
Marshall, John 53, 54
martial law 15
Martin, Julia 147
Mascarene, Major Paul 20, 22, 23, 24, 28, 31, 34, 35
Massachusetts 19, 43, 48, 49, 55, 58; divorce in 238–9, 244–5, 246, 247, 250, 255; law reform in 116; vagrancy convictions in 132
master and servant legislation 165, 305
masters of the rolls 44, 46, 50, 62, 106, 107, 108, 111
May, Ann 232
May, John 151
May, Peter 232
Meagher, Justice Sir Nicholas 50, 53, 56, 59, 66, 68
Measure, Jane 256
Melville Island 167
mercantilism 7
Merivale, Herman 236
mesne process 94, 95, 97
Methodists 102, 179, 246
Meuse, Francis 29
migration 128, 134, 169, 214
military hospital 219; military prison 167, 168
militia 15, 17
Miller, Anne 212
Miller, Mary 212

Milton, John 239
Minas (NS) 16, 17, 20, 21, 28, 30, 31, 32, 34
Mineral Exploration and Mining Association of Nova Scotia 312
Mines Arbitration Act (NS 1888) 303–19 passim
missionaries 20, 22, 29
Monk, George J. 46, 53, 56, 65, 67
Monk, James 65
Moore, Joseph B. 308
Morris, Alexander 64
Morris, Charles 44, 49, 53, 56, 60, 61, 62, 64–5, 66, 67
Morris, Isabella 61
Morrison, Mabel 293
Morse, J.S. 50
Morse, Sarah 50
Mosher, Major 249
Mosher, Mary 249
Mott, Elizabeth 278
Motton, Robert 204, 207
Mowat, Oliver 309
Moylan, J.G. 190
municipal government 147–8, 174, 182, 200; municipal law 201
Munro, Flora 293
murder 27, 164, 171, 174, 179, 180, 201
Murdoch, Beamish 8, 54, 96, 97, 105, 171, 239, 241, 250
Murray, Hugh 248
Myrer, Helen 251, 254, 255
Myrer, Richard 251

Napoleonic Wars 81, 92, 168
National Policy 133, 306
native peoples 5, 11, 13, 14, 20, 21, 28, 29, 30, 32, 66, 110; female petty offenders 215
Naval Hospital 243
Naylor, John 252
New Acadia 29
New Brunswick 11, 55, 60, 136, 140, 191, 331; attorney general 60; bankruptcy law 101; bar 52; Chancery 109, 111; child custody 289; divorce law 236, 237, 240, 258; divorce rates 240; married women's property law 88, 89, 114; resource regulation 327
New England 24, 47, 48, 49, 51, 66; bankruptcy law 93; colleges 52; influence on court system of Nova Scotia 48; influence on divorce law in Nova Scotia 238, 239, 247, 255. *See also* Massachusetts
New England Gas and Coke Company 315–16
Newfoundland 166, 182
Newfoundland Fencible Regiment of Foot 248
Newport (NS) 249
New South Wales 164, 170, 317
newspapers 82, 204; and law reform 114; on capital punishment 171–2; on Chancery 106, 109–11; on crime 166; on female petty criminals 222; on married women's property 86–7; on vagrancy 137, 144–5, 150–1; racism in 215
Newton, Hibbert 23
New York 11, 96; Chancery 108, 109, 111; law reform 116; married women's property law 87, 88, 89
Nicholson, Francis 16
Night Refuge for the Homeless 149–50
Norton, Caroline 276
Norton, Charles 291
Norton, Harriet 291
Nova Scotia Power and Pulp Company 333

Nova Scotia Railroad 183
Nova Scotia Society for the Prevention of Cruelty 252–3, 283
Nova Scotia Tramway and Power Company 333, 335, 337, 340, 341
Nova Scotia Water Power Commission 334, 335
nuisance laws 202, 203, 204, 207; and women offenders 204, 207, 211

oath of allegiance 13, 17, 20, 21, 25, 31, 33, 34
O'Brien, Mary 219
O'Connell, Norah 256
O'Connell, William 256
O'Neal, Nancy 166
Ontario: child custody 284; divorce law 240; divorce rates 240; labour law 305, 309, 317; legal history 5; resource regulation 327, 332, 338; vagrancy 144
Ontario Hydro-Electric Commission 333, 336
Ontario Trades Arbitration Act (1873) 309
Ormond, Norah 243, 246
Owen, William H. 312

Palmer, John 219
panoptic model 180, 181
pardons 165, 166, 170, 179, 190
Parliament: British 87, 186, 233, 236; Canadian 144, 192
paternity suits 165
patronage: and hiring of penitentiary guards 187; and judicial appointments 53, 55, 57–8, 60–1
Paul, Mary 215
Pemberton, Jeremy 46, 53, 56, 62, 67
penal reform 171
Pendergast, Mary 221
penitentiaries 163, 173, 178, 180, 186, 187, 191–2. *See also* prisons
Penitentiary Act (Can. 1868) 189
penitentiary commission 178
perjury 165, 190
petitions: for divorce 232, 243–58 passim; for release from debt 94
Philipps, Guilliam 23
Philipps, Colonel Richard 14, 17, 19, 20, 21, 22, 23, 24, 25, 31, 32
picketing 305
Pictou 87, 93, 241, 307, 308
Pioneer Lodge 312, 313, 314
Pipes, W.T. 115, 306
police 220, 288; assault on 203, 221; discretion allowed 202; and discrimination 215; and labour 306; and vagrancy 143, 146, 147, 148; in the United States 131, 148
Police Court (Halifax) 143, 173, 201, 220
Pollard, Elizabeth 244
pollution 329–30
polygamy 164
Poole, H.S. 311, 312, 315
Poor Law Amendment Act (UK 1834) 178
population: of Nova Scotia 82, 128, 147, 200, 207
Port-Royal (NS) 11, 24, 31
Potter, James 149–50
Potter, Sarah 219
poverty: classification of 143; Commissioners of the Poor 167, 174, 175; Elizabethan poor law 5; Halifax Association for Improving the Condition of the Poor 150; Overseers of the Poor 165, 167; pauper auctions 5; poor asylum 136, 144,

219, 220; poor-house 136, 139, 140, 149, 174, 178, 184, 217, 219, 222, 280; poor law (NS) 5; poor relief 5, 130, 135, 143, 146, 149, 178
Power, George G. 288–9
Power, Johanna 143
Power, Myrtle 288–9
Power Commission Act (NS 1919) 336, 339
Presbyterians 50, 51, 179, 246
primogeniture 88
Prince Edward Island 46, 48, 60, 100, 101, 140; divorce law 238, 240; labour law 305
prisoners 173–4, 179–90. *See also* prisons
prisons 129, 130, 140, 163–92 passim; administration of 168, 169; Board of Works, 180, 183; convict labour 129, 130, 143, 149, 166, 167, 173, 177, 182–3, 217; county jails 163, 168, 173, 184, 192; discipline in 143, 169, 174, 180, 181, 182, 185, 189, 217; inspection of 174, 186; for petty offenders 204–23 passim; military 179; as refuge 142–3, 149
Privy Council (UK) 14, 15, 16, 316
Probate, Court of: of England 8; of Nova Scotia 59, 61, 88
profanity 4, 201, 203; women and 212
property offences 174, 212; breaking and entering 180; burglary 180, 201; forgery 164, 171, 179, 180; grand larceny 28, 164, 165; highway robbery 171; horse-stealing 179; larceny 164, 179, 190; women and 201, 203, 204, 211, 212; petty theft 4; receipt of stolen goods 165, 180; sheep-stealing 180
prostitution 4, 130, 132, 134, 140, 141, 167, 200, 201–2, 204, 207–9, 210, 211, 213, 214, 219, 220, 221
Provender, Isaac 28
Provincial Workmen's Association (PWA) 304–19 passim
Pryor, Henry 91, 146, 147, 201, 204, 207, 208
Public Health Act (NS 1888) 330
Pubnico (NS) 14
punishment: changing attitudes towards 163–4, 168–74, 182, 186, 190–1, 192; for assault 203–4; for drunkenness 202–3; for profanity 203; for larceny 203; for vagrancy 28, 129, 130, 131, 144, 164–8, 202. *See also* capital punishment; corporal punishment; transportation
Puttum, John Lewis 170

quarantine 164
Quarter Sessions, Court of: of Nova Scotia 173
Quebec 14; divorce in 240; labour law in 305; vagrancy 144

racism 215, 221
Railway Labour Disputes Act (Can. 1903) 316
Ramezay invasion (1746) 28
rape 179, 190
Raymond, Francis 29
recidivism 135, 139, 140; of female petty offenders 216–22
Récollets 29
reformatory 136, 139, 166; in England 166
Reid, Rachel Amelia 279
Reid, William 279

Reiss, Erna 274, 275
religion: and married women's property law 91; impact on bankruptcy reform 100; of judges 50, 51; of divorce petitioners 246–7; of prison inmates 179; of vagrants 136–7
responsible government 49, 50, 51, 57–8, 62, 65, 82, 108, 109, 114
Richards, Francis 20, 29
Rigby, Samuel 47, 53, 55, 57, 59, 68
Riley, Elizabeth 202
riparian rights 326–44 passim
Ritchie, Amelia 61
Richie, Elizabeth Johnston 61
Ritchie, John N. 57, 59, 61, 68, 253, 330
Ritchie, John W. 53, 54, 55, 57, 58, 61, 63, 64, 67, 68
Ritchie, Joseph W. 252
Ritchie, Roland 61
Ritchie, Thomas 61
Ritchie, William Johnston 61
Rivett, Etienne 21
Roach, William 175
Roan, Joan 219
Robarts, Frederick 248
Robertson, George 248, 278
Robertson, Laleah 248, 278, 285
Robichaud, Prudent 26, 32, 33
Robie, Simon Bradstreet 44, 46, 48, 53, 55, 56, 61, 62, 63, 68, 106, 107
Roby, William 256
Rockhead Prison (Halifax) 128, 142, 184, 201, 202, 203, 212, 216, 217, 219, 220, 221, 222
Ross, Rebecca 280
Ross, Winifred 284
Royal Commission on Prisons 144
Royal Commission on the Relations of Labor and Capital 311
Russell, Benjamin 250

St Francis Xavier University 52
Saint John (NB) 89, 136, 140, 142, 145, 163
Salter family 61
Savage, Arthur 17, 23
Schmidt, Frederick 168
Schofield, Margaret 147
Scott, Susan 136
seigneurial system 31
Serjeant Talfourd's Act (UK 1839) 276
servants 28, 165, 166
Sessions, Court of: of Nova Scotia 184
Shannon, Samuel Leonard 102, 104, 105, 113
Sheehan, Edward 139, 141
Shelburne (NS) 167
sheriffs 14, 15, 31, 94
Shirreff, William 23, 24, 34, 35
Shubenacadie (NS) 141
Skene, William 23, 24, 25, 26, 34
Slattery, Mary 218, 221, 222
slaves 11, 84
smallpox 140
Smelting Act (NS) 332
Smith, Henry 48, 53, 57, 68
Smith, Thomas 142
social control 4, 129, 131, 164, 166, 190
sodomy: as grounds for divorce 233
solicitor general (NS) 56, 57, 62
Southack, Cypryan 23
Springhill mine 305, 312, 313, 315
Springhill Mining Company 305
Stafford, Kate 293
Stanford v. *Imperial Oil* 338
Stanley, Lord 182
Star Chamber 19
Stellarton (NS) 307
Stephen, Sir James 235–6, 237–8

Stewart, Alexander 44, 46, 50, 53, 55, 56, 61, 65, 68, 90, 100, 105, 107, 109, 110, 111, 112, 113, 114
Stewart, Amelia King 61
Stewart, Elizabeth Halliburton 61
Stewart, James 53, 56, 61, 67
stipendiary magistrates 140, 146, 201, 203, 207, 250, 253
Stipendiary Magistrates' Court 201, 204
Strange, Sir Thomas 45, 46, 48, 53, 54, 55, 56, 64, 66, 67
strikes 304–19 passim
suffrage 86, 283
Sulpicians 29
Superior Court (Quebec) 43, 50, 58
Supreme Court: of British Columbia 258; of Canada 42, 61; of Nova Scotia 43–5, 80, 99, 108, 166, 173, 174, 180, 237, 241, 253, 282–3, 286, 314, 315, 338, 340, 341; of the United States 42, 58
Sweeney, Martin 168
Sydney (NS) 248, 256
Sydney mines 311

Taylor, William 243, 244
temperance movement 91
Test Act (UK) 32
Thomas, Mary Ann 211
Thomas, Thomas 232
Thomas v. *Thomas* 243, 248
Thompson, John S.D. 47, 50, 53, 55, 57, 63, 64, 66, 68
Thorburn, N.S. 307
Tibeau, Louis 29
Timber Act (NS) 332
Tolliver, Mary Ann 208
Tolmy, Jane 165
Toronto 144, 210, 212, 213, 214, 215, 303; printers' strike 304; vagrants in 130
Townshend, Sir Charles 53, 57, 61, 65, 68, 111, 112, 113
Trades and Labor Congress of Canada 304, 317
trade unions 303–19 passim
Trade Unions Act (Can. 1872) 304
transportation 164, 169–70, 171
treason 28, 164, 201
Treaty of Utrecht (1713) 10, 15
typhoid 184

ultramontanism 14
unemployment 130, 146
Uniacke, James Boyle 97, 171, 250
Uniacke, Richard John 48, 53, 56, 57, 60, 63, 64, 67, 96, 97, 98, 100, 250
United Mine Workers of America 317
United States 42, 43; attitudes to criminals 176, 177; attitudes to punishment 172–3; bankruptcy and insolvency law 95, 96, 101, 115, 116; Chancery 108, 109, 111; child custody 290; divorce 252, 256, 257; economy and legal change 84, 97, 115, 131; female petty offenders 212; influence on Nova Scotia's legal system 85, 89, 108, 109, 111, 116; law reform in 81, 82, 83; married women's property law 83, 84, 85, 89; penitentiaries 173, 178, 192; police 148; resource regulation 328, 329, 332, 342; vagrancy 4, 130, 131, 152
Upper Canada 66, 96; attitudes to punishment 172–3; fears about crime in 173; married women's property law 114; penitentiary 163, 187

vagrancy: in Canada 129–30; in England 130, 132; in Halifax 200, 201, 204, 207–10, 211, 213, 220, 221; and crime 144, 147; causes of 144; classification of 128; economy 128, 131, 132–4, 138, 143, 152; imprisonment for 132–43, 207–10, 217; laws regarding 128–9, 202, 203; middle-class attitudes 143, 145, 146, 149, 150, 152, 153; newspapers on 144–5, 150–1; police and 143, 146, 147, 148; punishment for 129, 130; recidivism 135, 139, 140; seasonality of convictions 134–5, 142; and unemployment 130, 146; in the United States 130, 131, 143–4, 152
vagrants: in Nova Scotia 128, 167, 184, 221; age 135–6; ethnicity 136, 137; place of origin 137, 138; release 139–40; religion 136–7; sentencing 138–9
Vagrancy Act (Can. 1869) 129–30, 202
Vagrant Act (NS 1851) 202
Vale Coal, Iron and Manufacturing Company 308
Vale mine 307
venereal diseases 219
Vernede St-Poncy, Abbé Claude de la 30
Vetch, Samuel 17
Vice-Admiralty Court (England) 60
Victoria County (NS) 243
Victoria mines (Cape Breton) 315
Virginia 14, 17, 43, 166; impact on Nova Scotia's legal system 14–16
Virginia General Court 16, 17
Virginia instructions 14, 15, 16

Walsh, Mary 143
Warren, John 139
Water Act (NS 1919) 326, 332, 335–44 passim
Weatherbe, Sir Robert S. 48, 53, 55, 57, 59, 66, 68
Webster, Barclay 285, 286
Wenman, Richard 166
Western Canada: divorce law in 240
Weston, Anne 147, 217, 220
Westville (NS) 307
Wheeler, Ruth 234
Whidden, John 242
Whitaker, H. 192
White, Catherine 217
Whitney, H.M. 315, 316
Wilkins, Isaac 61
Wilkins, Lewis M., Sr 46, 56, 61, 67
Wilkins, Lewis M., Jr 53, 56, 61, 64, 67
Wilkins, Martin 53–4, 61
Williams, Amy 232
Williams, William 232
Windsor (NS) 107, 312
Winniett, William 15–16, 20, 24, 34
Winstanley, Ellen 217
Wiswall, Peleg 53, 56, 64, 67
women 66; as petitioners 243–4, 245; and social reform movement 223; and violence 211; employment of 211, 219–20; in the family 206; as petty offenders 204–23 passim; punishment 165; suffrage 86, 283; as victims of violence 211, 218–19; 'woman question' 83, 84, 89. *See also* married women's property; prostitution
Women's Christian Temperance Union (WCTU) 283
Woodend, Jemima 288, 291
Woodend, Robert John 288, 291
workhouse (Halifax) 129, 149, 167
wounding 164, 180

wrecking 164

Yarmouth (NS) 243, 288
Young, G.R. 108
Young, Sir William 48, 53, 55, 56, 57, 58, 59, 62, 63, 67, 98, 101, 102, 108, 110, 111, 112, 116, 150, 278, 285

PUBLICATIONS OF THE OSGOODE SOCIETY FOR CANADIAN LEGAL HISTORY

2011 Robert J. Sharpe, *The Lazier Murder: Prince Edward County, 1884*
Philip Girard, *Lawyers and Legal Culture in British North America: Beamish Murdoch of Halifax*
John McLaren, *Dewigged, Bothered, and Bewildered: British Colonial Judges on Trial, 1800–1900*
Lesley Erickson, *Westward Bound: Sex, Violence, the Law, and the Making of a Settler Society*

2010 Judy Fudge and Eric Tucker, eds., *Work on Trial: Canadian Labour Law Struggles*
Christopher Moore, *The British Columbia Court of Appeal: The First Hundred Years*
Frederick Vaughan, *Viscount Haldane: 'The Wicked Step-father of the Canadian Constitution'*
Barrington Walker, *Race on Trial: Black Defendants in Ontario's Criminal Courts, 1858–1958*

2009 William Kaplan, *Canadian Maverick: The Life and Times of Ivan C. Rand*
R. Blake Brown, *A Trying Question: The Jury in Nineteenth-Century Canada*
Barry Wright and Susan Binnie, eds., *Canadian State Trials, Volume III: Political Trials and Security Measures, 1840–1914*
Robert J. Sharpe, *The Last Day, the Last Hour: The Currie Libel Trial* (paperback edition with a new preface)

2008 Constance Backhouse, *Carnal Crimes: Sexual Assault Law in Canada, 1900–1975*
Jim Phillips, R. Roy McMurtry, and John T. Saywell, eds., *Essays in the History of Canadian Law, Volume X: A Tribute to Peter N. Oliver*
Greg Taylor, *The Law of the Land: The Advent of the Torrens System in Canada*
Hamar Foster, Benjamin Berger, and A.R. Buck, eds., *The Grand Experiment: Law and Legal Culture in British Settler Societies*

2007 Robert Sharpe and Patricia McMahon, *The Persons Case: The Origins and Legacy of the Fight for Legal Personhood*
Lori Chambers, *Misconceptions: Unmarried Motherhood and the Ontario Children of Unmarried Parents Act, 1921–1969*
Jonathan Swainger, ed., *A History of the Supreme Court of Alberta*
Martin Friedland, *My Life in Crime and Other Academic Adventures*

2006 Donald Fyson, *Magistrates, Police, and People: Everyday Criminal Justice in Quebec and Lower Canada, 1764–1837*

Dale Brawn, *The Court of Queen's Bench of Manitoba, 1870–1950: A Biographical History*
R.C.B. Risk, *A History of Canadian Legal Thought: Collected Essays*, edited and introduced by G. Blaine Baker and Jim Phillips

2005 Philip Girard, *Bora Laskin: Bringing Law to Life*
Christopher English, ed., *Essays in the History of Canadian Law: Volume IX – Two Islands: Newfoundland and Prince Edward Island*
Fred Kaufman, *Searching for Justice: An Autobiography*

2004 Philip Girard, Jim Phillips, and Barry Cahill, eds., *The Supreme Court of Nova Scotia, 1754–2004: From Imperial Bastion to Provincial Oracle*
Frederick Vaughan, *Aggressive in Pursuit: The Life of Justice Emmett Hall*
John D. Honsberger, *Osgoode Hall: An Illustrated History*
Constance Backhouse and Nancy Backhouse, *The Heiress versus the Establishment: Mrs Campbell's Campaign for Legal Justice*

2003 Robert Sharpe and Kent Roach, *Brian Dickson: A Judge's Journey*
Jerry Bannister, *The Rule of the Admirals: Law, Custom, and Naval Government in Newfoundland, 1699–1832*
George Finlayson, *John J. Robinette, Peerless Mentor: An Appreciation*
Peter Oliver, *The Conventional Man: The Diaries of Ontario Chief Justice Robert A. Harrison, 1856–1878*

2002 John T. Saywell, *The Lawmakers: Judicial Power and the Shaping of Canadian Federalism*
Patrick Brode, *Courted and Abandoned: Seduction in Canadian Law*
David Murray, *Colonial Justice: Justice, Morality, and Crime in the Niagara District, 1791–1849*
F. Murray Greenwood and Barry Wright, eds., *Canadian State Trials, Volume II: Rebellion and Invasion in the Canadas, 1837–1839*

2001 Ellen Anderson, *Judging Bertha Wilson: Law as Large as Life*
Judy Fudge and Eric Tucker, *Labour before the Law: The Regulation of Workers' Collective Action in Canada, 1900–1948*
Laurel Sefton MacDowell, *Renegade Lawyer: The Life of J.L. Cohen*

2000 Barry Cahill, *'The Thousandth Man': A Biography of James McGregor Stewart*
A.B. McKillop, *The Spinster and the Prophet: Florence Deeks, H.G. Wells, and the Mystery of the Purloined Past*
Beverley Boissery and F. Murray Greenwood, *Uncertain Justice: Canadian Women and Capital Punishment*
Bruce Ziff, *Unforeseen Legacies: Reuben Wells Leonard and the Leonard Foundation Trust*

1999 Constance Backhouse, *Colour-Coded: A Legal History of Racism in Canada, 1900–1950*
G. Blaine Baker and Jim Phillips, eds., *Essays in the History of Canadian Law: Volume VIII – In Honour of R.C.B. Risk*
Richard W. Pound, *Chief Justice W.R. Jackett: By the Law of the Land*
David Vanek, *Fulfilment: Memoirs of a Criminal Court Judge*

1998 Sidney Harring, *White Man's Law: Native People in Nineteenth-Century Canadian Jurisprudence*
Peter Oliver, *'Terror to Evil-Doers': Prisons and Punishments in Nineteenth-Century Ontario*

1997 James W.St.G. Walker, *'Race,' Rights and the Law in the Supreme Court of Canada: Historical Case Studies*
Lori Chambers, *Married Women and Property Law in Victorian Ontario*
Patrick Brode, *Casual Slaughters and Accidental Judgments: Canadian War Crimes and Prosecutions, 1944–1948*
Ian Bushnell, *The Federal Court of Canada: A History, 1875–1992*

1996 Carol Wilton, ed., *Essays in the History of Canadian Law: Volume VII – Inside the Law: Canadian Law Firms in Historical Perspective*
William Kaplan, *Bad Judgment: The Case of Mr Justice Leo A. Landreville*
Murray Greenwood and Barry Wright, eds., *Canadian State Trials: Volume I – Law, Politics, and Security Measures, 1608–1837*

1995 David Williams, *Just Lawyers: Seven Portraits*
Hamar Foster and John McLaren, eds., *Essays in the History of Canadian Law: Volume VI – British Columbia and the Yukon*
W.H. Morrow, ed., *Northern Justice: The Memoirs of Mr Justice William G. Morrow*
Beverley Boissery, *A Deep Sense of Wrong: The Treason, Trials, and Transportation to New South Wales of Lower Canadian Rebels after the 1838 Rebellion*

1994 Patrick Boyer, *A Passion for Justice: The Legacy of James Chalmers McRuer*
Charles Pullen, *The Life and Times of Arthur Maloney: The Last of the Tribunes*
Jim Phillips, Tina Loo, and Susan Lewthwaite, eds., *Essays in the History of Canadian Law: Volume V – Crime and Criminal Justice*
Brian Young, *The Politics of Codification: The Lower Canadian Civil Code of 1866*

1993 Greg Marquis, *Policing Canada's Century: A History of the Canadian Association of Chiefs of Police*
Murray Greenwood, *Legacies of Fear: Law and Politics in Quebec in the Era of the French Revolution*

1992 Brendan O'Brien, *Speedy Justice: The Tragic Last Voyage of His Majesty's Vessel Speedy*

Robert Fraser, ed., *Provincial Justice: Upper Canadian Legal Portraits from the Dictionary of Canadian Biography*

1991 Constance Backhouse, *Petticoats and Prejudice: Women and Law in Nineteenth-Century Canada*

1990 Philip Girard and Jim Phillips, eds., *Essays in the History of Canadian Law: Volume III – Nova Scotia*

Carol Wilton, ed., *Essays in the History of Canadian Law: Volume IV – Beyond the Law: Lawyers and Business in Canada, 1830–1930*

1989 Desmond Brown, *The Genesis of the Canadian Criminal Code of 1892*

Patrick Brode, *The Odyssey of John Anderson*

1988 Robert Sharpe, *The Last Day, the Last Hour: The Currie Libel Trial*

John D. Arnup, *Middleton: The Beloved Judge*

1987 C. Ian Kyer and Jerome Bickenbach, *The Fiercest Debate: Cecil A. Wright, the Benchers, and Legal Education in Ontario, 1923–1957*

1986 Paul Romney, *Mr Attorney: The Attorney General for Ontario in Court, Cabinet, and Legislature, 1791–1899*

Martin Friedland, *The Case of Valentine Shortis: A True Story of Crime and Politics in Canada*

1985 James Snell and Frederick Vaughan, *The Supreme Court of Canada: History of the Institution*

1984 Patrick Brode, *Sir John Beverley Robinson: Bone and Sinew of the Compact*

David Williams, *Duff: A Life in the Law*

1983 David H. Flaherty, ed., *Essays in the History of Canadian Law: Volume II*

1982 Marion MacRae and Anthony Adamson, *Cornerstones of Order: Courthouses and Town Halls of Ontario, 1784–1914*

1981 David H. Flaherty, ed., *Essays in the History of Canadian Law: Volume I*

www.ingramcontent.com/pod-product-compliance
Lightning Source LLC
LaVergne TN
LVHW090803070826
844660LV00022B/1061

9781442613591